E. M. Wilson.

D1587629

ANGLO-NORMAN LITERATURE
AND ITS
BACKGROUND

ANGLO-NORMAN LITERATURE
AND ITS
BACKGROUND

BY

M. DOMINICA LEGGE

OXFORD
AT THE CLARENDON PRESS
1963

Oxford University Press, Amen House, London E.C. 4

GLASGOW NEW YORK TORONTO MELBOURNE WELLINGTON
BOMBAY CALCUTTA MADRAS KARACHI LAHORE DACCA
CAPE TOWN SALISBURY NAIROBI IBADAN ACCRA
KUALA LUMPUR HONG KONG

© *Oxford University Press 1963*

PRINTED IN GREAT BRITAIN

PREFACE

THIS book is the result of an intention formed in undergraduate days, when Anglo-Norman studies were being
fostered in Oxford by the scholars whose pupil I am
proud to be—Paul Studer, E. G. R. Waters, and Mildred K.
Pope. That it has been written now is due to the prompting
of the late Miss Helen Darbishire. My gratitude goes out
to all of them.

It is a pleasurable duty to acknowledge my debt to the
late Professor Mildred K. Pope and Professor John Orr,
who read the early chapters in rough draft; to the many
scholars who have so generously allowed me to make free
with their work, both published and unpublished, whose
names are recorded as occasion arises; and to the members of
the Anglo-Norman Studies Special Subject Class at the University of Edinburgh during the past ten years, for their
helpful criticism. I wish also to record my thanks to Professor Pope for the gift of Anglo-Norman books from her
library, which has been invaluable; to the donors of the Mary
Somerville Research Fellowship at Somerville College; to the
Leverhulme Research Awards Committee for a Fellowship
without which the book would have taken much more than
twelve years to write; to the Edinburgh University Press for
permission to use material published in *Anglo-Norman in
the Cloisters* (1950); and to the Clarendon Press for undertaking publication and for all the patient help which I have
received from them.

M. DOMINICA LEGGE

Edinburgh
20 *July* 1963

CONTENTS

LIST OF ABBREVIATIONS

(Bibliographical references are given in full once in each chapter
in which they occur, except in the case of series listed below)

Acta Sanctorum:	published by the Bollandists, Venice, Antwerp, Paris, Brussels.
A.N.T.S.:	The Anglo-Norman Text Society, Oxford.
Archiv:	*Archiv für das Studium der neueren Sprachen und Literaturen* (Brunswick).
C.F.M.A.:	Les Classiques français du Moyen Age (Paris).
C.P.R.:	Calendar of Patent Rolls (Public Record Office, London).
Documents inédits:	Collection de Documents inédits relatifs à l'histoire de France, publiés sous les auspices du Ministère de l'Instruction Publique (Paris).
D.N.B.:	*Dictionary of National Biography*, ed. Sidney Lee (London).
Dugdale, *Monasticon*:	William Dugdale, *Monasticon Anglicanum*, ed. J. Caley, H. Ellis, B. Bandinel (London).
E.E.T.S.:	Early English Text Society.
o.s.:	Original Series.
e.s.:	Extra Series.
E.H.S.:	English Historical Society Publications (London).
Elliott Monographs:	Princeton University Press.
E.U.P.:	Edinburgh University Press.
Migne, *Patrologia Latina, Pat. Lat.*:	
	J. P. Migne, *Patrologia, cursus completus, Patres Ecclesiae Latinae* (Paris).
M.U.P.:	Manchester University Press.
Nelson's Medieval Classics:	General Editors, V. H. Galbraith and R. A. B. Mynors (Thomas Nelson and Sons Ltd., London, Edinburgh, Paris, Melbourne, Toronto, and New York).
Notices et Extraits:	*Notices et Extraits des manuscrits français de la Bibliothèque Nationale et d'autres bibliothèques* (Paris).
P.M.L.A.:	*Publications of the Modern Language Association of America*.
P.R.O.:	Public Record Office, London.

Rolls Series, R.S.:   Rerum Britannicarum Medii Ævi Scriptores, or
                             Chronicles and Memorials of Great Britain and
                             Ireland during the Middle Ages, published
                             under the direction of the Master of the Rolls
                             (London).

S.A.T.F.:   Société des Anciens Textes Français (Paris).

V.C.H.:   *The Victoria History of the Counties of England*
                             (London).

I

INTRODUCTION

ANGLO-NORMAN literature has not been ignored in the past, for of necessity it receives casual mention in every general history of Old French literature. Information can be gleaned from introductions to editions of texts. Besides, a few books have been devoted exclusively to Anglo-Norman. Johan Vising's *Anglo-Norman Language and Literature* (London, 1923) contains a bibliography of everything which could then be known. A badly-needed revision of the list of manuscripts which it contains has been in preparation for many years by Miss Ruth J. Dean. E. Walberg's *Quelques aspects de la littérature anglo-normande* (Paris, 1963) is chiefly concerned with the author's own chosen field, works of a religious nature, and the same is true of the present writer's *Anglo-Norman in the Cloisters* (Edinburgh, 1950), whose title speaks for itself. Writers on English literature have been slower and more grudging than those on French to acknowledge the existence and relevance of Anglo-Norman literature. The *Cambridge History of English Literature* hardly ever refers to it, merely mentioning from time to time an Anglo-Norman text as a source of an English work, but the editors did have the inspiration to obtain the permission of the Selden Society to reprint, as chapter xx of their volume i (1903), F. W. Maitland's remarkable essay on the *Anglo-French Law Language*, written to form part of the introduction to the *Year-Books of Edward II* (1903). Recognition was given to both Late Latin and Anglo-Norman literatures as part of the English heritage by W. H. Schofield in *English Literature from the Norman Conquest to Chaucer* (1st ed., London, 1906), and this is still useful if treated with discretion. Mr. R. M. Wilson included a brief chapter on 'The Anglo-French Background' in his *Early Middle English Literature* (London, 1939). The title sufficiently indicates his attitude to the subject, which is less

sympathetic than Schofield's. The chapter suffers from the
fact that no specialist in Anglo-Norman was consulted, and
too great reliance was placed upon Walberg's *Quelques
aspects*, which was avowedly an incomplete treatment of the
literature.

The study of Anglo-Norman literature is in a less satisfactory position than the study of the language. Since 1923,
when Vising's manual appeared, the late Professor M. K.
Pope's part V of *From Latin to Modern French* (Manchester,
1934, 1952, 1956) has covered phonology, orthography, and
morphology; versification is treated in the introductions to
The Anglo-Norman Voyage of St. Brendan by Benedeit, edited
by E. G. R. Waters (Oxford, 1928), and to *La Seinte
Resureccion* (Anglo-Norman Text Society, iv, 1943), contributed by Miss Pope; some light has been shed on syntax by
Professor John Orr's *Impact of French upon English* (Oxford,
1948, reprinted in *Words and Sounds*, Oxford, 1953, pp. 28–
42); finally an Anglo-Norman Glossary is being prepared.
The history of the use of the language has been treated from
various points of view by the present writer in 'Anglo-
Norman and the Historian' and by Mr. R. M. Wilson in
'English and French in England 1100–1300', in *History*
xxvi (1941), pp. 163–75, and xxviii (1943), pp. 37–60, and
again by the present writer in 'Ouster-le-mer', *Studies presented to John Orr* (Manchester, 1953), pp. 158–67, and
'The French Language and the English Cloister', *Studies
presented to Rose Graham* (Oxford, 1950), pp. 146–62.

With his supreme sense of drama the designer of the
Bayeux Tapestry ended his work with the words: 'Hic
Haroldus rex interfectus est et fuga verterunt Angli.' The
foot-soldiers are shown streaming away, hunted down by the
mounted invaders. Henceforward what was going to count
was the Mediterranean world of chivalry, Latin, Romance
languages, and the Church of Rome, and the Germanic tie
was loosed. Within a few years a Norman writer could put
into the mouth of Charlemagne's nephew the words:

> Jo l'en cunquis Escoce e Vales, Irlande
> E Engletere que il teneit sa cambre.

(For him I conquered Scotland and Wales, Ireland, and England,
that he held as his private domain.)

The face of England became dotted with castles whose inhabitants formed small courts in need of entertainment, maintained by people often connected with one another by ties of blood or marriage. Everything imported at the time of the Conquest and immediately afterwards was new and up to date. Motte-and-bailey castles were thrown up in a hurry, and the shell-keeps which succeeded them were common, but the latest fashion in castles developed in northern France was the tower-house, and some of the finest specimens ever seen anywhere were raised by the Conqueror. In the motte-and-bailey or shell-keep type of castle, it seems likely that the menials ate and slept in a separate building; in the tower-house they lived on a different floor. Conditions there favoured the production of the more intimate kind of literature, which can be termed 'courtly' in the widest sense of the word. Proof of the importance of the tower-house in Anglo-Norman society is given by the adoption of the 'soler', 'sollar' in English, which just means 'upper floor', in place of the continental French 'chambre', which meant originally the withdrawing-room behind the dais in the one-storied hall.[1] By 1100 the *chanson de geste* was a well-established form, soon to go out of favour in courtly circles. It continued to be written in France, but no trace of an Anglo-Norman *chanson de geste* survives. It belonged to the great hall where lords, attendants, and menials were present together; romances and other works in the octosyllabic rhyming couplet belonged to the chamber. Many of the earliest Anglo-Norman texts written for ladies were in this form. Anglo-Norman taste was not lagging behind continental, it was in the van.[2] There was a close resemblance between works of popularization and edification produced in England and in Normandy, and in some cases it is difficult

---

[1] Cf. M. K. Pope, 'Notes on the Vocabulary of the Romance of *Horn and Rimel*', *Mélanges Hoepffner* (Paris, 1949), pp. 69–70, M. D. Legge, 'Some Notes on Anglo-Norman Vocabulary', *Studies . . . presented to A. Ewert* (Oxford, 1961), pp. 221–3. Cf. S. Toy, *Castles of Great Britain* (London, 1953) and *A History of Fortification* (London, 1955), H. Braun, *The Story of the English House* (London, 1940), W. D. Simpson, *Exploring Castles* (London, 1957), and D. Allen Brown, *English Medieval Castles* (London, 1954).

[2] Cf. M. D. Legge, 'Archaism and the Conquest,' *Modern Language Review*, li (1956), pp. 227–9, and 'The Influence of Patronage on Form in Mediaeval French Literature', *Stil- und Formprobleme in der Literatur* (Heidelberg, 1959), pp. 136–41.

to differentiate.[1] The same kind of people, and very often the same people themselves, were patronizing writers on both sides of the Channel. There was soon, however, something which distinguished Anglo-Norman works from Norman ones. Those who settled in England, from the king downwards, were often younger sons. They felt a need to establish themselves and demanded history and romance, as well as Lives of saints, all of which dealt with the English past.

Feminine influence declined at the time of the disgrace of Eleanor of Aquitaine in 1173. She had already settled in Poitou, apparently for good, in 1170. It is about this time that there appear chronicles and romances written in the epic style. The demand for literature of this kind led to the copying of *chansons de geste*, for by this time most people, down to the very poorest, were bilingual.[2] It was, indeed, worth while writing plays in Anglo-Norman to perform outside churches. In the thirteenth century the sole surviving copies of the *Chançun de Willame* and the *Pelerinage de Charlemagne* were made, at the end of the century the Hanover manuscript of the *Destruction de Rome* and *Fierabras* was copied, and in the fourteenth century the Egerton version of the same two poems, which may possibly be of continental origin but was better known in England, for it is the source of the Middle English *Sowdone of Babylone* and, what has hitherto passed unremarked, may be the poem alleged to have been recited by The Bruce to his followers when crossing Loch Lomond.[3] The one exception to this apparent lack of interest in *chansons de geste* before the late twelfth century is the Oxford manuscript of the *Roland*. This is notoriously difficult to date: the hand appears to be of the second quarter of the twelfth century, but the scribe's clumsiness in handling his pen may be due to old age, and some would date it much later, thus bringing it nearer to the time of the revival

[1] Cf. Walther Suchier, *Zwei altfranzösische Reimpredigten* (2nd ed., Halle/Saale, 1949), pp. 1–18.

[2] Jocelin of Brakelond, *Chronicle*, ed. H. E. Butler (Nelson's Medieval Classics, 1949), pp. 33, 128, implies that by 1182 country folk almost invariably understood French.

[3] Cf. L. Brandin, *Romania*, xxviii (1899), pp. 489–507, and *Romania*, lxiv (1938), pp. 18–100; *The Sowdone of Babylone*, ed. E. Hausknecht (E.E.T.S., Extra Series, xxxviii, 1881); *The Bruce* by J. Barbour, ed. W. W. Skeat (Scottish Text Society, 1894), i. 67, 8.

of the epic style. The argument *a silentio* may be dangerous, and here one is faced with the difficulty that only four pieces of written French of pre-Conquest date are in existence; these are the Strasbourg Oaths, the sequence of *St. Eulalia*, the *Passion* poem, and the *Life of St. Leger*, and none of these is epic. Two of the earliest manuscripts of other French poems, *St. Alexis* and the *Roland*, happen to be Anglo-Norman.[1] Nevertheless no true *chanson de geste* seems to have been composed in this dialect.

The twelfth century was the era of small courts acting as centres of patronage, and the opening chapters of the main section of this book have had to treat texts in chronological order. This has enforced a little, but not very much, overlapping and recapitulation. The beginning of the thirteenth century saw two events which influenced the course of Anglo-Norman literature. The first of these was political; the loss of Normandy by John in 1204, which set the seal on the process which had been going on ever since the accession of Henry I. It was not upon the history of the language, as has been assumed, but on the history of the literature that the separation of kingdom and duchy had its effect. The other was religious: the Fourth Lateran Council of 1215, which gave great impetus to the work of instructing the laity and changed the tone of homiletic literature. It is significant that the vernacular at first chosen for this purpose was Anglo-Norman. English was used, but not for any work of importance for some time. By the end of the thirteenth century translations and adaptations into English were made on a considerable scale; the gap between the writing of a work in Anglo-Norman and its translation into English became narrower and narrower. Whether the *Ancrene Riwle* is based upon an Anglo-Norman original is a matter for doubt; it is remarkable that it should have been written or even translated into English as early as the first half of the thirteenth century, but it should not be forgotten that the English version was deemed insufficient, and several later Anglo-Norman translations, or retranslations, were made of it. All through the thirteenth century Anglo-Norman more than held its own;

[1] Cf. M. Delbouille, *Sur la genèse de la Chanson de Roland* (Brussels, 1954), p. 31, and M. D. Legge, 'Archaism and the Conquest', loc. cit.

it was only in the fourteenth that English really became a serious rival as a literary medium.

Throughout this book an attempt has been made to relate the literature to its background of society. Only pure literature is considered, and its development is traced from the beginnings, when a few texts were made at the request of individuals for specific purposes, texts made in competition not with English but with Latin works, to the end, when a sufficient range of English works existed to make it unprofitable to write in Anglo-Norman any more. At first Anglo-Norman belongs rather to the traditions of French literature, but it developed differently to suit English taste. Some kind of continuity of the old English tastes existed, and while the Anglo-Norman romances are finer and less artificial than the later continental ones, the Middle English ones are vigorous to the point of coarseness. Perhaps the upper classes became or remained more robust than their French counterparts; there is no evidence that these romances were rejected by them merely because they were written with a wider public in view. The wheel turned full circle, and conditions once again called for a literature to please all classes, just as they had when the *chansons de geste* were first composed. Chaucer's contemporary, John Gower, might see nothing incongruous in employing his three languages, Latin, French, and English, wherever he thought one more appropriate to his subject than another. Yet, nearly a century before, Guy of Beauchamp, Earl of Warwick, had given a whole library of books to Bordesley Abbey, about forty volumes, mostly of romances and epics in French. It looks as though he had spring-cleaned the house and thought that the abbey would give a good home to old-fashioned books which were too good to use as scrap.[1] There are other cases of gifts of books to monasteries less important than this one. Even the nobility seems to have lost interest in literature in French during the Hundred Years War.

[1] Cf. M. Blaess, 'L'Abbaye de Bordesley et les livres de Guy de Beauchamp', *Romania*, lxxviii (1957), pp. 511–18; A. de Mandach, *La Geste de Charlemagne et de Roland*, i (Geneva and Paris, 1961), chapter xiv (the conclusions drawn are to be treated with reserve).

II

THE EARLY TWELFTH CENTURY

SINCE the Norman Conquest took place in 1066, it may seem strange that the opening chapter of a history of Anglo-Norman literature should be entitled 'The Early Twelfth Century', but the history of vernacular literature in England is a blank between the arrival of the Conqueror and the accession of the youngest of his sons in 1100. The only substantial piece of writing in English for this period is the Anglo-Saxon Chronicle and that is not, strictly speaking, literature at all; such truly literary activity as we know of was in Latin. In Anglo-Norman there is nothing. Yet it is impossible to believe that the laity were deprived of any literature for over thirty years. Something must have been circulating in oral form, even if it was never written down. For English it is comparatively simple to imagine what was going on, but for French it is impossible to guess whether anything was actually composed in England or whether the speakers of French had to rely entirely upon imports from abroad like the *Chanson de Roland*. From 1100 onwards Anglo-Norman writers were amongst the pioneers of French literature, and it is difficult to believe that these authors sprang from nothing.

At this date learning to read meant learning to read Latin, and if any young noble was taught his letters he could not help learning some Latin too. If he read to himself or was read to in private, or had to transact any business, he probably knew enough Latin for the purpose, even if he could not write it. Similarly any girl who was given any education probably knew a little, but there must have been fewer girls who could read than boys. Women, moreover, led a more sedentary life and had more time for literature. It is therefore not surprising to find that great ladies were the chief patrons of the early Anglo-Norman writers.

The reign of Henry I produced two important Anglo-

Norman writers, whose output is so diverse that it suggests a demand for French texts which these authors were not the first to attempt to satisfy. They have this in common: they were producers of works of popularization and they wrote for court circles. What is lacking here is any sign that there was a literature of pure entertainment. This may be because poetry for entertainment was still largely a matter of oral tradition, whereas the compositions of clerks were of a kind more conveniently transmitted in writing. It is fortunate that the works of these two Anglo-Norman authors can be dated to within a few years, and that their names, if nothing much besides about their identity, were recorded. At this period the concealment of names from motives of prudence was not so necessary, even where religious questions were involved, as it became after the middle of the twelfth century.

Of the two men now to be considered one is represented by only one surviving work. The other seems to have been prolific, and several works survive which are either certainly his or may be attributed to him. One makes his appearance under the patronage of royalty, the other is to be observed in the process of winning royal favour. In spite of the different nature of the works which they chose or were requested to popularize, they may conveniently be treated in the same chapter. They were contemporary, they were both didactically inclined, and they were both patronized by a queen.

BENEDEIT AND THE *VOYAGE OF ST. BRENDAN*

A certain Benedeit was probably the earlier of these two writers; the earliest work was the verse *Voyage of St. Brendan*[1] and the first patron was Maud, queen of Henry I.

The author calls himself 'li apostoiles danz Benedeiz'. This conjunction of *apostolicus*, now used only of popes but in the twelfth century applied to any bishop, and *dominus*, a title given to prelates, the lesser nobility, knights, and Benedictine monks,[2] does not occur anywhere else.

---

[1] E. G. R. Waters, *The Anglo-Norman Voyage of St. Brendan by Benedeit* (Oxford, 1928).

[2] Not to Cistercians, as Waters says (p. xxvi). Cf. F. M. Powicke, *The Life of Ailred of Rievaulx by Walter Daniel* (Nelson's Medieval Classics, 1950), p. xii. There were no Carthusians in England at this date.

Probably Waters was right in assuming that Benedeit was a monk, that is to say a Benedictine, since there was no prelate of the name at this time. It has been suggested that *li apostoiles* may be an early case of a surname.[1] Benedeit was almost certainly of Norman extraction, and may even have been born abroad, but his language suggests that he had lived in England for some time.

The author not only names himself but tells us the name of the lady who had commanded him to write. It is Benedeit's misfortune that his description of himself has ceased to be clear, and that later scribes have confused the name of the patron for whom he wrote. Three call her Aaliz (Aliz, Aeliz), but a fourth (Bodleian Rawl. D. 913) names her Mahalt. The fifth scribe was a Frenchman and omits the dedication as being of no interest. Aaliz would be Adeliza of Louvain, whom Henry I married in 1121, and Waters, after some hesitation, pronounced in her favour. But Professor Ritchie went over the ground again not long ago and has shown cause for preferring Maud, the same king's first queen.[2] After a dignified but brief delay after he had seized the throne, Henry I announced his intention of strengthening his position by marrying a princess of the old English royal house. His choice fell upon a Scottish princess, Edith, renamed Maud, elder daughter of St. Margaret and Malcolm Canmore and great-niece of Edward the Confessor. She had been brought up by her aunt Christina, abbess first of Romsey and then of Wilton, and had worn the veil in order to escape embarrassing attentions. Evidence was called to prove her free to marry, and before the year 1100 was out the wedding and consecration were over. The marriage, however, was purely one of convenience, and after the birth of three children the queen established herself at Westminster, where she dwelt in great state, patronizing poets and musicians, especially foreigners, to the great disgust of native writers.[3] She was said to resemble her mother, who could dispute with ecclesiastics in Latin, and she herself was versed

---

[1] E. Walberg, 'Sur le nom de l'auteur du Voyage de S. Brendan', *Studia Neophilologica*, xii (1939), pp. 46–55.

[2] R. L. G. Ritchie, 'The date of the Voyage of St. Brendan', *Medium Ævum*, xix (1950), pp. 64–66.

[3] William of Malmesbury, *Gesta Regum*, ed. W. Stubbs (R.S., 1889), ii. 494.

in Latin. It appears that Benedeit had first written a *Voyage of St. Brendan* in Latin and then translated it at the queen's request, perhaps for the benefit of the ladies and maidens of her household, who would not have had the advantages of a convent education.[1]

The subject of the Anglo-Norman poem is not, as the manuscripts would have it, the Life of St. Brendan. Lives of saints followed a regular pattern, of which there are plenty of examples in later Anglo-Norman. It is rather, as Waters saw, translating the Latin title *Navigatio Sancti Brendani*, the *Voyage of St. Brendan*. The poem deals with not much more than episodes probably derived from an Irish Imram, formerly supposed to be the Imram Maelduin; but this is now thought to have been based on a story of St. Brendan.[2] Perhaps there were several Irish sources of the *Navigatio*, and it is idle to look for one particular Imram on which it is based. St. Brendan was an historical person who sailed oversea, but perhaps not farther from Ireland than the neighbouring coasts of Scotland and Brittany. The legend was and is a fascinating story and has never been better told than by Benedeit. It has everything the heart could wish for, except perhaps a love-interest. St. Brendan had that essential quality of a classic hero—he was of royal birth. In the best tradition, he left the world to become a monk, and was only persuaded to take the office of abbot by force. The poet dismisses all this in a few lines, and then gets down to business. Brendan, towards the end of his life, prayed for a sight of heaven and hell, a reason for his voyage which is Benedeit's invention. He went to consult Barinz, who had landed on an isle near Paradise while on a sea voyage. Now this is perhaps the first appearance in French literature of a stock-character in romance—the hermit who dispenses wise counsel; and the identification of Barintus with a hermit seems also to have been Benedeit's invention. Brendan, on his return, built a ship and carefully selected fourteen companions. At the last moment three more gained his reluctant consent to accom-

---

[1] M. D. Legge, '*Letre* in Old French', *Modern Language Review*, lvi (1961), pp. 333–4.

[2] Cf. M. Esposito, 'Sur la Navigatio Sancti Brendani', *Romania*, lxiv (1938), p. 339; C. Selmer, *Navigatio Sancti Brendani Abbatis* (University of N.-D., 1959).

pany him. These foreshadow the conventional three felons of romance, and they all came to a bad end. The description of the voyage contains a full tale of wonders—a deserted city of great splendour; the Easter feast upon the back of a sleeping whale, a beast whose disconcerting habit of drowning unsuspecting sailors was also known to the writer next to be mentioned, Philippe de Thaon, and who turns up again in the Arabian Nights; the paradise of birds, with its choir of fallen angels, which, as Professor Ritchie points out, Crestien de Troyes borrowed for *Yvain*;[1] the frozen sea; a magic and intoxicating spring, forerunner of so many others; fights between sea-monsters, griffins, dragons; the smithy of hell, so like the hell of St. Patrick's Purgatory; the volcano of Hecla, where Judas was imprisoned—a subject which remained popular in Old French literature; finally, Paradise itself. Here the poet spreads himself, and adds considerably to the account of the *Navigatio*. His description owes something to Genesis, something to Exodus, something to the Apocalypse, but almost as much to Claudian. It is fascinating to see how naturally Claudian's two springs, running with mingled poison and honey, turn into two rivers flowing with milk and honey, how Youth becomes an angelic guide, Juventus being replaced by *'le juvencel'*. Inevitably the walled garden is transported to the top of a mountain.[2] Nothing is left after this description for the poet to do but to record as briefly as possible the saint's return and death. The poem finishes even more abruptly than it began. There is no epilogue; it simply comes to an end with the subject.

Hitherto it has always been supposed that Benedeit was working upon the *Navigatio*, using perhaps a version which differed slightly from the one which survives—in nearly a hundred manuscripts, not all of which have been closely examined. It seems clear that Benedeit was a skilful editor. He made some omissions and a few modifications, even remembering that his omissions had to be covered in other ways, and he endeavoured to make his fantastic material

---

[1] *Chrétien de Troyes and Scotland*, the Zaharoff Lecture for 1952 (Oxford, 1952), p. 5; cf. E. Kölbing, 'Christian von Troyes *Yvain* und die Brandanuslegende', *Zeitschrift für vergleichende Litteraturgeschichte* (N.F. xi, 1897), pp. 442–8.

[2] For the influence of Claudian upon later French allegory, cf. C. S. Lewis, *The Allegory of Love* (London, 1938), pp. 74–76.

follow a more logical order. What is more important is that
he changed the tone of the story in two ways: he made it
more edifying by making the voyage a trial of faith, and at
the same time he added embellishments which show that
he shared in the beginnings of the courtly movement. For
example, he omits, as the editor points out (p. cii), matter of
interest only to clerks, 'reducing, for instance, the long list
of Canonical Hours celebrated on the Isle of Birds, and
omitting entirely the liturgical versicles which the Latin
author was putting into the mouths of his personages'. He
adds more reflections to drive home the lesson of any particular episode, thus treating the whole legend as a series of
fables. A couplet ending Brendan's speech to the monks after
the discovery of the Intoxicating Spring has the appearance
of a proverb:

> Fuium d'ici,
> Que ne chaiez meis en ubli.
> Mielz vient suffrir honeste faim
> Que ublier Deu e sun reclaim.   (819–21)

(Let us flee hence, lest you fall now into forgetfulness. Better
endure hunger with honour, than forget God and prayer to him.)

For the most part the cuts are judicious; only occasionally
does Benedeit omit picturesque details or episodes which
might have appealed to a lay audience. Additions and alterations are made with them in mind. The descriptions of the
Uninhabited City, of the Isle of Ailbe, and of Paradise have
been enriched. The walls of Paradise, for instance, are said
to be set with the precious stones of the Apocalypse. The
City was rich, great, and beautiful:

> E resemblout mult regal leu,
> D'empereür mult riche feu.   (268–70)

(And it was like a very royal place, the very rich fee of an emperor.)

Most telling of all, the silver bridle stolen by one of the
monks there, surely due to the Irish love of animals, becomes the more conventional golden goblet. By thus appealing to the senses of his audience the poet hoped to make
palatable the lesson which he had added to the adventure-tale
of the *Navigatio*:

Mais cum plus vunt, plus se peinent. (1104)

(But the farther they go, the harder they exert themselves.)

There is thus no doubt that Benedeit, at the queen's request, rewrote the story with a courtly audience in mind. But whether, as Waters thought, the modification was made for the Anglo-Norman version, or whether it was made before, in the version *en letre* of lines 10 and 11, which can hardly be anything else than Latin, it is impossible to decide. In either case the credit belongs to Benedeit.

The Anglo-Norman poem achieved immediate and lasting popularity. It was probably soon after its patroness's death that it was rededicated to her successor. Four complete manuscripts of it survive, besides one fragment. Of these, one (B.N., n. a. f. 4503) is perhaps as early as 1200, two are not much later, and the remaining two belong to the later thirteenth century. Of the two latest, one (Arsenal 3516) is a rewriting in the Picard dialect. What is perhaps more remarkable is that it was twice translated into Latin. One translation, into prose, exists in a copy of about 1200, and is thus at least contemporary with the oldest manuscript of the poem. The question arises as to whether this can be the version *en letre*. Waters assembled evidence which suggests that the Latin is translated from the Anglo-Norman and not the other way round, and the mistakes he lists (pp. cvii–cxii) do not suggest that they were slips on the part of an author translating his own work, though that is just possible. The wording of the prologue suggests that the Latin version preceded the Anglo-Norman. The other translation is into rhyming couplets. It survives in a fourteenth-century manuscript, but may be a century older than that. It is plainly later than the Anglo-Norman by a substantial interval, and the translator was aware of the differences between the *Navigatio* and the poem and made use of both. His Latin shows that he was habitually French-speaking, but naturally the evidence does not show whether he lived in France or England. It appears that Benedeit's Latin version, presuming that it existed, was not widely known and was early forgotten. His poem, on the other hand, was read in both France and England from the early twelfth to the fourteenth century. If it resembled the Latin, this is not a surprising state of affairs. A retelling of the legend so obviously aimed at a court audience, and so different from the accepted version, would be much more likely to survive in a vernacular language.

So much for the subject-matter. The form of the poem, too, may be called exciting. The *Brendan*, especially if Professor Ritchie's dating is accepted, has some claim to be the earliest extant French poem written in octosyllabic rhyming couplets, later to become the standard form of romance. It is even possible that this is one of the oldest long poems in Northern French to be written in any kind of octosyllable. The *Passion* and *St. Leger* are older, probably tenth-century, but they are in assonance, not rhyme, and were intended to be sung to a tune written for a liturgical hymn. The fragment of the *Alexander* by Alberic and the *Chanson de Sainte Foy* are written in *laisses*, and are both Provençal. *Sainte Foy* was written to one of the Gregorian tones for the Psalms and Canticles, which, though specially designed for the chanting of prose, can be adapted to verse. In Northern French, *Gormont et Isembart* may be older, but that is written in assonance and in *laisses*. Moreover, the only surviving manuscript is thirteenth-century, and there is no internal evidence to date this particular version of the legend, which was undoubtedly known in older forms. There are three or four lapidaries in octosyllabic couplets which are nearly as old, but though these are long poems they are not narrative.[1]

Not only is the *Brendan* perhaps the oldest poem written in the octosyllabic rhyming couplet, it is also the earliest with a substantial proportion—over one-third—of feminine lines. These lines, which had no exact counterpart in Latin verse, caused embarrassment and were avoided as much as possible by early French poets. That this avoidance was deliberate and not accidental is proved by the fact that in the William cycle and in *Gormont* the feminine line is sometimes used for the refrain or the orphan line, apparently for the sake of variety, though it is going too far to say that in substituting 'Lores fu mescredi' for 'Lors fu dimecres' a *remanieur* was

---

[1] Cf. Waters, op. cit., pp. xxix ff. The late G. Lote, *Histoire du vers français* (Paris, 1951), ii. 58 ff., does not distinguish between the octosyllabic line and the octosyllabic couplet. The difference is important.

sacrificing the regularity of the music,[1] about which we know nothing. *Chansons de geste* were declaimed or chanted, not sung, and the music probably had no more regularity than plainsong, but nothing can be proved about this at the moment. The feminine *laisses* of *Aucassin et Nicolette*, which were sung to a fairly regular musical phrase, were sung by the simple expedient of repeating a note. It is generally supposed that the *Brendan* was not sung or chanted, but its peculiarities may be explained by the view that it was. The poet has a way of dealing with the feminine lines which is rare in the history of French verse. He makes all his lines of equal length. Thus, to modern ears, the feminine lines have only seven syllables. This, says Waters (p. xxxv), 'carries the syllabic principle of French versification to an extreme, and neglects the principle of stress'. This objection disappears if it is conjectured that the verse was sung or chanted to a fixed tune and it is remembered that the feminine *e* was given even more value than it is today in singing. The *Brendan*, like the *St. Leger*, is distinguished by a regular application of a caesura. Each line breaks exactly in half, whether the fourth syllable occurs in the middle of a word, or consists of an article or preposition, or falls at a more convenient place. This again suggests the existence of a fixed tune which overrides the sense, and Waters points out the resemblance between this kind of versification and a line common in contemporary Latin lyrics. The same kind of thing may be observed in Provençal and French lyrics.[2] This is unlikely to have influenced Benedeit, though it must be remembered that other Anglo-Norman writers employ lyric versification in narrative, Thomas for instance in *Horn*.[3] He was perhaps influenced by his familiarity with Latin hymns, and indeed a model may be suggested. Waters says (p. xlii): 'Naturally it is impossible to point to any actual model which

---

[1] *Chanson de Guillaume*, ed. D. McMillan (S.A.T.F., 1950), ii. 76.

[2] e.g. short feminine lines are used in eight songs by Bertran de Born (Waters, op. cit., p. xxxvi), and in one by Gace Brulé (Lote, op. cit., i. 204). In Provençal songs the tunes consist of phrases corresponding to a line of verse. *Enjambement* is not infrequent, but the lines are usually 'pointed' in the manuscripts to show that the sense was to be subordinate to the requirements of the tune (Lote, i. 253 ff.). Modern singers have great difficulty in singing in this way, as can be heard on records of these songs.

[3] See below, pp. 96–104.

the author of the *Brendan* followed', but he overlooked a
hymn ascribed to Wido of Ivrea of about 1075, which has
the appearance of being of Irish origin.[1] There is a series of
three hymns in honour of Irish saints in a manuscript from
Ivrea, one of which commemorates St. Brendan and begins
thus:

Iam Brendani	sanctos mores
Canent fratres	et sorores.
Sub concordi	cantilena
Sibi serviat	camena.

The earliest French saints' legends were narrative written to
be sung to the tune of the Latin hymn proper to the day,[2]
and it is possible that the *Brendan* is one of the last in that
tradition. If the evidence of the *Renart* is to be believed, there
was a lay if nothing else of St. Brendan which could be sung.
In Branch I*b*, written about 1200, Renart pretends to be an
English jongleur. His repertoire consists of good Breton or
British lays, and lays of Merlin, 'Neptune', King Arthur,
Tristan, Chievrefeuille, Iseut, and St. Brendan.[3] Much later,
the French Cistercian Guillaume de Deguilleville employed
a similar type of line in his *Pelerinage de la Vie Humaine* and
possibly in another poem ascribed to him largely on the
grounds of its versification, the *Roman de la Fleur de Lis*.[4]
The *Pelerinage* was a reaction against the worldliness of the
Roman de la Rose, which it plagiarizes unmercifully, and it
therefore seems curious that the monk did not employ exactly
the same metre. Perhaps he was influenced by Latin hymns,
but perhaps he was also influenced by Benedeit, for he knew
the Brendan story either in its Latin form or possibly in the
Anglo-Norman poem. The scribes who copied Benedeit's
and Guillaume de Deguilleville's work tried to normalize the
feminine lines by adding an extra syllable. In the case of
Benedeit, the scribe who made the most alterations is, as

---

[1] Ed. E. Dümmler, 'Gedichte aus Irea', *Zeitschrift für deutsches Alterthum*, N.S.
xiv (1869), p. 256, and G. M. Dreves, *Analecta Hymnica Medii Ævi*, xlviii (1905),
pp. 88, 89. Cf., for Irish versification, F. J. E. Raby, *Christian Latin Poetry* (Oxford,
1953), p. 33.

[2] Cf. below, pp. 135–39.

[3] Ed. Mario Roques (Classiques Français du Moyen Âge, 1948), ll. 2435–40.

[4] The *Pelerinage* was edited for the Roxburghe Club by J. Stürzinger (1893, 95,
97); (*Le Roman de la Fleur de Lis*) ed. A. Piaget, *Romania*, lxii (1936), pp. 317–58.

might be expected, the Picard one, but the Anglo-Norman scribes made some adaptations, with the exception of the scribe of the fragment which has the dedication to Queen Maud. This is an argument for the authenticity of that dedication, since this scribe did his best to preserve the primitive form of the text, and it is unfortunate that so little of his copy survives.

When Waters remarked, after referring to Benedeit's peculiarities in versification, 'yet the technical perfection attained by the author indicates that he was using a well-established form', one may well be permitted to wonder, was he not rather experimenting? No doubt he was an experienced poet, otherwise he would hardly have been commissioned by the queen to write his French version of the legend. But was his experience in Latin or in French? The former is more likely, especially as he seems to claim that he had already written a Latin version of the legend, whether in verse or prose he does not say. But wherever he found his ideas on versification, it seems clear that he helped to popularize the octosyllabic rhyming couplet, which later in the century became, with the longer type of feminine line, the orthodox medium for romances. The modern kind of couplet was already in existence, but it was not used for courtly narrative poetry, and this, as has been pointed out, is what the *Brendan* was, in spite of the misleading fact that it deals with the legend of a saint.

Perhaps Benedeit's short and choppy lines may seem a little dry today, though at moments, as in his descriptions of the fight of the sea-monsters, he warms to the task like any Seneca, and there is liveliness in his descriptions of the smithy of hell and of Paradise. His repetition of the verb 'sigler'—'Siglent al vent', 'Siglet Brandan', 'Vunt s'en mult tost en mer siglant'—is undoubtedly effective. The way in which he links episode to episode by such introductory references to sailing and the sea is not devoid of stylistic sense, and by his omissions of anticipatory matter he makes his narrative more dramatic than the *Navigatio*. The appeal of the story needs no explanation. Sea journeys and wonders will always be popular, and here the *Brendan* is in the tradition of the *Odyssey*, the *Iter Alexandri ad Paradisum*, *Sinbad*

the Sailor, and such disparate things as the missionary journeys of St. Paul and the fourth and fifth books of *Pantagruel*.
Many of the stock details of romance are already here; the
hermit, the three felons, the garden, the spring, and the bird-
covered tree. But besides all this, the *Brendan* deals with one
of the great themes of human thought, the longing to see
the Land of the Blessed, the Hesperides, the Earthly Paradise, the Promised Land, call it what you will. 'O quanta
qualia' and more particularly 'Urbs Syon aurea', twelfth-
century poems both, have achieved and kept a popularity of
which their authors never dreamt, and might not have ap-
proved. The myth of St. Brendan's voyage still exercises a
fascination over all who come across it. Only scholars now
know it in Benedeit's version and for some reason they have
tended to put it on the shelves amongst lives of saints. It
belongs in another place altogether, with the great moments
of Old French literature, with *St. Alexis* perhaps, but also
with the Alexander romances, the poems of Crestien de
Troyes, and the *Roman de la Rose*.

PHILIPPE DE THAON

Li Cumpoz

Benedeit had a contemporary who belonged to a type all
too common in Anglo-Norman literature, dull but well-
meaning. Nevertheless this writer had one outstanding merit:
he was a pioneer, and wrote the first scientific popularizations in the French language.

This writer, Philippe de Thaon, was probably born on this
side of the Channel, but his family was Norman and presumably came from the village near Caen from which they took
their name. It is a little difficult to place Philippe's works in
chronological order, but *Li Cumpoz*[1] was almost certainly the
earliest of them. Scholars are less certain than they used to
be that this is to be acclaimed as the earliest surviving monument of Anglo-Norman literature, but it is still possible that
it was written shortly before the *Brendan*.

The main interest of *Li Cumpoz* lies in its prologue. It was
written, the author tells us, by Philippe de Thaon, and sent

[1] Edited by E. Mall (Strasbourg, 1873).

to his uncle, who was to amend any error of fact or wording. This uncle was named Honfroi de Thaon, and he was chaplain to Eudo, the king's steward. Eudo Fitz-Hubert, the son of Hubert de Rie, is better known as Eudo Dapifer.[1] He was steward to William I, William II, and Henry I, and was a supporter of the last two kings when in turn they seized the throne to the detriment of Robert Curthose. He was sheriff of Essex and held the town and castle of Colchester, where he founded the abbey of St. John.[2] Thus the mention of Eudo does not provide a useful *terminus a quo* but it does provide a *terminus ad quem* for the *Cumpoz*, for Eudo died near Rouen in February 1120, and was succeeded as steward by the notorious Geoffrey de Mandeville. In view of the fact that Philippe is known to have been active between 1121 and 1135, when Adeliza was queen, it can be supposed that he did not begin writing before the twelfth century, and here the *Cumpoz* supplies internal evidence that it was written in 1102, 1113, or 1119, for it postulates that the first of March was a Saturday and that the calendar had II in the column of concurrents. Professor Charles Haskins states categorically that it was written in 1119 without, however, giving any reasons for preferring this date.[3]

There is little to be said in favour of the *Cumpoz* as a work of art; nevertheless it may be more interesting than has been made out. After the dedication the prologue is thus divided according to the rubrics: 'Salutatio ad patrem'; 'Reprehensio allegorice per proverbia'; 'Redargutiones per proverbia'; 'Exhortatio auctoris'. This at once stamps Philippe as a pedant of the worst kind. There is no surer sign of pedantry in the Middle Ages than an excessive use of proverbs—the tradition, it will be remembered, survived into Lord Chesterfield's day, to be condemned as vulgar in polite conversation. After this lengthy prologue of 214 lines Philippe attacks his subject, the calculation of movable times and seasons. The

---

1 There is no article on Eudo in the *D.N.B.* His name occurs in every history of the period, but the fullest account of his career is contained in L. W. V. Harcourt, *His Grace the Steward* (London, 1907), pp. 14–16, 20, 22–23, 29–30, 34, 56, and J. Armitage Robinson, *Gilbert Crispin* (Cambridge, 1911), p. 136.

2 Dugdale, *Monasticon*, iv. 607.

3 *Studies in the History of Mediaeval Science* (Cambridge, Mass., 1924), pp. 84, 113, 330, 336–9.

poem, though written in a vernacular, is not intended for the laity, and the customary address to the public as *seignors* is replaced by one to his uncle as *maistre*. He names his sources with care: Bede, Helperic, Gerland, Turkil, and 'Nebroz' or Nimrod. The first three are to be expected; the last two were a mystery until they were identified by Professor Haskins.

Philippe's claim that he was carrying out St. Augustine's advice to the clergy may have been taken too seriously. Wright said: 'He informs us that he composed this book for the use of the priests of his time, and from the terms in which he speaks of them we may conclude that many of them were not able to study this science in the Latin of the original writers.'[1] It should be remembered, however, that Philippe was addicted to moralizing, and the appeal to St. Augustine is probably no more than the customary appeal to authority to give an air of respectability to what he was doing. The recitation of hard facts about the Signs of the Zodiac is embellished with allegorical interpretations which give them an ethical value but in no way aid the memory. There is no evidence that Philippe was writing for people who could not read Latin easily. The rubrics are in Latin, and Paul Meyer discovered a fragmentary manuscript which has considerable glosses in Latin. This fragment, of which he printed a fac-simile,[2] is late-twelfth- or early-thirteenth-century. It is easy enough to understand that a guide to the ecclesiastical calendar compiled from scattered sources and versified as a help to memory might have been found useful, but less easy to understand why the language chosen for it was French. There is one possible explanation which has not so far been considered, which may be deduced from the prologue:

Philipes de Thaün   At fait une raisun
Pur pruvaires guarnir   De la lei maintenir.
A sun uncle l'enveiet,   Que amender la deiet,
Se rien i at mesdit   En fait u en escrit,
A Hunfrei de Thaün   Le chapelein Yun
E seneschal le rei.   Iço vus di par mei.   (1–12)

(Philippe de Thaon has made a discourse to enable priests to keep

---

[1] *Biographia Britannica Literaria*, Anglo-Norman Period (London, 1846), p. 88.
[2] *Romania*, xl (1911), pp. 70–76.

the law of the Church. He sends it to his uncle that he may amend it, if there is anything wrong in fact or in writing—to Honfroi de Thaon, the chaplain to Eudo the king's steward. Here is what I have to tell you.)

Why was the work humbly dedicated to Honfroi de Thaon? Why was he assumed to be the person of all others capable of amending it? The answer lies, perhaps, in the position held by Honfroi. He was no parish priest, no monk, no ordinary. He was chaplain to the king's steward, who had charge of the household expenditure. This was before the great offices of state had become departments of the civil service. Each officer had, however, a staff of clerks to help him, and in those days, when few could read and write, chaplains were also private secretaries. This was so originally in the royal and noble houses, but the use of the word survived long in religious houses also; the Prioress's chaplain in the *Canterbury Tales* is a case in point. The steward's accounts would naturally be dated, like everything else, by the ecclesiastical calendar. They would be kept in Latin, but the vernacular of the office would be French. Possibly we have here an early monument of 'civil service' French, and it behoves us to beware of exaggeration when we say that after the Conquest English was replaced by Latin and not by French. This is really only true of the written language. *Language* Conversational English gave way to conversational French as English clerks were replaced by French ones. The steward himself, like other officers of the household at this date, was a layman, and if he took any interest in the workings of his department, everything would have to be explained to him in French, not Latin. There is a further small point worth mentioning in this connexion. One of Philippe's sources was Thurkil. For a long time this name meant nothing at all, but Professor Haskins has pointed out that there must have been a *Compotus*, now lost, compiled by Thurkil, the exchequer clerk who composed for a colleague a Latin treatise on multiplication, division, and fractions, perhaps between 1101 and 1117, but perhaps even earlier.[1] Here, then, Philippe is probably drawing upon a Latin work composed

[1] Op. cit., pp. 327–35. Cf. R. L. Poole, *The Exchequer in the Twelfth Century* (Oxford, 1912), p. 48.

for and used by another branch of the embryo civil service, and he may have thought it more useful to write in French. His purpose was to use a utilitarian treatise as the text for a sermon.

For this work Philippe, like some Norman writers, employed a line probably borrowed from the Latin hymns, a hexasyllabic rhymed couplet which may, alternatively, be considered a dodecasyllable with internal rhyme, in imitation of Marbode's Latin verses. The result is jerky and tiresome, and as will be seen, he himself later abandoned it as a medium. His style has been universally condemned as clumsy and childish. The clumsiness does not proceed from childishness but from pedantry. Philippe is unable to pass from one subject to another without announcing that he has finished the one and is now attacking another. This is not because he knows no other way of putting things, but because he has studied logic and rhetoric in the schools, and was perhaps engaged in teaching them, and does not realize that there is a time and a place for everything. He is pathetically anxious to do the right thing, in and out of season. Specimens of the twelfth-century schoolmen writing in a vernacular are rare, and Philippe is precious on that account alone. Moreover, there is evidence that he was very much to the taste of the public of the time, strange though this may seem.

The Bestiary and Lapidaries

The rest of the works by Philippe de Thaon are all of the same kind and probably intended for the laity. Evidently the allegorical parts of the *Cumpoz* had found favour, and, Philippe next approached the court, perhaps through Eudo. His second work was probably the *Bestiaire*,[1] since this is written in the same metre as the *Cumpoz*. It was dedicated to Adeliza of Louvain, the queen to whom the rededication of the *Brendan* was addressed, and must therefore have been written between 1121, the date of her marriage to the king, and 1139, the date of her remarriage to William d'Albini, Earl of Arundel, but more probably before 1135 when Henry I died, since she is described as 'reine corunee' and 'reine

---

[1]   Ed. E. Walberg (Lund and Paris, 1900). New edition in preparation by U. T. Holmes.

d'Engletere'. A suggestion that it was really written for Henry I, on the grounds that he kept a menagerie at Woodstock, is improbable. Such popularizations as this were more likely intended for ladies. The menagerie may, however, have been the starting-point for this allegory.[1]

This *Bestiary* is the oldest in the French language and is divided into two parts, a Bestiary proper and a Volucrary. Later Philippe seems to have wished to make it a tripartite work by adding a Lapidary. This, in its turn, is possibly the oldest Lapidary in French. The *Lapidary* known as the 'First Version' is of much the same date and is also originally Anglo-Norman. Philippe's third part is preserved in only one manuscript (Cotton Nero A. v), which happens to be the oldest of the three extant. The first forty-six lines are in the same metre as the *Bestiary* and the *Cumpoz*, the hexasyllabic rhyming couplet, which has been studied by Walberg and shown to be occasionally 'broken' even at this early date. Then suddenly Philippe announces:

> Or voil jeo mun metre muer
> Pur ma raison mielz ordener. (2889–90)

(Now I intend to change my metre in order to present my argument better.)

And the rest of the poem is in octosyllabic couplets. Unfortunately the folio containing the beginning of the part in octosyllables is missing, and it is not known whether there was any further explanation of the change. Later, a couplet makes plain that at one time the author thought of the three parts as a whole:

> Mustré ai or de treis manieres
> De bestes, d'oisels e de pieres. (3815–16)

(I have now demonstrated three manners, the manner of beasts, the manner of birds, and the manner of stones.)

It appears that between the first and second drafts of his *Bestiary* Philippe had discovered the virtues of the octosyllabic couplet. In this he wrote the *Lapidary* known as 'Apocalyptic', because it treats at length of the twelve foundation-stones of the Heavenly Jerusalem. He claimed for this that it was 'extrait de gramaire'—that is, from Latin, and at

[1] Cf. A. Krappe, *Modern Language Notes*, lix (1944), pp. 325-7.

the end of the section on stones in the *Bestiary* he refers the reader to it for fuller information. After this, he probably wrote the 'Alphabetical Lapidary', which was purely descriptive and contains no allegories but counted as a terrestrial Lapidary which he intended to have a 'celestial' sequel containing the allegories. Obviously this would have ranked in his estimation as his *chef-d'œuvre*, but if it was ever written, and there is no evidence that it was even begun, it has completely vanished. Professor Studer and Miss Evans identified it with the 'Apocalyptic Lapidary', but M. Langlois has since pointed out that this Lapidary lacks the prologue and the theological interpretations that Philippe had planned.[1]

The source of the *Bestiaire* is the *Physiologus* with a few additions.[2] After the description of each beast comes the explanation of its 'signefiance'. The name of many of the beasts is given in Greek, with an explanation usually derived from Isidore of Seville, quoted as Ysidorus in line 1109. What Philippe says about the name of the panther is unique and is quoted in the article on the animal in the *Encyclopaedia Britannica*, for it appears that no one has a better idea on the subject.

PANTERE est une beste	De mult precïus estre.
E oëz de sun num	Signeficatiun:
Pan en griu *trestut* est,	Kar de tel nature est:
Ele at multes valurs	Si at plusurs colurs . . . (461–8)

Pan c'est *tut*, Deus est *pan*.   (529)

(PANTHER is a beast of very precious nature. So hear the meaning of her name: *Pan* in Greek is *everything*, for this beast is of such a kind that she has many valuable qualities, and so is of many colours. . . . *Pan* is *all*, and God is *pan*.)

The queen's own name, too, is allegorized:

Aaliz sis nuns est;	Loenge de Dé est
En ebreu en verté	*Aaliz, laus* de Dé. (15–18)

(Her name is Adeliza; in Hebrew, in very truth, it is 'Praise of God'. Adeliza—*laus* of God.)

[1] P. Studer and J. Evans, *Anglo-Norman Lapidaries* (Paris, 1924), p. 262. Ch.-V. Langlois, *La Connaissance de la nature et du monde au Moyen Âge* (Paris, 1927), pp. 10–11.

[2] Cf. F. McCulloch, *Mediaeval Latin and French Bestiaries* (University of North Carolina, 1960), pp. 47–54.

This, of course, is nonsense. The name is the Germanic 'Adel-
haid', meaning 'nobility'. Philippe, struck by the chance resemblance of the name with *Alleluia*, has quietly slipped in
Isidore's explanation of the Hebrew word.[1] In extenuation it
may be pointed out that clerks wrestling to compose Latin
charters were in the habit of falling back on Biblical names
or some near equivalent. Thus Aulay (Olaf) can become
Amelec. In the case of bestiaries, it is possible that Philippe
set a fashion for allegorizing the name of the patron as well
as of the beasts. ⌋

The *Bestiary* remained popular for some time. One of the
manuscripts (Copenhagen Gamle Kungl. Saml. 3466) was
written at Paris, and was 'Gallicized'. Another (Merton
College 249) has a second dedication, added in a different
hand and written in octosyllables, to Eleanor of Aquitaine.
It has been suggested by Langlois that this may have been
the work of Philippe himself and written at the same time
as the Lapidary addition. But it seems unlikely that Philippe
was still active about 1152, and anybody would have been
capable of making use of the epilogue in octosyllables, as the
writer of the rededication did. The important point is that
the *Bestiary* must have been enjoyed in the same kind of
society for at least thirty years—a long life for a work of this
kind. It had one great advantage over the lapidaries in that
it lent itself to illustration; but the lapidaries too were popular. The 'Alphabetic Lapidary' was copied about 1200 in a
manuscript which belonged to Durham (Cambridge, Jesus
College Q. D. 2). A manuscript of a condensed version in
Latin prose was copied in Italy in the late thirteenth century.
The 'Apocalyptic Lapidary' exists in two manuscripts, both
Anglo-Norman, one written in the thirteenth century, the
other as late as the first half of the fourteenth. The 'First
French Lapidary', which was probably more or less contemporary with Philippe's and was also Anglo-Norman, was
copied in England from the beginning of the thirteenth
century till the beginning of the fourteenth; in the late
thirteenth century it was being copied in the Norman kingdom of Sicily, and it was also known in Champagne and in

---

[1] Cf. M. D. Legge, 'To speik of Science, Craft and Sapience', *Literature and
Science* (Oxford, 1955), p. 122.

north-east France. Like the 'Alphabetic Lapidary' it was not read only by the laity for whom it was devised. One manuscript (Cambridge, Pembroke College 87) belonged to Bury St. Edmunds, another (Gonville and Caius College 435) to St. Augustine's, Canterbury. This lapidary was the basis for four versions in French prose, the earliest of which was made in the mid-twelfth century. There was more French prose than the late Professor R. W. Chambers reckoned with, and it will be discussed in a later chapter.

Philippe de Thaon, dull though he was, was evidently a writer of some importance in his day, and even now he can be credited with a considerable output. His chief merit is, as has long been recognized, that he was a pioneer. He certainly wrote the first Computus and the first bestiary in French. Whether he or the author of the 'First French Version' wrote the earliest lapidary in French is a point of some interest. Did some rival steal a march on him, producing a work of the kind that Philippe thought that he had made his own? Did he thereupon perceive the superiority of the octosyllable over the hexasyllable and hurriedly adopt it for his remaining works, or did he have it forced upon his attention by his public?

Philippe's literary qualities are indeed not of a high order, but perhaps the epithets of childish and inarticulate applied to him by Waters[1] are inexact. His faults are those of a pedant, and pedantry may be clumsy, but is not inarticulate; it is sophisticated, not childish. Philippe and Benedeit are simply not to be compared, the one, a secular clerk trained painfully in the schools and devoting himself to popularizations in the vernacular, the other, a monk gifted with a poetic imagination, possibly a musician, telling a story as romantic as it was edifying. We should be grateful for the evidence of such variety in early Anglo-Norman. In view of what survives from this period it seems reasonable to suppose that the reign of Henry I saw the production of a considerable amount of didactic writing in French, the ground for which had been prepared by the philosophical and scientific stirrings of the godless and uneasy reign of William Rufus.[2]

---

[1] *St. Brendan*, p. iv.
[2] Cf. J. Armitage Robinson, *Gilbert Crispin* (Cambridge, 1911), p. 74.

III

STEPHEN AND THE ANARCHY

THE reign of Stephen is a period the mention of which ordinarily arouses feelings of revulsion, and it does not sound as though it would have been favourable to the development of a literature. Informed opinion, however, no longer condemns the whole reign as one of horror, and Dr. Austin Lane Poole has pointed out in a recent book[1] that from 1148 to 1153 the country was at peace. There is no reason to feel surprise at the fact that there is no break in the continuity of Anglo-Norman literature, not even during the Anarchy. It is true that little survives from this time, but what little there is continues to be in advance of what is extant from the Continent. Two writers certainly, and a third probably, belong to this reign, and each wrote a work which is the earliest of its kind in the French language.

GAIMAR AND THE *ESTORIE DES ENGLEIS*

Shortly after the death of Henry I there burst upon the world one of the decisive books in literary history, comparable in its effects to another great literary hoax based on Celtic myths, Macpherson's *Ossian*. By the year 1129 Geoffrey of Monmouth, a man probably of Breton origin, was at Oxford, where he became acquainted with the Archdeacon Walter at the collegiate church of St. George. According to his own story, he borrowed from the archdeacon a history in the British tongue, which he translated into Latin. Before this task was completed, Alexander, Bishop of Lincoln, persuaded him to translate into Latin the Welsh *Prophecies of Merlin* and so postpone the finish of the *Historia* until after the death of Henry I, for whose glorification the work had been planned. Setting a fashion in exploiting British myths, it ran like wildfire through

---

[1] *From Domesday Book to Magna Carta* (Oxford, 1955), p. 150.

England and Normandy, and it was as early as 1139 that
Henry of Huntingdon saw a copy at Bec.[1]

Even before this, that is to say, some time between the
death of Henry I in 1135 and the remarriage of Adeliza of
Louvain in 1139, a copy of the book was in the possession of
the northern baron, Walter Espec, at Helmsley. It was borrowed from him by a certain Ralph Fitz-Gilbert, a person of
importance in Lincolnshire who was granted lands by various
magnates to whom he may have been related. One of these,
whose illegitimate connexion he may have been, was Gilbert
of Gaunt, who was taken prisoner at the siege of Lincoln in
1140/1, and forced by Rannulf de Gernons, Earl of Chester,
to marry his niece the daughter of Richard Fitz-Gilbert of
Clare and Alice, daughter of Rannulf le Meschin, Earl of
Chester. These people will be mentioned later in this chapter.
Ralph Fitz-Gilbert had married Constance, a Hampshire
heiress,[2] who was a person of some education, with a taste for
literature. Gaimar says at the end of his work that she had
given a silver mark for the *Life of Henry I* written by David
for Adeliza of Louvain, and kept it and read it in her chamber. The wording suggests that she could herself read, and
there is no evidence as to the language of the poem. As
Gaimar compares this work to his own, it seems likely that
it was in French. Moreover, it is doubtful whether Adeliza
understood Latin, though, as we have seen, her predecessor
did.[3] It was Constance who borrowed Geoffrey's *Historia*
from her husband—who had himself borrowed it from
Walter Espec—and gave it to Gaimar to work upon. He
seems to have begun his book in Hampshire and finished it
in Lincolnshire.

With the possible exception of David, whose poem is not
extant, Gaimar is the oldest chronicler in the French language. That is something, but he is a pioneer in a particular

---

[1] For references cf. J. J. Parry and R. A. Caldwell in *Arthurian Literature in the
Middle Ages*, ed. R. S. Loomis (Oxford, 1959), pp. 72–93.

[2] For all that is known about Ralph see D. M. Williamson, 'Ralf son of Gilbert
and Ralf son of Ralf', *Lincolnshire Architectural and Archaeological Society, Reports
and Papers*, 1953, pp. 19–26. Cf. *Complete Peerage*, vii. 672–3.

[3] P. A. Becker, *Der gepaarte Achtsilber in der französischen Dichtung* (Leipzig,
1934), p. 39, thinks it was in Latin and that David was the Bishop of Bangor
(1120–39).

type of chronicle besides. He was the first to turn into a vernacular the kind of chronicle known as a *Brut*, from Brutus the Trojan, the legendary founder of the kingdom of Britain. Not content with this, he proceeded to supply a sequel bringing the history of the country down to contemporary times, ending with a rudimentary third part, a sketch of an account of the king who had just died. In so doing, Gaimar set the pattern of popular history for something like three centuries. This is a fact for which he has never been given sufficient credit.

As Gaimar left his work, it consisted of a *Brut*, opening with the story of the Argonauts and the Siege of Troy, and a story of the English, ending with a few lines on the late king. The *Brut*, except possibly for a few fragments,[1] has disappeared but there can be no shadow of doubt that it once existed, for the *Estorie des Engleis*[2] opens by declaring that it is a sequel to it, giving a very brief outline of its contents. This begins:

> Ça en arere, el livere bien devant,
> Si vus en estes remembrant
> Avez oï com faitement
> Costentin tint apres Artur tenement . . .   (1–4)

(Heretofore, in the book written some time ago, if you have it in mind, you have heard exactly how Constantine held the domain after Arthur . . .)

There is a further reference to the first book at the end of the poem:

> Treske ci dit Gaima de Troie.
> Il començat la u Jasun
> Ala conquere la tuison;
> Si l'ad definé ci endreit.
> De Deu seium nus beneit. Amen.   (6529–33)

(Up to this Gaimar spoke of Troy. He began at the point where Jason went to win the Fleece, and he has brought it to an end here and now. May God bless us. Amen.)

---

[1] Printed by R. Imelmann, *Laȝamon, Versuch über seine Quellen* (Berlin, 1906).

[2] Ed. A. Bell (A.N.T.S., 1960). The quotations are from the Rolls Series edition by Sir T. Duffus Hardy and C. T. Martin, made from B.M. Royal 13. A. xxi, the best, though not the oldest manuscript, especially from the historical point of view. Cf. my review, *Modern Language Review*, lvi (1961), pp. 264–6, and J. P. Collas, *Medium Ævum*, xxx (1961), pp. 109–10.

The disappearance of the *Brut* probably accounts for the failure to realize the importance of Gaimar in the development of the vernacular chronicle. It may have been called *L'Estorie des Bretuns*, since it is followed by a second part called *L'Estorie des Engleis*. The word *Estorie*, simple though it looks, is not easy to translate. It is both our 'history' and our 'story', and was used for a history which was also a story. So, the Life of William Marshall was called 'L'Estorie del conte'. On the whole, 'story' is preferable to 'history'. Gaimar's *Estorie des Bretuns* seems to have been deliberately suppressed. There are extant four manuscripts of the *Estorie des Engleis*, dating from the early thirteenth to the early fourteenth century, and every single one of them introduces it by a *Brut* chronicle. But this *Brut* is not by Gaimar but by Wace.[1] It is usually assumed that Wace, patronized as he was by royalty, enjoyed a vogue denied to the more obscure Gaimar, and it is indisputable that Wace was a livelier writer than his predecessor, though this, being a matter of taste, may not have counted for anything. What seems preferable today did not necessarily have more appeal yesterday. Another, subtler reason has been put forward by Dr. Bell.[2] According to Gaimar's epilogue, he used as source not only 'le livere Walter Espac'—generally identified with Geoffrey of Monmouth's *Historia*—but 'le bon livere de Oxeford' which had belonged to Walter the Archdeacon. This is the book on British history which he was using before he had access to the book borrowed from Walter Espec. It is curious that Walter the Archdeacon is supposed to have owned two book on British history, one in Latin used by Gaimar, and one in Welsh, translated by Geoffrey, but this is what Gaimar at any rate believed. Dr. Bell's suggestion is that Wace, by relying on Geoffrey, may have been more popular than Gaimar, whose rendering of Geoffrey was adulterated with the 'Oxford book'. But for centuries afterwards, in verse and prose, in Latin, French, and English, the popular history was to follow the pattern set by Gaimar, a *Brut*, a history of the English, and a third part bringing it up to date. Wace himself perhaps knew Gaimar's book, and followed his *Brut*

[1] Ed. I. O. Arnold (S.A.T.F., 1938, 1940).
[2] A. Bell, *Modern Language Review*, xxv (1930), pp. 56–57.

not by a history of the English kings, but by one of the Norman dukes, the *Roman de Rou*, which he seems to have intended to continue down to contemporary times, a project which, as he declared, was abandoned in disgust. Formerly it was assumed that Wace made use of Gaimar, but Dr. Bell is doubtful on this point, and in the absence of Gaimar's first book it is impossible to make a comparison between the two. Trice Martin, however, did point out[1] that Wace seems to be inspired by Gaimar's *Estorie des Engleis* in a faulty chronology of Rufus's reign. Whether Gaimar's *Brut* had any influence on works other than Wace is also a question which is difficult to answer, but it seems possible that it had.[2] It is true that works written at this date for private patrons might never circulate outside the family,[3] but little can be deduced from the gap of about a century between the composition of the *Estorie* and the first extant copy of it. Dr. Bell relies on this for his contention that there was a revival of Gaimar, but the situation is not unparalleled elsewhere. The gap in the case of Crestien is thirty to fifty years. Is it to be argued that he was unread during that period? Ralph Fitz-Gilbert was, after all, a far from obscure personage and anything written for his family could have circulated through the channels by which Geoffrey's *Historia* had reached him, in the reverse direction.

Gaimar's extant work has little value as history, much as a repository of tradition and as an example of history rewritten to conform to preconceived ideas. Professor Darlington has said that 'though it draws upon some other sources, it follows the Anglo-Saxon Chronicle sufficiently closely to entitle Gaimar to a place among the translators of that work'.[4] But Gaimar's additions are more important than this statement would suggest. It is naturally of interest that he should have made any use of English books, and have been capable of

---

[1] Ed. II, p. xxxvii.

[2] Cf. A. D. H. Bivar, 'Lyonesse: The Evolution of a Fable', *Modern Philology*, l (1952), p. 167.

[3] Cf. R. N. Walpole, *Philip Mouskes and the Pseudo-Turpin Chronicle* (University of California Publications, xxvi, 1947), pp. 364–7. For the Anglo-Norman version by William de Briane for Alice de Courcy cf. J. A. Noonan in *Studies . . . presented to M. K. Pope* (Manchester, 1939), pp. 247–51.

[4] R. R. Darlington, *Anglo-Norman Historians* (Birkbeck College, University of London, 1947), p. 6.

translating them, especially as his name, which has never
been accounted for, appears to be Norman. This, however,
was a time when the Norman settlers were taking an interest
in the past of the country and its heroes: the Norman-Welsh,
like Geoffrey, in the British, the Anglo-Normans in the English past. Gaimar apparently made use of two copies of the
Chronicle, possibly because he moved about; and besides the
Chronicle, a book that was not to be found in every house,
he had access to Danish traditions probably found in Lincolnshire.[1] It has long been known that he incorporated the
story of Haveloc into his book and had to juggle with
chronology to fit him into the list of English kings; but there
was formerly some doubt about the relationship between his
account, the Anglo-Norman and English lays, and the English version known as the Lambeth Interpolation. Dr. Bell
argues that both the Anglo-Norman lay and the Interpolation derive from Gaimar, who was responsible for localizing
the story. The fact that the lay is later than Gaimar has been
recognized for some time.[2] The adaptation is of technical
interest. Besides this famous story there are four other short
passages dealing with 'Danish' kings, apparently local legends
which Gaimar modified to fit in with contemporary views on
feudality and sovereignty. In these more original passages
he adopts a slightly more lively style, employing, for instance, direct speech. It is possible, too, that Gaimar had
access to Celtic traditions other than those of Geoffrey and
the 'Oxford Book'. Lives of Scottish and Irish saints, some
of them now lost, were being read in England. Interest in
them was at any rate partly due to Henry I's Anglo-Scottish
marriage and later connexions with Scotland. Geoffrey himself created the prophet Merlin out of a mixed ancestry
which included the prophet Lailoken, who had an encounter
with St. Kentigern, Glasgow's St. Mungo, just outside that
city. The two twelfth-century Lives of the saint which are in
part preserved are based upon material, now lost or destroyed,
containing heretical, and presumably romantic, accounts which
must have been available to people other than hagiographers.

---

[1] A. Bell, 'Early "Danish" Kings', *P.M.L.A.*, lxv (1950), pp. 601–40.
[2] E. Fahnestock, *A Study of the Sources and Composition of the Old French Lai
d'Haveloc* (New York, 1915). Cf. A. Bell, *Le Lai d'Haveloc* (M.U.P., 1925).

It is therefore a mistake, even at the present stage when so much obviously remains to be done, to dismiss the *Estorie des Engleis* as interesting for the language alone. It is true that Gaimar is one of the villains who, according to the late Professor R. W. Chambers, tried to destroy the prose tradition of England, though as will presently appear there was an Anglo-Norman prose of which he had not heard. By translations into Latin or French the writers of the twelfth century helped to send the English language into eclipse. They read and used English books. Later writers made little use of English sources, which had been superseded by translations and compendiums. No one troubled any more to write in local dialects anything intended to last. But there is more in it than this. Gaimar was a writer with ideas, and as he wrote, he learned. His narrative becomes less and less a dry restatement of his sources, more and more romantic and attractive. He tried, in true medieval style, to interpret the past in terms of the present, and he was loyal to his patrons and their family. He refers the reader to the superior knowledge of Nicholas de Trailli, nephew of Walter Espec. For him, Hugh Lupus, Earl of Chester, the father of Rannulf le Meschin and grandfather of Rannulf de Gernons, was a splendid magnate who had surrounded himself with nobler and richer men than the Emperor of Lombardy himself. He had equal praise for Hugh Lupus's boorish behaviour at the coronation of William Rufus, when he was too proud to carry one of the swords which four Norman earls had snatched from Welsh 'kings', and for Rufus's treatment of the episode as a joke and his selection of the Earl of Chester and his successors to carry the sceptre. On this occasion he celebrated the king's sense of humour which, in spite of its crudity, is to be reckoned one of his few redeeming features. Another of his characteristics, his love of luxury, is exemplified by Gaimar's description of the great feast given by the king in his 'New Hall' at Westminster—the scene of so many coronation banquets in the future. On this first occasion kings, earls, and dukes were present in plenty. No fewer than three hundred ushers manned the doors, and in their capacity as 'sticks-in-waiting' conducted the king's guests up the steps, instead of grooms, and accompanied those that bore the dishes and flagons from the kitchen, lest anyone should sample or disarrange them on the way. Each was sumptuously attired in vair or 'grey', or fine silk cloth from oversea. All held fiefs and honours, and had livery as befits courtiers. As the moralists of the time desired, Rufus is chiefly remembered for his vices. Yet he had gifts: he had a lively mind and encouraged scientific inquiry, and showed interest, to the horror of the Church, in Jewish philosophy. In Gaimar we see him invested with glamour by a generation passing into the age of romance. In his tastes he seems to foreshadow the successor who gave his 'New Hall' the appearance we know so well today: Richard of Bordeaux. It is not the recital of historical facts, but the preservation of contemporary gossip in high circles, which lends value to histories such as Gaimar's. His account of Rufus's end, dismissed as fiction by Freeman and others, is of special interest. The particular points to be noticed are as follows: Gaimar is at pains to describe a scene, before the fatal hunt, in which the foreigner Tirel indulges in light-hearted banter with the King, proving in the first place that they were on very friendly terms, and in the second that the King accepted Tirel's challenge to go oversea. He would keep his Christmas at Poitiers, 'Si jo tant vif', 'if I live so long'—a piece of dramatic irony. The King was jesting, but the other had treachery in his heart. The court then took part in a deer-drive. Tirel was dismounted near the King, and shot at a large stag, which he missed. At the same moment the King was pierced by an arrow which the other archers declared to be Tirel's. Colour was lent to this view by the fact that Tirel fled. The King, mortally wounded, wished to communicate and was given the conventional blades of grass by a huntsman. Three barons gave way to grief over the corpse, two of them members of the family of Clare and brothers-in-law to Tirel. Thanks to their care, the body was conveyed decently in an improvised litter to Winchester, where after it had lain in state it was buried with pomp and circumstance by Bishop Wakelin and other clergy. Now all this last part is clean contrary to the usual story that the body was deserted and ultimately thrown into a farm-cart for carriage to Winchester, where it was hustled into the ground without ceremony, and the fact that Wakelin was already dead makes it almost certain that Gaimar was inventing, though he may have made a slip. The exact truth about Rufus's death will probably never be known, but the most recent writer on the subject has summed up the matter thus:[1] 'There is, at the least, enough evidence to arouse the suspicion that the sudden end of Rufus was the result of a conspiracy formed and organized among members of the House of Clare, a conspiracy of which Henry himself was cognizant.' What we have in Gaimar is the version put about by that family, connexions of the patron for whom he was writing, and though it may not be true, it is certainly of historical importance. It is worth noting that on an earlier occasion Gaimar had given a more picturesque account than the one generally accepted of the death of a king through treachery. This is his description of the plot to destroy Edmund Ironside by means of a 'machine infernale'—'L'arc ki ne falt'.[2] It is possible that a story so strange may have been true.

In his poem Gaimar employed the octosyllabic rhyming couplet, which he probably transmitted to Wace, who handed it on to Benoit de Sainte More, historian and romancer, and so to all subsequent writers of classical and Arthurian romances. Syllabically, Gaimar's verse attained a high level of correctitude by continental standards, but the use of the caesura lends it monotony. Whether the work was intended to be read or sung, this is a legacy of the old singing days. Gaimar is important not only as the earliest author of an extant chronicle in French, but as one of the first writers to use the octosyllabic couplet as a matter of course. Even Wace experimented with longer lines in the *Roman de Rou*, Jordan Fantosme used a mixture of decasyllables and alexandrines, and much later Matthew Paris wrote a saint's life in alexandrines before definitely adopting the octosyllable. Benedeit, Gaimar, Wace, these are the ancestors of a metrical form used by writers of saints' lives and romances alike. It is a form which is not dead yet.

---

[1] A. Lane Poole, *From Domesday Book to Magna Carta* (Oxford, 1955), p. 114.

[2] Cf. M. D. Legge, 'The Unerring Bow', *Medium Ævum*, xxv (1956), pp. 79–83. William of Malmesbury knew a similar story: *Gesta Regum*, ed. W. Stubbs (R.S.), i. 217.

Bearing in mind that he was writing for a lay patron, and for a lady, Gaimar makes some attempt to make his work attractive by more and more frequent use of direct speech, and by occasional descriptions of clothes, furnishings, and drinking-vessels. He delights to recount at length stories such as those of Haveloc, Hereward, Taillefer, and the martyrdom of St. Edmund of East Anglia and the finding of his severed head by the wolf. He plainly enjoyed telling of King Edgar's wooing of Ælfthryth, and his subsequent marriage to her. His lines about Henry I show the way the wind was blowing—the courtly romance was not far in the future:

> Ço est d'amur e dosnaier
> De boscheier e del gaber,
> E de festes e des noblesces,
> Des largetez e des richesces,
> E del barnage k'il mena,
> Des larges dons k'il dona;
> D'iço devereit hom bien chanter,
> Nient leissir ne trespasser.   (6512–19)

(It is of love and the courtship of ladies, of sport in the woods and jesting, of feasts and noble behaviour, or largesses and riches, and of the great following of barons he maintained, of the generous gifts which he gave; of all this a man ought to sing, leaving out or passing over nothing.)

These references, apparently, were related to a side of the king's character that David, writing for the queen, had preferred, perhaps tactfully, to ignore.

Gaimar, dull though he sometimes may be, is a writer whose achievement in both form and content is magnificent. And it is well to remember that he was not writing for a royal patron, but for the wife of a country gentleman.[1]

SANSON DE NANTUIL AND THE PROVERBS OF SOLOMON

The second in date of the writers of this period wrote for a family connected with Gaimar's patrons. This is Sanson de

---

[1] Besides the works already mentioned, Dr. Bell has written on Gaimar in *Notes and Queries* (1921), pp. 104–5, *Modern Language Review*, xviii (1923), pp. 22–28, and *Medium Ævum*, vii (1938), pp. 184–98.

Nantuil, who from his name appears to be, like Philippe de Thaon, a member of a family which still prided itself on its continental connexions. Sanson is the author of a translation, with commentary, of the Proverbs of Solomon into French verse. This text is more interesting than it sounds, and it is a pity that it has never been edited.

The circumstances of its composition are romantic. Sanson explains, in his prologue:

> Ki ben en volt estre enqueranz
> Entendet dunc a cest Romanz
> Que al loenge Damne Dé
> E a s'enor at translaté
> Sanson de Nantuil, ki sovient
> De sa dame qu'il aime e creient,
> Ki mainte feiz l'en out preied
> Que li desclairast cel traited.
> Le num de ceste damme escrist
> Cil ki translation fist.
> Aeliz de Cundé l'apele
> Noble damme enseigne e bele.
> Ne quident pas li losengier
> Qu'ot eus se voille acompaigner,
> Kar trestut cil de sa contree
> Unt ben oï sa renumee.

(Whoso wishes to inquire about this, let him listen to this Romance version, which Sanson de Nantuil has translated to the praise and honour of Almighty God. He remembers his lady whom he loves and fears, who has many times prayed him to make this treatise plain for her. He who made this translation inscribes the name of this lady; he calls her Alize de Condet, a distinguished and beautiful lady. The flatterers need not think that he is joining forces with them, for all those in her neighbourhood have heard all about her fame.)

Sanson is shown by his prologue to be a writer in the courtly tradition, something which might not be guessed from his subject-matter. The choice, however, was not his, but the lady's, and it is necessary for the understanding of the text to recall what is known about her life.

Some account of Alice de Condet was given by the Abbé de la Rue, and after him by Thomas Wright,[1] but this has

---

[1] *Essais historiques sur les bardes* . . . , ii (Caen, 1834), pp. 132 ff. *Biographia Britannica Literaria*, Anglo-Norman Period (London, 1846), pp. 129-31.

now been superseded. All that can be deduced about her life has been collected by the late Canon C. W. Foster, in an appendix to the first volume of the *Registrum Antiquissimum* of the Cathedral Church of Lincoln.[1] The sketch which follows, necessary to give the background to this text, is mainly based upon that appendix.

The story begins with Rannulf le Meschin, Earl of Chester, son of Gaimar's Hugh Lupus. His daughter Alice, mentioned above, married Richard Fitz-Gilbert of Clare, and had two sons, the elder of whom later became first Earl of Hertford. In 1136 Richard was slain by the Welsh near Abergavenny, and his widow was besieged in a castle, from which she was rescued in romantic fashion by Miles of Gloucester, who led an expedition for the purpose at considerable risk to himself.[2] At this point Alice Fitz-Gilbert disappears, but Alice de Condet enters the scene, and Canon Foster has shown that there is good reason for thinking them to be one and the same. Rannulf's son and heir, Rannulf de Gernons, held lands in Lincolnshire, and was hand in glove with his elder half-brother, William de Roumare, who became Earl of Lincoln. Far from trying to oust one another from Lincoln, in the traditional manner of half-brothers, these two pooled their resources. In the course of their vacillations between the causes of the Empress Maud and Stephen, the Roumare family forfeited their earldom, but Rannulf emerged none the worse. Of him the *Complete Peerage* quaintly remarks: 'He distinguished himself as a soldier both on the side of the Empress Maud and of that of King Stephen, with the greatest impartiality.'[3] It is not likely that the sister of this ambitious baron would be allowed to remain a widow for long, and Robert de Condet, a Lincoln landowner and probably a relation of their mother, would provide an alliance which would strengthen the hands of Rannulf and William de Roumare. Robert died on 10 October, in 1140 at latest. His widow Alice, and his son and heir Roger, gave some land to Lincoln Cathedral for the

[1] The Lincoln Record Society, vol. xxvii (1931), pp. 277–95. I owe this reference to Dr. A. L. Poole, and my thanks are also due to Miss K. Major for her advice.

[2] *Gesta Stephani*, in *Chronicles of Stephen, Henry II, and Richard I*, ed. R. Howlett (Rolls Series, iii. 13), and K. R. Potter (Nelson's Medieval Classics, 1955), p. 12.

[3] Revised edition, iii. 166.

repose of his soul; this is mentioned in a Papal Bull of 6 February 1146, and the gift was confirmed by Roger when he came of age. At the end of 1140 Rannulf and his brother seized Lincoln Castle by a trick, and in December Stephen tried to propitiate them by rewarding them with grants. It is probably to this moment that a curious charter, which gives the probable clue to the relationship between Rannulf and Alice, ascribed by Canon Foster to 1149, really belongs.[1] In this Rannulf is granted the restoration of his castles and extensive privileges besides, and it ends with the statement that 'for the love he bore the said Earl Rannulf' he has restored to Alice de Condet all her land, including Horn-castria, after the destruction of the castle. Horncastria was formerly identified with Horncastle, but Canon Foster has shown that it is probably a mistake for Thorngate, made by the scribe who copied the charter—the original has unluckily disappeared—in 1325. It is difficult to understand the point of this clause unless it is assumed that there was close rela-tionship between Rannulf and Alice.

Shortly afterwards, before the Battle of Lincoln on 2 Febru-ary 1141, the arrangement about the castle of Thorngate was revoked. Evidently Stephen did not trust the site to a sister of Rannulf and William of Roumare. By a writ dated at Lincoln, and witnessed by—amongst others— Simon de St. Liz, who is known to have been present at the siege,[2] the king granted to the Bishop of Lincoln (Alexander, who deflected Geoffrey of Monmouth from the completion of his *Historia* and made him write the *Vita Merlini*) the ward-ship of Alice's son while under age, and the pledge which Alice gave the king of her castle of Thorngate in the suburb of Lincoln and all her other lands. Meanwhile Rannulf was holding grimly on to his gains, but in 1146, when he was at Stephen's court at Northampton, the king seized the oppor-tunity to make him give up Lincoln, and he purchased his liberty only by surrendering all his castles, and by giving hostages, one of whom was his nephew the Earl of Hertford,

---

[1] Printed by Canon Foster, and the subject of J. H. Round's article 'King Stephen and the Earl of Chester', *English Historical Review*, x (1895), pp. 87–91. The discovery of a fresh manuscript of the *Gesta Stephani* has led to a revision of the date. See A. L. Poole in *Gesta Stephani*, transl. K. R. Potter, pp. xvi–xxii.

[2] *Henry of Huntingdon*, ed. T. Arnold (Rolls Series), p. 270.

supposedly Alice's son. He in his turn purchased his liberty by pledging his castles next year, and joined his uncle, who, like Geoffrey de Mandeville on a previous occasion, was simply going amok.

Roger de Condet seems to have come of age and been made a knight between 1160 and 1165. The dates suggest that his parents were married in 1137 or 1138, a year or two after the death of Richard Fitz-Gilbert, and that Roger was born in 1138 or 1139, and was a year or two old at his father's death.

There is no mention of Sanson de Nantuil in any of the charters of Alice de Condet, but he was probably her chaplain. He was undoubtedly a man of education, and an ecclesiastic. As a writer, he is not to be despised. He handled the octo-syllabic couplet with grace, and his translation is far from dry, whatever Thomas Wright said of it. Besides the prologue and short extract which he printed, there is a longer passage published by Bartsch–Horning[1] which gives some idea of his quality. To be sure, it would be difficult to go wrong in the passage selected—from the seventh chapter—but it was to be feared that Sanson would overdo the commentary, and this he has managed to avoid. The scene has been well visualized:

> Des fenestres de ma meison
> Esgardei, ço dit Salemon;
> Par les chancelx gardai e vi
> Les petiz que jo la choisi.
> Les petiz vi, s'ei esgardé
> Un damisel mult forsené
> Par ces places le vi aler
> Joste un angle el vespre arester;
> Lez la veie de sa meison
> Alot regardant environ
> El seir obscur, quant avesprout
> E la nuit alques s'espeisout.
> Une moiller ad encontree
> Ki putement ert atornee,
> Apareillee a almes prendre.

---

[1] K. Bartsch and A. Horning, *La Langue et la littérature françaises* (Paris, 1887), pp. 150–8.

(From the window of my house I looked, saith Solomon; I looked through the bars and saw the simple ones I there descried. I beheld the simple ones and discerned a young squire void of understanding. I saw him pass through the streets and stop by a corner in the evening; he went the way to her house looking about him in the twilight, when it drew towards evening and the night was becoming very dark. And he met a woman who was attired like an harlot, ready to catch souls.)

Whether this work attained any sort of circulation cannot be estimated, though perhaps if it was published it might be easier to judge whether it had any influence. At least, the sole manuscript (B.M. Harley 4388) in which it has been preserved is not the original, but an early-thirteenth-century copy of this and various other twelfth-century moral treatises, which suggests that it was fairly well known.

The *Proverbs* may have been composed as a moral text-book for Roger de Condet, and they are the first work of this kind extant in the French language. Alice and Sanson would not know of anything outside the Old Testament where-withal a young man might cleanse his way. Grammar-school boys had their 'Cato', and quite soon this was to be trans-lated no fewer than three times into Anglo-Norman. That collection of supposedly moral tales, the *Disciplina Clericalis*, also translated into Anglo-Norman before the end of the century,[1] had perhaps not yet reached England. In the schools and universities parts of the *Nicomachean Ethics* were in use before the close of the twelfth century, and are men-tioned as a matter of course in Robert Curzon's Paris statutes of 1215.[2] But Roger de Condet was not a grammar-school boy or an undergraduate, he was what Montaigne called 'un enfant de maison', and it was perhaps for his instruction that his widowed mother turned to the one book that everybody knew, and in that book to the advice given by a king to his son. The *Proverbs* cannot be dated with precision, but they were perhaps written while Roger was still a page of twelve years old or so, which would make them of about 1150, after

---

[1] Ed. A. Hilka and W. Söderhjelm (Helsingfors, 1912).

[2] Philippe Delhaye, 'L'enseignement de la philosophie morale au xiie siècle', *Mediaeval Studies*, xi (1949), pp. 77–99; H. Rashdall, *The Universities of Europe in the Middle Ages* (ed. Powicke and Emden, London, 1936), i. 447; D. A. Callus in *Robert Grosseteste* (Oxford, 1955), p. 62; R. G. Gauthier, *L'Éthique à Nicomaque* (Louvain and Paris, 1958) i. 74* ff.

the reign of terror in which Rannulf had indulged. Writing of the similar behaviour of Geoffrey de Mandeville, the Peterborough chronicler was moved to blasphemy, crying that Christ and his saints slept. Seen against this background, the *Proverbs* seem like a flash of light in a dark world.

As for Roger, as far as can be told from the records, he lived a blameless and uneventful life as one of the Bishop of Lincoln's knights. He was dead by 1201, leaving a daughter and heiress married to Walter de Clifford, whose descendants became earls of Cumberland. And if it cannot be proved that the Proverbs of Solomon did him any good, it is at least certain that they did not do him any harm.

Once again we meet with a pioneer, the first to write for the instruction of the young in the French language.

The last writer who might be assigned to the reign of Stephen is the anonymous author of the *Jeu d'Adam*, one of the finest monuments of Old French literature, a fragment of great beauty of expression and subtlety in characterization. But this will be more conveniently treated in a chapter devoted to the Anglo-Norman drama, and full consideration of it is therefore postponed for the moment.

Before passing on to the great days of the Angevin Empire, a word must be said about the characteristics of the literature of the first half of the twelfth century. The production of it was in the hands of clerks, whether regular, secular, or merely literate. They, however, were not the only people concerned in its creation. Their patrons had a share. And these patrons were not only kings and queens, but all the adventurers who had come from oversea, and the wives that they had brought with them or married in the country. Soon after the Conquest England assumed the pattern which it was to have down to and even beyond the Industrial Revolution, until our own time. For England became and remained, as France did not, a land of country houses. They may have looked at this period more like pele-towers, but the life that was led in them was the life of the country house. Their owners turned up at the patronal feasts of neighbouring religious houses founded by themselves or their fathers as automatically as their successors attend the village church fête. A chaplain, resident or borrowed from the nearest monastery, combined his office with that of secretary, librarian, and tutor to the young. There was hunting when there was not fighting, there was chapel to attend every morning, games of chess and backgammon on wet afternoons, tales to be told when the tables had been removed, or when the quality had retired to what the French called the 'chambre' and the Anglo-Normans the 'soler'. And there was a need ✷ for books. There were children requiring polish when they emerged from the nursery, husbands and guests demanding entertainment, ladies left solitary for months at a time, pining for distraction. The lord and lady, perhaps more often the lady alone, went into consultation with the chaplain. Legends of the district, family traditions, books borrowed from friends and neighbours, lives of patron saints, tales and songs heard from wandering minstrels, all went into the melting-pot. Fashions came and went as people travelled to and from court, crossed and re-crossed the Channel, stayed with their friends and stormed the castles of their enemies. This last chapter has revealed a tangle of family relationships linking diverse authors and texts, and shown that wars and rebellions could not interrupt the flow. During the rest of the Middle Ages the universities and the towns played their parts in the demand for literature and its satisfaction, but the country-house background of so many important people's lives remains a factor which must never be forgotten. Did not Langlois feel,[1] when he was reading thirteenth-century romances, that he was caught up in descriptions of contemporary English house-parties? This continuity should help us to appreciate the literature brought into being by the society of the early twelfth century more easily than that which responded to the requirements of the sophisticated thirteenth century.

---

[1] Ch.-V. Langlois, *La Société en France au xiiie siècle* (Paris, 1904), pp. xxii, xxiii.

IV

THE COURT OF HENRY II

In the year 1154, just before Christmas, Henry of Anjou entered into his mother's inheritance and ascended the throne upon which his uncle Stephen had sat so uneasily. He was only twenty-one. With him came one of the most masterful women of the Middle Ages, eleven years his senior, Eleanor of Aquitaine, whom he had married two years before, and their infant son William. A few months later, the succession was made surer still by the birth of Henry, soon to replace his brother as heir and ultimately to bring discord to his family and two kingdoms. Henry II's reign lasted for thirty-five years, and the troubles of the last twenty-seven of these have coloured posterity's view of it. When, however, he came to the throne, he was known to the English as Henry Fitz-Empress, and the fact that he was the grandson of Henry I was more important than the possibility of the creation of an Angevin Empire. Henry himself pursued a double course. To England he intended to give peace and good government, while he occupied himself across the Channel in increasing his French possessions and so providing for his sons. For a few years all went smoothly, and it is important, when considering the literary history of the reign, to remember this. The Empress Maud had grown wiser since she lost her position as Lady of the English, and helped to guide her son's policy. Eleanor was prevented by a family of young children from seeking other outlets for her energy, and none of the princes was yet old enough to be a friend and patron of men of letters. As regards vernacular literature, the reign begins as a continuation to the reigns of Henry I and Stephen.

Perhaps one of the first writers in French to profit by the advent of a new sovereign was the unknown opportunist— Philippe himself or another—who resurrected the *Bestiary* of Philippe de Thaon and furnished it with a new dedication, to Eleanor of Aquitaine. She was a highly intelligent and well-educated person, and though it is a far cry from the songs of her grandfather to the didactic verse of the Anglo-Norman clerk, it is possible that the tribute did not cause her as much amusement as might be supposed. And for the moment the English regarded her simply as the successor of Adeliza of Louvain and Stephen's pious queen, Matilda of Boulogne.

Over in Normandy the Jerseyman, Wace, the *clerc lisant*[1] then living at Caen, was busy with his poem based on Geoffrey of Monmouth's *Historia*. It was finished, as he tells us himself, in 1155, and presented, according to his translator Laȝamon, to Queen Eleanor. As has already been mentioned,[2] this *Brut* became fashionable and caused the disappearance of Gaimar's. Its influence upon romance on the Continent and in England is difficult to estimate, partly because its ideas were already in the air, partly because writers may have drawn directly upon Geoffrey, partly because Gaimar seems also to have been known,[3] and it is now impossible to tell how much it was quoted.

THOMAS AND *TRISTAN*

One of the most important romances in Old French, let alone Anglo-Norman, is the *Tristan* by Thomas.[4] It has had perhaps more influence on subsequent literature than any other.

This version of the Tristan story has been the subject of much recent work[5] both as regards its date and its nature. In the past, attempts were made to date the romance by comparing it with other works believed to be of the same

---

[1] For this expression see M. D. Legge, *Modern Language Review*, xlvii (1952), pp. 554–6. To the examples there given should be added the *Roman de Troie*, i. 2993.

[2] Cf. above, p. 30.

[3] Cf. A. D. G. Bivar, 'Lyonesse, the Evolution of a Fable', *Modern Philology*, l (1953), p. 167.

[4] Edited by J. Bédier (S.A.T.F., 1902, 1905). New edition on Bédier's principles by B. H. Wind, *Les Fragments du Tristan de Thomas* (Leyden, 1950), and by the same editor in the Textes Littéraires Français (Geneva and Paris, 1960). The quotations are from Bédier. F. Whitehead, 'The Early Tristan Poems', R. S. Loomis, *Arthurian Literature in the Middle Ages* (Oxford, 1959), has now become rather dated because of subsequent publications.

[5] Cf. the list given by Dr. Wind, 1960, pp. 12–14.

period. The first of these is Béroul's *Tristan*. Unfortunately Béroul cannot be dated,[1] and it would be fallacious to assume that an apparently less courtly version is necessarily the older. In any case, there is no evidence that either writer was acquainted with the work of the other. The second romance which might be of help is Crestien's *Cliges*, again a work which cannot be dated. It is, roughly, an 'anti-Tristan', but the great question is, Against which *Tristan* was Crestien reacting? Crestien himself had written a poem 'Del Roi Marc et d'Iseut la Blonde', he tells us in *Cliges*, but this is an odd title and it may have been a *lai* like that called 'Le rey March' in the thirteenth-century list of lays published by Miss G. E. Brereton.[2] According to M. Fourrier, Crestien knew both versions, the 'common' represented by Béroul and the 'courtly' represented by Thomas, but most of his strictures seem to be directed against the latter.[3] This appears to be a just estimate. Much has been made of the triple pun on 'la mer' which occurs in *Cliges* and in Gottfried von Strassburg. The history of this pun has been traced back to Plautus,[4] and Gottfried may not have found it in Thomas, but borrowed it from Crestien or some other writer in French or Latin. It simply cannot be used as an argument. In the third place Thomas has been accused of borrowing from Marie de France. This is difficult to sustain. It is quite impossible to write on similar subjects in rhyming octosyllables without verbal coincidences, and since Marie cannot be dated, there is no knowing whether the borrowing was not the other way, if borrowing there was. The only certain relationship between Thomas and another writer is his obvious dependence on Wace, in particular on his *Brut*. This is fortunate, since Wace tells us that his chronicle was finished in 1155, thus giving us a *terminus a quo* for Thomas. Not only are there various reminiscences, but the whole

---

[1] Cf. G. Whitteridge, 'The date of the *Tristan* of Béroul', *Medium Ævum*, xxviii (1959), pp. 167–71.

[2] *Modern Language Review*, xlv (1950), pp. 40–45.

[3] *Le Courant réaliste dans le roman courtois du moyen âge*, i (Paris, 1960), pp. 153–4.

[4] M. M. Jirmounski, *Archivum Romanicum*, xi (1927), pp. 218, 219; R. Louis, 'A propos du *Tu autem* dans un poème latin d'Hugues le Primat', *Romania*, lxxi (1950), p. 100.

episode of Arthur's combat with the giant is related at unnecessary length. Thomas breaks off with the words:

> A la matire n'afirt mie,
> Nequedent boen est quel vos die
> Que niz a cestui cist esteit
> Ki les barbes aveir voleit
> Del rei e de l'empereür
> Cui Tristrans servi a cel jur,
> Quant encore esteit en Espaigne
> Ainz qu'il repairast en Bretaigne.   (781–8)

(It does not concern my subject, nevertheless it is good that I should
tell it you, for he whom Tristan was serving at this time, when he was
in Spain before repairing to Brittany, was nephew to him who wanted
to have the beards of the king and the emperor.)

Others have sought to date the romance on historical
grounds. There is no clue to its patron, save the fact that
it is obviously aimed at an English audience. The praise of
London, so often quoted, was a commonplace in the England
of Henry II. It is mentioned in Wace's *Brut*, but there is
more detail in the description of the city in Fitz-Stephen's
introduction to his life of Thomas Becket,[1] written about
1174. Of more or less the same date is a reference by Jordan
Fantosme: for rich barons and gay and generous ladies
Norwich is almost beyond equal:

> Fors la cité de Lundres, a nul ne set sa per. . . .
> Gentil rei d'Engleterre, kar pernez a penser
> Cum vus devez Lundres e les baruns amer.   (912, 918–19)

(Save the city of London, to none is her equal known. . . . Noble
King of England, pray give thought to how you should love London
and the barons.)

London was not at this date the capital, and Thomas shows
both pride and knowledge in his account of the port:

> Kaherdin sigle amunt la mer,
> E si ne fine de sigler
> De si la qu'il vent a la terre
> U vait pur la reïne querre:
> Ço est l'entree de Tamise;
> Vait amunt od sa marchandise;

---

[1] *Materials for the History of Thomas Becket*, ed. J. C. Robertson (R.S.), iii. 2–13.

En la buche, dehors l'entree,
En un port ad sa nef ancree;
A sun batel en va amunt
Dreit a Lundres, desuz le punt;
Sa marchandise iloc descovre,
Ses dras de seie pleie e ovre.

Lundres est mult riche cité,
Meliur n'ad en cristienté,
Plus vaillante ne melz preisiee,
Melz guarnie de gent aisiee.
Mult aiment largesce e honur,
Cunteinent sei par grant baldur.
Le recovrer est de Engleterre:
Avant d'iloc ne l'estuet querre.
Al pé del mur li curt Tamise;
Par la vent la marchandise
De tutes les terres qui sunt
U marcheant cristien vunt.
Li hume i sunt de grant engin.
Venuz i est dann Kaherdin
Ove ses dras, a ses oisels,
Dunt il ad de bons e de bels.   (2639–66)

(Kaherdin sails up the sea and ceases not from sailing until he comes
to that land whither he goes to fetch the Queen, that is, to the Thames
estuary; in the mouth, outside the entrance, he has anchored his ship
in a port and goes in his boat as far as London, below the Bridge.
There he displays his merchandise, folds and outspreads his silken
cloths.

London is a very rich city, there is none better in Christendom,
worth more or better prized, furnished with more well-off people.
They greatly appreciate largesse and honour, their bearing is bold and
free. It is the treasury of England; there is no need to seek it further.
The Thames runs by its wall-foot; thither comes the merchandise
from all the lands there are where Christian merchants go. The men
there are of great skill. There has arrived Sir Kaherdin with his cloths,
his hawks, which are both good and fine.)

The emphasis on the commercial importance of London
is remarkable. The only other local knowledge displayed in
the fragments of Thomas concerns the sea-route between
London and Normandy (lines 2790–810). The details here
are also precisely given. The audience is apostrophized as

seignurs, which may imply that the poem was written for a court. All this suggests that if, as has frequently been proposed, the romance was written for Eleanor of Aquitaine, it belongs to the beginning of the reign, soon after the completion of the *Brut* in 1155 and probably before she settled at Poitiers, apparently for good, in 1170. It would seem that the early part of this period is the more likely. *Tristan* is a tale to interest the young, and even in 1155 Eleanor was over thirty, but it is the sort of bitter-sweet story which would ⊁ appeal to her, and the dialectic nature of Thomas's version would be to her taste. The matter must, however, rest there.[1] More recently, M. Anthime Fourrier has combated the argument for an early date.[2] Unfortunately for his cause, the evidence he has produced is nearly all from the later derivatives of Thomas. Thus, there is no mention of Caerleon in the Fragments, so there is no point in calling attention to Henry II's visit to the place. The magic pillow used by Brangwain may indeed be an imitation of Camille's pillow, but the episode occurs only in the *Saga*. The Plantagenet arms of Tristan also are peculiar to the *Saga*. It is Gottfried who refers to Dublin as a 'houbetstat', and at this date the word was not the equivalent of the modern *Hauptstadt*,[3] so that the fact that Dublin became the capital of Ireland after 1170 is irrelevant. It is true that Thomas calls the sovereign of Spain King and Emperor, but 'Emperor' was the by-name of Alfonso VII, who died in 1157, and if the title means anything here it implies a reference to him, and not to his grandson, the next to be crowned emperor. It is therefore impossible to date this romance by historical allusion.

Nothing whatever is known about the writer. Attempts to identify him with the Master Thomas of *Horn* or the Thomas of Kent who wrote the *Roman de Toute Chevalerie* belong to the realm of speculation. It may be an odd coincidence that all but one of the authors of romances in England in the twelfth century whose names are known were called Thomas, but it is not impossible.

---

1 Cf. R. Lejeune, 'Le Rôle littéraire d'Aliénor d'Aquitaine', *Cultura Neolatina*, xiv (1954), p. 35, p. 31; M. D. Legge, *Bulletin de la Société internationale arthurienne*, vi (1954), pp. 95–96.   2 *Le Courant realiste...*, especially pp. 38, 55, 65, 108.
3 I am beholden to my colleague, Mr. W. L. Wardale, for advice on this point.

It is unlucky that both the full-length romances of *Tristan* in French verse should survive only in mutilated form. The beginning and end of Béroul are lost, but a substantial proportion remains, preserved only in one manuscript. The case of Thomas is more complicated. The whole of the beginning is lost, there are only short fragments of the middle, but the end is preserved in its entirety. Some of the manuscripts overlap here. In his great edition Bédier supplied a framework for these fragments by a prose version of the derivatives of Thomas—the Norse *Saga*, Gottfried von Strassburg's poem, the Northern English *Sir Tristrem*, the *Folie Tristan d'Oxford*, the *Tavola Ritonda*, and the French prose romance, with a commentary on their divergences. Unfortunately, he proceeded on the fallacy that when any episode occurs in more than one of these, it must have been in Thomas, and this view has found general acceptance. But this is not necessarily the case. As Thomas himself tells us, he deliberately omitted episodes in which he was not interested, and later writers with different tastes may have felt compelled to reintroduce what belonged to the common stock of the Tristan legend. The *Saga* embellished the end with a piece of folklore, the intertwining of the bushes springing from the graves of Tristan and Iseult. Some have supposed that this has been omitted from the extant copies of the romance of Thomas, but the end as it stands is perfect. The fact that this addition is found elsewhere than in the *Saga* can be proved here to be of no value for the reconstruction of the poem as it left Thomas's hands.

The Fragments are usually distributed under five heads. These are as follows: (i) The lovers surprised by Mark in the orchard, their parting after Iseult has given Tristan her ring. (ii) Tristan's dilemma on his wedding-night to Iseult of Brittany, after his ring has been shaken from his finger by his shirt-sleeve; Iseult surprised by Cariado, when singing a *lai*. (iii) Tristan's meditation before the statue of Iseult he has had made. Mark's power over Iseult and her lack of love for him. The other Iseult's betrayal of her virgin state at the water-splash. (iv) Tristan and Kaherdin's ambush of Iseult. (v) Brangwain's explosion of rage and jealousy during a return of Tristan. His detection during some games, and his

flight to Brittany. (At this point Thomas describes his treatment of the legend.) The appeal for help from Tristan le
Nain and the mortal wound received by Tristan in coming
to his aid. Kaherdin's departure with the ring to fetch Iseult.
The jealousy of the other Iseult. Kaherdin's arrival in London and the success of his mission. The storm on the return
and the lie about the colour of the sail told by the other Iseult.
Tristan's death followed by the arrival and death of Iseult.
Finally, an epilogue.

   The passage in which Thomas describes his method is as
follows:

> Seignurs, cest cunte est mult divers,
> E pur ço l'uni par mes vers
> E di en tant cum est mester
> E le surplus voil relesser.
> Ne vol pas trop en uni dire:
> Ici diverse la matyre
> Entre ceus qui solent cunter
> E del cunte Tristran parler.
> Il en cuntent diversement:
> Oï en ai de plusur gent.
> Asez sai que chescun en dit
> E ço qu'il unt mis en escrit,
> Mes sulun co que j'ai oï,
> Nel dient pas sulun Breri
> Ky solt les gestes e les cuntes
> De tuz les reis, de tuz les cuntes
> Ki orent esté en Bretaingne.   (2107–23)

(Lords, this tale is told very diversely, and therefore I have blended
it by my verses and say as much as is needful and will leave aside the
rest. I do not want to make it too smooth: here the matter varies
amongst those who are wont to tell the tale and speak of the tale of
Tristan. They tell it in divers fashions. I have heard it from many
people. I know very well what each one says of it and what they have
put in writing, but according to what I have heard, they do not speak
according to Breri who is wont to know the deeds and the tales of all
the kings and all the counts who ever were in Brittany.)

   From this it appears that Thomas had heard many versions   ✶
of the story, some told orally and some put in writing, but
there is no means of knowing whether these were *lais*
or romances or both. There was, it seems, a multiplicity of

incidents and discrepancies. The claim to follow 'Breri', who may or may not be the Bledhericus of Giraldus Cambrensis, is the introduction to a piece of invention on the part of Thomas, as anyone who knows the Middle Ages will recognize. It is possible that the public resented, as children do, the disappearance of favourite episodes, and that these were reintroduced by later hands. There may even have been an expanded version of Thomas from which the derivatives descend.

It is obvious that the *Folie d'Oxford* owes much to Thomas, but of all the episodes described in the *lai*—the combat with the Morholt, the visit to the Irish court, the fight with the dragon, the potion (told twice over), the tracks in the snow, the strewing of the flour, the gift of Petit-Creu (but without his bell), the harp and the rote, the ambush in the tree, the discovery in the cave, the gift of Husdent to Iseult, the discovery in the orchard and the gift of the ring—only this last occurs also in the Fragments. Here there is a significant difference. Thomas refers only to 'cest anel', but this is not enough for the later and more romantic writer, who feels obliged to add a cliché:

vostre anel
d'or esmeré ben fait e bel.   (953–4)

(Your ring of fine gold, well wrought and beautiful.)

It cannot be proved that the other episodes are related according to Thomas, and indeed it is possible that Thomas was not so clumsy as has been made out, and had substituted the discovery in the orchard for the discovery in the cave, on which it is manifestly based. The cave may have been in the original version, and the bower a variant invented by Béroul, who was interested in the life in the forest.

The label 'courtois' so long applied to Thomas has begun to seem of late something of a misnomer. Béroul is courtly in his way, and prides himself on the fact, as when he puts forward a more courtly version of Tristan's fight with the lepers. When Béroul is courtly it is in external matters. Thomas is not interested in material things; it is his attitude which is courtly. Today, it appears that he is more clerkly than courtly. He never describes the physical appearance of the characters: there is nothing like the sentimental description of Iseult led to the stake, with her tightly laced bliaut of silk, her hair falling to her heels and braided with gold thread, over which Béroul lingered. The description of Tristan's wedding is perfunctory: the church service and the feast which follows are accorded the barest mention, and only the field sports after the banquet arouse any enthusiasm in the author. In the hall of statues the sight of Iseult's ring awakes memories, Tristan remembers her expression when they parted, but nothing else about her. The contrast between the treatment of the ring given by Iseult to Tristan by Thomas and the *Folie d'Oxford* has already been mentioned. It is the sight of this ring which recalls Tristan to his senses when he is married to the other Iseult, and it is noteworthy that he takes notice of it only when it is pulled from his finger by his shirt-sleeve when he is being undressed. When describing the passage of Iseult's retinue Thomas gives a list of the household, with no description, until at the end he says that the nobility and gentry were singing songs, and the lovers amongst them were discussing affairs of the heart. The one tender passage about Iseult occurs when Cariado finds her singing a *lai*:

> La reine chante dulcement,
> La voiz acorde a l'estrument,
> Les mainz sunt beles, li lais bons,
> Dulce la voiz, e bas li tons.   (843–6)

(The lady sings softly, her voice is in tune with the instrument, her hands are fine, the lay good, sweet the voice, and the key low.)

The appeal is to the ear, not the eye. Iseult of Brittany is betrayed into revealing the nullity of her marriage by her reaction to the splash of cold water on her thigh. It is inconceivable that the romance of Thomas ever contained descriptions of the cave in the forest, the hall of statues or the intertwining bushes. For all the interest he takes in visual images, Thomas might have been blind. Touch and hearing are the only senses which play any part in his work.

The story of Tristan and Iseult is not one which it is easy to rewrite in terms of courtly love, and neither Béroul nor Thomas was successful in doing so. The primitive element

in Thomas has tended to be overlooked. The life in the forest
as told by Béroul appears primitive, but this quality, like
so much in Béroul, is on the surface. Where Thomas is
primitive is in the character of Iseult. She is passive because
her position does not permit of anything else. She is not, like
Tristan, a free agent. Thomas, like Crestien, knows the pun
on *cor* and *corpus*, but whereas it is usually the husband
who possesses the body but not the heart of his wife, as in
Cliges, in *Tristan* it is the wife who possesses the husband's
body, but refuses his heart:

> Ele a le cors, le cuer ne volt.   (1039)

She possesses it because she is not in a position to refuse it
and there is no question of choice. Crestien has a later attitude
and puts a condemnation of Iseult into the mouth of Fenice:

> Amors en li trop vilena,
> Que ses cuers fu a un entiers,
> E ses cors fu a deus rentiers.   (3112–14)[1]

(Love in her showed basely, for her heart belonged wholly to one,
but her body was shared between two owners.)

Fenice makes use of an old dodge to cause her husband to
think he possesses her when he is asleep, and to modern ideas
there is little to choose between the two heroines. The Iseult
of Thomas is, however, rendered cowardly by fear, and her
cowardice may drive her to cruelty, as in her treatment of
Brangwain. The initiative is always with Tristan:

> Isot ma drue, Isot m'amie
> En vus ma mort, en vus ma vie.

(Iseult my dear, Iseult my love, in you my death, in you my life.)

So Gottfried echoed the words of Thomas:

> La plus bele raïne, s'amie,
> En cui est sa mort e sa vie.   (1061–2)

(That most fair queen his love, in whom is his death and his life.)

In *Cliges*, as in the *Folie d'Oxford*, the woman is treated far
more on a level with the man. Thomas had the clerk's
attitude.

> Tristrans murut pur sun desir,
> Ysolt, qu'a tens n'i pout venir.

[1] Ed. by A. Micha, C.F.M.A. (1957).

> Tristrans murut pur sue amur,
> E la bele Ysolt pur tendrur. (3121–4)

(Tristran died for longing, Iseult because she could not reach him in time. Tristran died for his love, and the fair Yseult for pity.)

The emotions ascribed to Tristan and Iseult here are not equipollent. The onlooker sees most of the game, and it is not surprising that one of the most valuable judgements on Thomas comes from a specialist in Middle English. For Mr. T. C. Rumble, Thomas 'is writing for a highly sophisticated courtly audience', whereas he still classes Béroul and Eilhart as minstrels, who see everything in black and white and love nazardous and adventurous episodes. Thomas 'makes of his version little more than a greatly extended poem in the *débat* tradition'. Of the dilemma in which Tristan places himself by his betrothal, he says: 'he concludes each separate phase of his analysis with the conventional courtly device of a *demande d'amour*'.[1] This appreciation fits in with M. Jonin's view of Thomas as above all things a clerk, and with Signora V. Bertolucci-Pizzorusso's study of his rhetorical and scholastic manner.[2]

If, however, Thomas had produced nothing but an exercise in dialectics calculated to appeal to the sophisticated courts of the twelfth century, it would be difficult to explain why it is this version rather than the other which has had the most lasting success. Bédier made an odd miscalculation when he considered the poem to have been a failure. The evidence of the eight fragments from five different manuscripts shows that it was worn to pieces, and the derivatives in five languages prove that it was modernized and translated, even adapted almost out of all recognition, but always demonstrating its lasting appeal. It is the ultimate source of Wagner's libretto, and here the wheel has almost turned full circle, for Wagner, unlike the immediate successors of Thomas, was interested in the heart and not in adventures. He even reduced the element of mysticism which was

---

[1] 'The Middle English *Sir Tristrem*', *Comparative Literature*, xi (1959), p. 222.
[2] 'La retorica nel "Tristano" di Thomas', *Studi mediolatini e volgari*, vi–vii (1959), pp. 25–61. Cf. P. Jonin, *Les Personnages féminins dans les romans français de Tristan* (Aix-en-Provence, 1958).

Gottfried's contribution to the pedigree of this version. It is generally assumed that Thomas relied upon the potion as the mainspring of his tragedy. In fact, Thomas reduced the part it plays to the barest minimum. It is not mentioned in Tristan's monologues, nor—and this is still more unexpected—by either Iseult or Brangwain in their quarrel scene. In the Fragments there is only one mention of it, by Tristan on his death-bed:

> Dites li qu'ore li suvenge . . .
> Del beivre qu'ensemble beümes
> En la mer quant suppris en fumes.
> El beivre fud la nostre mort,
> Nus n'en avrum ja mais confort;
> A tel ure duné nus fu
> Nostre mort i avum beü.   (2486, 2493–8)

(Tell her that she should now remember . . . the drink which we drank together on the sea, when we were overcome by it. In that drink was our death, we shall never more have solace from it; at that hour it was given to us, we drank our deaths with it.)

Even here the potion forms just one item in a list, and is hardly more than a variation on the play on *amor* and *mors*, a favourite theme down to Ronsard and Sponde, 'Car l'amour et la mort n'est qu'une mesme chose.' Where Thomas is outstanding is in his characterization. For him, love's physical aspect is all-important. Tristan's two internal debates are superb, and one of his arguments in favour of his marriage is, it is to be noted, jealousy of Iseult, who has at least physical satisfaction with Mark. Mark himself is a bewildered figure. The quarrel between Iseult and Brangwain is a masterpiece, and so is the jealousy of Iseult of Brittany. Thomas does not forget the loneliness of the three principal characters, who have all cut themselves off from friends, country, and kindred through this tragic business. He sees this story as an *exemplum* and his object is to provide a mirror for lovers:

> Tumas fine ci sun escrit:
> A tuz amanz saluz i dit,
> As pensis e as amerus,
> As emvius, as desirus,

A enveisiez e as purvers,
[A tuz cels] ki orunt ces vers.
Si dit n'ai a tuz lor voleir,
[Le] milz ai dit a mun poeir,
[E dit ai] tute la verur
[Si cum] jo pramis al primur.
E diz e vers i ai retrait:
Pur essemple l'ai issi fait
E pur l'estorie embelir
Que as amanz deive plaisir,
E que par lieus poissent trover
Chose u se puissent recorder:
Aveir em poissent grant confort,
Encuntre change, encontre tort,
Encuntre paine, encuntre plur,
Encuntre tuiz engins d'Amur!   (3125–44)

(Thomas brings his writing to an end here: in it he greets all lovers, the dolorous, the amorous, the envious, the desirous, the pleasure-seeking, and the wayward, all those who hear these lines. If I have not said what everyone wanted I have said the best I can, and all the truth, just as I promised at the beginning. I have told it in words and verse: I have done this for an example, and to make the story pleasing, which ought to be agreeable to lovers, and so that they can find in places things in which they can see themselves reflected: may they be fortified thereby, against change, against wrong, against trouble, against tears, against all the wiles of love!)

Evidently Thomas had also written a prologue, which, if it had survived, might have given us more information about himself. This epilogue, however, defines the version as an *exemplum* of what Mme Lejeune calls 'amours contrariées'.[1] He may have intended to write a tale of courtly love, but the love he depicts remains passion.

There survived into the nineteenth century the fragments of five manuscripts, varying in date from the late twelfth to the mid-thirteenth century. They represent at least four different traditions. None was of the kind which could be described as a presentation copy, and only one had miniatures, reported to have been coarsely executed. All are Anglo-Norman with the possible exception of Cambridge University Library Add. 2751 (3), which is so short that its

---

[1] 'Le Rôle littéraire ...', pp. 41–42.

dialect is difficult to determine, but which shows no specifi-
cally Anglo-Norman features. Two had strayed to Italy, and
one to Alsace. These have disappeared. The 'Turin fragments'
were in private hands, their whereabouts when copied were
not divulged, and editors have perforce to be content to use
the diplomatic edition of Fr. Novati.[1] The 'Strasbourg fragments' were burnt with the rest of the library by the Germans
in 1870. The most substantial remains are now happily
united in the Bodleian and thus are easily accessible. They
are Douce d. 6 and French d. 16 (the 'Sneyd fragments').
The three smaller sets of fragments have all been recovered
from bindings. The popularity of works written for a small
circle of the chosen did not last long in the Middle Ages.
Either they disappeared altogether, or, like the *Roland* and
this *Tristan*, they survived only in modified form. If Thomas
was patronized by Eleanor, he would, like Wace, have
suffered from her disgrace. Her daughters were probably
responsible for introducing the version to Spain, Germany,
and Sicily, and her grandson Henry III for introducing it to
his ally, Haakon IV of Norway.

In form, *Tristan* follows what had become the convention
of romance, the octosyllabic couplet. Possible signs of the
early date of the poem are the fact that the couplet is rarely
broken and the presence of the caesura, which occurs in
more lines than might appear from Bédier's edition, which
he made before he had formulated his famous principles. He
has sometimes smoothed it away by emendation of the line.[2]
In both these practices Thomas is more archaic than Béroul,
but this does not necessarily mean that he was the earlier
writer. The versification of Thomas is not, however, monotonous. He obtains variety, as may be seen in the epilogue
and in the monologues, by making the caesura sometimes
coincide with the structure of the sentence and sometimes
not. The division of a line between the parties to a debate or
speakers in dialogue is a rhetorical device much employed
by writers of romance in Anglo-Norman, and it is, as we
shall see, one of the outstanding merits of the *Adam* play. It

[1] *Studj di filologia romanza*, ii (1887), pp. 369–515.
[2] Cf. B. H. Wind, 'Quelques remarques sur la versification de Thomas', *Neo-
philologus*, xxxiii (1949), pp. 85–95.

was not so often employed by Crestien, and there is more of it in *Perceval*, his last romance, than in his earlier ones.

It is unlucky that so much mystery should surround the circumstances in which this romance was produced, for, even in this fragmentary condition, it is one of the most outstanding of the works written in Anglo-Norman, and one which has had the greatest success and influence outside the country of its origin.

THE *TRISTAN* OF BEROUL

The version of *Tristan* by Béroul is sometimes referred to in histories of Old French literature as being, like that of Thomas, Anglo-Norman. It was, however, written in true Norman dialect, the only surviving manuscript (incomplete, alas) is also in Norman, and there is no clue to the writer's patron. Nevertheless, it seems likely that it was written for an Anglo-Norman public. The name Godoine has been borrowed for one of the three felons; another, Andret, is said to be a native of Lincoln, a centre of rebellion and trouble in the days of Stephen. Durham is one of Arthur's capitals, and this is no part of tradition. Like Crestien in *Perceval*, Béroul makes use of the evil reputation of Galloway, the bourne from which no knight returns, and this is therefore a piece of local colour known on the Continent. Less widely known, in all probability, was the pilgrimage to St. Andrews. The route across the 'Sea of Scotland' by the Queensferry Passage was taken by pilgrims from England in the twelfth century, as the Monk of Durham relates. Beyond, they were in Scotia proper, or Albany. This reference to

> Saint André, que l'en vet querre
> Outre la mer, jusque en Escoce   (3132–3)

has usually been misrepresented by French and English scholars unfamiliar with medieval topography.[1] This allusion, more than any other, suggests that Béroul had in mind an audience living in England, and may have been residing there at the time.

---

[1] Cf. M. D. Legge, review of R. L. G. Ritchie, *The Normans in Scotland*, in *Modern Language Review*, li (1956), p. 112.

THE BARKING ST. EDWARD

The other purely Anglo-Norman poem associated with the early years of the reign of Henry II is very different from the romance of Tristan. It is the *Life of Edward the Confessor* by a nun of Barking.[1] The *terminus a quo* of this work is 1163, the date of Ailred's Latin Life, of which this is a version, written in commemoration of the translation of the relics of St. Edward. Dr. Södergård is undoubtedly right in maintaining against Dr. Abson and Professor A. T. Baker that it must have been written before 1170, when the troubles of the reign began. In two passages reference is made to the reigning king. The first, lines 105–30, is an interpolation into the genealogy of Edward the Confessor in which stress is laid upon the Norman origin of Edward's mother. 'Le glorius rei Henri' descends from this holy line of Normandy, and has freed England and enriched religion. Such words are only appropriate if written fairly soon after Henry's advent. Prayer is made that his heirs may have the same wisdom and valour as their good ancestors, Count Robert, Richard the Good, and William the noble Bastard. Such a prayer would make little sense if composed at a time when the king's sons had ceased to be young and unformed, and even less when they had turned against their father. The second passage occurs much later on, lines 4969–5006. This time stress is laid on the English ancestry of the glorious Henry. Through the marriage of his grandfather, 'li boens Henris', to Edward's great-niece, 'la bone Mahalt', the ancient lineage was restored, not by need or fear, but by the force of love alone. Through marriage the rightful heirs have resumed their inheritance. By an awkward symbol the tree is described as being reunited to the trunk, and as having flowered at the birth of the empress.[2] Her son, the glorious Henry, therefore unites the two races and is of the ancient lineage of

---

[1] This has been twice edited: first, in an unpublished thesis for the Doctorate of Philosophy in the University of Sheffield by the late Mr. Percy Abson; secondly, in *La Vie d'Édouard le Confesseur*, by Östen Södergård (Uppsala, 1948).

[2] Dr. Södergård is a less sound guide at this point than Dr. Abson. He has mixed up the Empress Maud with her mother. In reading his notes and introduction it is as well to remember that he comes fresh to English history. He has even invented an Archbishop of Warwick (Everewic, Eboracum)!

Edward the Confessor. Then follows another prayer that his
heirs in their turn may be granted the qualities of their ancestors : 'God save our King, their father, and our Queen,
their mother. Maintain them in true health, in peace, joy and
plenty, and give them strength to beat down all those who
think to war upon them.' So ancient is the vocabulary of the
hymn which is now used as words to the National Anthem.
None of this passage could have been conceived after the
breach with the queen and the princes.

The text, therefore, can be dated with fair certainty between 1163 and 1169, and was probably written nearer the
former than the latter date, when Ailred's *Life* was new, and
before the beginning of the quarrel with the Church at Clarendon in 1164. The poem is anonymous, and deliberately so,
but its writer owned to being a nun at Barking.

> Se nul de vus est desiranz,
> Ki avez oï cest rumanz,
> De saveir en quel liu fust fait
> E ki de latin l'ait estrait, . . .
> En Berkinges en l'abeïe
> Fu translatee ceste vie,
> Pur amur Saint Edward la fist
> Une ancele al duz Jhesu Crist.
> Mais sun num n'i vult dire a ore,
> Kar bien set n'est pas digne unkore
> Qu'en livre seit oï ne lit
> U si tres saint num ad escrit.   (5296–311)

(If any of you who have heard this romance are desirous of knowing
the place in which it was made, and who took it out of the Latin..., this
life was translated at Barking, in the abbey; a handmaid of sweet Jesus
Christ did it for the love of St. Edward. But she will not say her name
at present, for she knows very well that she is not yet worthy that it
should be heard or read in a book where she has written such a holy name.)

One of the miracles told by Ailred concerned a nun at
Barking. Here his translator treats her source freely, having
heard the miracle described by the nun herself:

> Ceste merveille ad puis oïe
> Une dame en nostre abeïe,
> Ki Berkinges est apelee.
> Iloec esteit nunein velee

E unkore est tresqu'a cest jur
En sancté e en grant valur,
Certes, e de li oï ai
Cest miracle que vus dirai,
E nepurquant anceis l'esscrist
Cil ki la vie en latin fist.   (6442–51)

(Later on there heard tell of this marvel a lady in our abbey, which
is called Barking. She was a veiled nun there—indeed, she is still there
to this day, in holiness and worth, and from her I have heard this
miracle about which I shall now tell you—and yet he who made the
Life in Latin wrote about it before.)

In the twelfth century the abbesses of this famous house
were appointed by the king. Amongst holders of the office
were Maud, queen of Henry, and Maud, queen of Stephen.
How far these were titular appointments is not clear.
Henry II put in office Adeliza, sister of Eustace and Payn
Fitz-John. Eustace was Judge and Constable of Chester.
He was faithful to the empress. He obtained grants from
Rannulf II, Earl of Chester, and was associated with Walter
Espec. He was slain by the Welsh in 1157. Payn was one
of Henry I's new class of officials. He was associated with
Miles of Gloucester, whose son eventually married his daughter. Unlike his brother, he was on Stephen's side. In 1137 he
too fell at the hands of the Welsh.[1] Henry II may have
wished to reward the family for Eustace's devotion to his
mother's cause. It will be noted that the Fitz-Johns belonged
to the circles that patronized Anglo-Norman literature in
Stephen's reign. Adeliza presumably died in 1173, when the
king appointed somebody of more lowly origin, Mary, the
sister of the murdered Thomas Becket, as an act of repara-
tion. About 1175 the courtly sequence was renewed with a
third Maud, Henry II's daughter. Adeliza Fitz-John was
therefore probably abbess at the time when the *Life* of
St. Edward was written, and indeed it may have been done
at her request, either for presentation to the court or for use
amongst the ladies of the abbey, who seem to have had a need
for French books in their aristocratic assembly.

This *Life* is one of the earliest in Anglo-Norman verse to
follow what became the set pattern. It begins with the *Life*

---

[1] For these and other details, see the article in *D.N.B.*

proper of the king, introduced in this case by a brief genealogy from the time of Alfred the Great. (It should be recalled
here that Marie de France, who probably wrote later on for
the court of Henry II, attributed to King Alfred the English
fables which she professed to be translating. There may have
been a revival of interest in the hero during this reign, for
political reasons.) This introduction is preceded in the Anglo-
Norman translation by a pious prologue which appears to
have been shortened, for the late Professor Baker owned a
fragment of the beginning of the *Life*, in which the author
apologized for the shortcomings of her French. Most unfortunately this fragment has never been seen since Professor
Baker's death. Some lines of it are often quoted without their
being fully understood.

> Si joe l'ordre des cas ne gart
> Ne ne juigne part a sa part,
> Certes n'en dei estre reprise,
> Ke nel puis faire en nule guise.
> Qu'en latin est nominatif,
> Ço frai romanz accusatif.
> Un faus franceis sai d'Angletere,
> Ke ne l'alai ailurs quere.
> Mais vus ki ailurs apris l'avez,
> La u mester iert, l'amendez.   (1–10)

(If I do not keep the order of cases, or join part to the right part,
indeed, I ought not to be taken to task, for I cannot do it in any way.
What is nominative in Latin, I shall make accusative in Romance. I
know a false French of England, for I have not gone to seek it elsewhere. But you, who have learnt it elsewhere, must amend it where
there is need.)

By 'vus', she may mean the king and queen, both born and
bred on the Continent. It should further be noted: first, that
protestations of insufficiency are conventional and not meant
to be taken seriously; secondly, that the author does not say,
as is often made out, that she is aware of the breakdown of the
two-case declension in Anglo-Norman, but that the Latin
declension-system is vanishing in French, and that the accusative is prevailing over the nominative; thirdly, that the
wording, given the subject and the author's vocation, may
owe something to the famous apology of Gregory of Tours.

Qui nullum argumentum utile in litteris habes, qui nomina dis-
cernere nescis; saepius pro masculinis feminea, pro femineis neutra, et
pro neutris masculina commutas, qui ipsas quoque praepositiones, quas
nobilium dictatorum observari sanxit autoritas, loco debito plerumque
non locas. Nam pro ablativis accusativa, et rursum pro accusativis
ablativa ponis.[1]

The *Life* proper of St. Edward occupies 5,224 lines. Then
follows an epilogue of 40 lines, ending with a doxology and
Amen. The remaining 1,330 lines of the poem are taken up
with a description of the posthumous miracles—evidence of
sanctity. Both the *Life* and the account of the miracles are
based on Ailred, and this arrangement is the classic one
particularly appropriate in the case of a recently canonized
saint. The result here, as so often, gives an impression of a
lack of proportion which is characteristically medieval, but
for which there is an obvious reason. The *Life* proper is
clearly given the preference, and is complete in itself, ending
here with a pious epilogue. The miracles occupy a kind of
appendix, which was perhaps not always read.

The text as we have it exists in two main manuscripts,
neither of which is complete. The older, an early-thirteenth-
century manuscript now in the Vatican (Reg. 489), begins
at line 1463 and goes on to the end. The other, part of the
Campsey collection (Welbeck 1 C. 1), begins after the prologue already referred to and breaks off before the death of
the Confessor, at line 4240. It is late-thirteenth-century. Both
are Anglo-Norman. In Vising's manual these two manuscripts are listed as being of different versions (nos. 126,
127). The credit of identifying them belongs to Professor
Baker's pupil, the late Dr. Abson. Unfortunately his thesis
was never published, and the identification remained unknown until the present writer published a note on the
Vatican manuscript in *Medium Ævum*, vi (1937), p. 31. Dr.
Abson used the Welbeck manuscript as the basis of his text;
Dr. Södergård has, probably wisely, preferred the one in the
Vatican. Professor Baker's fragment was also Anglo-Norman.
The late Professor Arnold pointed out that lines 69–4482
exist in a third manuscript, for they have been substituted
for lines 14763–74 of Wace's *Brut* in a manuscript of that

[1] *Liber de Gloria Beatorum Confessorum.* Migne, *Patrologia Latina*, lxxi, p. 830.

text.[1] Dr. Södergård was the first who was able to make use of this fragment. It proves two things: that somebody considered the Barking *Life* of the Confessor preferable to Wace's account, and that the text was circulating on the Continent, for the scribe was not an Anglo-Norman but a native of northern France. He finished his work in May 1292. Further proof that the *Life* was known across the Channel is afforded by the existence of a prose version which was published by Paul Meyer in *Romania*, xxxix (1911), pp. 532–69.

The poem is written in the octosyllabic couplet of romance, but of the early Anglo-Norman variety. That is to say, the couplet is rarely broken, and in over 60 per cent. of the lines, according to Dr. Södergård's calculations, there is a caesura after the fourth syllable. There are only 732 feminine rhymes out of 3,340. The feminine *e* is supernumerary, however, and for the most part the lines are syllabically regular. Numerous allusions make it plain that the work was intended to be heard.

As a work of art this *Life* of Edward the Confessor has little merit. The self-effacing author is no great poet. She follows her original closely for the most part, and her additions are chiefly moralizations of no striking interest. But at least she was competent, and the apology for her sex which she felt called upon to make is superfluous:

> Si requiert a toz les oianz,
> Ki mais orrunt cest soen rumanz,
> Qu'il ne seit pur ço avilé,
> Se femme l'ad si translaté.
> Pur ço nel deit hoem pas despire
> Ne le bien qu'il i ad desdire.
> Merci crie, si quiert pardun
> Qu'el' emprist la presumtïun
> De translater iceste vie.
> Des qu'ele n'est mielz acumplie,
> Or emblasmez sun numpueir,
> Kar aquité s'ad sun vuleir.　　　(5312–23)

(So she requires all who hear, all who will ever hear, this romance of hers, that it should not be despised for this reason, that a woman has

---

[1] See his edition, S.A.T.F., i. ix.

thus translated it. For this alone one should not be contemptuous of it, nor condemn the good to be found there. She cries mercy, and asks pardon for her presumption in undertaking to translate this Life. That it has not been better accomplished, blame her lack of power, for her wish she has performed.)

Many a man could and did do worse.

As history the text has, naturally, no value except as a fairly close rendering of Ailred. It has, however, an importance of its own. It is proof of the popularity of Ailred's *Life* that a translation of it should have been made almost at once. Works by nuns are rare in England and unknown on the Continent, and this poem is a considerable effort. It was known on the Continent, and at some time was preferred to a section of Wace's *Brut*. A Picard copy of the version in prose was made as late as the middle of the fourteenth century, perhaps two centuries after the poem had been written. Lastly, as is now well known, it is one of two important verse Lives produced in the Abbey of Barking.

CLEMENCE OF BARKING'S *ST. CATHERINE*

A more difficult problem is posed by the second saint's Life written by a Barking nun, Clemence's *Life of St. Catherine*.[1] This poem is often mentioned as the sole example of a poem by a nun, but though frequently referred to, it is rarely read, and has not hitherto been easily accessible.

In Vising's Manual this text is listed as twelfth-century, and the *Life of Edward the Confessor*, which he had had no opportunity of reading, as thirteenth-century. Now, however, as has just been seen, it is known that the latter is twelfth-century. The two texts are probably not very far apart in date, and both may have been produced in the time of Abbess Adeliza Fitz-John, but they are very different in character.

The occasion for which the *Life of St. Catherine* was written is not apparent. Barking was not dedicated to her, but she was, naturally, a most suitable subject for a poem written in a convent, especially one in which the nuns had some pre-

---

[1] J. U. Jarnik, *Dvě verse starofrancouzské legendy o sv. Kateřině Alexandrinské* (Prague, 1894). New edition in preparation by Mr. William MacBain (unpublished thesis, University of St. Andrews), for the Anglo-Norman Text Society.

tensions to literacy. *St. Edward* was a fairly close translation of a recent Latin Life, with additions of a pious nature. *St. Catherine* is the adaptation of an earlier French translation of a standard Latin Life. The additions, far from being pious, ✳ are courtly and suggest that this modernized version was written after *Piramus* and Thomas's *Tristan*. Nowhere else save in this text do such courtly passages occur in a saint's Life.

Echoes of courtly literature are found throughout, such as in the couplet:

> Par un mecresdi devia,
> Vie perdi, vie truva. (2303–4)

(She departed this life on a Wednesday, then she lost her life, then she found life.)

Here the influence is on the form rather than on the sense. But what is truly astonishing is the tone of the additions to the lamentation of the Emperor over the defection of his wife, converted by Catherine:

> Laissier ne puis que ne t'ochie,
> Asses m'iert puis por mort ma vie.
> Comment morroies tu sans moi?
> Ne jou ne puis vivre sans toi. (2163–6)

(I cannot help but slay thee; my life will afterwards be nought but death. How shouldst thou die without me? How can I live without thee?)

> En tristur demenrai ma vie
> Quant jo vus perdrai, bele amie. (2175–6)

(In sadness will I lead my life, when I lose you, fair friend.)

Lines from the description of the Heavenly City might come from Thomas's epilogue:

> Cuntre dulur i ad cunfort
> Encuntre enui joius deport. (1720–1)

(Against grief there is comfort, against vexation joyous pleasure.)

Unfortunately, since neither *Piramus* nor *Tristan* can be dated with certainty, the existence of these lines gives only the vaguest indication of period, merely showing that the poem must have been written when such sentiments were expressed in fashionable literature. They recall similar lines in *Chevrefoil* and *Eliduc*.

The author appears to be less modest than the writer of *St. Edward* and names herself in the epilogue:

> Jo ki sa vie ai translatee
> Par nun sui Clemence numee,
> De Berkinge sui nunain. (2677–9)

(I who have translated her life am called Clemence by name, I am a nun of Barking.)

Clemence or, as the Picard scribe called her, Dimence, is otherwise unknown, and this seems a pity. It would be interesting to know if she had written *St. Edward* when she was younger and when courtly ideas had not yet reached Barking.

St. Catherine begins with the sort of prologue typical of the twelfth century, stating that knowledge must not be kept hidden, and then going on modestly to pray for help in the task of translating from Latin into Romance the Life of a true friend of God:

> Ele fud jadis translaté
> Sulunc le tens bien ordené,
> Mais ne furent dunc si veisdus
> Les hommes, ne si envius
> Cum il sunt al tens ki est ore,
> E apres nus serrunt uncore.
> Pur ço que li tens est mué
> E des humes la qualité
> Est la rime vil tenue
> Car ele est alquans corrumpue.
> Pur ço si l'estuet amender
> E le tens selunc la gent user.
> Nel ament pas pur mun orgoil . . . (35–47)

(It [the Life] was translated before, well-ordered according to the time. But men were not then so wicked or so envious as they are at the present time, and as they will be still more after us. Because times have changed, and the quality of men has altered, the rhyme is esteemed vile, because it has become somewhat corrupted. Therefore it has to be amended and the time passed suitably to the people. I am not amending it on account of my vaingloriousness . . .)

Here again the ideas are typical of the twelfth century.

Old-fashioned things fall into contempt not because they are antiquated, but because people have deteriorated and will continue to do so. The question posed by the passage is whether an earlier translation did in fact exist, and if it did, whether it is still extant.

Clemence is not the only author to claim that she is re-writing an existing text. A continental writer of the thirteenth century, a certain Gui, translated the Life of St. Catherine from Latin into Romance for the benefit of a nun.

> Un clerc translatee l'avoit,
> Mes, por ce que normant estoit
> La rime qui fu faite ençois,
> Si ne pleisoit mie aus François.

(A clerk had translated it, but, because it was Norman, this rhyme which was made in former times was not pleasing to the French.)

The only known manuscript of Gui's poem was in private hands and has disappeared, but fortunately La Curne de Sainte-Palaye made a transcription of it which is obviously fairly accurate.[1] The Norman Life referred to, quite apart from the fact that a nun would hardly be described as a clerk, (the epilogue might have disappeared), is plainly not that by Clemence. On the other hand, there are resemblances which suggest that it was probably the poem on which she was working. The courtly additions are not in Gui's version. The late E. C. Fawtier-Jones thought that she had discovered the Norman original of both poems in a manuscript in the John Rylands Library. This is unfortunately only a fragment, which is of the second half of the thirteenth century, but the text is certainly older than that, and she may have been right in her claim that it belongs to the early twelfth century. It is a curious text, perhaps intended to be mimed. A sign of age is that it is in assonance, not rhyme, and much of it is in rough alexandrines. The dialogue, however, shows some variety. The Emperor orders the execution of the Empress in decasyllables, St. Catherine speaks in octosyllables. The rubrics are obviously intended to be read. Perhaps the dialogue was sung. Thus the fragment, though not

---

[1] B.N. MS. Moreau, 1716. Cf. P. Meyer, *Notices et Extraits*, xxxiii, 1re partie, pp. 61 ff.

a play, has features in common with the two twelfth-century mysteries, the *Jeu d'Adam* and *La Seinte Resureccion*, but it lacks the skill and beauty of these. The writer thought that the manuscript might have come from Harmondsworth, a cell of Sainte-Trinité-au-Mont, Rouen, the Latin source having been composed at Sainte-Trinité by a monk in the mid-eleventh century.[1]

The Life by Clemence is preserved in three manuscripts, only two of which were known to the first editor of the text. The oldest of these is Anglo-Norman and is catalogued as twelfth-century (B.N. n.a.f. 4503). It is probably of about 1200. In style it is archaic, the verse being written as prose. Of the three manuscripts it probably preserves a version closest to the original text, but unfortunately it has been deliberately shortened. The passages omitted are always couplets or multiples of couplets, so that the rhyme-scheme is intact and the omission is disguised. It is, however, quite clear from internal evidence that the aim was to concentrate attention on St. Catherine and to omit passages that have little to do with her. Thus the 'editor' skips heavily when it comes to Porphyrius, and here he once goes astray, for in omitting the description of the burial of the Empress by Porphyrius he has destroyed a link with what follows. This is perhaps the only occasion where the omission does violence to the sense. It is not clear whether the scribe was responsible for the mutilation of the text. The copies of the *Brendan* and the *Alexis* in this manuscript are also shortened, more clumsily, but Waters[2] was perhaps unfair to lay all the blame on the scribe for 'losing patience'. In the case of *St. Catherine* at any rate something more than mere loss of patience seems to have been at work.

Next in date probably comes a manuscript of the thirteenth century in which the text has been virtually rewritten in the Picard dialect (B.N. fr. 23112). The passages deliberately omitted in the Anglo-Norman manuscript are here present, but the Picard scribe was guilty of gross careless-

---

[1] See her article, intended to be the first of a series interrupted by her untimely death, in *Romania*, lvi (1930), pp. 99 ff.

[2] E. G. R. Waters, *The Voyage of St. Brendan by Benedeit* (Oxford, 1928), p. xiii. Mr. MacBain is also severe on this scribe.

ness, and many lines are missing, often single lines or odd numbers of lines.

The third manuscript, that unknown to Jarnik, is Anglo-Norman. It forms part of the Campsey collection of saints' Lives, belonging to the Duke of Portland at Welbeck Abbey (1. C. 1). It is closer to the earlier than to the later manuscript but, unluckily, is incomplete and omits the epilogue. All three probably go back to a common ancestor, but the two Paris manuscripts are more akin to one another than to the Welbeck manuscript.

The relationship between the two saints' Lives written at Barking is difficult to determine. The date of *St. Edward* can be fixed between fairly narrow limits. *St. Catherine* is a typical production of the late twelfth century. *St. Edward* follows its Latin source fairly closely, and any alterations and additions betray a moralizing tendency. *St. Catherine* is a fresh or modernized translation—it is not quite clear which—of a Latin Life, and the changes make it more courtly. This suggests, though it cannot prove, that it is later than *St. Edward*. The sentiments recall the *Tristan* of Thomas, and the octosyllables are of the same type. The same doxology is found at the end of both Lives:

> Ki regne e vit e regnera
> E est e ert e parmeindra.

The versification of both poems was probably 'correct' by continental standards, except for a few lines of seven syllables—probably a sign of twelfth-century date. Later scribes have made it less correct.

In Mr. MacBain's opinion both Lives may be the work of one poet,[1] a view which has been disputed ever since they became known. Now that both have been the subject of modern studies the identity of their author has been shown to be a possibility.

St. Edward follows the conventional pattern of a saint's Life, the life proper and a separate section on posthumous miracles. *St. Catherine* has no section on miracles; two on the

---

[1] 'The Literary Apprenticeship of Clemence of Barking', *AUMLA*, Journal of the Australasian Universities Language and Literature Association (Christchurch, N.Z.), ix, 1958, pp. 3–22.

day of her burial which are recorded count as part of the life, as usual in such cases. As a literary production *St. Catherine* is superior and is interesting for the curious blend of piety and courtliness, this courtliness striking an odd note in a work of praise to a virgin saint. On the other hand, *St. Edward* has the interest of belonging amongst the texts, religious and secular, which exploit English native traditions. Both were known on the Continent, *St. Edward* being turned into prose there and also becoming incorporated in a version of Wace, replacing the part which tells of St. Edward in the original, and *St. Catherine* taking the more accustomed path of Anglo-Norman literature into north-eastern France. In view of the writer's half-hearted protestations about the incorrectness of her French, it is interesting to observe that it put no stumbling-block in the way of her work being accepted in France.

MARIE DE FRANCE—THE *LAIS*

It is possible that the *Lais* of Marie de France belong to the same period as the *Tristan* of Thomas. Some, if not all, were written in England. It seems unlikely that they were written all at one time, but attempts to put them in chronological order have not met with great success. The collection ultimately made is dedicated to a king, but whether this was Henry II, the Young King, or King John is a matter of dispute.[1] Of the twelve *lais*, six are set on the Continent, five in Britain, and the setting of the twelfth is left vague. The titles of six are proper names and five of the others have titles referring to characters in the story. *Bisclavret* is said to be Breton, and to mean 'Garwaf' in Norman. *Laustic* is also Breton, and is said to mean 'russignol' in French and 'nihtegale' in 'dreit engleis'. *Chevrefoil*, the only *lai* whose title does not directly refer to a person or persons, has only the French title at the beginning, but this is translated into English at the end as 'Gotelef'. (This word is not attested.) Whether these translations have any particular significance or whether they

---

[1] Cf. the edition by A. Ewert (Oxford, 1944); R. Lejeune, 'Le Rôle littéraire d'Aliénor d'Aquitaine', *Cultura Neolatina*, xiv (1954), pp. 35, 39, 'Le Rôle littéraire de la famille d'Aliénor d'Aquitaine', *Cahiers de civilisation médiévale*, i (Poitiers, 1958), p. 320.

are just literary devices is a matter for conjecture. The only complete manuscript (B.M. Harley 978), which is also the oldest, is Anglo-Norman, and the *lais* were certainly popular in England. A Norse version was made from a source which was probably Anglo-Norman. Marie may have written for patrons on both sides of the Channel, but the probabilities are that English ones counted for more with her.

The subject of *Chevrefoil* is the lying in wait for the passage of Iseult by Tristan, which also occurs in a slightly different form in the romance of Thomas. It is matter of dispute whether either writer knew the work of the other, or whether each derived the episode independently from the general mass of Tristan legend.

Lanval was translated into English and in the fifteenth century was much expanded by Thomas Chestre in *Sir Launfal*. *Le Fresne* was translated with the title *Le Freine*, which perhaps points to the popularity of the original, since *The Ashtree* would have been more appropriate to the subject.

From the evidence of these texts, few though they are, it would appear that for the first fifteen years or so of the court of Henry II and Eleanor of Aquitaine there was a period of calm and literary activity on both sides of the Channel. It was worth while for hopeful writers like the refurbisher of the *Bestiaire* and Wace to try to catch the eye of the new queen.

V

1170 AND AFTER

THE quarrel with Becket and his murder in 1170 were
the prelude to the break-up of the English courts as
they had existed from the time of Henry I. Not for
nothing did Miss Kate Norgate date her chapter 'The New
England' from this fatal year.[1] The shock and dislocation
and their effect upon public opinion had considerable influence upon the history of literature.

The king and queen had been separated for two years and
for three years more Eleanor was to hold court in France
and to patronize writers in French. In 1173 came her capture and in 1174 the captivity in England which caused her
complete withdrawal from the world for ten years.[2] Writers
could no longer count on receiving remuneration from that
quarter. Wace ceased from trying to engage the attention of
Henry II. Crestien de Troyes, who had perhaps written his
Erec about 1170 for the court of Henry II and his family, ✳
followed the fortunes of Marie de Champagne.[3] Meanwhile,
Eleanor's younger daughters were being the means of spread-
ing the literary ideas of their mother's court all over Europe,
through the marriages arranged for them by Henry II. In
1168 Matilda's marriage to Henry the Lion of Saxony introduced the Tristan story to Germany. For her court Eilhart
von Oberge made the version which is in part akin to Béroul's, while Gottfried von Strassburg made use of the version
of Thomas. Next year Eleanor's marriage to Alfonso VIII
of Castile carried the Tristan and Arthurian material to
Spain, and finally in 1176 Joan's marriage to William II

---

[1] *England under the Angevin Kings* (London, 1887), ii. 431.

[2] See the itinerary drawn up by Mme Rita Lejeune, 'Le Rôle littéraire d'Aliénor
d'Aquitaine et de sa famille', *Cultura Neolatina*, xiv (1954), pp. 50–57.

[3] A. Fourrier, 'Encore la chronologie de Chrétien de Troyes', *Bulletin bibliographique de la Société internationale arthurienne*, ii (1950), pp. 69–88, but cf.
J. Misrahi, ibid. xi (1959), pp. 90–101.

of Sicily made it known in Italy.[1] In England itself there was a reaction. Henry II patronized Benoit de Sainte-More, perhaps for the benefit of the Young King and queen.[2] Other writers remembered how Becket, when he became archbishop, turned away from minstrelsy and such things, which he had patronized as chancellor, and turned from fairy-tales to truth. It was the lack of a queen's entourage which may✳ have led to a revival of the kind of form suited to the great hall, as opposed to the solar, and it is at this point that poems in *laisses* of long lines became the fashion in Anglo-Norman literature.

JORDAN FANTOSME

One of the earliest manifestations of this state of affairs is the chronicle of the years 1173 and 1174 by Jordan Fantosme,[3] which begins significantly with the words: 'Oëz veraie estoire'. This poem has never been adequately considered in relation to its background, and it has never been realized that it is a work of art as well as a recital of events. Wild statements have been made that Fantosme was a sort of war-reporter, partly owing to various clichés having been misinterpreted to mean that Fantosme was an eyewitness of some of the events. Vising has deplored his shortcomings as a poet. It is time to attempt an explanation of the existence and nature of this remarkable work.

First, as to its date. There can be no doubt whatever that it was written within the period 1174–82, when Henry's sons began to quarrel anew, and likewise before the Young King's death in 1183. It reads like a paean of praise for the restoration of peace in 1174, and that is probably what it is. The date of composition is most likely 1175 or even the end of 1174.

The author names himself five times in the course of the poem—twice (lines 521, 903) as Jordan Fantosme and thrice

---

[1] Cf. R. Lejeune, 'Le Rôle littéraire de la famille d'Aliénor d'Aquitaine', *Cahiers de civilisation médiévale*, i (1958), pp. 319–37; for influences on continental art cf. T. S. R. Boase, *English Art 1100–1216* (Oxford, 1953), pp. 91, 190, 192, 204.

[2] Cf. M. D. Legge, 'The Influence of Patronage on Form in Mediaeval French Literature', *Stil- und Formprobleme in der Literatur* (Heidelberg, 1959), pp. 136–41.

[3] Ed. R. Howlett, *Chronicles of the Reigns of Stephen, Henry II, and Richard I* (Rolls Series, 1886), iii. New edition in preparation by I. MacDonald (A.N.T.S.).

(lines 668, 674, 1152) as Fantosme. There seems no reason
not to agree with the thirteenth-century scribe who wrote
above the name at line 1152 the words 'auctor libri'; there
is no point in supposing that there was a Latin original which
was by Fantosme. Whether Jordan Fantosme was born in
England or not is unknown, but the probabilities are that
he was. He is first heard of in youth as one of the four
favourite pupils of the philosopher Gilbert de la Porrée
who was Chancellor of the Schools of Chartres, later taught
at Paris, and finally became Bishop of Poitiers, dying in
1154. Fantosme is depicted, beardless and haloed, sitting
at his master's feet, in the famous miniature in the twelfth-
century Saint-Amand copy of Porrée's commentary on Boethius.[1] Fantosme followed in Porrée's steps to the extent of
holding an office equivalent to being Chancellor of the
Schools at Winchester, where he was one of the clerks of
Bishop Henry of Blois, the younger brother, but opponent,
of King Stephen. The saintly appearance of the youth in the
miniature is deceptive, for Fantosme turned out to be a
difficult and tactless man. It has long been known from a letter
of John of Salisbury to Pope Hadrian IV[2] that a certain
John Joichel was accused by Fantosme of having opened a
school in the diocese of Winchester without his authority,
and this gives a hint that Fantosme was capable of antago-
nizing others. In 1160 he is mentioned as being at Fareham
with Bishop Henry, so that he had evidently weathered that
storm, but some time before 1171 he was in worse trouble.
A certain clerk named Herbert accused him of being the
cause of the death of his father, whatever this may mean.
Pope Alexander, to whom Fantosme had appealed, committed the case to Bartholomew Bishop of Exeter and
John Dean of Chichester. Fantosme refused to appear and
obtained letters forbidding Herbert's witnesses to give
evidence, and he was in consequence suspended. The Pope
issued a fresh commission to the Bishops of Exeter and

---

[1] There is an excellent coloured reproduction in H. Suchier and A. Birch-
Hirschfeld, *Geschichte der französischen Literatur* (Leipzig and Vienna, 1900),
plate opp. p. 126. The names written below the figures are not shown, but Fantosme
is seated on the dexter side of the miniature. For Porrée's philosophy cf. O. Lottin,
Psychologie et morale aux xiie et xiiie siècles (2nd ed., Paris, 1957), i.

[2] Printed by Howlett, op. cit., pp. lxii–lxiii.

Bath with instructions to suspend Jordan and compel the witnesses to appear, and if he proved guilty of active intimidation to deprive him.[1] Apparently Fantosme had been making astute use of the jealousy between secular and ecclesiastical courts, but, whatever the rights and wrongs of the affair, and the outcome is not known, his actions were hardly those of a man with a clear conscience. However, the trouble must somehow have blown over once again. In 1171 the king came back to England after Becket's murder and visited the old Bishop of Winchester when the dying man rebuked his cousin for his share in the tragedy. After his death the see was vacant or three years, and it was not until 1174 that Richard of Ilchester, 'the friend of St. Thomas', was consecrated. From the report Fantosme gives of a conversation between Bishop Richard and the king (lines 1533–1622) and of another between Richard de Lucy and the bishop (lines 1626–33) it is plain that he was in no disgrace, but was probably the bishop's confidant, and may possibly have written the Chronicle at his suggestion.

The poem is written in long *laisses* in the rhyme which was replacing assonance, and for the most part in what passed in England for alexandrines. There are two passages in different metres, one of 119 lines in decasyllables and another of 26 in lines of fourteen syllables. These passages are complete in themselves, but there is no need to suppose that they are interpolations, and none to 'correct' them,[2] for similar mixtures are not unknown elsewhere—in the case of *Aiol*, for instance, which is not necessarily a conflation of two poems. It is worth noting that the period 1170–75 is believed to have been the time when Wace made his last attempt to retain popularity by writing or rewriting a section of the *Rou* in the same kind of metre.[3]

Fantosme's literary allusions are confined to mentions of

---

[1] Letters summarized by Adrian Morey, *Bartholomew of Exeter* (C.U.P., 1937), pp. 54–55 and 77.

[2] As has been done by P. A. Becker, in *Zeitschrift für romanische Philologie*, lxiv (1944). For an examination of Fantosme's versification and its possible derivation from Latin see I. MacDonald, 'The Chronicle of Jordan Fantosme', *Studies . . . presented to A. Ewert* (Oxford, 1961), pp. 254–8.

[3] J. H. Philpot, *Maistre Wace* (London, 1925), pp. 83–84; cf., for difficulties about the exact dating, A. Holden, 'L'authenticité des premières parties du *Roman de Rou*', *Romania*, lxxv (1954), pp. 28–29.

King Charles and his twelve companions, of whom Oliver
and Roland are named separately (lines 114–15), and of
Thibault de Balesgué, the Saracen leader.[1] There are no
references to Arthur or to any other romantic hero, or even
to Alexander. Names of epic characters occur in the works
of Crestien de Troyes, but it looks as though Fantosme's
avoidance of any other sort of name was deliberate.

In form, therefore, this Chronicle resembles the later and
more popular *chansons de geste*, but there is nothing popular
or coarse about the theme. The fact that this poem is a contemporary relation of events of historical importance, entering at times into great detail, must not be allowed to obscure
the fact that it was conceived as a work of literature. It describes a tragedy brought about by *hubris*. The principal
characters are kings and princes—Henry and his son the
Young King, William the Lion and his brother Earl David.
The subject of the tragedy is reversal of fortune. The action
begins with the rebellion of the Young King and William
the Lion's support of it, nearly ending in disaster for Henry,
and it ends with the capture of William the Lion and Henry's
triumph. The springs of the action are in the characters
themselves. Henry is directly accused of having treated his
son unfairly after the fatal coronation:

> La crut guerre senz amur, Damnes-Deus la maldie!   (20)
>
> (Thence grew war without love, the Lord God curse it!)

The Young King's subsequent misdeeds were thus his
father's fault. Evil begets evil. The Young King secured the
help of William the Lion by promising him Carlisle, while
his father lost it by refusing him Northumberland. William,
however, was sowing the seeds of his own undoing by allow-
ing himself to be swayed by greed in resolving his dilemma
in owing allegiance to both the old and the young kings.
There was thus wrong on both sides. At first William carried
all before him, but success fed his pride and the Scots waxed
ever more violent. On the receipt of bad news from the
north Henry returned to England from the Continent, and

---

[1] Possibly the only occasion where Thibault is so named, the usual qualifications
being 'd'Arabe, Aufrique, Espagne, Perse, l'Esclavon'. Cf. E. Langlois, *Table des
noms propres dans les 'chansons de geste'* (Paris, 1904). Balaguer was thought of as
the limit of Saracen power in Spain.

received from the Bishop of Winchester fresh details of losses and defections when he landed. It is at this point that Fantosme shows that he is more than a student of Donatus's commentaries on Plautus, and the story ceases to follow the pattern of tragedy pure and simple. The insistence which the thirteenth century was to place upon confession and penitence is here foreshadowed:

> 'Saint Thomas, dist li reis, Guardez-mei mun reaume!
> A vus me rent cupable dunt li autre unt le blasme!'
>
> (1605, 1606)

('Saint Thomas,' said the king, 'guard my kingdom for me! To you I yield myself as guilty of that for which others bear the blame.')

The moment the king alluded to his guilt things took a turn for the better for him.

There are two points to be noted here. First, Fantosme had carefully suppressed all mention of Becket's murder at the beginning of the poem. The king is at fault, but only because of his treatment of the Young King after his coronation. Neither Becket's opposition to that ill-starred affair nor his ultimate assassination is even hinted at. Fantosme does not refer to Henry's act of penitence at Avranches, which had already taken place before his return. He deliberately secures a dramatic effect by making Henry's call upon St. Thomas appear spontaneous, and the repetition of the act of penitence at Canterbury follows naturally upon the invocation. On the very day on which the scene at Canterbury was enacted, William the Lion was taken prisoner at Alnwick. Physically, he was pinned down by his fallen horse, morally

> Le pechié des Escoz li fait encumbrement.   (1791)
>
> (He is weighed down by the sins of the Scots.)
>
> Ne fait a demander si Deus en est marriz,
> E si il ad le rei Willame enhaiz;
> Pur le pechié de lui sunt plusur malbailliz
> E il meïsmes i fud icel jor descumfiz.   (1906–9)

(There is no need to ask if God is vexed at it, and if he has hated King William. On account of his sin many are in evil case, and he himself was there discomfited that day.)

Here Fantosme's views on free will are in the Porretanian

tradition. When the messenger brought the news to King Henry, the latter exclaimed:

Deus en eit mercié,
E Saint Thomas martyr e tuz les sainz Dé!   (2017–18)
(God be thanked for it, and Saint Thomas the Martyr and all the saints of God!)

Fantosme was living not only in a Christian world but in a feudal one. Henry had made his fine with God, 'La guerre est ore fenie'.[1]

The poem of Fantosme exists in only two manuscripts, one belonging to Durham (C. IV. 27) and the other to Lincoln (A. IV. 12). In both it follows the chronicle of Gaimar. It has thus been preserved in two of the districts most closely connected with the fighting.

Enough has perhaps been said about the worth of this poem. It has a certain rugged grandeur, and its stylistic and metrical shortcomings should be viewed as a reaction against artificiality. Its historical value is beyond dispute. For many things it is authoritative and it was used as a source by William of Newburgh. There are, as is inevitable in any medieval chronicle, minor inaccuracies of dating, and Fantosme has suppressed mention of Avranches and telescoped the relief of the siege of Rouen to heighten his dramatic effect, but for the most part he sticks to fact. He can hardly be blamed for his discreet and indirect allusions to Becket in a work addressed to the

Gentil rei d'Engleterre a la char tres hardie.   (5)
(Noble King of England with the right brave face.)

Besides the qualities of its epic nature the chronicle has some other literary merits. The scene where the messenger forces his way into the palace after the king has gone to bed, in order to give him the news of Alnwick, is superb. It possesses a quality rare in medieval literature—suspense, and is impressive in its realism. Then it has a classical conciseness. It is true that conversations, which must be largely imaginary, are reported at great length, but it has only four lines of introduction, with the abrupt opening: 'Oëz veraie

---

[1] Cf. William the Lion's dedication to St. Thomas of the Abbey of Arbroath: R. L. Mackie, *Arbroath Abbey* (Edinburgh, H.M. Stationery Office, 1954), pp. 3, 4.

estoire', and the epilogue consists of the hemistich: 'La guerre est ore fenie.'

Fantosme's chronicle is unique. There is nothing quite like it on either side of the Channel. It is, however, possible that Peter of Langtoft, writing in the early fourteenth century, was influenced by the form chosen by his predecessor.

DENIS PYRAMUS[1]

Almost at the same time as Fantosme was writing there was a clear case of recantation. Whether the identification of Denis Pyramus with Master Dionysius the Cellarer be correct or no, he was certainly a monk who had once been a ✳ court poet writing love lyrics and songs in the manner of the troubadours and was now feeling the need for repentance. It was the Enemy who had formerly led him astray:

> Mult ay usé cum pechere
> Ma vie en trop fole manere,
> E trop ay usé ma vie
> En peché e en folie.
> Kant courte hantey of les curteis,
> Si fesei les serventeis,
> Chanceunettes, rymes, saluz,
> Entre les drues e les druz. . . .
> Ceo me fit fere le enemy,
> Si me tync ore a mal baily.
> Jamés ne me burderay plus.
> Jeo ay noun Denis Piramus,
> Mes jurs jolifs de ma joefnesce
> S'en vunt; si trey jeo a veilesce,
> Si est bien dreit ke me repente,
> En autre ovre metterai m'entente. . . .   (1–20)

(I have spent much of my life like a sinner, in a very foolish manner, and I have spent my life much in sin and folly. When I frequented the court with the courtly, I made sirventes, songs, rhymes, and messages between lovers and their beloved. . . . The Enemy made me do this, and I now consider myself in an evil plight. Never will I jest again. My name is Denis Pyramus, my gay days of my youth are passing and I approach old age. So it is fitting that I should repent; I shall turn my mind to other things.)

[1] Ed. H. Kjellman (Göteborg, 1935); cf. for further references M. D. Legge, *Anglo-Norman in the Cloisters* (Edinburgh, 1950), pp. 7, 8.

He prays for the help of the Holy Ghost in providing a work which will be not only pleasurable but profitable. In a passage of thirty-four lines he explains that kings, princes, courtiers, earls, barons, and 'vavassours', to say nothing of ladies, love lays, tales, songs, and fables which prevent them from brooding and from harbouring melancholy thoughts. He singles out two writers who have particularly offended, 'Cil ki Partonope trova', of which 'la matire resemble sounge', and 'Dame Marie'

> Ki en ryme fist e basti
> E compensa les vers de lays,
> Ke ne sunt pas de tut verais. (36–38)

(Who made and constructed and thought out in rhyme the verses of lays, which are not at all true.)

It is not for nothing that the anonymous author of the *Partenopeus de Blois* and Marie de France, writer of lays, are coupled together. *Partenopeus* is a fairy-story as *Lanval* and *Guigemar* are fairy-stories. All are fundamentally variations on the fairy-mistress theme.[1]

Denis now proposes to tell a story which is not only agreeable to hear but good for the soul. Moreover:

> Un dedut par vers vus dirray
> Ke sunt de sen e si verray
> K'unkes rien ne pout plus veir estre. (69–71)

(I will tell you a pastime in verses which are full of wisdom and so true that nothing can be truer.)

These verses are about the infancy and miracles of St. Edmund, which Denis could not be expected to know are the wildest fiction.

In his prologue to the second part of his poem Denis explains that the task of translation has been laid upon him by the elders of the monastery:

> Denis Piramus, ki l'ad translaté,
> Nel tient pas a fais ne a baratté,

---

[1] There has been no edition of *Partenopeus de Blois* since that by A. C. M. Robert (Paris, 1834, 'the Crapelet edition'). For the subject see H. Newstead, 'The Traditional Background of *Partenopeus de Blois*', *P.M.L.A.*, lxi (1946), pp. 916–46, where it is convincingly argued that the pseudo-Greek element is of less importance than folk-lore.

> Li seint espirit me seit grace
> Ke jeo renablement la face,
> E gré me sace de ma peyne
> E Dieus e seint Edmund demeyne,
> E del eglise li segnur,
> Ki me unt enchargie cest labur.   (3279–86)

(Denis Pyramus, who translates it, does not account it a burden or
a trouble. May the Holy Ghost grant me grace to perform it reasonably, and may God bear goodwill to me for my pains, and Saint
Edmund himself and the seniors of the Church who have laid this
labour upon me.)

The idea of writing about this king in French was not new.
Gaimar, one of Denis's sources, hurried over this part of
his story:

> Mes si Gillemar eust leisir,
> Il parlast plus del seint martyr.
> Pur ço que aillurs en est la veie,
> E les leçons, e l'estorie
> Si l'ad leissé ceste feie
> Pur l'estorie k'out comencé.   (2925–30)

(But if Gaimar had had the opportunity he would have spoken more
about the holy martyr. Because his life is found elsewhere, and the
lessons and the story, he has left this affair alone this time, for the sake
of the story he had begun.)

These words suggest that several works on St. Edmund,
presumably in French, were in circulation as early as the time
of Gaimar. One of these may have been the *Passion of St. Edmund* in four-line octosyllabic stanzas—a form which may
indicate an early date—supposed to be about mid-twelfth-
century.[1] The adventures of St. Edmund in early life, and
even more the tale of his severed head crying 'Here, here,
here', discovered guarded by a faithful wolf, were naturally
popular, and a carol with the passion of St. Edmund
as subject was long current.[2] In the case of Denis there
were other attractions. In the first place there is little doubt
that he was a monk of St. Edmund's, and was writing about
the patron saint of his house. In the second, as a contemporary

---

[1] Ed. A. Nabert (Greifswald, 1915); cf. below, pp. 244–6.
[2] E. Duncan, *The Story of the Carol* (London, 1911), pp. 66–67 (B.M. Sloane
MS. 2593). Nigel Wireker makes fun of this incident, *Speculum Stultorum*, i. 2136.

of Henry II, whose descent from Alfred was emphasized, as we have seen,[1] he would feel that the commemoration of a saint who was revered by Alfred and who worked miracles against the Danish invaders was appropriate to the times. In the third, he, like Gaimar, exploited traditions about the Danes which seem to have been still current in East Anglia in the twelfth century but were afterwards completely forgotten. We shall see that a third text written in this century also makes use of East Anglian material.

Denis Pyramus's sources, listed by Dr. Kjellman, are Wace's *Brut*, Abbo de Fleury's *Passio Sancti Edmundi*, possibly in a fuller version than is extant, Ording's *De Infantia Sancti Edmundi*, Hermannus's *Liber de Miraculis Sancti Edmundi*, and Gaimar. In the case of this last the disappearance of the first part of the chronicle is once again to be regretted, as more use may have been made of it than can now be assessed. Ording had been prior of Bury in 1148–56, so the use of his *De Infantia* is only to be expected. The other sources are, however, also obvious ones. The debt to Wace is not advertised and does not amount to very much, and indeed it is impossible to say whether some things which seem to be reminiscences of Wace may not really have been derived from Gaimar. The 'de eyr en eyr' of line 73 looks like a quotation from Wace's prologue, but this in its turn may have been inspired by Gaimar. From Wace onwards it becomes part of the *Brut* tradition.

The *Life of St. Edmund*, unfortunately, survives in only one manuscript (Cotton Domitian A. xi), written in England in the thirteenth century, the end of which has disappeared. Presumably not very much is missing, but there may have been an epilogue in which the poet gave more details of himself.

Unlike Fantosme, Denis uses the octosyllabic couplet. He makes use of a certain number of English words, chiefly sea-terms, which are the subject of an interesting study by the editor. The sea-voyage to England is described with much detail. This love of the sea and of voyages is characteristic of Anglo-Norman literature. Kjellman speaks of 'le roman maritime français du xiie siècle', but this really is a misnomer.

---

[1] Cf. above, p. 60.

The texts which he assembles under this head—*St. Brendan*, *St. Edmund*, *St. Giles*, and *Tristan*—all either originated in England or were written to please English taste. The style of Denis Pyramus has something to recommend it. His narrative powers are good and he handles the couplet, which sometimes leads to aridity, with skill. There are occasional purple passages to the taste of the time, like the comparison between the life of a saint and that of a fruit-tree bearing sweet-scented blossom (lines 3299–301). Such things are inevitable in a narrative written by a self-confessed lyric poet. Denis had a gift for composition. He does not slavishly follow one source at a time but dovetails them into one another. His narrative follows the conventional pattern of a saint's Life—a first part describing the life and immediately posthumous miracles, the second summarizing the account of the miracles wrought by the dead body, the evidence prepared for the process of canonization.

THE ROMANCES OF HUE DE ROTELANDE

There are two ways of condemning a literary fashion, by censure and by burlesque. So far, in this chapter, only the first method has been considered. The second was represented in Anglo-Norman by a light-hearted writer of romance, Hue de Rotelande, who presumably belongs to the same race of Norman-Welsh clerks as the greater and no doubt better-born Giraldus Cambrensis and Walter Map. Like them, he was witty and cynical. Probably born at Rhuddlan, he lived at Credenhill near Hereford. He wrote two romances, *Ipomedon*, in which there is a reference to the siege of Rouen in 1174, and its sequel *Protheselaus*,[1] for Gilbert Fitz-Baderon, Lord of Monmouth 1176/7–1190/1. The romances must, therefore, have been composed between 1174 and 1191, and attempts have been made to narrow the gap between these two dates. It is to be supposed that Hue wrote *Ipomedon* to catch the eye of some patron, possibly Gilbert who derived his name from the family of Clare, his mother being Rohaise, daughter of Gilbert de Clare,

---

[1] *Ipomedon*, ed. E. Kölbing and E. Koschwitz (Breslau, 1889); *Protheselaus*, ed. F. Kluckow (Göttingen, 1924); cf. F. Lecoy, 'Un épisode de *Protheselaus*', *Romania*, lxxvi (1955), pp. 477–518.

Earl of Pembroke,[1] and a connexion of Eudo Dapifer, of Alice
de Condet, and possibly also of Gaimar's patroness. He belonged, therefore, to circles where French literature was in
demand, and, according to Hue, had a library of books both
in Latin and in French. Vising dates *Ipomedon* '*c.* 1185' and
its sequel 'shortly after'. This latter statement seems plausible, but the great difficulty is to date *Ipomedon*. There are
various clues which require to be followed.

There is first of all the setting. This has been ascribed to
the vogue for Classical and Byzantine romances, and Hue
has been accused of plagiarizing most of the continental
writers of the twelfth century.[2] In reality it was inspired by
the marriage of Henry II's daughter Joan, betrothed to
William II of Sicily in 1164 and married in 1176. Most of
the action takes place in the provinces of the Norman kingdom of Sicily—Apulia, Calabria, and Sicily. These were
names which were well known in England in the last third
of the twelfth century. Secondly, the allusion to the siege of
Rouen (lines 5348–9) which took place in 1174 gives a
certain *terminus post quem*. Thirdly comes a reference to
Walter Map (lines 7173–91) in connexion with an episode
which recalls one in the *Lancelot*. It has been assumed that
this passage must have been written after 1180, the date of
the *De Nugis Curialium*, but it undoubtedly refers to Walter's
real or supposed authorship of a *Lancelot*. Fourthly, there is
an allusion to a Welsh king—'I have an idea that they called
him Ris' (lines 8939–48)—who may be intended for Rhys
ap Griffith who supported Henry II in 1174 but rebelled
against him ten years later. He was, however, quickly reconciled, and Vising has pointed out that the lines would
more aptly fit the last true king in Wales, Rhys ap Tewdur.[3]
To his arguments it may be added that Rhys ap Tewdur
more than once attacked Rhuddlan Castle, and was besieging
it in company with King Griffith ap Cynan in 1086 when
the latter cut off Robert of Rhuddlan's head. He was the
father of Ness. In 1093 he was killed by the Normans at the

---

[1] Cf. H. L. D. Ward, *Catalogue of Romances* (London, 1883), i. 729.

[2] But cf. L. M. Gray, 'Hue de Roteland's *Ipomedon* and Chrétien de Troyes',
P.M.L.A., xxxii (1917), pp. 468–91.

[3] C. H. Carter in *Haverford Essays* (Haverford, 1909), pp. 237–8; J. Vising in
Kritischer Jahresbericht, xii (1909–10), ii. 140–1.

Battle of Brecknock. Legends attached themselves to his name, and he is sometimes credited with a Breton origin and to him was ascribed the invention of the Round Table.[1] All things considered, Hue may have had both these Welsh leaders in mind, but it may be pointed out that where Hue refers to other contemporaries of his, he does not use the word 'jadis' in connexion with them, as he does of the Welsh king. Lastly comes the vexed question of whether or not he used the *Roman de Thebes*. Many of the proper names in his romances occur also in *Thebes*, but it might be argued that Hue took them straight from Statius. Against this interpretation of the resemblance between the nomenclature of the two romances must be set the lines from the end of *Ipomedon* which look like a reference to *Thebes* itself:

> De ceste estorie, k'ai ci faite,
> Est cele de Tebes estraite.
> A Thebes fut Ipomedon,
> Aillurs querrez, si vus est bon,
> Cument ilokes li avint.   (*Ip.* 10539–43)

(From this story, which I have here fashioned, is derived that of Thebes. Ipomedon was at Thebes; seek elsewhere, if you like, what happened to him there.)

This certainly looks like an allusion to a French poem, and one of recent date, much in the fashion. In the old days, when *Thebes* was happily thought to be the oldest of the romances of antiquity, and to be of about 1150–5, the question of whether Hue could have known it or not did not arise, though it did seem puzzling that he should have mentioned it as something everybody was reading more than twenty years later. Now, however, the dating of *Thebes* has been thrown into the melting-pot. Basing his arguments on internal evidence, F. E. Guyer would place it later than *Eneas*, *Cliges*, and *Yvain*—1167–70 in his opinion.[2] If the latest dating of the romances of Crestien is accepted, this argument would make *Thebes* perhaps as late as 1181. R. Harris has proposed another line of attack which would also result in its being 1181 or even later. His contention rests upon a

---

[1] *D.N.B.* and E. A. Freeman, *William Rufus* (Oxford, 1882), i. 122–6.
[2] The 'Chronology of the Earliest French Romances', *Modern Philology*, xxvi 1928–9), pp. 257–77, cf. his *Romance in the Making* (New York, 1954).

supposed allusion to the 'quarantaine le roi', which may or
may not have been instituted in 1180.[1] The dating of this,
however, is a crux, and it is not certain that the reference
is to a royal institution and not to a mere convention, later
given the force of law.

The balance of argument seems to be in favour of a date
after 1180 for the *Roman d'Ipomedon*; but before leaving the
question, it must be pointed out that the lines mentioning
the siege of Rouen appear to refer to a recent event, and
suggest that Hue's patron or patron-to-be took part in the
fighting:

> A Herefort, a ces estaus,
> Pot teus seer e sei vanter
> De la grant guerre d'ultre mer,
> Quant Room fut de reis asis,
> Dunt (a) tant fut truble le pais —
> Sun nun ne voil pas ci numer.   (*Ip.* 5346–51)

(At Hereford, at his dwelling, could such a one sit and pride himself
on the great war overseas, when Rouen was besieged by kings, by
which the country was so disturbed—I will not mention his name
here.)

Thebes has been thought to be of great antiquity because it
lacks an interest in courtly love. Its main theme is family
strife, and this was also used by Hue in *Protheselaus*. This
subject would have been topical during the appalling feuds
between the sons of Henry II and their father and amongst
themselves, which lasted from 1173 until 1189.

Whatever Hue owed to other writers, he cannot be described as anybody's disciple. His attitude towards romance
may be compared with that of the author of *Aucassin* or of
Jehan Renart. There is the same quizzical view of elegant
society, the same amusement at the behaviour of the young,
the same descent into fabliau-esque. Only, the other writers
belong to the next century. Hue is first in the field and gives
the impression that he knows more about courtly life from
within than the other two, who always seem to be looking on,
half-comprehending, from outside. Crestien has the same
air of being at ease in high company.

---

[1] 'A *terminus a quo* for the *Roman de Thebes*', *French Studies*, xi (1957),
pp. 201–13.

Ipomedon tells the story of the heir to the kingdom of Apulia who falls in love with the description of the Duchess of Calabria, only known by the nickname of La Fiere. His methods of approach are at once conventional and ludicrous. First of all, he spends three years incognito at the Calabrian court. La Fiere, finding herself attracted by an unknown squire, drives him away, which enables him to return later to take part in one of the Three Days' Tournaments, beloved of romancers. Naturally, he is the victor; equally naturally, he vanishes after the victory. In the meantime he is leading a complicated existence at the court of the Queen of Sicily. Later again he rescues La Fiere from a knight who is besieging her, but of course refuses to reveal himself, and the romance might have been prolonged indefinitely if a follower of a long-lost brother of his had not betrayed him. As his father is now dead, Ipomedon is able to marry La Fiere and become King of Apulia without further trouble. The plot of *Protheselaus* owes more to the story of *Thebes*. Ipomedon had two sons, Daunus, heir to Apulia, and Protheselaus, heir to his mother's duchy. This is seized by Daunus, and he only regains it with the aid of the Queen of Sicily, now widowed, who loves him for his father's sake. Her name turns out to be Medea. Complication is supplied by means of a false letter, substituted for one which is intercepted, and the course of true love is also interrupted by the machinations of the Pucelle de l'Isle, who falls in love with an unwilling Protheselaus and imprisons him. The romance ends with the expected combat between the brothers, in which Daunus receives his death-wound, but for all that it is a happy ending, for the two are reconciled. Naturally, Protheselaus and Medea marry, and have a large family whose adventures Hue looks forward to telling at a future time. It will be noticed that in *Protheselaus* there are more accidents which achieve ends which in *Ipomedon* are brought about by the behaviour of the characters.

It will be evident from this sketch that Hue was not interested in his plots. Anything would do. Nor was he interested in character-drawing. There is more of this in *Ipomedon* than in *Protheselaus*, but little enough even there. Yet neither Ipomedon nor La Fiere is quite a stock character.

Ipomedon is a youthful Don Quixote and La Fiere a 'Précieuse ridicule'. There are two minor characters with less nonsense about them. One plays a large part in the first part of *Ipomedon*, and then vanishes from the scene to reappear in *Protheselaus*. This is Jason, a young nephew of La Fiere. Unlike Ipomedon, Jason is a real squire and not a prince in disguise. He is young enough to be made miserable when, one day at table, he is teased in Ipomedon's place. He is unable, like the grown-ups, to put a gloss on the attack against himself, and is the picture of helpless offended dignity. For Ipomedon he has a romantic, schoolboy sort of devotion, and does his best to favour the relationship between him and La Fiere. It is he who reports Ipomedon's departure to her. Designated as the squire whose duty is to supply fresh lances to the man who does best in the tournament, he is delighted each day to find he has been serving Ipomedon. The other sensible character is Ismeine, Duchess of Burgundy, La Fiere's lady-in-waiting. She, too, is a creature of flesh and blood. Finding herself falling in love with Ipomedon, she has no false sentiment, but acts with the effrontery of the heroines of the *chansons de geste* who serve as models to the young ladies of romance—'Il est impossible de rappeler toutes les demoiselles qui, dans les quêtes en prose et en vers, s'offrent à Lancelot, Perceval, Gauvain etc.'[1]

While *Ipomedon* has been classed as a love-romance, *Protheselaus* has been set among the *romans d'aventures*. This is rather a superficial view. *Ipomedon* has a zest and a sparkle which *Protheselaus* lacks. The former was perhaps written for fun, the latter to earn bread and butter. The one is almost a parody of the courtly romance, the other reflects the taste of a particular individual or family, as has already been mentioned. It has been questioned whether the oft-quoted reference to Walter Map alludes to his supposed *Lancelot* or to his *De Nugis Curialium*. Setting aside the question of dating, for *Ipomedon* may have been written before the *De Nugis* was begun, it is evident that they belong to the same world. Flippancy was a characteristic of the court which in

---

[1] Italo Siciliano, *Villon et les thèmes poétiques du Moyen Age* (Paris, 1934), pp. 148–50.

the opinion of Petrus Blesensis resembled hell, and in *Ipo-medon* one side of courtly life finds expression.

Ipomedon exists in two more or less complete manuscripts, one thirteenth-century (Cotton Vespasian A. vii) and the other, written by Johan de Dorkingge, early fourteenth (Egerton 2515), both Anglo-Norman, and two fourteenth-century fragments (Rawlinson Misc. 1370), also Anglo-Norman. Fairly recently, a continental fragment of the mid-fourteenth century was discovered.[1] Only the two manuscripts and one of the fragments were used by the editor, and there is room for a modern edition. Of *Protheselaus* there are only two manuscripts (Egerton 2515 and B.N. fr. 2169), one incomplete, and two fragments (Rawl. Misc. 1370 and Rawl. d. 913). In two of these it follows *Ipomedon*. No continental version of *Protheselaus* is known, but it is mentioned by Wolfram von Eschenbach. There seems little doubt that *Ipomedon* has always been the more popular of the two romances. There are three Middle English versions of it, and it is mentioned in lists of romances in *Richard Cœur-de-Lion* and by Chaucer. Its influence may be traced in other romances and on Malory.[2] It is closest, curiously enough, to Ulrich's *Lanzelet*, which may have been based on the *Lancelot* of Walter Map.

Hue was an excellent versifier. He uses the octosyllabic ✳ couplet in a particularly jaunty manner, especially in *Ipo-medon*. He was well schooled in rhetoric and makes effective use of repetition. In a descriptive passage of the 'Three Days' Tournament' (*Ip.*, lines 4821-44), for instance, he uses the adjective 'meint' twenty-four times in twenty lines, but with many variations in its position in the line. This occurs in a description of action. More conventional, perhaps, but no less skilful, is La Fiere's meditation on 'orgoil' (*Ip.*, lines 4587-611). 'Par mun orgoil' is repeated six times in seven lines and the word 'orgoil' comes ten times in twenty-seven lines. The repetitions in *Protheselaus* are more mechanical and become tedious. Hue shows his greatest skill in dialogue, which for liveliness may be compared to that of the Adam

---

[1] C. H. Livingston, *Modern Philology*, xl (1942), pp. 117-30. Cf. M. Esposito, *Revue des bibliothèques*, xxiv (1914), pp. 196-7.

[2] Kluckow, op. cit., pp. 40-43, Carter, op. cit., p. 245.

play. Here, by way of illustration, is Jason's report to La Fiere of the departure of Ipomedon:

> Mout l'avisa la damoisele
> Et dit: 'Apportez vus novelle?'
> 'D[amois]ele, mout qe me poise,
> Kar a mon us est trop malveise.'
> 'Coment, quel es[t]? Dites le moy!'
> 'Dame, mout volunters, par foy:
> Votre vadlet s'en est aleez
> Et par moy vous salu' assez!'
> 'Ly quels?' 'Vostre vadlet estrange:
> Ja mes n'avrez de ly eschange!'
> 'Alez?' 'Oyl!' 'Pur quey?' 'Ne say!'
> 'Ky ly mefist?' 'Nuls!' 'Si fist!' 'Nay:
> Eins est son songe, k'ad songé,
> Dount a mervaille est desheité.'   (*Ip.* 1413-26)

(The Damsel stared hard at him and said: 'Do you bring news?' 'Damsel, that which grieves me much, for it is a sad loss for me.' 'Why, what is it? Tell me!' 'Lady, very willingly, in faith. Your squire has gone away and greets you many times by me!' 'Which one? 'Your foreign squire: you will never have his like in exchange!' 'Gone?' 'Yes!' 'Why?' 'I know not!' 'Who did him wrong?' 'No one!' 'Yes, they did!' 'Not at all: but it is his dream, which he has dreamt, by which he is wonderfully cast down.')

The quickening of the exchanges and the cadence of the conclusion are strikingly well done. Nor is this the only example.

Hue is also capable of linguistic jokes. When La Fiere confesses to Ismeine that she is in love with the 'vadlet estrange' she sighs in the middle of the word, so that Ismeine thinks that she is talking about a man called 'Vehalet' (*Ip.*, lines 1499–1518). This is an improvement on the *Roman d'Eneas*, where Lavinia pronounces the three syllables of Eneas separated by sighs (lines 8553 ff.), for there the riddle is plain, and Hue, as usual, gives the affair a comic twist. There is a similar complication in *Protheselaus*. When Tristan has to take an assumed name he reverses the syllables of his own and passes as Tantris. Melander advises Protheselaus differently:

> 'Prothes' vus nomez, n[e]ent plus
> Et si relaissez l'-eläus'!   (*Proth.* 2366-7)

This abbreviated version later causes Medea emotion:

> Cum el öi 'Prothes' nomer,
> Tot le cors li prent a trembler:
> Ço fut del nun le començail.
> En suspirant fait un b[a]ail
> Et dit: 'Ad del nun n[e]ent plus?'
> 'Nenal!' fait Prothes[e]laus. (*Proth.* 3252–7)

(Call yourself 'Prothes', no more, and let the '-elaus' drop. . . . When she heard 'Prothes' mentioned, she began to shiver all over. It was the beginning of the name. She caught her breath in a sigh and said: 'Is there no more of the name?' 'No more!' said Protheselaus.)

In *Protheselaus* there is more fighting, in *Ipomedon* more love-scenes. Perhaps the theme of sleeplessness plays a bigger part there than in any other romance. The scene where first of all La Fiere retires to bed, but not to sleep—

> Cocher se vodra, kar tens est;
> Cocher se poet, mes de dormir
> N'i avra geres de leisir (*Ip.* 948–50)

and then Ipomedon follows suit—

> [I]cil est coché en son lit,
> Mes il dormi assez petit (*Ip.* 1131–2)

(She wants to go to bed, for it is time. She may go to bed, but will scarcely have a chance to sleep. . . . He has lain down in his bed, but slept little.)

is exaggerated to the point of being ludicrous. Later on, when Ismeine comes to him in the night with improper suggestions, Ipomedon bites her hand and worries it, a method of extricating himself from an embarrassing situation which would hardly have occurred to Perceval (*Ip.*, lines 8839–54). A flippant cynicism, especially with regard to women, which is even more apparent in *Ipomedon* than in *Protheselaus*, adds spice to both romances, and the epilogue to *Ipomedon* is too shameless to be quoted here. One of the attractions, again more conspicuous in the earlier romance, is a zest for life and society. Hue delights even more than Crestien, and as much as Jehan Renart, in details—rich clothes for Ipomedon, poor ones for the 'curleu', food, plate, the rolling of hauberks, the squire deputed to hand out fresh lances as a jouster breaks them.

When all is said, however, the most interesting point about Hue de Rotelande is his topical allusions, not only in his dedication of *Protheselaus* to the baron 'Ly gentils de Monmue, Gilbert, le fiutz a Badelon', but in *Ipomedon* to the

> grant guere d'ultremer,
> Quant Room fut de reis asis   (*Ip.* 5348–9)

(the great war overseas, when Rouen was besieged by kings);

to a known canon of Hereford:

> Hugh de Hungrie par dreit
> S'en deust mut ben entremettre,
> La glose set de cestre lettre   (5518–20)

(Hugh of Hungary ought rightly to undertake it—he knows the gloss on this text);

and, most interesting of all, to Walter Map, where he raises the question of truth and fiction in connexion with his imitation of the 'Three Days' Tournament' in *Lancelot*:

> Ore entendez, seignurs, mut ben:
> Hue dit, k'il n'i ment de ren,
> Fors aukune feiz, neent mut:
> Nuls ne se pot garder par tut;
> En mendre afere mut suvent
> Un ben resonable hom mesprent.
> El mund nen ad un sul si sage,
> Ki tuz jurs seit en un curage,
> Kar cist secles l'ad ore en sei:
> Nel metez mie tut sur mei!
> Sul ne sai pas de mentir l'art,
> Walter Map reset ben sa part;
> Nepurquant a la meie entente
> Ne quit pas, ke nul de vus mente.
> Seignurs, ke de rime entendez,
> Si jo mesprenc, ne me blasmez:
> A escient pas nel ferai.   (7173–89)

(Now understand this, lordings, clearly: Hue says, that he never tells a lie in it; well, hardly ever, and then not much. No one can keep himself entirely from it. In the least affair a quite reasonable man very often does wrong. There is not a single man alive so wise that he can always be of the same mind, for he is of this world. Don't lay it all on me! I'm not the only person who knows the art of lying, Walter Map is very good at it too. Nevertheless, I don't believe willingly that any of you tells lies. Lordings, who understand the art of poetry, if I do wrong, don't blame me, I won't do it on purpose.)

Professor Livingston has tried to shed doubt on the authenticity of these lines,[1] but his 'faulty text of A' is that supplied by the oldest manuscript, and the other manuscript used by the editor is an abbreviated version. It is a pity that Madame Lejeune makes no reference to this passage in her account of Ulrich's *Lanzelet*.[2]

Hue alleges that he translated *Protheselaus* from a Latin book belonging to Gilbert Fitz-Baderon, who had many books in his castle, both Latin and French (*Proth.* 12707–11). That is just a conventional compliment. The prologue of *Ipomedon*, modelled on the kind of thing which came into vogue with the romances of antiquity, is intentionally comic, and Hue makes fun of their pretensions:

> Moult me mervail de ces clers sages,
> Ky entendent plusurs langages,
> K'il ont lessé ceste estorie,
> Ke mis ne [l]'ont en memorie;
> Ne di pas, q'il bien ne dit
> Cil, qi en Latin l'ad descrit,
> Mes plus i ad leis ke lettrez:
> Si li Latin n'est translatez,
> Gaires n'i erent entendanz:
> Por ceo voil [jeo] dire en romanz
> A plus brevment qe jeo savrai,
> Si entendrunt clerc e lai. . . .
> Fors la verrour n'y acrestrai,
> Dirai brefment ceo que j'en sai.
> Ke grant ovre voet translater,
> [B]refment l'estuet ou[t]repasser,
> Ou si ceo noun, trop s'anoiront
> Cil, ki d'oir talent avront.   (*Ip.* 21–46)

(I am very much surprised at those wise clerks, who know many languages, but have left this story alone, and have omitted to pass it on. I don't say that he didn't tell it well, the writer of the Latin version, but there are more laity than clerks. If the Latin isn't translated, they will hardly understand it. Therefore I want to tell it in French as shortly as I can, so that both clerks and laity will understand it. . . .

---

[1] Loc. cit., p. 118.   [2] Loc. cit., p. 335.

I shan't add anything to the truth, but tell what I know shortly. He who
wants to translate a great work, ought to get through it as briefly as
possible, or else those who wish to hear it will be very bored.)

There are moments when Hue's common sense is very
refreshing.

THE *HORN* OF MASTER THOMAS

A third romance belonging to much the same period is
of a very different character, and has some claim to be considered the finest of the Anglo-Norman romances. It has more
the flavour of the best kind of *chanson de geste* than any other,
and though it lacks the crusading spirit of the *Chanson de
Roland* and it would be ridiculous to compare the two, it has
a spirit of its own and commemorates the desperate courage
of men fighting for hearth and home.

The *Romance of Horn*[1] was written by a certain Thomas,
probably not to be identified with the author of *Tristan* or
with Thomas of Kent, author of the *Roman de Toute Chevalerie*.[2] In line 3 he calls himself 'Mestre', thus laying
claim to have been a clerk. He cannot have proceeded to
priest's orders, since at the end he speaks of his son. *Horn*,
according to Thomas, was designed to form the central
portion of a trilogy. It had been preceded by a *Romance of
Aalof*, Horn's father, and it was intended that it should be
followed by a *Romance of Hadermod*, his son.

> Seignurs, oi avez le[s] vers del parchemin,
> Cum li bers Aaluf est venuz a sa fin.
> Mestre Thomas ne vult k'il seit mis a declin
> K'il ne die de Horn, le vaillant orphanin,
> Cum puis l'unt treit li felun Sarasin.   (1–5)

(Lords, you have heard the lines of the parchment, how Aaluf
wight came to his end. Master Thomas does not wish it to be laid aside
before he tells of Horn, the valiant orphan, how the wicked Saracens
treated him thereafter.)

> Entritant de sorjorn cum iluc sorjornat,
> Le vaillant Hadermod de Rimel engendrat,
> Ki Asf[r]iche cunquist e qe pus [i] regnat
> E ki tuz ses parenz de paens [i] vengat;

[1] Ed. M. K. Pope, i (A.N.T.S., IX–X, 1955), ii.
[2] Cf. below, pp. 105–7.

De pruesces e de sen trestuz les ultreat,
Cum cil purrat mustrer ki la estorie savrat.
Icest lais a mun fiz, Gilimot, ki·l dirrat,
Ki la rime apré mei bien controverat —
Controvures ert bon: . . .   (5225–33)

Or en die avant ki l'estorie saverat!
Tomas n'en dirrat plus, 'Tu autem' chanterat:
'Tu autem domine miserere nostri'.   (5238–40)

(During his stay, while he remained there, he begot on Rimel the valiant Hadermod, who conquered Africa and afterwards reigned there, and avenged all his family on the pagans. He surpassed them all in prowess and wisdom, as he who knows the story can show. I leave this to my son, Gilimot, to tell, who can well devise it in rhyme after me, he will be a good artist: . . . Now let him who knows the story well say more if he likes! Thomas will tell no more of it, he will sing 'Tu autem'—'Tu autem, domine miserere nostri'.)[1]

The implication is that Thomas was no longer young when he wrote *Horn*, and this may account for the mixture of archaisms and neologisms in his language. There are indications, according to Miss Pope, that Thomas or his family was connected with Poitou like Jordan Fantosme. This may be coincidence or it may be, as Madame Rita Lejeune would prefer to think, that the influence of Eleanor of Aquitaine was responsible.

There is no trace of a *Romance of Hadermod* in any language, but the previous existence of *Aaluf* may be deduced not only from the opening words of *Horn*, but from further references to the story in the course of the romance. An allusion to it in *Waldef*[2] has not much value as evidence. *Aaluf* is listed with *Tristan* and the *Brut* as a work translated from English. It is not clear whether any reliance can be placed upon this statement and what it was intended to convey is not clear. It is uncertain whether by *Aaluf* the author did not really mean *Horn* itself, since this is declared to be a sequel and is part of the saga of the family of Aaluf.

---

[1] The versicle which followed the lesson at Compline, also used at the end of meal-time readings in religious houses. Cf. *Girart de Roussillon* and the lyric *Cyl qe vodra oyr mes chauns*, of which the last lines are: 'Ly *tu autem* est en ce vers, Ly respounz soit de joye. Amen.' Cf. below, p. 342, and L. Sainéan, *La Langue de Rabelais* (Paris, 1922), i. 371, 372.

[2] Cf. below, p. 144.

The relationship between the Anglo-Norman text and the various English poems on the subject is obscure. The Anglo-Norman is considerably the oldest extant version, but has probably undergone more revision than *King Horn*. In his introduction to the edition of that poem,[1] Joseph Hall suggested that the origin is a tradition going back to the English invasion of the south-west, a stage best represented by *King Horn*. Later, the story was carried to the north during the period of the viking raids and altered to fit conditions there. The *Romance of Horn*, with the addition of courtly elements to please French taste, *Horn Child*, and the ballads all belong to this, the 'Scandinavian' version. W. H. Schofield tried to localize the geography of *King Horn* in the north-west of England, but his theories are of no use for the other versions.[2] Personal names have been the object of a study by W. H. French,[3] who maintains that most of them are of Germanic, not Norse, origin. The wisest conclusions on the subject are drawn by H. G. Leach. The story as we know it 'has quite outlived any historical events that it may record'. It is a tale of 'exile and return', such as was popular amongst the peoples of the north. It may have been first told by people of Norwegian descent in western England. 'However, the theories concerning the origin of *Horn* are little more than guesses.'[4]

The immediate source of Thomas's poem may have been in English, but there is no means of telling this. The part played by Thomas in adapting the story has been ignored, and the 'Scandinavian' version probably owes more to him than has been realized. It is Thomas who identified Westir with Ireland:

> Seignurs, or est Yrlande, lors fu Westir noméé.   (2184)
> (Lords, now it is Ireland, then it was named Westir.)

In *King Horn* Westerness is part of the British mainland. Moreover, it was Thomas who introduced Dublin into the story, and in his romance it has great prominence. Horn lands near by at an unnamed port, the landfall being marked

---

[1] Oxford, 1901.
[2] 'The Story of Horn and Rimenhild', *P.M.L.A.*, xviii (1903), pp. 1–83.
[3] *Essays on King Horn* (Cornell Studies in English, 1940).
[4] *Angevin Britain and Scandinavia* (Harvard, 1921), pp. 328–31.

by a natural rock, more than a league distant from Dublin, which can be approached by an open plain. Later, the pagans land apparently at the same spot, which is linked to Dublin by a metalled road. The pagans make two attacks on Dublin and are repulsed only at great sacrifice. These battles seem to have been inspired by the heroic defence of Dublin by Miles de Cogan described in the poem *Dermot and the Earl*[1] and by Giraldus Cambrensis. Perhaps *Horn*, a man's poem in both form and content, was written in connexion with the Christmas festivities of 1171, when Henry II spent the period between Martinmas and Christmastide in a castle constructed of wattles in the Irish manner outside the walls of Dublin.

The proper names used by Thomas seem to be derived from various sources, and he has a disconcerting habit of using the same name for different characters either because he was working on two versions of the story or because his invention gave out, as Malory's was to do later. The continental names seem to be connected with events which took place several centuries before those which occurred in the Ireland that he knew. Aaluf is the same as Olaf, and he is said to be the grandson of Baderolf, Emperor of Germany. His mother's name was Goldburc. He thus appears to be the same person as Havelok, but the connexion between the story of Horn and the story of Havelok is a mystery which perhaps the recovery of a romance of *Aaluf* might help to clear up. Gudborc or Goldeburc is also the name of the Queen of Ireland. The King of Ireland—really only the King of Dublin—is called Gudreche, Gudred, &c., and surely owes his name to Gothred Sitryggson, King of Dublin, with whom Lanfranc (who mistook him for the King of Ireland) was in correspondence in 1074. The name must have been familiar in England, too, from the fact that Gothric, King of Man, was the father of Olaf Bitling, who was a refugee at the court of Henry I from 1098 to 1103. The Archbishop of Dublin's name, Markier or Marcher, bears some resemblance to Malchus, the name of the Winchester monk who became Bishop of Waterford and was translated to Cashel in 1106, to Malachy, and to Maurice, names borne

[1] Cf. below, pp. 303–4.

by the bishops of Down and Derry in Henry II's own day. The 'Irish' in this poem are all Danes—the Ostmen—and the Africans or pagans who attack them are Danes from overseas. These were the Saracens who had killed Aaluf. The Bretons who gave shelter to Horn after the massacre are also Danes. The King of Brittany, Hunlaf, bears a name used for a Dane in *Beowulf*. His daughter, Rigmel, Rigmenil, &c., has a name which is a form of Ragnhildis, well known as that of a daughter-in-law of Somerled. The Treasurer, however, is called Moroan or Moruan, like the King of Brittany overthrown by Louis the Pious in 810. The Archbishop is named Taurin, like the seventh-century Bishop of Nantes. Modin or Modun, Horn's cousin and rival, has, it seems, the same name as two Earls of Caithness, Moddan, Muddan, or Mumtan, one of whom was the grandfather of Olaf Bitling's wife. Of the pagans, Rodlac and his nephew Rollac recall the name of Rollaug Ragnvaldson.[1]

The topography appears to be Viking. Countries are usually known only by their coasts. Horn's home, Suddene, the Anglo-Saxon name for what one might call the South Riding of Denmark, has apparently shifted to England, and has variously been identified with Dorset and Devon. It is clearly to the north-west of Brittany, since Horn is driven to the latter by a nor'-west wind. 'Bretaigne' is Little, not Great Britain. Its port is Costance which must stand for Coutances. This happens to be in Normandy, but it is in the same bight as St-Malo. The court of Brittany is kept at Lions, perhaps the county of Leon and not some specific town in it—Morvan was Count of Leon before being elected chief of the Bretons. Westir, the name applied by the Vikings to the Hebrides, Man, and Ireland, is here used for Ireland alone, as has already been mentioned. Modun's country, Feneneie, Fenoie, Fenie, or Finee, is probably Finland. Other countries mentioned are also connected with Vikings and their settlements—Norway, Frisia, Russia, Burgundy, Portugal, and Italy. Miss Pope has mentioned that Thomas appears to have first-hand knowledge of the coastal parts of Brittany. The same applies to Dublin. If Thomas had not

---

[1] For these last three names cf. *The Orkneyinga Saga*, translated with notes by A. B. Taylor (Edinburgh and London, 1938).

himself visited these parts he must have had information from people who had. A curious point is that the Angevins are represented as treacherous villains, attacking Horn's benefactors, the Bretons. This sounds hardly tactful if the romance was written for Henry II's court, but perhaps for Angevins one should read the Young King and his party.

Briefly, the story of the romance is as follows: Aaluf was a foundling brought up in Suddene by King Silaus. Like his double Havelok, he was really a prince, and when it was discovered that he was the son of the Emperor of Germany, Silaus married him to his daughter Suanburc and left him his kingdom. When his son Horn was a child the kingdom was invaded by Saracens. Aaluf was slain, Suanburc escaped to a cave overlooking the sea where she lived in poverty for years, while Horn and other children were exposed in a rudderless boat. They drifted to Brittany where the king's daughter Rigmel fell in love with Horn. Disgraced and banished, he took refuge in Ireland under an assumed name, might have married an Irish princess, but returned to save Rigmel from marriage to a man she disliked. While he was again absent in an attempt to recover his kingdom and find his mother, Rigmel was abducted, but again Horn returned in time and forgave his enemies. The story thus has a happy ending, and there seems little need to prolong it with a story of Hadermod.

There are some obvious resemblances to the *Tristan* story, but the spirit of the romance is very different and there may be no connexion between the two. Rudderless boats and visits to Ireland under an assumed name are hardly proof of any direct borrowing. There are some clumsy features of the narrative which seem to be signs of hasty adaptation. The repetition of proper names has already been mentioned. Much more disconcerting is the treatment of the character of Wikele, who is one of Horn's young companions at the beginning of the poem, is knighted by Horn and becomes one of his closest followers, then is said to be Horn's cousin, joins Modun against Horn, is forgiven once, but takes advantage of Horn's absence to abduct Rigmel, and meets with a traitor's death and exposure at the hands of Horn. Although some of this is also found in *King Horn*, Wikenhild, as he is called there, is never said to be Horn's cousin. For some reason, which must remain obscure for lack of further evidence, Thomas makes matters worse by introducing this complication. Possibly he intended to heighten the dramatic effect of his treachery, which is already emphasized in the 'Scandinavian' versions by the existence of a loyal brother of Wikele.

It is as well to point out that the 'courtly' element added by Thomas has nothing to do with courtly love. All the interest is concentrated on the men's characters. Horn is of angelic beauty and wears fine clothes. It is Rigmel who is dazzled by his beauty and not the reverse. She puts on her best clothes to attract him. Of course she is beautiful, but in a thoroughly vague way. Horn at first rejects her advances; but having once accepted a pennon sent to him by her, he remains loyal to the end, and soon consents to exchange rings. He has no eyes for the Irish princesses, and refuses an offer of the hand of one of them, together with the kingdom. To say that either Horn or Rigmel felt the emotion known as 'courtly love' would be ridiculous. Rigmel is obliged to make the running because as a motherless girl she cannot appear in Hall. The Irish princesses can make brief appearances there because they are chaperoned by their mother.[1] Horn responds to Rigmel, after some hesitation, because he has to get married to somebody, but once his course of action is decided he cannot be deflected from it. Tristan's dilemma is unthinkable in his case. But to say the truth, Horn is a somewhat dull hero. If he has a fault, it is pride, but his character is only slightly sketched. Thomas was interested in events, not character. Yet the romance itself is far from dull. If the author was not interested in the relationship between a young man and a girl, he is moved by the relationship between prince and follower and between mother and son. Miss Pope found some of the fighting for Dublin worthy of comparison with the Battle of Maldon. The Ostmen are 'li nostre', and Egfer's death is described with real pathos. Where the version of Thomas, dismissed

---

[1] Cf. M. D. Legge, 'The Influence of Patronage on Form in Mediaeval French Literature', *Stil- und Formprobleme in der Literatur* (Heidelberg, 1959).

by Mr. French as 'a florid transformation', excels is in parts
where he has given himself a free hand:

'Amis', çoe dit Egfer,   'ke vaut or(e) vostre plur?
Ne vus aiderai mais   en cembel n'en estur,
Kar ui sui avenu   a mun de[e]rein jor,
Mes merci vus en rende   li haut creator
Ke m'avez si vengé   del felun traïtur
Ki m'ad mort. De sauté   n'i ad mes nul retur.'   (3510–15)

('Friend', said Egfer, 'what skills your weeping now? I shall aid
you no more in tourney or in battle, for I am come to my last day.
But the high Creator reward you for avenging me on the wicked
traitor to whom I owe my death. Henceforth, health will return no
more.')

Francisque Michel, who edited all the texts for the Bannatyne Club in 1845, found the recognition scene between Horn
and his mother extremely moving.

The romance, written in *laisses* of alexandrines, has perhaps more in common with the *chansons de geste* than any
other Anglo-Norman poem, but it does not imitate them in
all its technique. There are no 'laisses similaires'. The
nearest approach to them is the repetition of an opening line.
Laisse 164 begins:

Paien sunt descunfit, vers lor nefs fuiant vont,

and laisse 167:

Paiens sunt descunfiz, morz [e] mis a turment.

The attitude of the Christians to the pagans is reminiscent
of the jeering tone used in the *Roland* and *Gormont*. The only
literary allusions are to the *Roland*, *Gormont*, and *Ogier le
Danois*. As regards the versification, rhyme and assonance
are mixed, and it would be rash to deduce from this the
previous existence of an assonanced version. The mixture
occurs elsewhere, even in Béroul. There is a high proportion
of lines with a 'lyric' caesura, which is found in narrative
poetry more often in Anglo-Norman than in French. Alliteration is used to a certain extent, but only as an ornament.
The line:

N'en chauf n'en chevelu ke bien ne seit ferant!   (4353)

is a proverbial expression. If Thomas had an English source, English heroic poetry had no influence on him. There is in fact no evidence of a knowledge of English in his romance. The pun on the word 'horn' in line 4206, and his knowledge of the oath 'Witegod' in line 4013, prove nothing. (Wace's allusion to Wassail and Drinkhail does not mean that he knew English, a language which he compares to the barking of dogs.) The poem is 5,250 lines long, but is not monotonous. It is a straightforward tale, with plenty of addresses to the audience of 'seignurs'. There are no dragons or supernatural happenings. A dream of swine signifying people is received with jeers (lines 4644–64). Material things are interestingly described, and from the point of view of social history are worth studying. Clothes, buildings, feasting, sea-faring, games, and music all play a part. Particularly important are the passages describing harping and the singing of lays (laisses 135–7) and a contest of putting the stone (laisses 124–9). Descriptions of this game, practised in order to strengthen the muscles, are not rare, but what is remarkable here is the way the excitement of the spectators is depicted. Here, as in the battle-scenes, the author seems to identify himself completely with the people about whom he is writing, something which is not universal in medieval literature. One word of caution must be added. Thomas always makes it plain that he is telling about something which happened a long time ago, and at times tries to add local colour; but for the most part he is putting a saga into modern dress.

The romance survives in three main manuscripts (Cambridge Univ. Lib. Ff. 6. 17, Bodleian Douce 132, B.M. Harley 527), none, unfortunately, complete, and in two small fragments (Cambridge Univ. Lib. Add. 4407, 4470). All are Anglo-Norman, written in the thirteenth century. Although no trace of a continental copy survives the text must have reached France, for it was adapted, with change of nomenclature, as *Ponthus et Sidoine*, a fifteenth-century prose work written by Ponthus de la Tour Landri for the purpose of glorifying his own family. This, in its turn, was translated into German, Flemish, and other languages, besides English.

THOMAS OF KENT—*LE ROMAN DE TOUTE CHEVALERIE*

Alexandrine *laisses* are also used for the third Anglo-Norman romance by a writer named Thomas, the *Roman de Toute Chevalerie* by Thomas of Kent,[1] which treats of Alexander. In the absence of an edition it is difficult to assess the place and value of this once very popular work. The date at which it was written is impossible to guess. It is independent of the continental romances and goes back to Latin sources. It is not merely a romance but, as the title implies, an *exemplum*; and Thomas had a moral purpose in compiling it. In the past it was too easily dismissed as derivative, the fact that a version of the *Fuerre de Gadres* and, in one manuscript, a passage from the French romance were interpolated into it after its composition not having been recognized.[2] The name of the author of the *Fuerre*, Eustace, has led to scribal confusion, and the *Roman de Toute Chevalerie* is still sometimes attributed to a mythical Eustace of Kent. To Lambert le Tort, writing about 1170,[3] is generally given the credit for first using the dodecasyllable in connexion with Alexander, whence the name alexandrine. It is possible that he was preceded in this by Eustace and by Thomas of Kent. A recent attempt to date the *Roman de Toute Chevalerie* by a supposed reference to the *Roman d'Eneas*, itself impossible to date more closely than some time before a period 1175–81, failed to carry conviction.[4] The form of the romance seems to suggest that it belongs with the other works mentioned in *laisse* form to the time of Eleanor's imprisonment, but it may be earlier. A close study of the language and versification might help, though such evidence is untrustworthy, especially where Anglo-Norman is concerned.

As for the author himself, he has proved elusive. It is not always sufficient to know the name of a writer when trying

---

[1] Extracts in P. Meyer, *Alexandre le Grand* (Paris, 1886), ii. 273 ff.; latest bibliography in G. Carey, ed. D. J. A. Ross, *The Medieval Alexander* (Cambridge, 1956), pp. 35–36. Edition in preparation by B. Foster.

[2] Cf. the text of the *Fuerre*, Elliott Monographs, v (1942). Cf. D. J. A. Ross, 'New Medieval Versions of French Alexander poems', *Medium Ævum*, xxviii (1959), pp. 48–49.   [3] Elliott Monographs, iii (1949), p. 1.

[4] B. Foster, *French Studies*, ix (1955), pp. 154–8. Cf. ibid., pp. 348–9.

to establish his identity. Neither his Christian name nor his surname was uncommon. It seems unlikely that he was the Thomas who wrote *Horn*, who was a more inspired poet and has a different style. It is more difficult to feel sure that he was not the author of *Tristan*. Here, the different metre employed rules out any close stylistic comparison, and certain vague resemblances in the ideas expressed in the prologue and epilogue have been noted.[1] A St. Albans illustrator believed him to have been a Benedictine monk, and resemblances between his sources and those used for a later Latin compilation made at St. Albans may indicate that he belonged there.[2] But this is conjecture. If he was the author of *Tristan*, he may, as Benoit de Ste More is believed to have done, have changed his matter and style to suit the changed climate of the English court.

The moralizing nature of this text, which is one of the reasons for the way it is neglected today, did not prevent it from being very popular. It survives in four manuscripts, one being a short fragment. None is earlier than 1250, and two are fourteenth-century. Three probably go back to the same St. Albans prototype. Two of these (B.N. fr. 24364, Cambridge, Trinity College O. 9. 34) contain very similar illustrations, and the third (Durham C. iv. 27B) has the same captions without the illustrations. The most complete of these three has been quite unjustifiably included amongst *Les Plus Beaux Manuscrits français à peintures de la Bibliothèque Nationale* (Paris, 1937). Possibly a manuscript of this type served as model for the paintings which Henry III caused to be made in the queen's chamber at Nottingham Castle.[3] The text was probably unknown abroad, but at home it served as the source for the English *Kyng Alisaunder*,[4] dated before 1350. The copy used by the author of that version did not contain the interpolated

---

[1] *Anglo-Norman in the Cloisters*, pp. 35–43. Cf. B. H. Wind's 'Faut-il identifier Thomas avec Thomas de Kent ?', *Mélanges Li Gotti* (Palermo, 1962).

[2] Mr. Ross objects that this illustrator thought his name was Eustace. As, however, he was working nearly a century after the romance was written, the tradition that he was a monk may have outlived the knowledge of his name. Cf. *French Studies*, ix (1955), p. 351.

[3] M. Bateson, *Mediaeval England* (London, 1903), pp. 150–2.

[4] Ed. G. V. Smithers, E.E.T.S., o.s. ccxxvii (1952), ccxxxvii (1957).

Fuerre de Gadres. The use of the name Eumenidus for Eme-
nidus in a reference to the Alexander story in the *Histoire
de Guillaume le Maréchal* (line 8446) shows that its author,
writing in 1226, made use of the version of the *Fuerre* interpolated into the *Roman*, possibly therefore the *Roman* itself.
This author, a Norman by birth, probably worked in England. The interpolations, the wide spread in the dates of
the surviving manuscripts, and the existence of an English
version, are all proof of the lasting popularity of this now
neglected work. It must be confessed, however, that part
of its popularity was due to the suitability of all books about
Alexander for illustration. The gradual deterioration in the
language and versification at the hands of the scribes[1] suggests that the pictures came to be regarded as being more
important than the text. Such, to an even greater degree, was
the fate of the text of the translation of the Apocalypse.[2]

THE *FABLES* OF MARIE DE FRANCE

Before leaving the study of the question whether there
was not a reaction against the courtly trend of literature, a
passing reference must be made to the *Fables* of Marie de
France. These were dedicated to an Earl William who has
never been identified. Clearly, in this case, she was writing
for a man and not a court personified in a king. It has been demonstrated how carefully the fables were selected, and the
morals composed, with the responsibilities of a magnate in
view. This is indeed aristocratic, but not courtly, literature.[3]

This courtly literature, however, did not disappear altogether, and its survival and revival will be discussed in the
next chapter.

---

[1] F. B. Agard, *Romanic Review*, xxxiii (1942), pp. 216–65.
[2] Cf. below, pp. 236–9, 241–2.
[3] E. A. Francis, 'Marie de France et son temps', *Romania*, lxxii (1951), pp. 78–99.

VI

THE END OF THE TWELFTH CENTURY

THE end of the twelfth century and the beginning of the thirteenth saw the production of a number of works, both secular and religious, which it is impossible to assign to any particular reign. Towards the end of the reign of Henry II there was probably little royal patronage, and it is perhaps symptomatic that an important author like Hue de Rotelande wrote for a magnate, almost unknown to history, on the Welsh border. Richard and John were continental and southern in their tastes. Richard was a poet in his own right and kept in touch with his half-sister, Marie de Champagne. His relations with the troubadours are well known. He was rarely in England for any length of time. John had luxurious tastes, but is not known to have been inclined to literature. It is true that he once sent in a hurry for a 'Romance of the History of England', a copy of Gaimar, perhaps, and that he borrowed from the Abbot of Reading some Latin books and owned a Pliny, but none of these was written for him. Henry III was a great builder and very fond of wall-paintings copied from books, as the Angers tapestry is copied from the Anglo-Norman Apocalypse, but absolutely nothing is known about his taste in literature.[1] His patronage of Matthew Paris was utilitarian.

The works to be discussed in this chapter cannot therefore be arranged chronologically. There is no clue in any of them, except the last to be mentioned, which could lead to the identification of any patron for whom they may have been written.

---

[1] See especially A. L. Poole, *From Domesday Book to Magna Carta* (Oxford, 1955), p. 243; F. M. Powicke, *Henry III and the Lord Edward* (Oxford, 1947), ii. 573; V. H. Galbraith, *The Literacy of the Medieval English Kings* (British Academy, 1935).

AMADAS ET YDOINE

At first sight the truest expression of the courtly spirit in Anglo-Norman appears to be the romance of *Amadas et Ydoine*,[1] thought to have been written between 1190 and 1220, but possibly earlier. The study of this romance is complicated by the fact that in its entirety it survives in a modernized and abbreviated Picard manuscript, and only fragments of the original Anglo-Norman text remain. Classed as a *roman d'aventure*, it is in reality a serious work and its exaggerated courtliness conceals a lesson. The continental scribe or *remanieur*, as Monsieur Le Gentil has pointed out without perhaps making all the implications clear, has sometimes altered the text in order to make it accord more closely to the accepted courtly conventions.

The chief characters have allegorical names. They are just lovers like the anonymous pair in Jehan Renart's *Lai de l'Ombre*. Amadas is a youth of a lower rank than the object of his devotion, smitten with love at first sight at an awkward moment when he is carving before the high table, with the result that he drops the carving-knife. This is a breach of etiquette of which Chaucer's Squire would not have been guilty. The lady is called Ydoine, an 'idonea persona' in the context. The same name is used in the satirical debate *Melior et Ydoine*. When he hears of her marriage to another, Amadas becomes ill through unrequited love. Ydoine, after rejecting the suit of one so humble, becomes so fitting a heroine that she succeeds in reserving her 'cuer' and her 'cors' for the same man (line 6940). She is married to a Comte de Nevers, but keeps him at bay by witchcraft. A demon knight steals the ring with which she had plighted her troth to Amadas, and puts her under a spell so that she appears to be dead. Here one thinks of Thisbe and Juliet, but still more of Fenice. Amadas rescues her after a fight in

[1] J. R. Reinhard (Classique français du Moyen Age, Paris, 1926). Cf. his 'Amadas et Ydoine', *Romanic Review*, xv (1924), pp. 179–266, and *The Old French Romance of Amadas et Ydoine* (Durham, N.Y., 1927); G. Paris, 'Sur *Amadas et Ydoine*', *Miscellany presented to F. J. Furnivall* (Oxford 1901), pp. 334–5, and *Mélanges de littérature française au moyen âge* (Paris, 1912), pp. 328–36; P. Le Gentil, 'A propos d'Amadas et Ydoine', *Romania*, lxxi (1950), pp. 359–73; F. M. Warren, 'Notes on the Romans d'Aventure', *Modern Language Notes*, xiii (1898), pp. 343, 344.

a cemetery, an episode which recalls *L'Atre Perilleux*, the theme being probably derived from a common source. All ends happily without further appeal to mortality. The Comte de Nevers gracefully renounces Ydoine and marries a daughter of the Comte de Poitiers, with whom he had apparently been in love all the time without knowing it. Ydoine and Amadas are able to marry, have many children, and live happily ever after.

The author, to do him justice, shows a certain skill in combining these several different but much-used themes and does contrive to give an air of freshness to the mixture. The plot gives him various occasions for moral reflections. There is the inevitable passage on the nature and power of love, and particularly on the troubles of secret love (lines 497–506). There is an outburst against the deceitfulness of women, which to modern ears accords ill with the exaltation of the lady but which is in tune with contemporary feeling (lines 7037–97). References to Fortune are fairly frequent, and free use is made of personification, as for instance of Love, Pity, Nobility, and Fear (lines 1102–6). Interest is shown in clothes, food, plate, and other luxuries, but there is little about fighting. Technical details of this are confined to two episodes, the fight in the cemetery and a tournament at Lucca. This is a very different state of affairs from that in Hue de Rotelande's romances. Occasionally little details of social life emerge—it is apparently taken as a matter of course that Ydoine can read (lines 1276–7). During Amadas's madness the people of Lucca jeer at him and make him run the gauntlet in the streets every day (lines 2701 ff., 3121 ff.).

Of character-drawing there is little or none. At the beginning Ydoine is the typical 'Fiere', cruelly rejecting the suit of the Squire of Low Degree—or, at least, of lower degree than her own. Pity, nobility, and fear when Amadas is apparently dead for love combine to melt her heart and turn her into the *idonea persona* worthy of such devotion. When, later on, she falls ill in her turn, she becomes so selfless as to invent for herself—and kill—three illegitimate children, whose fathers, to add to the horror, were her first cousins, in order to prevent Amadas from killing himself after her death (lines 5027 ff.). Amadas is at first a youth as hard-hearted as the diamond from which his name is in part derived. The perfection of Ydoine turns him into the ideal 'amador', sick for love and mad from disappointment. While he is sick his abnegation is complete:

> 'Beaus sire Deus, pur quai fui né?
> . . . . . .
> Murir ne vivre ben ne puis,
> Ne nule part confort ne truis.
>
> . . . . . .
> La mort ne m'at pas en baillie
> Cum jo vudraie, kar ainz jur
> Serait finie ma dolur,
> De cest mal serai delivre;
> Issi ne puis lunges vivre.
> U me estuvera tut guarir,
> U a curt terme de dol murir.
> La guarisun jo n'i vai pas.'
> Atant suspire et dit: 'Allas!
> Si jo par ma rage me oci,
> Dunt sai jo ben certes de fi
> Que, quant ma vie est del cors issue,
> Finablement serat perdue.
> Jo n'os me memes ocire,
> Et vivre issi est gref martire.
> Mais ore sai ben cum le ferai,
> Renablement de dol murai:
> Jo m'en irai tut drai a lui
> Hardïement crier merci;
> Ele s'en aïra forment,
> Par ire et par mautalent
> Fera venir ses pauteners,
> Ses serfs malveis et ses fuers;
> Devant lui me ferat hunir,
> Tresquo la mort batre et laidir.
> Feble sui et sanc mellerai,
> Ignelepas de dol murai,
> Kar jol prendrai a si gref fes
> Quo vivre ne purai aprés;
> Jo n'i vai autre guarisun,
> Fors murir par cest achaisun.
> Puis aint ma dame u bas u haut,
> Aprés mes jurz ren ne me chaut.'   (V. 1065–1110)

('Fair Lord God, why was I born? . . . I can neither die nor live, nor find comfort anywhere. . . . Death has not the power over me that I would wish, for before daylight my grief should be over, I should be free of this pain; I cannot live long in this way. Either I must be entirely healed, or die of grief within a short term. Healing I do not perceive.' Then he sighs and says: 'Alas! If I kill myself in my raving, then I am quite certain that, when my life [soul] has left my body, it will be lost for ever. I dare not kill myself, and to live thus is grievous martyrdom.—But now I know well how to do it, I shall die reasonably of grief. I will go straight to her and boldly cry her mercy; she will become very angry, and call in her anger and ill-will for her grooms, her wicked serfs and knaves, she will have me shamed before her, beaten and ill-treated to death. I am feeble and shall falter; straightway I shall die of grief, for I shall take it as such a heavy burden that I cannot live afterwards; I see no other possible way of health, save to die for this cause. Then, whether my lady loves high or low, it will not matter to me when my days are ended.')

Here we have the soliloquy dealing with the dilemma and the casuistical solution, which Thomas had exploited long ago in his *Tristan*. But there is something new, the desire to be reasonable and the contemplation and rejection of suicide as a way out. Galiene in *Fergus*, written perhaps about 1209, also considered killing herself, but from family pride refrained. Amadas believed that death would end his sufferings, since love was all on one side. There would be no briar-bushes to twine above the graves of himself and Ydoine.[1]

The Comte de Nevers is a ridiculous nonentity. Ydoine had to be married to another to satisfy the conventions of courtly love, just as the heroine of the *Lai de l'Ombre* had to have a husband. Jehan Renart adroitly left the husband out of the story, a possibility when writing a lay. The author of *Amadas* had to bring him on the stage, but he is just too good to be true, first of all meekly accepting his wife's refusal to consummate the marriage and then discovering a convenient latent passion for the daughter of the Comte de Poitiers.

The question has been raised often enough whether

---

[1] I do not know why Miss West exclaims of the two last lines 'than which it would be hard to find a less courtois remark'. C. B. West, *Courtoisie in Anglo-Norman Literature* (Oxford, 1938), p. 121.

Amadas is a truly *courtois* romance, or whether it is merely a *roman d'aventure*. The truth lies somewhere in between. There is no such thing as a *courtois* romance, for the simple ✗ reason that courtly love belongs to the lyric and cannot be satisfactorily treated in a romance. It is scarcely true to say, as Reinhard did, that the poet 'forcefully repudiates Chrétien's and André [Capellanus]'s main thesis that love is illicit and adulterous'.[1] Crestien never held anything of the sort, and tried in *Cliges*, but less successfully, to reconcile courtly love with the kind of love which ends in marriage.

The author was, of course, well read in classical literature. He makes parade of his erudition, referring to the three Fates, Pyramus and Thisbe, Lucretia and Collatinus, Paris and Helen, Lavinia and Aeneas, Dido, Achilles, Alexander, and so on. Presumably the mention of Lavinia shows that he was acquainted with the *Roman d'Eneas*, but there is no proof that he was influenced by Crestien de Troyes. Resemblances between this romance and *Cliges* and *Yvain* are more likely accidental, and demonstrate that certain topics were in fashion at the end of the twelfth century. What distinguishes *Amadas* from other romances is the author's intention to create an example. It does seem probable that he knew the *Tristan* of Thomas, and he certainly follows the tradition of the exemplary tale proclaimed in Thomas's epilogue.[2] *Amadas* was said above to be a serious work; the author is a moralizer, neither flippant nor cynical. His first few lines recall the *Pervigilium Veneris*.

Amadas enjoyed immense popularity, and there is a formidable list of works in which it is mentioned drawn up by Reinhard. It was well known in the Low Countries from the thirteenth to the fifteenth centuries, probably having travelled, like so many other texts, from northeastern France across the border and so to Holland. The name of Amadis de Gaule may be a reminiscence of Amadas. Curiously enough, it seems to have been quoted only once in a continental French text, *Gautier d'Aupais*. It was in England, the land of its birth, that it achieved its greatest renown. The author had intended to add the example of

---

[1] 'Amadas and Ydoine', *Romanic Review*, xv (1924), p. 193.
[2] Cf. above, pp. 56–57.

Amadas and Ydoine to the list of faithful lovers. To the names from classical sources just mentioned he himself added two modern pairs, the inevitable Tristan and Yseult and, more surprisingly, Roland and Aude. The train of events which was to turn the Roland of Roncesvalles into Orlando Furioso, a hero suffering, like Amadas himself, from love's delirium, was already in motion. As he had hoped, his successors in their turn added the names of Amadas and Ydoine. First in the field was the poet of the *Donnei des Amants*, mentioned later in this chapter, and last was Gower in his *Confessio Amantis*, late in the fourteenth century. In *Sir Degravant* and in *Emare* their story is embroidered. None of Crestien's lovers made their mark in this way. The author would have appreciated the *Luve Ron* of the thirteenth-century Thomas of Hales.[1] In the 'Ubi sunt' stanza of this religious and didactic poem he sets Amadas and Ydoine with Paris and Helen, Tristan and Yseult. This is just where their creator would have wanted them to be.

The romance itself is preserved in three manuscripts. As has already been stated, the only complete one is Picard and is late thirteenth-century. The writer has corrected Anglo-Normanisms.[2] There is a long Anglo-Norman fragment (Vatican Pal. 1871) and a double fragment (Göttingen Univ. Philol. 184) belonging to the early part of the same century. Like so many popular works of the Middle Ages, it seems to have been torn to pieces. There is no English translation or version extant, and the names seem to have become known through the French romance. But it is unnecessary to suppose that everyone who mentions them had read the romance; they were just two names added to a stock list which was repeated over and over again.

The poem is written in the conventional octosyllabic rhyming couplets, with few eccentricities. The style is not unattractive, but there are too many appeals to the 'signeur' to whom it is addressed, and too many clichés like

> Que vous iroie plus contant?

and

> Il n'est dame ne pucele

---

[1] See below, pp. 227–8.   [2] Cf. the articles by G. Paris and P. Le Gentil.

and so on. There are apparently reminiscences of Thomas's
Tristan:

> 'Ma vie est en vus et ma mort' (V. 799)
>
> 'Ne jo en vie ne jo en mort
> Ne puis truver de rens confort'. (V. 1075–1076)

There is little conversation except in the encounter between
the demon knight and Amadas (lines 5671 ff.). The versification is not so skilfully handled as in the romances of Hue
de Rotelande. Rhetoric is used occasionally, as in the para-
doxical play on *cuvrir* and *descuvrir* (V. lines 569–84).

What is one to say about the value and merits of this
romance? It is plain that it enjoyed a popularity which
appears beyond its deserts. The public, however, does not
necessarily demand the best in any age. The extreme con-
ventionality, presented, however, in a fresh and original
way, and the easy if undistinguished style would have their
appeal. It is easy to imagine that many who would feel uncomfortable in the presence of Tristan and Iseult would feel
more at home with the tribulations of Amadas and Ydoine.
There is something almost morbid in this preoccupation
with suffering, but it was the order of the day. It was not so
long since Petrus Blesensis had written in his *De xii Tribula-
tionibus* 'Da, Domine, nobis auxilium tribulationum'. In the
Middle Ages secular literature always follows in the wake of
ecclesiastical, and Thomas of Hales was not the only religious who drew parallels from one to the other. The last
word on *Amadas* must be left to the Middle Ages themselves. The author meant to describe a pair of ideal lovers.
The testimony of three centuries proves the measure of his
success.

AMIS E AMILUN

Amadas et Ydoine was not the only courtly romance with
a didactic flavour which belongs to this period. It was presumably towards the end of the century that an Anglo-
Norman version of a favourite medieval story, *Amis et Amiles*,
was produced, with the title *Amis e Amilun*. (It is confusing
that the Anglo-Norman Amis corresponds to the French
Amiles, Amilun to Amis.) The original seems to have been
a coalescence of two folk-themes. The first is one of two

friends as alike as identical twins, who change places, even their own wives being deceived. The other is of a man who sacrifices his children so that their innocent blood may heal the leprosy which has afflicted his guilty friend. The substitution leads to perjury which is wiped out by the sacrifice, and this is rewarded by the resuscitation of the children. What starts as a comedy of situations becomes in the hands of writers of romance a psychological study in characterization, while clerics turned the heroes into saints.

When this tale was first made the subject of an Old French poem it was probably in the form of a *chanson de geste*. A late twelfth-century poem of this kind does indeed exist, but it cannot be the earliest form of the story and is very likely later than the Anglo-Norman romance. *Amis et Amiles*[1] is written in assonant *laisses* of alexandrines, ending with a feminine 'orphan' line. The story has become attracted into the Charlemagne cycle, and is said to be well known to the pilgrims going to St. James, but, *pace* Bédier, the original setting was Lombardy and had nothing to do with the pilgrim route to Compostella. There are some obvious reminiscences of the *Chanson de Roland*.

Amis e Amilun[2] treats the story in quite independent fashion and must be derived from some earlier version. This was probably also Anglo-Norman, and the source of the Middle English poem, which resembles it more closely than it does the French poem, but preserves or reinstates primitive features which have been refined away in the Anglo-Norman romance, as will presently appear. The romance is designed for a different kind of public from that of the *chanson de geste* and has a false air of courtliness. It is written in the conventional octosyllabic rhyming couplet of romance.

The prologue begins with the lines:

> Ki veut oïr chançoun d'amur,
> De leauté e de grant douçur,
> En peis se tienge pur escouter;
> De trueffle ne voil mie parler.
> De dous juvenceus vus dirrai,
> Si com en escrit le trovai. . . .   (1–6)

---

[1] Ed. C. Hofmann (Erlangen, Paris, and London, 1852).
[2] Ed. E. Koelbing, *Amis and Amiloun* (Heilbronn, 1884).

(He who wishes to hear a song about love, about loyalty, and of great sweetness, let him hold his peace to listen; I have no intention of talking about trifles. I will tell you about two youths, just as I found it in writing. . . .)

The poet therefore acknowledges that the essential fact of the story is that it tells of two youths. In his version, how-ever, they are neither saints nor just brothers in arms—'Il bons compaingnons'—they are heroes of romance:

> Bien out en eus Nature ovré
> Angeles resembleint de beauté.   (15, 16)

(Well had Nature wrought in them, for beauty they appeared like angels.)

This is perhaps a clerkly touch. Thomas speaks of Horn's angelic beauty several times, and he was a particularly clerkly author.[1] A love-interest is nevertheless added to the plot, without distortion. In the French *chanson* Belyssant, daughter of Charlemagne, makes advances to Amiles in the accustomed forthright fashion. When repulsed, she tricks him into receiving her into his bed. They are spied upon and betrayed by the wicked steward, given the conventional name of Hardré. Amiles has acted quite innocently, but he is not expected to be chaste, merely to respect the person of his master's daughter. Belyssant does not require love from him, but physical satisfaction. In the romance Amis is read a lecture by his friend who is about to depart:

> Lessez orgoil e envie,
> Si vus gardez de glotonie,
> Amez bien vostre seingnur,
> Ne suffrez k'il eit deshonur!
> Mult li devom amur e fei,
> Kar mult ad amé vus e mei!   (95–100)

(Let alone pride and envy and keep yourself from gluttony. Love your lord, do not suffer him to be dishonoured. We owe him love and fealty, for much has he esteemed you and me.)

These injunctions are preceded by a warning against the steward—here anonymous.

---

[1] M. K. Pope, *The Romance of Horn* by Thomas (Anglo-Norman Text Society, vol. ii (forthcoming).

Gardez vus de sa felonie
Ne aiez a li compaignie,
Kar ki s'acompaingne a felon,
Ne porra trover si mal nun;
Kar pis ne poeit avenir,
Kant compaign vult autre trahir.   (87–92)

(Beware of his treachery. Do not become friends with him, for a person who is friendly with a felon will meet with nothing but ill. For nothing worse can happen than when one friend will betray another.)

This is the kind of didactic attitude in courtly literature which was to reach a climax in the allegory of Guillaume de Lorris.

Left to himself, Amis is courted by the daughter of his master, a mere count in this version. Not wishing to behave badly towards the count, he rejects her advances and meets with the characteristic reaction of a 'Fiere', furious because she has condescended so low and met with a rebuff. In the end they agree to meet secretly, as lovers upon equal terms, and are spied upon and betrayed.[1] In the meantime Amilun has gone to his own estates and by advice of his knights married a suitable heiress, a business affair in which love plays no part. At the end of the poem the wife of Amis endures the horror of the murder of her children for the sake of her husband's friend. The wife of Amis in the *chanson de geste* pretends to welcome home her husband and is imprisoned for her past treatment of him when he was smitten with leprosy. In the romance, the return of Amilun is more complicated. He forgives his erring barons, who had cast him out but now repent, but he shuts up his wife in a tower until she dies, because she tries to hide herself from him through fear and shows no repentance. The author does not insist upon this point, but there is a contrast here between the behaviour of the wife who has married a man she loves 'par amurs' and that of the wife who has made a *mariage de convenance*. In the *chanson* Amis has a young son, Girart, who is bullied by his mother. In the romance Amilun

---

[1] It is difficult to see why MacEdward Leach, *Amis and Amiloun* (Early English Text Society, 1937), p. xxvi, thinks that the Anglo-Norman and Middle English texts are less courtly and more primitive than the French at this point.

is tended only by a faithful squire, a relation of his, and he and his wicked wife have no children.

It is unlikely that this version of the story ever circulated on the Continent. It is contained in three manuscripts, all Anglo-Norman. One (Cambridge, Corpus Christi L) is early thirteenth-century, another (B.M. Royal 12. C. xii) fairly closely related to it, is early or mid fourteenth-century. The third (Carlsruhe Durlac 38) is late fourteenth-century, and is characterized not only by frequent omissions but by long supplementary passages which the editor probably rightly considered to be interpolations. In one Amilun and his wife are credited with a son, Florentyn, who has no part to play, as Girart has in the French version. It seems likely that even the earliest manuscript does not represent the earliest version of the story known in England, since the fourteenth-century English *Amis and Amiloun* may have been derived from a more primitive form of it. This romance is in tail-rhyme stanzas of twelve lines each. The main points of difference between it and the Anglo-Norman poem are: the heroine is called Belisaunt, as in the *chanson*, but she is the daughter of a duke, not of Charlemagne. The tone of the whole poem is less courtly, and has more in common with the *roman d'aventure*. The introductory allusions to love and friendship are omitted, Amiloun's parting injunctions to Amis are confined to a warning against the steward and to a swearing of friendship. The barons do not urge Amiloun to marry. Belisaunt's anger with Amis proceeds from mere frustration, and not from pride of rank. The boy Owein is not a vague relation, but the traditional sister's son. The wicked wife has remarried with a neighbouring knight, and Amiloun, with the help of Amis, inflicts on his return a heavy defeat on the barons, which inevitably recalls Ulysses' fight with the suitors. There is no contrast between the behaviour of the wife and that of the barons. The last editor of the English text, as has been said above, seems to have been over-hasty in classing it and the Anglo-Norman poem together as identical in tone and more primitive than the French version.

The main interest of the Anglo-Norman *Amis e Amilun* lies in the transformation of a simple legend, suitable as a subject for a *chanson de geste* or a moral tale, into a romance capable of appealing to a sophisticated public with a formed taste for courtly literature. The poem has no particular stylistic merits, but no particular defects either. There are no rhetorical tricks or flourishes, no lengthy moralizings to hold up the action, no clever representations of dialogue. The author's sole concern is to tell his tale as straightforwardly as possible, while considering the tastes of his patrons. Since he is concerned with two heroes he has to speak of them alternately; he is forced to adopt a method which later on becomes characteristic of the prose romances. He breaks the thread of his narrative and picks it up again with such warnings as:

> Ore vus dirrai d'Amilun   (151)

and

> Ore lerra d'els ma matire,
> De Sire Amis vus voudrai dire   (179–80)

and so on.

A curious device is twice employed. Two characters are known by nicknames. They have names used by their families, but are known to the household by nicknames which describe their qualities. This is an elaboration of the theory of names characteristic of the twelfth century. The first of the young people with two names is the Count's daughter:

> Nomer vus dei bien la pucele:
> Son dreit nun fu Mirabele;
> Mes Florie fud appellee
> De ceus ke furent de sa meisné.   (247–50)

(I must tell you what the maiden was called. Her rightful name was Mirabele; but the people of her household called her Florie.)

The second is the faithful page:

> Le nun vus dirrai de l'enfant:
> La gent l'apellent Amiraunt,
> Mes Owein esteit son dreit noun.   (887–9)

(I shall tell you the child's name. The household called him Amiraunt, but his rightful name was Owein.)

Owein is the name by which his lord calls him. These two names occur in the English poem, but the maiden is invariably there called Belisaunt, as in the French, and she is a less courtly character.

The versification has few peculiarities. The couplet is rarely broken, a sign of antiquity or archaism. The rhymes show one hesitation which is particularly Anglo-Norman. A word ending in a vowel followed by a feminine *e* may be treated either as a feminine or as a masculine ending. Thus, *meisné* can rhyme both with *privé* and with *appellee* (lines 150, 250). The final *e* was probably not being pronounced in such cases, a development which took place so much later in France that such rhymes are considered daring even today.

In the history of Anglo-Norman literature, adorned as it is by so many interesting romances, *Amis e Amilun* does not occupy a place in the front rank. It is, however, a charming re-telling of a legend found fascinating throughout the Middle Ages, and has for the modern reader the advantage of being only 1,250 lines long. In the history of the legend it occupies an important place. Neglected by Bédier, and misunderstood by MacEdward Leach,[1] it is deserving of fuller study. As comparison of the Anglo-Norman and the Middle English versions has shown, even the earliest of the Anglo-Norman manuscripts which has come down to us appears to be reminiscent of a version which differed from that which preceded the French *chanson de geste*. In view of this fact, and the existence of more than one Latin version, the exact relationship of all the extant forms of the legend will probably never be clarified.

Two minor works, a *Folie Tristan* and the *Donnei des Amants*, betoken perhaps a revival of interest in the Tristan story during the reigns of Eleanor's sons. The earlier of these is probably the *Folie Tristan d'Oxford*.

THE *FOLIE TRISTAN D'OXFORD*

The two lais known as the *Folie Tristan* are too well known, thanks to the work of Bédier and Ernest Hoepffner,[2]

---

[1] J. Bédier, *Les Légendes épiques* (3rd edition, Paris, 1926–9), iv. 178–94; Leach, op. cit. A recent study of the legend is to be found in *Amis et Amiles; an exploratory survey*, by J. A. Asher (Auckland University College Modern Language Series No. 1, 1952).

[2] J. Bédier, *Les Deux Poèmes de la Folie Tristan* (S.A.T.F., 1907); E. Hoepffner,

to justify a long account of the Oxford version here and they have been the subject of much recent work, but something must be said of its peculiar quality, especially as, slight as it is, it is one of the most artistic of Anglo-Norman works.

The subject of the *Folies* is the most popular of the means adopted by the exiled Tristan to obtain access to Iseult. He does this either by disguises—disguises which may have inspired some of the themes in the *Roman de Renart*—or by lying in wait for Iseult by the roadside—the subject of Marie de France's *Chevrefoil*. The disguise as a fool has a great advantage later exploited in the *Sotties*; the fool, being mad, has unusual licence of speech, and this gives an apportunity for a development of one of the main characteristics of the Tristan story, the double entendre. The popularity of this idea is attested not only by the existence of the two lais, but by episodes in four of the extant romances, the French prose romance and three of the German ones.[1]

The relationship between the *Folies* is difficult to determine. It seems more likely that the Folie d'Oxford (Fo) is dependent on the Folie de Berne (Fb) than the other way about, but the probabilities are that both go back to a common source now lost. Fb was probably a Norman text copied by a Burgundian scribe.[2] The poet seems to have known some form of the romance which resembled Béroul's. Fo was both written and copied in Anglo-Norman. The author knew either the Fb or its source, but altered events to bring them into line with the romance of Thomas, with certain exceptions described by Professor Hoepffner. He kept episodes like the training of Husdent which were unknown to or omitted by Thomas. More than once the two *Folies* are nearly word for word the same, notably in the description of Husdent's recognition of his master (Fb lines 512–18, Fo lines 915–19). This does not prove Fo's dependence on Fb: the passage may have become classic and go back to a common source. Fo is more courtly than Fb, just as Thomas is more courtly than Béroul, but this does not prove that it

La Folie Tristan de Berne (Paris, 1949) and *La Folie Tristan d'Oxford* (Strasbourg, 1943). There is a bare mention in *Arthurian Literature in the Middle Ages*, ed. R. S. Loomis (Oxford, 1959), p. 144.

[1] Bédier, op. cit., p. iii.   [2] Hoepffner, Fb, p. 35.

was written later. The great difficulty in the way of deciding the relationship between the *Folies* is the impossibility of dating either. Fb is probably later than Béroul, Fo is almost certainly later than Thomas, but since neither Béroul nor Thomas can be dated with any precision, this does not advance the matter much.

Summing up the relationship between Fo and Thomas, Professor Hoepffner says: 'Un fait est certain: si la Folie était signée Thomas, personne n'hésiterait à identifier son auteur avec l'auteur du roman. . . . En tout cas, si ce n'est Thomas lui-même, c'est bien son *alter ego*.'[1] The close comparisons between the romance and the lai, however, made by Bédier, lead rather to the conclusion that the author of the *Folie* was some other poet, deliberately copying Thomas. If that was the case, the gap in time betwen the writing of the romance and the date of the *Folie* could be much greater than it would be if both poems were written by the same man.

In manner, wording, language, and versification the two works resemble one another very closely, and the fact that the unique surviving copy of the *Folie* was written as a sequel to Thomas by the scribe of the Douce fragment, naturally does nothing to lessen the resemblance. Only now and again does some modernizing trifle suggest that the *Folie* poet was writing later and had not completely assimilated the habits of his predecessor. It is more than ever clear since the analysis of Thomas's versification by Dr. Wind[2] that Thomas almost invariably broke his line in the middle. Many of the lines in the *Folie* are of the same type, and couplets occur which might well have been written by Thomas and may indeed have been inspired by lines now lost, as for instance:

> Ysolt, pur vus / tant par me doil,
> Ysolt, pur vus / ben murir voil.   (171–2)

At other times, however, there is no caesura. It has disappeared in what seems to be an adaptation of a passage in the romance:

> Vers Engleter / e curt a tref.
> Vint jurz, vint nuz, / i a curu.
>   (Thomas, 2590–1)

---

[1] Fo, pp. 37 and 39.   [2] See above, p. 58.

> Tut droit vers Engleterre curent,
> Dous nuiz e un jur i demurent.   (Fo, 91, 92)

It is as though the poet of the *Folie* had not noticed the caesura, obsolete by his day, and only reproduced it by accident.

Professor Hoepffner has compared the subject-matter of the *Folies* and pointed out how superior the composition of Fo is to that of Fb. Some of his remarks, however, are inspired by his belief that Fo is based directly upon Fb, and though it is plain to see that the poet of Fo was a more conscious artist than the author of Fb, it is not certain that he was improving upon that particular model. There is, as has been said above, more courtliness in Fo than in Fb, but it is an exaggeration to describe Iseult's recognition of Tristan as a humiliation—'C'est elle, la dame qui s'humilie devant l'homme et qui humblement implore son pardon. . . . Cette attitude . . . est en effet tout le contraire de la conception courtoise.'[1] It is a misconception to place Iseult's behaviour on the same level as Brangain's; the poet has carefully differentiated the two. Brangain falls at Tristan's feet and asks for pardon for her 'vilenie', a temporary lapse from her habitual 'courtoisie'. Iseult accuses herself of madness and falls in a swoon. In Fo the underlying belief in the inconstancy of women which appears contradictory to the courtly conception of the relationship between men and women is not only accepted but insisted upon:

> 'Dame reine,
> Mult fustes ja de bone orine,
> Quant vus m'amastes seinz dedeing.
> Certes, de feintise or me pleing.
> Or vus vai retraite e fainte,
> Or vus ai jo de feinte atteinte,
> Mais jo vi ja, bele, tel jur
> Ke vus m'amastes par amur.'   (851–8)

('Lady queen, you were formerly of noble character, when you loved me without disdain. Indeed, now I complain of falsehood. Now I see you have retracted and withdrawn, now I have convicted you of playing false. But once upon a time I saw, fair one, a day when you loved me in true courtly fashion.')

---

[1] Fb, p. 24.

It is the author of the Fo, not of the Fb, who underlines the contrast between the woman and the dog:

> 'Ysolt, melz li suvient
> Ke jol nurri si l'afaitai,
> Ke vus ne fait, ki tant amai.
> Mult par at en chen grant franchise
> E at en femme grant feintise.'   (934–8)

('Iseult, he remembers better that I looked after and trained him, than you do, whom I loved so much. There is great nobility in a dog, and great deceit in a woman.')

These are harsh words, but they denote, what is lacking in Fb, some interest in women. In Fb Iseult is just the object of Tristan's love, and the story is told from the man's point of view. In Fo interest is almost equally divided between the hero and the heroine of the story. Iseult does not merely fail to recognize Tristan, she is uneasy and frightened and takes refuge in running away from the situation. She is 'fainte', 'faint-hearted', and the faint-hearted woman is one of the creations of courtly literature. The faint-hearted woman *par excellence* is Chaucer's Cryseide: 'there is a flaw in her, and Chaucer has told us what it is: "she was the ferfulleste wight that might be".'[1] The poet of Fo has been accused of clumsiness in making Tristan continue to speak in a feigned voice long after it appears to be necessary. But it is done to test Iseult; only after she has acknowledged him and proved her sincerity does he reveal himself:

> 'Dame raïne,
> Belë estes e enterine.
> Des or ne m'en voil cuvrir,
> Cunuistre me frai e oïr.'
> Sa voiz muat, parlat a dreit.   (971–5)

('Lady queen, fair are you and sincere. From henceforth I will conceal myself no longer. I shall make myself known and heard.' He changed his voice, he spoke in his own again.)

Perhaps not sufficient attention has been paid to the fact that the whole setting of the two *Folies* is different. Fb opens with the lines:

> Mout est Tristanz mellez a cort
> Ne set o aille ne ou tort. . . .

[1] C. S. Lewis, *The Allegory of Love* (Oxford, 1938), pp. 189–90.

> Formant redoute le roi,
> Que rois Mars forment lou menace.   (1-4)

(Tristan is much embroiled at the court, he does not know where to go or turn. . . . He greatly fears Mark the king, for King Mark greatly threatens him.)

The beginning of Fo is quite different:

> Tristan surjurne en sun pais,
> Dolent, murnes, tristes, pensifs,
> Purpenset soi ke faire pot,
> Kar acun cunfort lu estot.
> Confort lu estot de guarir,
> U, si ço nun, melz volt murir.   (1-6)

> Quant il pert la reïne Ysolt,
> Murir desiret, murir volt.
> Mais sul tant ke ele soüst
> K'il pur la sue amur murust.
> Kar si Ysolt sa mort saveit,
> Siveus plus suëf en murreit.   (19-24)

(Tristan remains in his country, lamenting, mournful, sad, melancholy. He bethinks himself what he can do, for some comfort is needful to him. He must have comfort to save him, or else he had rather die. . . . When he loses Queen Iseult, he desires, he wills to die, provided only that she should know that he died for love of her. For if Iseult knew about his death, at least he would die the more sweetly.)

The emphasis in Fb is on the external circumstances which have separated the lovers. Tristan expresses the wish to see Iseult before he dies, but the idea that one might die for love never enters his head. Similarly at the end of Fb the joy of the reunited lovers is purely physical:

> A cez paroles, sanz grant cri,
> Con vos avez ici oï,
> Entre Tristanz soz la cortine:
> Entre ses braz tient la raïne.   (569-72)

(At these words, without much clamour, as you have heard here, Tristan enters beneath the bed-curtains. In his arms he holds the queen.)

According to Professor Hoepffner, 'la fin abrupte du

poème (Fo) correspond tout à fait à celle non moins abrupte de Fb'.[1] But the tone is quite different:

> Ysolt entre ses braz le tint.
> Tel joie en ad de sun ami
> K'ele ad e tent dejuste li
> K'el ne set cument cuntenir:
> Nel lerat anuit mes partir,
> Dit ke il avrat bon ostel
> E dous lit ben fait e bel.
> Tristran autre chose ne quert
> Fors la raïne, u ele ert.
> Tristran en est joius e lez:
> Mult set ben k'il est herbigez.   (988–98)

(Iseult holds him in her arms. She has such joy of her lover that she has and holds close to her that she cannot contain herself; she will not let him go that night. She says that he will have good lodging and a soft bed well made and fair. Tristan seeks nothing save the queen, wherever she will be. Tristan is joyful and happy over it: he knows very well that he has found shelter.)

In short, in his zeal to establish the priority of Fb, Professor Hoepffner has been inclined to underrate the peculiar qualities of Fo. There is, however, more in the comparison between the texts than the question of date, and two recent studies have treated it from different points of view. Monsieur J. Horrent has undertaken the defence of Fb.[2] Undoubtedly Fb is the shorter version, and therefore in some ways is more pointed, and Professor Hoepffner's dismissal of it as incoherent was too sweeping. M. Horrent makes out a fair case for giving the author credit for his choice of episodes described by Tristan. Mr. Alfred Adler in a still more recent article[3] characterizes Fb as being of the town and Fo as being of the court. If this attitude is accepted there is no need to argue about priorities.

It is not enough, however, to say that Fo is more courtly than Fb. It is also more courtly than the Thomas version.[4]

---

[1] Fo, p. 143.

[2] 'La composition de la Folie Tristan de Berne', *Revue belge de philologie et d'histoire*, xxv (1947), pp. 21–38; cf. 'A propos de Gallerous', *Moyen Age*, lii (1946), pp. 43–72.

[3] 'A Structural Comparison of the Two "Folies Tristan"', *Symposium*, vi (1952), pp. 349–58.   [4] Cf. above, pp. 52–53.

It is perhaps reasonable to assume that because it contains episodes which are in the *Saga*, it derives these from the romance of Thomas. The manuscript of Fo is thirteenth-century, and, though the language of the text suggests that it is twelfth-century, it may belong to a period thirty or forty years later than Thomas, and a desire to add to Thomas's selections may have been felt. Fb is a *lai* of the 'grotesque' type, whereas Fo is sophisticated. It is sufficient to refer to Tristan's allusions to his parentage. In both versions the Fool claims to have had a whale for his mother, but whereas in Fb he adds that his father was a walrus, Fo has an allusion to a nursing tigress, an obvious reminiscence of Virgil's Hyrcanian tigress.[1]

One of the absurdities, the shears which Tristan loved because they were a present from Iseult (lines 205–9), is probably not the fault of Fo, though it does not occur in Fb, for the shears are mentioned by Jehan Renart in the *Lai de l'Ombre*, and there is no reason to suppose that he was relying on Fo, for in *L'Escoufle* he mentions other disguises of Tristan —as a fool, a leper, and a false pilgrim.[2]

The *Folie d'Oxford* exists only in a thirteenth-century copy, the Douce manuscript (d. 6), which contains the longest fragment of Thomas's romance. Fortunately, this is the work of a careful scribe. Inevitably he has made the state of the language and versification appear worse than it is, but most of his verbal mistakes are easily corrected and he has left only one gap of serious dimensions, which interrupts the comparatively unimportant description of the castle of Tintagel.

LE DONNEI DES AMANTS

The other work which owes much to the Tristan story is the little treatise *Le Donnei des Amants*.[3] The word *Donnei* is simply the Provençal *domnei*, 'courtship of ladies', and at once gives indication of the kind of literature to which it belongs. The poet, a clerk, wandering in a meadow in the

---

[1] *Aeneid*, iv. 367.

[2] *Le Lai de l'Ombre*, ed. John Orr (Edinburgh, 1948), lines 124–7; *L'Escoufle*, ed. H. Michelant and P. Meyer (S.A.T.F., 1894), lines 3131–3.

[3] Edited G. Paris, *Romania*, xxv (1896), pp. 497–541. The unique MS., Cheltenham 3713, is temporarily inaccessible.

springtime, catches sight of a damsel waiting for her lover, and decides to eavesdrop at the interview. The lover, a pedantic being who can only have been another clerk, is disappointed at obtaining no more than a kiss, and enters upon a disputation with a view to convincing the lady that it is her duty to grant him further favours. He makes use of many *exempla*. Even amusing tales, says the poet, may conceal a lesson, and such stories are particularly useful for young people, for whose benefit he repeats them. The lover gets much the worse of the argument, the damsel having no difficulty in proving that most of the *exempla* are inept. Unluckily the end of the poem, which survives in only one manuscript, is missing, and there is no means of knowing whether the clerk was rebuffed, or whether he was able to produce better arguments and overcome the damsel's reluctance, or whether, as is likely, the poet acting as moderator in the dispute summed up and gave a solution to the problem, and if he did, which side he came down on.

Harsh words have been said about the amorality of this poem. Gaston Paris wrote:[1]

Ce morceau est doublement intéressant. D'abord il nous montre quelle influence la littérature romanesque inaugurée au xiie siècle dans la société anglo-française pouvait exercer sur les mœurs. Cette influence était naturellement pernicieuse, comme l'a été et l'est celle de romans d'époques plus récentes.

This is, to our ideas, a curious view of the function of fiction, which does not exist solely to instruct, and moreover there is no evidence that anyone was ever corrupted by reading the *Donnei des Amants*. This is to take a joke altogether too seriously. It is true that the lady's objections appear to be on the ground of expediency and 'Thou shalt not be found out' is for her the important commandment:

> 'Ben le sachez de verité
> Ke tote vostre volunté
> Feïsse jo sanz [nul] retur,
> Ne dotasse perdre m'onur.
> Je ferai quant jo pora[i] fere,
> E ren ne me vodra retrere;

---

[1] Loc. cit., p. 527.

> Mes liu e tens de[it ben] gaiter
> Ke grant chose volt comencer.'   (445–52)

('Know well in truth that I would have done all your will without any turning back, had I not feared to lose my honour. I shall do it when I can, and nothing shall make me withdraw; but one must look well for the right time and place if one wants to undertake some great action.')

She does not even feel the twinge of conscience that momentarily troubled the lady in the *Lai de l'Ombre*:

> 'Sire', dist ele, 'n'est pas droiz
> Que je ainme vos në autrë home,
> Que j'ai mon seignor molt preudome,
> Qui molt me sert bien et enneure.'   (*Ombre*, 492–5)

('Sir,' said she, 'it isn't right that I should love you or any other man, for I have my lord who is most worthy, and he serves me well and honours me.')

However, as has been said above, there is no knowing how the poem ended. In any case, such things were often mere exercises in rhetoric, designed to amuse. Irony entered in to an extent not always realized,[1] and it is possible that such works were deliberately ambiguous and meant to be taken in two ways. Cynicism is not necessarily the same thing as immorality, though it would be an exaggeration to say that situations like the one described in the *Donnei* were uncommon.

The main literary interest of the poem lies in its allusions. The lover produces a list of ladies who have suffered for their lovers, and it consists of the names Helen, Dido, Ismena, Ydoine, and Iseult. The author probably had in mind the romances of *Troy, Eneas* and *Thebes, Amadas et Ydoine* and Béroul or a forerunner. Gaston Paris was not certain whether *Thebes* or Statius himself was being followed. *Amadas et Ydoine* provided a puzzle, as in his day it was thought to be thirteenth-century. Iseult is said to have been ready to be burnt on a pyre for Tristan's sake, and among the extant romances this episode occurs only in Béroul and Eilhart,

---

[1] Cf. D. W. Robertson, 'The Subject of the *De Amore* of Andreas Capellanus', *Modern Philology*, l (1953), pp. 145–61)—a stimulating if not entirely convincing argument.

though it may have occurred in some other which has disappeared. Later on there is a reference to a *Folie*, but this
again may be to some lost version, since it includes a detail
preserved nowhere else—the throwing of broth over the
supposed fool. Other allusions may be to Latin texts or
translations—of Aesop and Petrus Alfonsi. It seems likely
that the work of the latter was known in some expanded
version which has vanished.

The most famous of the *exempla* quoted does not occur
elsewhere, but it is hardly to be supposed that it is original,
since all the others are well-known stories. It has been suggested that it is based on a *lai*, to which the name of *Tristan
Rossignol* has been given. The subject is one of Tristan's
returns from exile to seek an interview with Iseult. In this
case he comes back quite alone, and sits under the pine-tree
beside the pool in the garden—the usual trysting-place. He
had learned long ago to imitate the song of birds: the nightingale, the popinjay, the oriole, and all the birds of the wood-
lands. The artificial nature of this list may perhaps be cited
in evidence against those who see in this power the vestiges
of a Celtic original of the tale. What is far more likely is that
there is some connexion between this story and the *Laustic*
of Marie de France. Iseult, hearing the bird-song, leaves
Mark's side and goes out. She is observed by a dwarf, who
attempts to interfere and receives a buffet for his pains. This
treatment has been described as uncourtly, and to denote
some primitive character in the original Tristan material, but
it is in fact in the best courtly tradition.[1] Except for this one
jarring note this ranks with *Chevrefoil* as the most fanciful
of the stories about Tristan's returns.

As a stylist the poet has little to recommend him. There is
hardly any magic or lyrical quality in his verse, except
perhaps just once, when he remembers the couplet of all
others from Thomas's *Tristan* which no one in the Middle
Ages was ever able to forget:

> 'Ostez! Pur Deu, ma bele amie!
> Ne estes vus ma mort, ma vie?'   (383–4)

('Stop! For heaven's sake, fair friend! Are you not my death, my
life?')

[1] Cf. M. D. Legge, 'Toothache and Courtly Love', *French Studies*, iv (1950), p. 52.

But even here the tone is different. His scholastic background makes him tedious. The young people to whom he professes to be addressing himself would hardly have been attracted by his opening references to the wise words of David and Solomon. The dialectic technique and the use of *exempla* are bluntly stated to be for instructional purposes. Worst of all, the *Tristan Rossignol* episode is interrupted by a passage forty lines long on the derivation of *gelus* from *geler*. This digression is worthy of Jean de Meung, and though the author probably prided himself on the ingenuity of this argument it is aesthetically a blemish.

> Gelus est nomé de gelee,
> Ke l'ewe moillé tent fermee.
>
> .   .   .   .
>
> Ewe corante si ferm lie,
> Ke ne se put remüer mie,
> Coure de li ne departir
> Plus ke dame de chambre issir
> Ke gelus tent en sa baillie.   (551–2, 559–63)

(The jealous man gets his name from frost, which holds the wet water. . . . It binds the running water so fast that it cannot move, run from it or leave it, any more than a lady can leave her chamber if she is in the power of a jealous man.)

The Anglo-Norman nature of this poem is not in doubt. The rhymes, the contracted forms, and a certain number of forms peculiar to that dialect—*cnivet* (794), *wendace* (812), and *eindegré* (1033, 1176), and so on—all go to prove it. Yet it is interesting to note that this is a clear case of the relationship between Provençal and Anglo-Norman literature in the twelfth century.

THE *LAI DU COR*

Two *lais* which exploit the Matter of Britain have probably been wrongly claimed for Anglo-Norman. The first is the burlesque *Lai du Cor* by Robert Biket,[1] who says he had

---

[1] Latest ed. by H. Dörner (Strasbourg, 1907). For the dialect cf. P. Richter, 'Versuch einer Dialektbestimmung des Lai du Corn', *Ausgaben und Abhandlungen aus dem Gebiete der Rom. Phil.*, xxxviii (1885), and ed.; for the date cf. P.A. Becker, 'Von den Erzählern neben und nach Chrestien de Troyes', *Zeitschrift für romanische Philologie*, lvi (1936), pp. 247–51 and S. Hofer, 'Bemerkungen zur Beurteilung des Horn- und des Mantellai', *Romanische Forschungen*, lxv (1953–4), pp. 38–48.

learnt the story from an abbot, which perhaps indicates its satirical intent. The story is a variant of the test of chastity, and closely resembles that of the *Mantel mautaillié*, with a horn instead of a mantle providing the test. The setting is King Arthur's Whitsunday Court at Caerleon; the hero is Garadue (Caradoc), said to be the original teller of the tale. His wife came from Cirencester, for some unknown reason. Becker argued that the lai must be posterior to the First Continuation of *Perceval*, where the same tale is told but with a background which explains the choice of hero and heroine, but there was probably a common origin. Caradoc, besides being the name of the hero,[1] is also that of the Welsh writer who first told of the abduction of Guinevere, which may have some bearing here. S. Hofer has tried to prove that the lai was written after Marie de France, Wace's *Brut*, and *Erec*. The parallels he quotes are not convincing arguments for dependence. An argument for a date earlier than Marie is the use of the hexasyllable instead of the octosyllable used in other lais, but this is not altogether satisfactory, though it is remarkable that the prologue is in octosyllables because it has been borrowed from the *Mantel mautaillié*, which looks as though the *Cor* was earlier than the *Mantel* and adapted later. The most telling argument for a date considerably later than the middle of the twelfth century is that it is difficult to imagine that a burlesque should be composed of something which hardly existed.

The only manuscript (Bodleian Digby 86) is late thirteenth-century, and due to an Anglo-Norman scribe. Richter believed that the original was Picard, Dörner suggests with more plausibility that it was Norman. It certainly seems unlikely that the writer was Anglo-Norman, but he probably worked in England.

A new edition of both the *Cor* and the *Mantel* together would be helpful.

THE *LAI DEL DESIRÉ*

The *Lai del Desiré* is later and is a true lai. The subject is a variant of the fairy-mistress story, but it differs from

---

[1] Cf. R. S. Loomis, 'The strange story of Caradoc Brechbras of Vannes', *Bull. bibl. de la Soc. int. arthurienne*, xii (1960), pp. 133-4.

Lanval, Guigemar, Guingemor, and *Graalent Mor* in attributing a son and daughter to Desiré and his fairy. She brings the children to court when they are grown up, the son to be knighted and the daughter to be married, and then goes away to fairyland, taking Desiré with her. The *Lai* exists in two manuscripts, the older of which, and the first to be published,[1] is Anglo-Norman (Cheltenham 3713, temporarily inaccessible). The later manuscript (B.N. n. a. f. 1104) is in Francien, and has now been published in an uncritical edition by Miss E. M. Grimes.[2] She seems to have preferred this manuscript because the French is more 'correct', but it may be doubted if it really preserves a text closer to the original than the other, for it has been modernized. For instance, in one passage indirect has been substituted for direct speech. It might be a continental *remaniement* of an Anglo-Norman text, but in view of the fact that the language of the text in the Anglo-Norman manuscript cannot be proved to have been insular, this does not appear likely. Like the *Lai du Cor,* it may have been written for an English public.

This lai is not Arthurian. The scene is the court of the King of Scotland in Calatir, and the Kings of Moray and the Lothians are also mentioned. No other countries play any part. It is possible that the author obtained his geography, and perhaps other details, from the lost first part of Gaimar.[3]

Though these two texts may not, properly speaking, be Anglo-Norman, they were known in England and, indeed, it is only thanks to an Anglo-Norman scribe that one of them is extant.

GUISCHART DE BEAULIU'S *SERMON*

The gayer and more irresponsible society becomes the more likely it is that puritans will arise to find fault and to point a moral. This picture of courtly literature in England at the close of the twelfth century would be incomplete without a reference to what is perhaps the most sombre text

---

[1] F. Michel, *Lais inédits* (Paris, London, 1836).
[2] *The Lays of Desiré, Graelent and Melion* (New York, 1928).
[3] A. D. H. Bivar, 'Lyonesse: the Evolution of a Fable', *Modern Philology*, l (1953), p. 167.

written in Anglo-Norman, the *Sermon*, or rather the *Romaunz*   ✳
de Temtacioun de Secle, by Guischart de Beauliu.[1] Possibly addressed by a monk of Beaulieu Priory, a cell of St. Albans,
to a great lady of the neighbourhood, Dionysia Hacon, who
was bed-ridden for some years shortly before 1200, it passes
in review all the temptations of this world. This gloomy
work was not intended to repel. It begins:

> Entendez ça vers mei, les petiz e les granz,
> Un deduit vos dirrai, bel est e avenanz.

(Hearken to me, both great and small, I will tell you something
amusing, it is good and agreeable.)

The world is seductive, it is foolish to give way to it. When
people die, they wish they had behaved better. The Devil is
always on the look-out. Unjust princes go to hell, so do the
rich, perjurers and traitors.

> Li secles est mut vielz e si est trespassanz
> Frailles est e malveis, tuit s'en vait declinanz.   (11–12)

> Remembre vus d'emfer ki mult est tenebrus
> Malveis ostal i ad horibles e hisdus.   (221–2)

(This world is very old and therefore passing away. It is frail and
wicked, it is decaying fast. . . . Remember hell, which is quite dark;
there is bad lodging there, horrible and dreadful.)

Those who do not believe in death are no true Christians.
What, then, is to be done? Nothing, but to give up everything. Even the saints cannot ransom us. The rich man has
wealth, hawks, hounds, horses, minstrelsy, and can contemplate his treasures, live with his wife:

> Ço est delit del cors ke vus m'oiez conter,
> É est la mort al alme ki ne se set garder.   (281–2)

(This is the delight of the body about which you hear me tell, and
it is the death of the soul which does not know how to look after
itself.)

There is no perfect love in this world, but God died for us.
Adam was the first sinner. David's line is our salvation.
Paradise is a fine place, and he who is housed therein is
happy. There is no need of castles there. It is full of martyrs—

[1] Ed. A. Gabrielson (Uppsala and Leipzig, 1909), cf. *Anglo-Norman in the
Cloisters*, pp. 31–35.

Peter, Paul, Stephen, Vincent, Lawrence, and many more.
The Day of Judgement will be terrible. God will describe
his Passion. This leads to an account of the Temptation, the
Creation, and other matters some of which have already been
treated. But the sinner should not despair

> Ki de queor se repent e merci volt crier
> E par confession tuz ses pechez laver.   (949–50)

(Who repents in his heart and will cry mercy, and wash away all
his sins by confession.)

Here is the first hint of the doctrine which, as we shall see,
becomes of paramount importance in the thirteenth century.
The poem goes on to talk of the two angels who look after
men, one good and the other bad, who juggle with the judgement scales. Good deeds help, in particular alms and bridge-
building, both appropriate for the wealthy and powerful.
A treasure is received at baptism. This world is wicked and
treacherous. Guischart has given up bodily ease, he has no
love for this world:

> Par la fei ke jo dei ma dame Dionise
> Cest secle est trestut felon ke jo n'en sai devise.   (1519–20)

(By the faith I owe the Lady Dionysia, this world is so entirely
wicked that I do not know how to describe it.)

Then the author goes back to the Fall and the Life of Christ
and tells them all over again.

> Tant i avrait a dire ja par mei n'ert conté,
> Ne tut li clerc de France ki melz i sunt letré
> Ne[l] dirreient od mei el plus lung jorn d'esté.   (1813–15)

(There is so much to say that will never be related by me, and all
the most learned clercs in France would not tell it either, in the longest
summer's day.)

After a further contrast between the pains of hell and the
joys of heaven, the poem closes with a prayer:

> Ore penst chascon de sei, ne dirai plus avant,
> Mais preiez dampnedeu si cum il est poant
> Ki tut tens fu e ert e co[n] trovum lisant,
> E fud por noz pechez enz en la croiz pendant,
> Ke le cors en conseilt, as almes seit garant,
> Ke nus puissum senz fin od lui estre manant,

E Deus le nus otreit par sa pi[e]té grant,
Ke nus por noz pecchez lui ne seum perdant.
Cil ki por nus dunat [e] sun cors e sun sanc,
Vus salt e beneie de [si] ci en avant.   (1914–23)
          Amen.
Ici fine le Sermun Guischart de Beauliu.

(Now let each one take thought for himself, I will say no more.
But pray Almighty God, as he is powerful, who was from all time and
shall be as we find in our reading, and was once hung on the cross for
our sins, that he may help our bodies and save our souls, so that we
may dwell with him for ever. And God grant us by his great pity that
we may not be lost to him through our sins. He who gave for us his
body and his blood, save and bless you from henceforth. Amen. Here
ends the Sermon of Guischart de Beauliu.)

From the foregoing brief analysis it will be seen that there
is very little arrangement and much repetition in this poem.
The author's sincerity is apparent, his lack of a sense of composition evident. The reader will look in vain for justifica-
tion of the claim that this work is a 'deduit', an amusement.
The sources, some of them English, have been listed by the
editor. The spirit is that of Bernard of Morlaix, and seems
to belong to an earlier period than that of a poem which
bears a close resemblance to this *Sermon*, the *Vers* of Thibaud
de Marly.[1] This poem, shorter, better composed and with
more topical allusions, by a grandson of Henry I who became a Cistercian, can be proved by internal evidence to date
from between the canonization of Becket in 1173 and the
death of Henry II in 1189. It cannot be proved that either
writer made use of the other's work. All that can be said
is that there is so close a resemblance between the two that
there may have been direct influence, that Thibaud de Marly
appears to have been writing at a later date than Guischart
de Beauliu, and that both appear to have flourished in the
last quarter of the twelfth century.

In form the *Sermon* resembles a *chanson de geste*. It is in
laisses of alexandrines in rhyme mixed with a little assonance.
There are a few English words and words confined to Anglo-
Norman to be found in it. Some affinities with Provençal are

[1] Ed. H. K. Stone (Paris, 1932).

not unexpected in an Anglo-Norman text of this period. The usual contrast obtains between the decaying state of the declension system and the archaic conjugation of verbs. Perhaps the author might not be too pleased to learn that one result of his review of worldly pleasures, the pains of hell and the delights of paradise, has been that his text proved a gold-mine for contributors to the Anglo-Norman glossary.

Four manuscripts (B.M. Harley 4388, Egerton 2710; Bodleian Digby 86; B.N. fr. 19525), none complete, still exist. All are thirteenth-century Anglo-Norman. Two are closely related. The total number of lines must have been about 1,923, divided into forty *laisses*. There is no manuscript evidence that the poem was known on the Continent, but Thibaud de Marly might have had access to it through the fact that his mother was an illegitimate daughter of Henry I, and could have been in touch with Anglo-Norman courts.

The *Sermon* has been treated here because, unlike the other verse sermons of the period, of which presently,[1] it is addressed to court circles and is in a different form. The address is to 'seignurs', but this does not mean that it was not written at the request of a lady, the Lady Dionysia who may have been the wife of Walter Hacon. The word is sometimes used as a general term, sometimes for the 'elders' of a religious house. Judging from the extant remains, it was popular. Guischart, like Denis Pyramus, was probably a poet turned monk. This gloomy poem is another attack on the wickedness of society and the dangerous love of light literature. The sequel will be treated in subsequent chapters. Only this example finds its rightful place here.

---

1 See below, pp. 180–1.

VII

THE 'ANCESTRAL ROMANCE'

O N the Continent attempts have been made from time
to time to establish a relationship between the creation of a *chanson de geste* and the patronage of a particular family. The fallacy of this contention was sufficiently
demonstrated by Joseph Bédier in a letter published by
Charles Livingston in 1942.[1] The patronage of great ladies
led to the writing of romances which are pure fiction, without any local or family background, though it is sometimes
possible to try to date these through topical allusions.[2] In
England and Scotland the peculiar pattern of society after
the Conquest seems to have led to the invention of a type
of romance which is truly of *origine lignagère* and deserves
a chapter to itself. It arose in the twelfth century, and though
it continued to be popular until into the fourteenth, its
characteristics remained the same and the whole subject
is therefore conveniently treated here. This type of romance
may have filled the place of the 'family' chronicle in France.

The Normans and others who acquired estates in England
did not regard themselves as belonging to the country, even
if they spent most of their time in it and founded religious
houses there. 'Home' was across the Channel and 'home'
was where they wished to die or at any rate be buried. It can
be seen from the pages of Dugdale how often the Norman
founder or benefactor of an English monastery retired to be
nursed in old age in some French house with which he had
a family connexion, or was buried with his fathers there. One
of the advantages of having come over with the Conqueror
was that it enabled a man to make provision for the cadets of

---

[1] 'L'origine "lignagère" des Chansons de geste: Lettre inédite de Joseph Bédier
écrite en 1913', *Romanic Review*, xxxiii, 1942, pp. 319–35.

[2] Cf. above, pp. 85–88, and A. Fourrier, 'Encore la chronologie des œuvres de
Chrétien de Troyes', *Bulletin bibliographique de la Société internationale arthurienne*,
ii, 1950, pp. 69–88, 'Remarques sur la date du "Conte del Graal" de Chrétien
de Troyes', ibid. vii, 1955, pp. 89–101.

the family. The eldest son could inherit the continental lands while his next brother fell heir to the 'acquest' in England. So, of the famous Beaumont twins, the elder, Waleran, became Count of Meulan while the younger, Robert, became Earl of Leicester. The example had been set by the Conqueror himself. He is buried at Caen, and his eldest son Robert became Duke of Normandy and the younger King of England—a state of affairs only partially provoked by family quarrels. Matters became complicated when Rufus died childless, murdered probably with the connivance of the youngest brother, but Henry, being on the spot, seized the crown for himself. His marriage to Maud, the fiction that she was the heiress of Edward the Confessor, and the resulting cult of Alfred the Great were exploited to the full and had, as has been noted above, an influence on Anglo-Norman literature. Henry was buried, not somewhere abroad, but in his own foundation of Reading. To provide him with predecessors going back far beyond even the Anglo-Saxons, Geoffrey of Monmouth planned his *Historia Regum Britanniae*. After his death the situation was confused until the accession of Henry II. Although Henry was hailed as Fitz-Empress, he began the whole process over again. His eldest son was to succeed his mother as William XI of Aquitaine, his second son was to be Henry III of England. After William's death Henry was to have had part of his inheritance, and the third son Richard became Count of Poitou under his mother's tutelage. Ultimately, but not before they had caused frightful trouble and jealousy, these elaborate plans were brought to naught by deaths among the sons, but the fact that they had been made must not be overlooked. 'Henry II was a Continental monarch (why else should he lie buried at Fontevrault?) as much at home in Tours or Angers as in Westminster' writes Professor Jacob.[1] The consciousness of being English amongst the king's subjects has been ascribed to the loss of Normandy by John, but the process had begun much earlier. It is perhaps difficult to realize the homesick feelings of families isolated in castles and on manors, surrounded by people who did not even speak the same language, and without the comfort of

[1] E. F. Jacob, *Henry V and the Invasion of France* (London, 1947), pp. 8–9.

going to church surrounded by the stone effigies of relations whom they hoped to join. Poets would benefit by this feeling and could supply interesting legends of the past glories of the new home and even suggest a connexion with some famous figure of the past, preferably a king and saint. The simplest way of ministering to this need would be to take some old story or stories and provide a local setting. How much the resulting legends would be taken seriously it is impossible to say. Certainly, in some cases, the families pretended to believe in them, and, after all, it was a time which could produce and swallow any number of forged charters. Some self-deception may have taken place, just as later on Michel Eyquem could bring himself to advance the remarkable theory that his family had conferred their name on their birthplace, Montaigne.[1]

GUILLAUME D'ANGLETERRE

The earliest of what may be termed the 'ancestral romances' is very likely *Guillaume d'Angleterre*. This happens to be the work of a continental writer, and neither of the two extant manuscripts of it is Anglo-Norman. Yet the setting and story could only have appealed originally to an English patron. The author has been identified by many with Crestien de Troyes, but the fact that he twice names himself 'Crestiiens' in the prologue, and a few resemblances in vocabulary, particularly in rhyme-words, are not necessarily sufficient to outweigh the difficulty in believing that anything so dull in composition and so flat in style could possibly have come from a master hand. Moreover, the resemblances are not evenly distributed through the work. Crestien de Troyes was looked up to by his contemporaries, and had no monopoly of the name. Some imitator may even have gone so far as to borrow it. But all this is by the way. The romance, as Miss E. A. Francis has pointed out,[2] was probably written for one of the Lovel families, but she was unable to decide between the claims of the Castle Cary family, which had a

---

[1] *Essais*, III, ix.
[2] In *Studies in French . . . presented to R. L. Graeme Ritchie* (C.U.P., 1949), pp. 68–71; cf. C. Foulon, 'Les Tendances aristocratiques dans le *Roman de Guillaume d'Angleterre*', *Romania*, lxxi (1950), pp. 222–37.

marriage connexion with Scotland, and the Titmarsh family, connected with Bury St. Edmunds. As the pretended source of the romance is a book of history to be found in that abbey, it is probably the Titmarsh family who are in cause. And the Titmarsh family had more need of a fake ancestry than the other. Some time before 1170—which is a possible date for the romance—William and his eldest son Waleran handed over the English lands of the family to the younger son William, who thereby became the founder of the family famous later on as the Lovells of Minster Lovell. Waleran inherited the continental estates.[1] The interest in Bristol and in Scotland cannot be accounted for, unless the writer was hoping to please both Lovel families, but it may be pointed out that nothing is known of the parentage and connexions of Isabel, wife of William Lovel the younger.

The principal character of the romance has nothing to do with any historical King William and the story is a retelling of that ancient and ever-popular theme known as the Eustace–Placidas adaptation of the legend of Apollonius of Tyre. It is possible that a version of this story attached to a king of England was already in existence, and was given a local setting by Crestien, who made use of the names William and Lovel to suit his own purpose. This source, if it existed, must have been in either Latin or French, to explain the names Marin and Lovel. The later *jongleur* version of the story, the *Dit de Guillaume d'Angleterre*, which has been somewhat rashly claimed as a *remaniement* of the romance, lacks the local interest, and there are reasons for thinking that it is independent. For instance, in Crestien the vital ring by which husband and wife are reunited appears out of the blue. In the *Dit* poignancy is added to its history by the fact that the queen had given it to her husband when she thought she was dying. This hardly seems the invention of a clumsy *remanieur*.[2]

The story occurs twice in Castilian, once in an abridged prose translation, with slight modifications, of Crestien,

---

[1] *Complete Peerage*, viii. 209–12.

[2] Ed. Francisque Michel, *Chroniques anglo-normandes*, iii (Rouen, 1840), pp. 183, 206. Cf. *Guillaume d'Angleterre*, ed. M. Wilmotte (C.F.M.A., lv, 1927), lines 2443–93.

made in the fourteenth century, and again in an extraordinary sixteenth-century jumble which may go back to a source beyond Crestien, since it lacks most of the localization and contains other variations. In it the ring is sent to William by the queen after her capture, and this does have the appearance of a clumsy alteration or addition. The editor thought that this text was based on a Latin original written by a Frenchman. Guillaume is used as an *exemplum*, along with Roland, to illustrate betrayal, by Robert de Blois in *L'Enseignement des Princes*, written at the end of the thirteenth century.[1] It is curious, in view of the fact that the legend is invariably associated with England and Scotland, that there does not seem to be any trace of it in Anglo-Norman or English.

WALDEF

Guillaume d'Angleterre is a modest production of a mere three thousand lines or so. Later writers were not so restrained. It was probably in the nineties that an anonymous author was responsible for the *Estoire de Waldef*, which runs to 22,304 lines, and even then is not complete. On account of its length, and the difficulty of obtaining access to the unique manuscript,[2] it has had to wait over-long for an edition. Its contents, however, have been known in outline from the publication of a Latin abbreviated translation in prose by a monk of Thetford, made in the fifteenth century from a Middle English version, now lost, eked out by the French, which was apparently then complete.[3]

The story is not only long, but complicated. It begins with Julius Caesar, but the Roman Conquest is briefly dealt with:

> Qui l'estoire savoir voldra,
> Lise le Brut, illoc l'orra.   (23–24)

[1] The Spanish texts are edited by H. Knust, *Dos obras didácticas y dos leyendas* (Madrid, La Sociedad de Bibliófilos Españoles, 1878), and *L'Enseignement des Princes* in J. H. Fox, *Robert de Blois* (Paris, 1948).

[2] Formerly in the Phillipps collection at Cheltenham, it is now in the possession of M. Martin Bodmer of Geneva, who made it available to Mr. R. Anderson for a forthcoming edition.

I am deeply grateful to Mr. Anderson for lending me his transcription before publication. Professor Walther Suchier has now deposited in the library at Göttingen the transcription made by his father.

[3] Johannes Bramis, *Historia Regis Waldei* edited by R. Imelmann (Bonn, 1912)

(If anyone wants) to know this history, let him read the *Brut*, he will hear it there.)

For this is the story of Waldef. Nevertheless, about two thousand lines are devoted to the love-stories of his parents, King Bede and the sister of the King of Normandy, and of his aunt. Bede dies while Waldef is still a baby, a wicked steward marries his mother and tries to get the foundling Florenz to murder him. The two escape abroad. When Waldef is grown up he marries Ernild, daughter of the King of Lincoln. They have two sons, Guiac and Gudlac. The country is torn by perpetual wars. Waldef hears that his whole family has been captured by Saracens. Guiac is brought up at Cologne, Gudlac in Morocco. At line 7142 the writer says that his 'dame' has bidden him pause, but that he will presently continue, giving a synopsis of the story down to line 7196. After many more battles Waldef is re-united with his wife, who, exceptionally in this kind of story, has not been married to someone else, but has been servant to a hermit. She is immediately carried off again by more Saracens, this time to Dublin, where she staves off remarriage for a year. This enables Waldef to find her again after a long voyage. After many adventures their two sons have met, without knowing one another. They join forces and attack their father. An angel acts as *deus ex machina* and the family is reunited. The two sons, however, are restless and soon leave to raid the Continent. During their absence Waldef is defeated and perishes at Rochester. Gudlac returns and rescues his mother, while Guiac goes off on a pilgrimage to expiate his sin of pride. According to Bramis Gudlac is crowned King of London—having married the daughter of the last king—while Guiac, returning after seven years, is crowned not only Emperor of Germany, but Emperor of Rome as well.

The writer claims that *Waldef* is translated from an English source, well beloved by the English, small and great, before the Conquest, like the *Brut*, *Tristan*, and '*Aalof*.' Some people have taken this statement seriously, others have argued that there never was an Old English *Brut* or *Tristan*, and that the whole claim is probably fabricated. The truth probably is that the author did have an English source or sources, and that he also utilized Wace's *Brut*, Thomas's *Tristan*, and *Aaluf*, which may have included *Horn*. So much is clear from internal evidence as well. The fact that the originals of the *Brut* and *Tristan* were probably, so far as they existed, Celtic and not Anglo-Saxon was a detail irrelevant for his present purpose. He further claims to be translating at the request of his 'duce amie', but it is Bramis who is responsible for the statement that this was because she knew no English. But whether she knew English or not, she might not have been able to understand Anglo-Saxon a century old. It is possible, however, as will presently appear, that she was a foreigner.

> Ne me vuel ore pas numer
> Ne le non m'amie mustrer.
> Si jo le livere puis parfere
> E a bon chief peüsse trere,
> Le nun m'amie e le mien
> Saverai jo demustrer mult bien.   (87–92)

(I do not wish to name myself now, or reveal the name of my friend. If I can finish the book, and bring it to a conclusion, I can then let out the names of my friend and myself.)

Revealing names at the end of a text was a common practice, and it is unfortunate that the end of *Waldef* is missing. It is, however, strange that the manuscript translated by Bramis did not mention any names, and perhaps they were never revealed, unless there was an epilogue omitted in his text.

The names of Waltheof and of Guthlac, one of his sons, suggest that the romance might have some connexion with the monastery of Croyland. There is nothing in the story, or in their careers, which bears this out, and if there is a connexion with any monastery, it is with the Cluniac Priory of Thetford, where Bramis later translated it. Thetford was founded by Roger Bigod in 1103 after the loss of his elder son in the White Ship. In 1140 or 1141 he was created Earl of Norfolk and Suffolk, an earldom which corresponded with the old kingdom of East Anglia. The Bigods were a family of Norman origin, but the name is not territorial and may have been a nickname. Several Bigods are mentioned in England after the Conquest, but it is not known which of them was the ancestor of the Earls of Norfolk. The first two earls married Anglo-Norman wives. The parentage of Ida, wife of the third earl, Roger who died in 1221, is again a mystery, and she may have been a foreigner. His son Hugh married Maud, elder daughter of William Marshall, and, according to M. André de Mandach, the name Marshall occurs in the manuscript.[1] It was during the life of the third earl that *Waldef* was probably written, whether it was actually for his wife or not. The language, analysed by Professor Ham,[2] indicates a date at the extreme end of the twelfth or the extreme beginning of the thirteenth century. The evidence that the 'duce amie' may have been a Norman is the love-story of the King of Normandy's sister. She falls in love at first sight with Bede, and thinks much about the beauty of Englishmen in general. Bede, 'd'amur suspris', returns to his lodging and casts himself on his bed, a prey to despair. The maiden, also 'susprise d'amur', is restless, often going to the window from which she can see Bede's lodging.

> 'Haï le païs d'Engletere:
> Tant par sunt ore de mal eire
> La gent que de vus sunt estreiz;
> Trop par sunt une gent de pes
> Qu'a femme ne sevent parler
> Ne lur servise abaunduner.
> Mais trop sunt beals e alingné
> E trop ont il en euls bunté;
> De male eschole sunt apris;
> Ne dusent hors de lur païs
> En estranges terres aler,
> Quant ne sevent a gent parler.'   (1071–82)

('Alas the country of England: the people who come from you are very ill-bred. They are such very silent people that they cannot speak to a woman, nor undertake their service. But they are very beautiful and well-made and there is much goodness in them. They are very badly brought up. They ought not to go out of their own country, into foreign lands, since they don't know how to speak to people.')

This amusing passage raises the question whether there was some particular point in it.

---

[1] *La Geste de Charlemagne et de Roland* (Geneva, 1961), p. 267.
[2] E. B. Ham, 'The Language of the *Roman de Waldef*', *Medium Ævum*, iv (1935), pp. 176–93.

The romance is less wearisome than the number of lines would suggest, and it is a thousand pities that it has not been made available sooner. The abridgement by Bramis fails to convey, as Professor Ham has pointed out, the peculiar flavour of the original, and is not much more than a catalogue of battles and adventures. The writer of *Waldef* possessed, alone amongst the category of authors considered here, the sense of pathos. No doubt the expression of it is crude and overdone, but the remarkable thing is that it is there at all, and can still make some appeal. Lamentations over lost relations and dead friends follow the conventional pattern. No doubt Virgil would have handled better Guiac's regret at being forced to kill the arrogant young son of the King of Portugal, but his address to the boy is not, like the action of Darius or the Dauphin, intended as a taunt:

> 'Unchore puis tu od ta pelote
> Od les enfanz mult mielz juer
> Ke ore en cest estur juster.'   (20092–4)

('You would yet be better playing with your ball with other children, than jousting in this combat.')

The most touching passage occurs after the reunion of Waldef and his wife with their two sons. When they leave, Waldef indulges in a conventional lament. His wife, also distraught by grief, strives to console him with these words:

> 'Bien vus di ore pur verité,
> Que ces sunt d'estrange regné:
> Ne furent unques voirs nos fiz,
> Ainz sunt estrange aventeïz
> Qui venu sunt en cest païs.
> Par lur enging nus ont suspris
> Pur atreire vostre tresor
> E tut vostre argent e vostre or.
> Puis qu'il orent vostrë avoir
> Ne voloient plus remanoir.
> Leisiez les aler a malfé:
> Ja ne viengnent a salveté
> Ne a havene ne a droit port
> Car par euls avomes la mort!'   (15315–28)

('I tell you now in very truth, that they belong to a foreign kingdom: they were never true sons of ours, but are foreigners who have come into this country. They overcame us by trickery to win your treasure and all your silver and gold. When they had obtained your wealth they did not wish to stay any longer. Let them go to the Devil: may they never reach safety or haven or their right port, for through them we receive our death.')

This is the only occasion when a writer handling the Apollonius of Tyre theme seems to have realized that children kidnapped as babies and brought up in foreign and often heathen lands might give their parents pain once the joy of the reunion was over. Their parents, separated as adults, are able to begin again where they left off. Some use is made of dramatic irony. The feelings experienced by Waldef and his sons, when they fight, are described by the author much as, later on, the author of the *Huth Merlin* described the emotions of the brothers Balin and Balan. When Waldef is fighting Guiac he says to him:

> 'Vus n'estes mun fiz ne mun eir.'   (14096)
>
> ('You are neither my son nor my heir.')

The reader has just been told that he is both.

It has been assumed, on the evidence of the Latin version, that *Waldef* must be nothing but a weary succession of battles and separations. Seriously considered, the story is a terrible one. In all probability based upon an English poem telling a story of the saga type, it reflects conditions in East Anglia in the tenth and eleventh centuries. It has something in common with Gaimar and Denis Pyramus's *Life of St. Edmund*. The careers of Bede and Waldef have some points of resemblance with those of Ethelred the Unready and Ulfkell Snilling.[1] Nearly every town is ruled by a king or petty king, or a duke or count, hoping for a crown. No one can leave home with any certainty that he will not find it destroyed or occupied by the Danes or some rival king on his return. The happy-go-lucky way in which people do leave home is proof of a dreadful indifference to fate that is born of familiarity. Mobility and the possibility of surprise are conferred by the fact that most of the raiding is done from the sea. Rival fleets, too, are apt to run into one another

---

[1] Cf. F. M. Stenton, *Anglo-Saxon England* (Oxford, 1947) pp. 375, 377–8, 387.

unexpectedly. It is curious, as Dr. Bell has hinted,[1] that there
seems to be no memory of this awful time in East Anglia
or Yorkshire. On the coast and in the islands of the west,
the vikings are part of yesterday, and it is impossible to look
seawards without an uncomfortable feeling that something
unexpected is going to appear, but the raids persisted much
longer there and may have kept alive the awareness of the
danger from the sea. Casualties in the armies are heavy, but
mortality amongst leaders is rare, for a beaten king, like a
Chinese warlord, simply offers to transfer his allegiance to
the victor, with whom he is quite likely to remain firm friends
ever after. Occasionally his kingdom may be confiscated and
given to some relation or follower who has not yet acquired
one. The scramble for kingdoms is so well recognized that
when Gudlac is first offered the crown of London, he modestly
declines it on the grounds that his elder brother has not yet
obtained one. The clerical status of the author has caused him
to do his best with this intractable material. Guiac's repentance may be his own addition. Almost certainly he is responsible for the introduction of the story of Hero and Leander,
and perhaps for the action of the Danish leader who inter-
venes to postpone a fight between the brothers on the sea:

> 'Seingnurs,' fet-il, 'entendez ça.
> Il n'est pas us de chevalier
> Que combatre doivent en mer:
> Mais ço est us de mariner
> Qui ne servent d'altre mestier.
> E si vus croire me vulez,
> Ceste batalle relerrez
> Desi que vus terre truissiez
> U vus combatre peüssiez.'   (12600–8)

('Lords,' said he, 'listen here! It is not the habit of knights to fight
on the sea: that is the habit of sailors who follow no other trade. And
if you will believe me, you will put off this battle until you find land,
where you may fight.')

The conception of the sailor as a gentleman was still far off.
Yet it is this, of all Old French texts, which conveys most
a sense of the sea. The Saracen fleets in the *Roland* and the
Willame are seen from the land. In *Tristan*, *Horn*, and even

---

[1] 'Gaimar's Early "Danish" Kings' (*P.M.L.A.*, lxv, 1950), p. 634.

S. Gilles, the sea is a means of getting from place to place.
In *Tristan*, and far more in *Guillaume d'Angleterre*, there are
tantalizing glimpses of merchant venturers making their
way from port to port. In *Fouke FitzWarin* there are not only
merchants but pirates. But in *Waldef* the sea plays a part
such as had not been seen since the *Brendan*. The reader
sometimes sees the viking fleets from the land, but is more
often on board taking part in a raid. A clearer picture of the
activities of merchants emerges. When Gudlac comes to
years of discretion in Morocco, all he knows about himself
is that he is English. He wants to run away, and finds some
merchants in port. They are Irish, and he asks them if they
have ever heard of a certain England. They reply that they
were there only six months ago, and intend to return there,
if they are granted a favourable wind. He accompanies them,
but the wind plays them false and a storm drives them to
Denmark. Their cargo brought to Morocco was wine, salt,
corn, and squirrel fur.

The characters in the romance are almost innumerable,
and either the Anglo-Norman writer or his predecessor has
been hard put to it to find names to go round. Some are
familiar in other contexts—Waldef himself and Gudlac, and
Bern, Felix, Fergus, Hardacunut, Hildebrand, Merlin,
Salemun, Swein, and Tierri. But as has been remarked, there
are also many eponyms. There is Atle of Attleborough, Bede
of Bedford, Canute of Cambridge, Castor of Caister, Howard
of Hereford, Osmund of Oxford, Rut of Roudham, and so
on. But there is not a Cole of Colchester or a Lear of Leicester.
It is difficult to say whether there is any genuine tradition
at work here or whether the names were invented to fit this
particular story.

The one undoubted contribution of the Anglo-Norman
writer is the introduction of a courtly element, and here he
is, naturally, inspired by the *Tristan* he names. When
Bede's sister Odenild has fallen in love with Dereman, he
is murdered by Frodelin and the news throws her into
despair:

> 'Ne serroit ore pas reison
> Que vus murisiez si pur moi
> Si jo ne murusse pur toi:

> Si vus murrez, jo i murrai:
> Par el eschaper ne purrai.'   (540–4)

('It would not now be right for you to die thus for my sake, unless I should die for yours. If you die, I shall die at once. There is no other way of escape.')

She lives, however, to bear a son, brought up as a foundling and recognized only near the end, by means of the conventional ring which had been tied round his neck. The love at first sight between Bede himself and the Norman princess has already been mentioned. It may be added here that the maiden has a certain pride:

> 'Ne sui pas fille de burgois
> Que change amur a plusur gent
> Pur lur or ne pur lur argent.'   (1310–12)

('I am not a burgher's daughter, to change my love from man to man, for their gold or silver.')

It is not inconsistent with the courtly view of women that a little later on a story is introduced which illustrates the untrustworthiness of tattling women, for the author was at moments a moralist. Waldef himself makes a *mariage de convenance*, but becomes involved, in fairy-tale fashion, with two other suitors, and has to fight one of them (one proves enough). He pays tribute to the prevailing view of love in the middle of his duel:

> L'escu enbrace e treit le brant.
> Vers s'amie puis reguarda
> La rien el mund que plus ama.   (3728–30)

(He takes his shield by the grips and draws his brand. Then he looked towards his love, the creature in the world he loved the best.)

Waldef's sons have no love-affairs; Gudlac marries the King of London's daughter and so acquires a kingdom. Guiac, according to Bramis, had numerous descendants. His wife was presumably a foreigner. The foundling Florenz, after his abortive attempt to marry his own mother, which may owe its origin to the Oedipus story, marries a princess and has a son named Lioine. He accompanies Waldef's sons on their continental expedition and acquires a friend called Tierri, who lives with his old father and a sister in a hut since the destruction of their castle. It might have been expected that Lioine would fall in love with the maiden, and indeed, he does go so far as to think that he might have done so if he had felt inclined, but the author has reserved him for another fate. He and Tierri return to the siege of Ratisbon, and the emperor's daughter sees him from her vantage-point on the battlements and sends a messenger to him with presents. He is to swim his horse over the estuary when he sees a lamp that she will hang from her window. Lioine does so and is greeted by a page who equips him with dry garments before he goes upstairs. The night is passed as one might expect, and Lioine takes his leave only when the watchmen wind their horns at daybreak—the author is well acquainted with the *alba*. (A game of hunt-the-source might be played in order to find out whether there is any line of descent from *Waldef* to *Romeo and Juliet*!) Lioine promises to return:

> Mes einz qu'il guarde se durrunt
> Lur amur mult chier comparrunt.
> Amdui murrunt a grant tristur.
> Allas tant mar fu lur amur!   (18895–8)

(But before they can realize it they will pay dearly for their love. Both will die in great sadness. Alas! So ill fated was their love.)

Since in the Middle Ages there was no such thing as an accident, a wicked chamberlain steals the lamp one night and rows away with it in a boat out to sea, luring the young man to his doom. Gradually time passes, and when his horse begins to founder he understands what is happening:

> Comanda soi a Jesu Crist.
> Unc ne suna aprés un mot.
> La mer en soi trestut l'enclot.
> La peri: ço fu grant damage;
> Unques humme de sun parage
> N'iert tant regreté en sun tens,
> Kar sa mort pleinstrent tutes genz.   (19396–402)

(He commended his soul to Jesus Christ. Never after did he utter a word. The sea swallowed him up quite. There he perished; it was a great loss. Never was a man of his rank so regretted in his time, for everyone lamented his death.)

Indeed, when his body was cast up there was universal grief and astonishment. The princess gives way to grief:

> 'Bien sai, Lioine, que par vus
> Enbelira li ceuls la sus.
> En cele seinte compangnie
> Averez la pardurable vie.
> A vus vendrai ja, beals amis,
> Ensemble serrum a tuz dis.
> Nos almes ensemble serrunt
> E nos dous cors ci remeindrunt.
> Pur ço ai jo mult grant desir
> Ke jo ore puisse murir,
> Que jo a vus venir peüsse
> E k'entur vus tuz dis fusse.'
>
> . . . . . .
>
> En estrengnant e en beisant
> A Deu rendi l'alme a itant.
> Or est pis que il einz ne fu.

(19613–24, 19641–3)

('I know well, Lioine, that the heavens above will be beautified by you. In that holy company you will have everlasting life. I shall now come to you, fair friend, and we shall be together for ever. Our souls will be together and our two bodies will remain here. Therefore I have a great desire to die now, so as to come to you and be ever at your side. . . .' Embracing and kissing [his body] she yields straightway her soul to God. Now is it worse than it was before.)

There is then a magnificent joint funeral, conducted by two archbishops, three bishops, and a host of lesser clergy. It almost looks as though the author had intended to make Lioine marry his friend's sister, and had then changed his mind and identified Lioine with Leander. No trace of an Old French 'Hero and Leander' can be found, but the story is referred to in the *Roman de Troie*, lines 22121–6, where the young man is called Leandés. Such a brief summary suggests that the story was already known to lay persons.

It will have been seen how unchristian and at times amoral the story of Waldef is, but sometimes the clerical status of the author betrays itself. A striking instance is the repentance of Guiac. After his conquest of Germany and first coronation as emperor, he announces his intention of going east, to conquer Rome and cross the Sea of Greece and remain there for a time. A mysterious palmer enters, and accusing him of sinful pride, tells him that he can never reach the Earthly Paradise, nor fight angels, and that in St. Michael he will meet his match. The news arrives of Waldef's death, which looks like a judgement:

> 'Pur ço m'aparçoue jo mult bien
> Ke cest siecle ne me valt rien.'   (21721–2)

('By that I perceived right well that this world is worth nothing to me.')

He resigns his crown. Gudlac tells him that he should devote himself to good works—the founding of religious houses, the building of roads and bridges, the clothing of the brethren. Salemun reminds him of his ancestor Alexander. But Gudlac changes clothes with the palmer—there is another reminiscence of *Tristan* here—and goes off alone. Then, it is an angel who reveals to Ernild the identity of her two sons, though humanity reasserts itself when Ernild throws herself between her husband and son, and shows her bared breasts in appeal to the two youths.

It is probably a proof that there was one main English source for *Waldef* that the author has reported episodes which were plainly not to his taste. The little Waldef's murder of his playmate in a quarrel is glossed over lightly because it is no use crying over spilt milk. Florenz's action in dashing out the brains of the seven-year-old son of his father's murderer is half-heartedly excused as a piece of legitimate vengeance. Florenz's attempt to starve his stepfather to death in order to marry his unrecognized mother is one thing, but her calm acquiescence in the performance of the ceremony while her husband is still alive is another; though it is necessary for the story that the mother should be reunited to her husband and live happily ever after. Ernild's outburst when her sons leave has already been quoted, but it must be remarked that before that Waldef had tried to persuade them to stay, arguing that there was no need to go overseas to find kingdoms to conquer because there were at least six kingdoms on this side of the Scottish border waiting to be conquered. Such sentiments seem hardly in keeping with the Christian and humane ideas expressed elsewhere.

No fabulous monsters appear, though angels are mentioned several times. Once, Gudlac kills a polar bear which is
about to eat some Danish children. Waldef has one 'animal
dream' of thousands of wild boars.

The versification was discussed by Professor Ham, and
in the absence of a controlling manuscript it is difficult to
take the matter further. The form is the octosyllabic couplet,
and the octosyllables seem to have been correct if Anglo-
Norman pronunciation is taken into account. The repetition
of the same rhyme more than twice (in one case ten times,
lines 5611–20) is characteristic of Norman and Anglo-
Norman texts. *Enjambement* is employed rarely as a stylistic
device. The effective line 'La peri: ço fu grant damage' will
have been noticed. Like Crestien and other twelfth-century
writers, the poet uses the caesura as a rhetorical device, occasionally in two lines running:

> Com est le Bruit, com est Tristram.   (47)
>
> Uns rois i ot, de Rome iert né.   (95)
>
> Dunc se pasme, dunc se demente,
> Si se cleime: 'Lasse, dolente!'   (573–4)

The vocabulary is interesting, including some uncommon
words. *Dan* as a title carries no derogatory significance; this
is characteristic of texts of south-western France and of
Horn.[1]

This romance seems not to have reached the Continent.
The English poem used by Bramis was evidently a Middle
English translation from the Anglo-Norman, and followed
it very closely. At that time it covered only half the romance,[2]
and may never have been completed. It was divided into
three fits, and Bramis says that he divided the rest into three
parts to match. Later in the fifteenth century a Latin epitome,
incomplete as we have it, was made.[3] In this, the proper
names occur in peculiar forms. Atle appears as Attalus. In
Geoffrey of Wells the Latin form is Athla. In view of the
way the epitome has treated the other names, the equation

---

[1] Cf. M. K. Pope, 'Titles of Respect in *Horn*', *Studies . . . presented to J. Orr*
(M.U.P., 1953), pp. 226–32.

[2] 'As far as the fourth part.' This means the beginning, and not, as is usually
assumed, the end. This is clear from the statement about the six divisions.

[3] Ed. J. G. Smyly, *Hermathena*, xviii (1919), pp. 240–328.

Attalus=Attila, which has given rise to the belief in a legendary combat between Attila and Unwen, may not be well founded.[1]

Whatever may be said in extenuation of it, *Waldef*, like the 'récit de Théramène', remains much too long. As it was written to be read aloud, for days and weeks on end, the author is forced to recapitulate from time to time. The modern reader can proceed much faster and look back if necessary. The material would have been better split up amongst several romances.

BOEVE DE HAUMTONE

About the same time, perhaps, comes *Boeve de Haumtone*, one of the better-known Anglo-Norman texts, thanks to the monumental edition by Albert Stimming.[2] Though this belongs to the class labelled romance, it is, like *Horn*, cast in the form of a *chanson de geste* and is designed to be recited or intoned before a large company. It opens with the words:

> Seingnurs barons, ore entendez a mei,
> Si vus dirrai gestes, que jeo diverses sai,
> De Boefs de Haumtone, le chevaler curtays.
>
> .   .   .   .   .   .
>
> Si vus volez oyer, jeo vus en dirray.   (1–5)

(Lords, now pay attention to me, and I will tell you of deeds, of which I know many, of Bevis of Hampton, the courteous knight. . . . If you will listen, I will tell you some of them.)

Whether or not the poem was actually sung to music, the writer knew that 'to sing' was the right verb to use in this connexion. The text was, however, written and apparently read, not recited by heart.

> Seignurs, iceo quens Guioun dount vus chaunt . . . .   (13)
>
> Nostre chançon finist, ne dure plus avant;
> Jeo ne vus dirrai plus en dist ne en chant.
> Issi finist la geste, ke bien est complie,
> De Boun de Hampton od la chier hardie.
> Jeo le vus ay lui, e vus l'avez oye.
> Rendez m'un servise si freyez curteysie.   (3845–50)

---

[1] Cf. A. Bell, 'Gaimar's Early "Danish" Kings', pp. 609–10.
[2] *Bibliotheca Normannica*, vii (Halle, 1899).

(Lords, this Count Guy about whom I am singing to you . . . .
Our song ends here, it lasts no longer; I will tell you no more in narrative or song. Here ends the geste, which is well completed, of Bevis
of Hampton of the bold bearing. I have read it to you and you have
heard it. Give me my due for it and you will be doing a courtesy.)

Not content with handing the hat round at the end, the
minstrel demands a 'refresher' before he is well into his
subject:

> Issi com vus me orrez ja a dreit conter,
> Si vus me volez de vostre argent doner,
> Ou si ceo noune, jeo lerrai issi ester.   (434–6)

(It is thus as you will hear me relate aright, if you will give me
some of your money. And if you don't, I shall leave off here.)

The origin and dating of this romance are matters of
difficulty. The story became very popular and there are no
fewer than three continental versions of the poem, all edited
by Stimming.[1] We speak of one Anglo-Norman version, but
in reality there were two, sufficiently different to make col-
lation impossible. They survive in two long fragments, one
(B.N. n. a. f. 4532) containing the beginning and the other
(Firmin-Didot) the end of the romance. In the middle there
is an overlapping passage, which shows how different these
two versions were from one another. This suggests that there
was a considerable lapse of time between the composing of
the text and the making of the two copies, and that the
original may have been rather simpler and without the
'jongleur' remarks quoted above. Perhaps this original also
inspired the continental poems, for it is a matter of dispute
whether the archetype was Anglo-Norman or continental.
Certainly the extant Anglo-Norman fragments are not the
originals of any French version. These come from different
districts, Rheims, Beauvais, and Picardy. The twelfth-
century Provençal *Daurel et Beton* borrows from some Bevis
poem. All this makes it difficult to believe that there was not
in Northern French, most likely in Anglo-Norman, a form
of the romance which went back to some time well inside
the twelfth century. It is curious that in the earliest part of
the romance the *laisses* are very short, and the English

---

[1] In the Gesellschaft für romanische Literatur, nos. 25, 30, 41, 34, 42.

version reproduces these in the form of short stanzas. This
perhaps indicates that the text was at some time expanded,
but the English translator knew it in its present form.

The popularity of the story is largely due to the amount
of incident worked into it. The usual hunt for sources has
resulted in a long list, and it has been suggested that the core
is a lost saga. The beginning has some resemblance to the
Hamlet theme, but it might be unwise to press the analogy.
In any case, the author succeeded in composing a fresh story
out of popular ingredients, which he welded together with
a considerable amount of skill. The hero is Bevis, who at the
beginning of the tale is ten years old. His father Guy, Earl
of Hampton, has just been murdered by the Emperor of
Germany to please his former love, the daughter of the King
of Scotland, wife to Guy. She wishes to make away with the
child, who addresses his mother in terms unbecomingly
strong in one so young, but he is saved by his governor
Sabot. He is sold to Saracen merchants, so that in course
of time he falls in love with Josiane, daughter of the Saracen
King Hermine. She presents him with a sword, Morgleie,
later on show at Arundel Castle, and a horse called Arundel,
the Swallow. However, all is not to end happily yet. Bevis is
imprisoned by Bradmund King of Damascus and Josiane is
married to Yvori de Monbrant. Bevis escapes and reappears
disguised as a palmer, to be recognized by Josiane, who in
the meantime has contrived to live with her husband for
seven years in a state of chastity, thanks to a magic silk belt.
The pair escape, and at Cologne Josiane and a giant, Esco-
part, are baptized. After various adventures the emperor is
cast into a pit of molten lead, Bevis's mother flings herself
from the top of a tower, and he and Josiane are married at
Haumtone, but not to live happily ever after. They are
forced to flee from the English court, and Josiane gives birth
to twin boys. The family is then separated and Bevis is
obliged to contract himself in marriage to a queen. Josiane,
disguised as a man, turns up in the nick of time, the twins
reappear, Yvori de Montbrant is vanquished, and Bevis is
crowned King of Montbrant by the Pope. One of the twins,
Miles, marries the daughter of King Edgar of England and
succeeds him, the other, Guy, succeeds King Hermine and

ultimately his own father. The castle of Arundel, built by
Bevis, is called after the noble horse, who is one of the
principal characters.

The last detail may provide a clue to the romance in its
present form. It is lacking in the continental versions, and
even in the Anglo-Norman poem seems dragged in merely
because of the existence of the castle. Now this has always
been held, apparently mistakenly, to occupy a special position, which the Duke of Norfolk has recently tried to regu-
larize by a Private Bill. In the twelfth century it was held by
the Constable of Sussex, and was granted to the Queen
Dowager, Adeliza of Louvain. Consequently, her second
husband, William de Albini, held it in right of his wife. His
mother, it is perhaps pertinent to note, had been a Bigod. In
1154 Henry II confirmed him in the earldom of Sussex and
gave him the honour of Arundel. He died in 1176, having
long lived a bachelor existence, for Adeliza had left him in
1150. After bearing him seven children she had retired to her
family abbey of Affligam in Flanders, suffering apparently
from some complaint from which she died the next year.[1] It
is possible that a poem flattering to the newly-created Earl
of Sussex, and written in a style suitable for a masculine
company, was composed for William de Albini some time
between 1154 and 1176.

The brief outline of the story given above is enough to
show the affinity between the *Bevis* and *Guillaume d'Angleterre*, the *Willame*, *Aiol*, the *Prise d'Orange*, and countless
other epics and romances. As so often in Anglo-Norman
romance, an emperor and a king of Scotland play some part.
But there is no historical background, and there is nothing
to connect the story with any event in the reign of King
Edgar. The name may have been inspired by a memory of
the Ætheling, who survived into the reign of Henry I. The
poem is more interesting than might have been expected.
It has a vigorous and businesslike air. The poet wastes no
time, though he is fond of the picturesque. There are no
lengthy descriptions, but plenty of lively dialogue. Clothes,
food, and furniture might not exist, but the imagination is
fed by hints that the beasts of the chase include leopards,

[1] *D.N.B.*

lions, and other wild beasts, not forgetting cartloads of
bears. Well-known names like that of Baligant are casually
introduced. The style has no nonsense about it, but is never
dull, though the epithets are trite. Bevis is very often given
his title of 'de Hauntone', but he is also 'le chevaler curtays'
or 'vaylant', or is described as being 'o le vis ber'. Josiane is
'la pucele o le cors honuré' or 'a cler vis'. Yet such is the pace
of the narrative that these clichés do not offend. When it is
considered that so much incident is compressed into the
3,850 lines of Stimming's edition, compared with the 10,614,
19,127, and 16,391 lines of the continental versions, the
author's powers can be appreciated. Yet he is never dry, and
his poem is evidently not a summary of a longer text. It is the
continental versions which are padded with romanticism and
loaded with the descriptions of ladies' dresses so dear to the
later generations. It is nonsense to pretend, on the evidence
of mere date of copying, that these are earlier versions of
the story than the Anglo-Norman fragments. There can be
little doubt that there once existed a twelfth-century Anglo-
Norman text, now surviving in thirteenth-century form.
On the Continent the contents were brought up to date, in
England only the form.

For some reason, even in its flatter manifestation, this
story became as widespread as any. The Anglo-Norman
version has given rise to a Middle English romance in more
than one *remaniement*, a Welsh translation, a Norse saga,
and an Irish version based on the English. Then there are
the three continental poems, and versions in Dutch, Italian,
Russian, Rumanian, and Yiddish.[1]

Boeve is written in *laisses* of dodecasyllables mixed with
decasyllable, linked by assonance. Exceptionally in Norman
or Anglo-Norman, -*en* is in assonance with -*an*, but this is
not in itself sufficient to prove an ultimate continental origin
for the text. The assonance of -*u* with -*o* is not now held to
indicate a north of England provenance. Some assonances
seem to be late and may be due to thirteenth-century altera-

---

[1] Cf. Stimming, *Der A.-N. B. de H.*, and C. Boje, 'Über der altfranzösischen
Roman von *Beuve de Hantone*', *Zeitschrift für romanische Philologie*, Beiheft xix
(1909), especially table, p. 22; A. Baugh, 'Improvisation in the Middle English
Romances', *Proceedings of the American Philosophical Society*, ciii (1959), p. 432.

tions, but the archaisms are more striking. Feminine endings are rare, and for the most part the *laisses* are very short. Of the two manuscripts, one is fourteenth-century and the other thirteenth, but, as sometimes happens, it is the later which better preserves the character of the original.

As a specimen of literature the Anglo-Norman *Boeve* is undoubtedly superior to contemporary work of the same kind produced on the Continent. It belongs, however, to a class and period which were something less than first-rate.

FERGUS

These are all the 'ancestral romances' which can be ascribed to the twelfth century, but the type remained fashionable in the thirteenth. *Fergus*, like *Guillaume d'Angleterre* the work of a continental writer, belongs to this class.[1] The story of a boy brought up in ignorance, who becomes a knight and makes a brilliant marriage, it was probably written for Alan of Galloway, perhaps to commemorate his marriage with Margaret, daughter of Earl David and niece of William the Lion, in 1209.[2] Most of those who have worked on this romance have concentrated on the Galloway connexion, and looked for origins in the Celtic mists. They have forgotten that the princes of Galloway were not Gallowegians (a word which was synonymous with thief) and that the historical Fergus was a viking given lands by David I. What was of more importance by the time of Alan was that he was heir of the Morvilles, and therefore constable of Scotland and an English magnate. His name is on Magna Carta as a witness. Hence, in the romance Melrose and the borders play a more important part than Galloway itself. The author names himself 'William the Clerk', and so may have been the 'beloved and familiar clerk' sent by Alan to Henry III in 1220. In that case he was Prior of the Isle, that is, St. Mary's Priory of Austin Canons at Traill.[3] This writer is probably not the

---

[1] Ed. E. Martin (Halle, 1872).

[2] Cf. M. D. Legge, 'Some Notes on the *Roman de Fergus*', *Transactions of the Dumfriesshire and Galloway Natural History and Antiquarian Society*, xxvii (1950), pp. 163–72.

[3] Traditionally one of Fergus's Five Foundations. Mr. D. E. Easson found no reference to it before 1219/20, *Medieval Religious Houses, Scotland* (London, 1957), p. 82. But Roland of Galloway had granted it a church in the twelfth century

same as Guillaume le Clerc de Normandie, writer of the *Besant de Dieu* and *Tobie*. Neither of the surviving manuscripts is Anglo-Norman, and the romance was later translated into Dutch, so that the only traces of it are continental. Yet for topographical detail it holds the palm amongst all the romances, and can only have been written by someone whose knowledge of Scotland was first-hand. It is—let it be remarked in passing—very readable. Reminiscences of the works of Crestien will be forgotten where there is so much brilliance of invention and realism in the setting.

GUI DE WAREWIC

The same cannot be said about the next work to be mentioned, truly Anglo-Norman this time, which yet became one of the most widely known and influential of texts written in England—*Gui de Warewic*.[1] The story seems to be pure fabrication, perhaps by a canon of Oseney to flatter Thomas Earl of Warwick, heir through his mother of the d'Oilli family, constables of Oxford, patrons of the abbey, some time between 1232 and 1242. Just as the borders play a more important part in *Fergus* than Galloway, so do Oxford and Wallingford loom larger in the later work than Warwick, which seems only known to the author through hearsay. Not only was it expedient for the canons of Oseney to please their new patron, but the Earl of Warwick was already in possession of lands which had belonged to the d'Oillis, and, as in the case of the Lovels and Bigods, a romance dealing with the past glories of the family would be welcome.

Guy of Warwick never existed, but his name may be derived from Wigod of Wallingford, Edward the Confessor's cup-bearer, one of whose daughters married Robert d'Oilli; and some of his exploits may be borrowed from Brian Fitzcount, husband of his other daughter, who defended Wallingford in 1139. The fight between Guy and the Dane Colebrand at Winchester is supposed to have been inspired by the Battle of Brunanburgh. It became, in England, the most popular incident in the story, but does not stand out as

(Register House Charters, no. 14). I have to thank Mr. Grant Simpson for this reference.

[1] Ed. A. Ewert (C.F.M.A., lxxiv, lxxv, 1933).

much as might be expected in the original Anglo-Norman romance.

The poem falls into two main parts, but to think of it as two romances tacked together would be to misinterpret the writer's intention. The first part is an ordinary story of courtly love, uninteresting because it was written when the fashion for such things was long past. It is thoroughly artificial. The young Guy falls in love with his social superior, Felice. This name comes out of a real pedigree, but in the context is emblematical. The youth suffers from the appropriate sleeplessness and loss of appetite, and despair overtakes him when he is rejected. The poet is versed in the rules of rhetoric, and is no stranger to the use of internal debate:

> Amur le fait a tere chaïr,
> Amur le fait tost tressaillir,
> Amur le fait oster ses dras;
> Sovent se claime chaitif e las.   (401–4)

(Love causes him to fall to the ground, love makes him shiver and shake, love makes him tear off his clothes; he often calls himself wretched and weary.)

> 'Ahi! mort, u demuers tu?
> Ja m'a amur si vencu!
> Purquei ne viens e si me prens?
> De tut ai mes perdu les sens.'   (409–12)

('Ah! Death, where delayest thou? Now has love vanquished me! Why dost thou not come and take me away? I have for ever quite lost my senses.')

And so on, in the tradition of *Amadas* and *Ipomedon*. The practised reader will here expect an echo of *Tristan*, and will not be disappointed. Guy falls on his knees and begs for mercy:

> 'Vus estes ma vie e ma mort,
> Sanz vus n'avrai jo confort;
> Asez vus aim plus de mei,
> Murrai pur vus a grant desrei.'   (321–4)

('You are my life and my death, without you I shall lose my strength. I love you much more than I do myself, I shall die for you in great madness.')

All is in vain; Felice reminds him that he is a mere steward's
son. Guy then goes off to the Continent with his governor,
Heralt. He wins the prize in tournament after tournament
and returns in triumph to claim Felice as his bride. She,
however, points out to him that he is not yet a proved knight.
He, therefore, gets himself knighted by her father and goes off
again to offer his sword to anyone in distress anywhere in
Europe or Africa. This journey lasts for seven years and takes
over 6,500 lines to describe. In the course of it Guy acquires
his companion in arms, Tierri de Guarmeise (Worms). In after
times the story was sometimes thought of as *Guy and Thierry*.
Extraordinary combats take place. At one point Guy rescues
a lion from a dragon and, like Yvain, is haunted by the grateful
beast until someone tactfully murders it; at another he is within an ace of marrying the emperor's daughter, in a fit of absence of mind. However, he returns to England at last and
marries Felice. A fortnight later, without more than a pious
hope that a son would be born to him, he is off again.

> Ço fu en mai, el tens d'esté,
> Que Gui ert en Warewic la cité.   (7563–4)

> A une vespree, que bele esteit,
> Gui en une tur munta,
> En halt as estres se pua;
> Le pais envirun a esgardé
> E le ciel, qui tant ert esteillé,
> E le tens, qui ert serré e cler.
> Gui comence dunc a penser
> Cum Deus li out fait grant honur   (7568–75)

> E cum aveit sun cors pené
> Loinz en estrange regné
> Pur une femme qu'il tant amat,
> Pur qui tant mals duré ad;
> Mais unc pur sun criatur
> Qui fait li ad si grant honur,
> Ne s'entremist de lui servir;
> Mais ore s'en voldra repentir. . . .
> En sun corage se purpensa
> Que tote sa vie changera
> E en Deu servise se mettra.
> Atant es vus sa moiller!   (7583–95)

(It was in May, in summer time, that Guy was in the fortress of Warwick. . . . One evening, when it was fine, Guy climbed on to a tower and leaned against the parapet on the top; he surveyed the country round about, and the sky, which was so starry, and the weather, which was so serene and bright. Then Guy began to reflect how God had done him great honour, . . . and how he had laboured far away in a foreign kingdom for a woman he so greatly loved, for whom he had endured so many evils, but never for his creator who has done him such great honour, did he undertake to serve him. But now he will repent of it . . . in his heart he bethought himself that he would change his whole life and put himself in the service of God. And now, lo and behold his wife!)

This reference to the unfortunate Felice introduces an argument between husband and wife which recalls that between Alexis and his bride in the later, expanded version. The lady gives Guy a gold ring (the reverse of what happens in *St. Alexis*) and laments his departure:

> 'Deu! fait ele, que ferai,
> Quant mun seignur perderai,
> La ren del mund que plus amai?
> E jo coment vivre purrai?'   (7739–42)

('Oh God!' said she, 'what shall I do when I lose my lord, the person in the world I love the best? And I, how shall I live?')

Guy goes to Jerusalem and other distant parts, under an assumed name. As indicated at the moment of his conversion, he finds just as much fighting as before, only this time he fights for God and not for love of a lady. In the meantime Guy's son Reinbrun, who was being brought up by Heralt, is stolen at the age of seven by merchants from Russia, who are afterwards cast up by a storm on the coasts of Africa. Anlaf of Denmark invades England, and the traitor Duke Modred of Cornwall gets rid of Heralt by pretending that he has sold Guy's son. This sends Heralt off to look for the boy, thus leaving the way open for Modred to besiege Wallingford, which, however, is defended by the steward Edgar. To return to Guy: he meets Thierry again, and saves him from a false accusation. He then returns to England, to find out that Athelstane is besieged by Analf at Winchester. The situation is saved by the famous fight between Guy and Colebrand. After his victory Guy retires to Warwick, where he

lives like St. Alexis on the charity of his wife, who has passed
the interval in good works. Worn out by his privations, he
does not long survive, and when on the point of death sends
his ring to Felice, who recognizes it, and, overcome by grief,
follows Guy to the tomb.

> Ensemble sunt en la compaignie
> De Nostre Dame, Sainte Marie;
> E issi nus doinst Deu servir
> Ke en sa glorie puissum venir. Amen. (11629–32)

(They are together in the company of Our Lady, St. Mary. And
may God grant us so to serve him that we may come to his glory.
Amen.)

This is by no means the end of the poem. After a curious
passage stating that Thierry exhumed Guy's body and took
it to Worms, we turn to the adventures of Heralt. It goes
without saying that he finds Reinbrun only when the two
have engaged in mortal combat. What is more unexpected
is that Heralt's son Aselac, who has never been mentioned
before, and has been all the time brought up by his grandfather, the Earl of Leicester, appears on the scene in search
of his father, and he too is recognized only after a fight.
When this fresh complication has been cleared up all three
are able to return to England and regain their home.

> De ceste estorie voil fin fere;
> Plus ne voil desore retraire;
> Bel essample i puet l'um prendre,
> Qui bien le set e velt entendre,
> De prouesce amer e lealté tenir,
> De tuz bens faire e mals guerpir,
> Orguil e richesces aver en despit.
> De Guiun nus aprent l'escrit,
> Ço fut la sume de sa valur,
> Qui tut guerpi pur sun criatur;
> E cil qui en la sainte Trinité
> Uns Deus est par sa pité
> Nus doinst en tere lui servir
> Que a lui en glorie puissums venir. Amen.
>   (12913–26)

(I will bring this story to an end, I do not wish henceforth to tell
any more of it; from it one may take a good example, if one knows it

well and has the will to understand it, of loving prowess and keeping faith, of doing all things good and forsaking the evil, of having contempt for pride and wealth. The writing teaches us of Guy, the sum of his worth, how he forsook all for his creator's sake; and may he who is one God in the holy Trinity grant us in his pity to serve him on earth so that we may come to him in glory. Amen.)

No version of the story extant today goes back to anything other than the Anglo-Norman romance. The historical background seems to be one of the sketchiest. It has been suggested that the poet borrowed from no fewer than nine *chansons de geste* and romances.[1] This is tantamount to saying that he raided the stockpot. Long as the romance is, it may once have been much longer. Was the end formerly, as it appears to be in the Auchinleck manuscript, a separate romance? And how is one to account for the sudden appearance of Heralt's son from nowhere? The reference to an earl of Leicester recalls the fact that some of the lands of Robert, Earl of Leicester, were acquired by Henry, Earl of Warwick, his younger brother, so that this looks like another piece of lore culled from the family archives. The whole of the postscript dealing with Heralt and Reinbrun has an air of hurried compression absent from most of the earlier part of the romance.

Ellis's judgement on the romance,[2] published in 1805, has been endorsed by all subsequent critics: 'Guy of Warwick is certainly one of the most antient and popular, and no less certainly one of the dullest and most tedious of our early romances.' Why, then, did it have such an enthusiastic reception all over Europe? There are two Anglo-Norman redactions of it, the earlier, that published by Professor Ewert, in five manuscripts, and the other also in five. One glance at the table of criss-cross contaminations on his p. xvi is enough to show that these ten are forlorn survivors of a numerous tribe. All ten are Anglo-Norman, but the poem was known in France and was turned into prose at the beginning of the fifteenth century. This was twice printed in the sixteenth, and one of Jean Louvet's mysteries, written in 1537, is based upon it. Part of the story made its way into

---

[1] Cf. the edition by A. Ewert, p. viii.
[2] *Specimens of Early English Romances*, ii (London, 1805), p. 4.

the *Gesta Romanorum*, whence it travelled to Germany. The first twenty-seven chapters of the Catalan *Tirant lo Blanch*, later translated into Spanish, Italian, and French, are devoted to the story of 'Guillem de Varoyc'. In England the Anglo-Norman poem was translated into English several times,[1] and from English into Irish. Guy's fame inspired the homiletic *Speculum Guy de Warwyk*. The fight with Colebrand was made the subject of a separate lay, and the story of Guy remained popular in verse, prose, and on the stage until, in our own day, it was relegated to the nursery in the Told-to-the-Children series. Guy was adopted as a Christian name by the Beauchamp family, who built Guy's Tower at Warwick Castle. The castle still contains various relics of the hero—his weapons and armour, his porridge-pot, and a rib of the dun cow, a late arrival in the legend. The hermitage is supposed to have been at Guy's Cliff. Moreover, the fight at Winchester became part of English history for four hundred years, thanks to the ingenious adoption of it by Peter of Langtoft.[2] Langtoft explains how Anlaf, defeated at 'Brunnanburg sur Humbre', fled back to Denmark and then returned with Colebrand to besiege Athelstan at Winchester, thus blending the two invasions of Olaf Cuaran and Olaf Tryggvason, the confusion of which gave rise to the romance.

> Adelstan priait a Deu omnipotent,
> Ke aider ly vousist, et Deu benignement
> En sounge of ly parlait, et dist ke prestement
> Ke al matyn troverayt un velz palmer et lent
> A la porte del seu, et cely seurement
> Parfrait la bataille pur Deu omnipotent,
> Si pur Deu ly priast; ço fut verrayment
> Guy de Warwik, sun livre dist coment
> Il tuayt Colebrand, par quai tut quitement
> Anlaphe rethorna a cel fez dolent.[3]

(Athelstane prayed Almighty God to be willing to help him, and God spoke benignly to him in a dream, and told him that immediately in the morning he would find at the south gate a palmer old and slow, who would assuredly undertake the battle for God Almighty, if he prayed him for God's sake; this was really Guy of Warwick, his

---

[1] Cf. A. Baugh, loc. cit., pp. 432–3.
[2] See below, pp. 278–80.
[3] Ed. T. Wright, Rolls Series, i. 330–2.

'Book' tells how he killed Colebrand, whereby Anlaf was quit and returned home in grief that time.)

The poet had no sense of style, and repeats himself incessantly. His poverty of invention is proved by his habit of making the same devices serve over and over again. There is no character-drawing; in fact there are no characters, only types and lay figures. The colourless girl Felice, abruptly turning into a Lady Bountiful, could only have been drawn by someone who had entered religion very young and had been bewildered ever since by sermons on temptation. What, then, could be the cause of the strange fascination this story has exerted?

The answer is contained in the epilogue. The romance, long as it is, is quite genuinely an 'exemplum'. With the exception of the Reinbrun part, it has a unity which has been missed. It is the story of the progress of a man from childhood through an apprenticeship in arms to real fighting, first for a lady and then for God. This man is a layman, not a religious, and even when he has ceased to lead an active life will come back at God's command to save his king and country. It is this singleness of purpose which distinguishes Guy from the other figures in the romance. If the author was really a canon of Oseney, he may already have seen on the library shelves the Oxford *Roland*, but that as a model was out of date. The Crusade he knew was not the First, but the Third, with its disgraceful quarrels and the failure to retake Jerusalem. The sieges which were of recent memory were not by the Danes, but by the partisans of Stephen or Matilda. There were no patriots, only robbers and adventurers changing sides when it suited them. Within the memory of canons of Oseney, their patron Robert d'Oilli II had invited the Empress to Oxford Castle, whence she escaped two months later across the ice in white camouflage to Abingdon and Wallingford. It was an age which needed an 'exemplum' of loyalty, and Guy of Warwick not only provided it, but did so in such a way that its success was not ephemeral. However much the author may be condemned and despised, he provided what was wanted, and did so with a stern sense of duty. Adventure he supplied in plenty, but no hint of immorality.

It is possible that he had a model. The statement that there were no patriots at that time must be qualified. There was one. One single man was respected by friend and foe alike for his uncompromising loyalty. It does not seem a large ration for the two countries of England and France, but one was all they could produce between them. William Marshall began life as a second son, landless and poor, a 'chevalier qui vit de proie', one of a despised class who supported themselves by pot-hunting at tournaments. His career, though not the motives for it, was then and after curiously like that of Guy. Through the deaths of his father and elder brother he became marshal, and, through the king's providing him with an heiress above him in station as a bride, Earl of Pembroke and Striguil. Chosen as a companion of the Young King, whom he knighted and on whose behalf he went on a crusade, he served Henry II after his death and fought for him against Richard until the end. Richard understood that his loyalty had nothing personal about it, and continued to treat him as his father had done. In old age, when other people begged him to remember that he had done his part, he became the champion of the infant Henry III and routed the Dauphin Louis at the Fair of Lincoln in 1217. He died probably not long before *Gui de Warewic* was written. He was altogether a more human and gracious person than Guy, a good dancer and singer, and possessed of a rather robust sense of humour. As far as can be told, however, he never fell in love. All things considered, Guy could be an idealized William Marshall. It is unlucky for the author of *Gui* that there is a standard of comparison in the shape of what may be called the authorized biography of the marshal,[1] which is a great deal more interesting in every way. But it was unknown to him, and after all is a private production for record, not light reading. There are no dragons in it.

The state of the versification in the extant manuscripts reduced Professor Ewert to despair and he rightly renounced any attempt to correct it or even to advance an opinion on the poet's intentions. He certainly aimed at an octosyllabic couplet, but how much of the variation in length of the lines

---

[1] *L'Histoire de Guillaume le Maréchal*, éd. P. Meyer (Société de l'histoire de France, 3 vols., 1891, 1894, 1901).

is due to the scribes must remain unknown. The complicated relationship of the manuscripts suggests that they may have had much to do with the present appearance of the text. The line used was not the old twelfth-century one with a caesura. The lines quoted above, beginning:

Vus estes ma vie e ma mort

contrast rhythmically with the

Isolt ma drue, Isolt ma mie,
En vus ma mort, en vus ma vie

of their prototype. Outbreaks into decasyllables, as in the longish passage in Version I, lines 10069–112, also show a weak rhythmical pattern and sometimes disappearance of the caesura. There is a decasyllabic passage, curiously enough, added to or preserved in Version II which is not in Version I. It seems more likely that the poet mixed his metres as Fantosme and the continental author of *Aiol* had done, rather than that he was working over an earlier form of the poem in decasyllables. The passages show no trace of *laisse* formation; sometimes the same rhyme is repeated four times, but this occurs also in the octosyllabic parts, and is a well-known characteristic of Norman and Anglo-Norman texts. All one can say of the present sad state of the text is that, from the point of view of versification as from every other, it has suffered from over-popularity. For this popularity, the public must share the blame with the author.

FOUKE FITZWARIN

The remaining romance of the ancestral type survives only in a fourteenth-century version. It is the truest of them all and has been the least popular. It is the story of *Fouke Fitzwarin*.[1] In its present form the romance was probably rewritten before 1314, for Fulk Fitzwarin V. The unique manuscript (B.M. Royal 12. C. xii) dates from soon after 1322. The original poem, which recounted the adventures of Fulk III, could not have been earlier than the accepted date of his death, 1256, and is unlikely to have been later than 1264, the date of the death of Fulk IV. Incorporated in the prose

---

[1] Ed. L. Brandin (C.F.M.A., lxiii, 1930).

text are two quotations from the Prophecies of Merlin, which have been intentionally left in verse. The *remanieur* left so many rhyme-words in his text that long passages can easily be reconstructed in octosyllables. These octosyllables, as one could expect in a mid or late thirteenth-century Anglo-Norman poem, varied in length from seven to nine syllables according to French reckoning. It requires very little ingenuity to detect the original poem which underlies a passage like the following: 'Willam, quant ce oy, surryst e dist: "Bele nece, bien avez dit et je vous ayderay a mon poer de tel seignour purchacer e ci vous dorray Blanchetour et quanqe apent ou tut l'onour, quar femme que ad terre en fee serra d'assez plus desiree." '

The romance opens with a reference to the months of April and May, when a man's fancy should turn to remembering the deeds of his ancestors. It then gives an imaginative account of the Conquest and of William the Conqueror's pacification of the Welsh march, during the course of which he learns about the single-handed combat between Coryneus and Geomagog, in a spirited description. After a further historical sketch the subject of the romance is introduced. One Guaryn de Meez wins the prize at a tournament at the Peak, after which he marries one of the nieces of William Peverel. He thus becomes heir to Blauncheville (Whittington in Shropshire) and has a son named Fulk. The adventures ascribed to him, however, really belong to his son, Fulk II. The bulk of the romance describes the rebellion of the third Fulk against King John, his exile and wanderings in France under an assumed name, his turning to piracy, his return disguised as a merchant, his further adventures and final return and pardon. A perfunctory description is given of his two marriages, the birth of several children, and the founding of New Abbey at Alberbury. It was there that Fulk was buried when he died, after the death of his second wife and his blinding by a vision.

Cesti Fouke remist sept aunz veogle e soffri bonement sa penaunce. Dame Clarice morust e fust ensevely a la Novele Abbeye. Aprés qi mort, Fouke ne vesqui que un an e morust a Blaunchevyle; a grant honour fust enterré a la Novele Abbeye. De la alme de cui Dieus eit merci! Joste le auter gist le cors. Deus eit merci de tous, vifs e mortz! Amen.

(This Fulk remained blind for seven years and endured his penance bravely. Dame Clarice died and was buried at the New Abbey. After whose death, Fulk lived for only a year and died at Whittington; he was buried very honourably in the New Abbey. On whose soul God have mercy! Near the altar lies the body. God have mercy on all men, alive and dead! Amen.)

This ending suggests that the author of the original text, and possibly the *remanieur* also, was a monk at the New Abbey, a Benedictine house founded by Fulk II. The chronology and points of detail are confused. It is not surprising, in the context, that a monk should not be able to get the identity of the founder of his house right. Professor Brandin has pointed out all the discrepancies between truth and fiction in his introduction and index of proper names. Accuracy was something which never worried the Middle Ages, and once again one can see here illustrated the background of innumerable forged charters.[1] Miss Francis has shown, indeed, that there may be a purpose behind the distortion of the truth here.

The romance, unlike some of the others, remains readable. The introduction of so many real people with well-known names—Kings, Peverels, FitzWarins, and others—makes the reader feel at home even today. There are exciting moments, such as Coryneus's great fight with the Devil and Fulk's adventures during his sea-voyages. The mixture of real wonders with false, a description one minute of the frozen seas of the north and the next of a dragon ravaging Wales in the time of King John, has its own fascination. The author was a lively narrator, witness his retelling of the old story of the sailor who was not afraid of death by drowning, although all his family had met their end in that way. He gives spirited accounts of the tournament and the battle:

Lors resonerent lé tabours, trompes, busynes, corns sarazynes, qe les valeyes rebonderent de le soun. Lors comença le tornoy dur e fort. La poeit um vere chevalers reverseez des destrers e meynte dure coupe donnee e meynte colee!

(Then there resounded the drums, trumpets, pipes, and Saracen horns, so that the valleys re-echoed with the sound. Then began the tourney that was hard and fierce. There might one see knights flung backwards from their chargers, and many a hard stroke given and many a blow.)

The writer who turned the poem into prose worked clumsily, but the result, with its traces of rhythm and rhyme-words, has a sparkling attraction of its own. Nobody could ever use the words 'dull' or 'tedious' about *Fouke FitzWarin*.

This romance never became widely known, and never seems to have reached the Continent. Leland knew a French poem which was probably the lost original of the extant prose version, and a poem in English, which Wright pointed out must have been in alliterative verse, probably also based upon it, though it does not seem to have been a slavish translation.[1] It might be argued that this lack of popularity was due to the purely local appeal of the subject, but this applies to others of these romances. The explanation probably lies in the late date of its composition.

It is now time to ask what features these 'ancestral' romances have in common. They were all apparently written to lend prestige to a family which, for one reason or another, could be regarded as parvenu. The hero is regarded as the founder of a family, and must preferably be a king, or become one at the end of the story. There must be a period of exile, if possible involving wanderings over sea, with mention of exotic places, their fauna, and other details. This may be combined with the Eustace–Placidas theme. In the case of *Fergus*, its place is taken by the period of madness in Ettrick Forest, derived from the Merlin story. The author may take an existing story and adapt it to fit his needs, or create a new one, or he may make use of genuine history. Whether his fable is derived from truth or fiction, he will ornament it with signs and wonders. At least one fight with a dragon is almost *de rigueur*. The burial of the hero in a monastery is almost universal. Courtoisie finds little place, and only lip-service is paid to it. Since the object in writing at all seems to be to describe the founding of a family, marriage is bound

---

[1] *Fulk Fitzwarine*, ed. T. Wright (Warton Club, 1855), pp. viii, x, xi.

to play an important part; love-affairs outside matrimony are out of place. But besides this, all the writers seem to take a curiously detached view of girls and women, almost as though they had never met any outside a book. (*Waldef* is exceptional in this respect.) They do seem to know a certain amount about fighting, but this knowledge could be more easily acquired from books than an insight into human nature. The explanation may be that nearly all these romances were written by members of the regular clergy, inmates of houses founded or patronized by the family for whom these stories were concocted. Perhaps the most surprising thing is the widespread popularity of most of them. Although created for a specific and local purpose, they had sufficient topical interest to become part of universal literature. Nevertheless, today it is difficult to understand the fortunes of some. The fame of Roland and Tristram can be understood much more easily than the reputation of Bevis of Hampton or Guy of Warwick. But it is just a matter of taste, the hardest thing in the world to understand.

VIII

RELIGIOUS LITERATURE AT THE TURN OF THE CENTURY

THE OXFORD AND CAMBRIDGE PSALTERS

AT the beginning of Vising's list of Anglo-Norman works stand two versions of the Psalter,[1] known as the Oxford and Cambridge Psalters. The Oxford Psalter is a translation of the Gallican, the Cambridge of the Hebrew version. The oldest manuscript (Bodleian Douce 320) of the Oxford Psalter comes from Montebourg, that of the Cambridge Psalter (Cambridge, Trinity College R. 17. 1) from Canterbury. This forms part of the magnificent edition of the three versions of the psalms by the sacristan Eadwin about 1160. Another, probably later, translation of the Gallican version was discovered by M. Charles Samaran, unfortunately surviving only in a fragment. M. Samaran believes that all three translations were made in England, and the first two at Canterbury.[2] All are in prose and the first is the ancestor of nearly all the subsequent French translations of the Gallican version. They may have begun life as glosses—indeed, the Cambridge Psalter is arranged in parallel columns to the Latin text—but they soon acquired independent life. They are true specimens of French prose, unlike the Arundel Psalter, also twelfth-century, where the French acts as an interlinear gloss, and for the most part the Latin word-order is kept.[3]

LI IV LIVRE DES REIS

More interesting, both from a literary and a linguistic point of view, is the magnificent *IV Livre des Reis*.[4] Five

---

[1] *Anglo-Norman Language and Literature* (London, 1923), p. 41.

[2] 'Fragment d'une traduction en prose française du Psautier composée en Angleterre au xiie siècle', *Romania*, lv (1929), pp. 161–73; Y. Le Hir, 'Sur des traductions en prose française du Psautier', *Revue de linguistique romane*, xxv (1961), pp. 324–28.

[3] Ed. A. Beyer, *Zeitschrift für romanische Philologie*, xi (1887), pp. 513 ff.; xii (1888), pp. 1 ff.

[4] Ed. E. R. Curtius, *Gesellschaft für Romanische Literatur*, xxvi (Dresden, 1911).

manuscripts of this are extant, and only the oldest and best is Anglo-Norman. Doubt has been shed upon the Anglo-Norman character of the text, but Dr. Curtius cleared this up by analysing a series of mistakes made by the continental scribes which could only be due to their unfamiliarity with Anglo-Norman spelling, forms, and vocabulary.[1] The archetype had *u* for *o*, which could equally well be Norman as Anglo-Norman, but the fact that it had *madles* for *masles*, rendered by *malades*, is decisive. The form *avres* (cattle), rendered *autres*, is additional evidence, for even *avers* is rare in Norman, and *avres* is never seen.

The most curious feature of this text is the use of rhyme. It cannot be a prose version of a poem, for there are whole passages in lines of 4, 5, 6, 7, 8, 9, 10, 11, 12, and 14 syllables. The lines linked by rhyme are usually in threes, but there are examples of passages of 4, 5, 7, and 8 lines.[2] These rhythmical and rhyming passages are obviously intended to be ornamental. Unrhymed rhythmical prose occurs in Old English, and rhyme was later introduced into Old English in imitation of medieval Latin prose.[3]

Prose was well developed in England before the Conquest, and it may be no accident that the earliest major examples of French prose were written there. As it was more usual in French to employ verse for lay use, the introduction of rhythm and rhyme into the *IV Livre des Reis* may have been a sort of compromise. Mr. C. A. Robson, in contending that French prose originated in Paris at a later date,[4] is a less safe guide than Dr. Curtius, who recognizes the long English tradition of vernacular prose which probably lies behind it.

The translation is fairly literal, though not slavish, and, as is only to be expected in a translation made for the laity, it incorporates in the text additions which come, some from the Glossa Ordinaris, some from the Glossa Interlinea, and others from various commentaries. Attention is called to these passages in the margin. The oldest manuscript is freely

[1] Op. cit., pp. lxxxix–xcii.
[2] Ibid., pp. lxxxii–lxxxviii.
[3] Cf. J. de Ghellinck, *La Littérature latine au moyen âge* (Paris, 1939), ii. 156–66.
[4] *Maurice de Sully and the Medieval Vernacular Homily* (Oxford, 1952), especially pp. vii, 3.

bestrewn with accents, as a guide to the person who had to read it aloud.

The allegorical significance of the Old Testament is pointed out as in the following example:

'É jo susciterai á mun oes pruveire fedeil ki sulunc mun quer se deduirra. Entendez la signefiance. Içó fud dit de Jesu-Crist, ki de sei meïmes dist: "Jo faz tuz jurs íçó que á mun pere plaist." A sun oes edifia Deu le pere maisun de lealté, çó est Sainte Eglise, ki tuz jurs devant Jesu-Crist serra é en prosperite cunversera.' (p. 8)

('And I will raise me up a faithful priest, that shall do according to that which is in mine heart and in my mind. Attend to the meaning: This was said of Jesus Christ, who said of himself: "I do always those things that please my father" [John viii. 29]. For him God the Father built a sure house, that is Holy Church, which will always walk before Jesus Christ and dwell in prosperity.')

The poetical quality may be deduced from an extract from David's lament for Saul and Jonathan:

'La saiette Jonathas', fist David,' 'unches ariere ne turnad, é la spéé Saül en vain al fuerre ne repairad. Saül é Jonathas amiables e bels furent en lur vie, é a la mort ne se sunt partiz. Plus furent ignels ke li egles é plus fort que líuns. Vus, filles de Israel, plurez pur Saül, ki vus vesteit des riches guarnemenz é dunat vus d'or les riches áürnemenz. Cument chaïrent en bataille li bon vassal? Jo duil sur tei, cher frere Jonathas, bels é amiables, que jó amoue si cume la mere sun fiz qui n'ad mais un. Áï! Cume chaïrent li bon champïun é perirent ces bones armes é li bons cunreidz?' (p. 62)

('The arrow of Jonathan', said David, 'turned not back, and the sword of Saul returned not empty to the scabbard. Saul and Jonathan were lovely and pleasant in their lives, and in their death they were not divided: they were swifter than eagles, they were stronger than lions. Ye daughters of Israel, weep over Saul, who clothed you with rich apparel and gave you rich ornaments of gold. How are the mighty fallen in the midst of the battle! I am distressed for thee, my brother Jonathan, very pleasant hast thou been unto me, and I loved thee as a mother loves her son, who has but one. Alas! How are the mighty fallen and the good weapons and the good accoutrements perished!')

While this passage will stand comparison with both the Vulgate and the Authorized Version, it contrasts favourably with Louis Segond's Modern French, and the final verse in his translation will suffice to demonstrate the superiority of the oldest French version:

'Je suis dans la douleur à cause de toi, Jonathan, mon frère! Tu faisais tout mon plaisir; ton amour pour moi était admirable, audessus de l'amour des femmes. Comment des héros sont-ils tombés? Comment leurs armes se sont-elles perdues?'

The dates and distribution of the manuscripts are interesting. The oldest manuscript (Mazarine 54), as has been said, is Anglo-Norman. It is the only one which contains only the Books of Samuel and Kings; all the others contain other books of the Old Testament. It is late twelfth-century, and was soon in the possession of the French royal family. Blanche, daughter of Philip V, probably took it with her when she entered the Convent of Longchamp as a child in 1315. She took the veil three years later and died there in 1358.[1] How or when it crossed the Channel is not known, but it may have been a present. There are two manuscripts in Francien, one late thirteenth-century and one fourteenth; one Walloon, perhaps early thirteenth; and finally a Picard manuscript, probably late fourteenth-century. This gives some idea of the influence wielded by the anonymous Anglo-Norman translator, who was really responsible for much of the knowledge of the Old Testament amongst the French laity of the Middle Ages.

THE *ANGLO-NORMAN BIBLE*

What is known as the *Anglo-Norman Bible*[2] belongs to the fourteenth century. In its present state it is incomplete, but was apparently a prose rendering of both Testaments. According to Berger,[3] the Great Bible made by Jean de Sy for John of France, which afterwards belonged to Charles of Orleans, is a revision of this text. The king may have acquired a copy of the Anglo-Norman text during his captivity in England after the Battle of Poitiers, and put Jean de Sy to work on it. The interesting fact here is that Anglo-Norman at its worst was recognized in France as French, even though it was thought capable of improvement, and the

[1] Le Roux de Lincy, *Les Quatre Livres des Rois*. Collection de documents inédits (Paris, 1841), pp. xlvii–xlviii.

[2] An edition of the *Acts of the Apostles* from this is in preparation by Elizabeth Ratcliffe.

[3] S. Berger, *La Bible française au moyen âge* (Paris, 1884), pp. 237, 243.

influence of Anglo-Norman literature upon French was still continuing in the fourteenth century.

GENESIS

To the same period belongs a verse rendering of *Genesis*,[1] of no great merit.

BIBLE STORIES

A very popular series of stories taken from the Bible, with Jerome's commentary on the Vulgate, was made about 1200 in *laisses* of decasyllables, with assonance, and was later turned into prose. These stories seem to have reached the Continent. So far, only extracts have been published.[2]

GENESIS AND EXODUS

Of about the same date is a poem derived from Genesis and Exodus, also later turned into prose.[3]

Besides these more important translations there were from early times verse translations of the psalms and canticles and some prayers. A metrical psalter, in stanzas of six hexasyllables, was made in England in the twelfth century.

SERMONS IN VERSE

There were also sermons in verse. Guischart de Beauliu has already been mentioned as being a writer for courtly circles,[4] but his work reached a wider public than the family for which it was written. The sermon known as *Deu le Omnipotent* is more popular in character. It consists of 122 stanzas of hexasyllables, rhyming aabccb, and was probably conceived as an imitation of the sermon *Grant mal fist Adam*. The stanza form here is the same, except that the lines are pentasyllabic. Although all the extant manuscripts are Anglo-Norman (B.M. Harley 4971, Arundel 292; Cambridge, Corpus Christi 405), this appears to have been composed in Normandy, possibly as early as the mid-twelfth century.

---

[1] Extracts, P. Meyer, *Romania*, xxxvi (1907), pp. 184–204.
[2] Cf., besides S. Berger, op. cit.: F. Bonnardot, *Romania*, xvi (1887), pp. 182–213; P. Meyer, *Notices et Extraits*, xxxiv, pp. 210–11; J. Bonnard, *Traductions de la Bible en vers* (Paris, 1884), pp. 92 ff.
[3] P. Meyer, *Romania*, xvii (1888), p. 140.   [4] See above, pp. 134–8.

The subject is the Fall of Man (curiously enough, this is a fall without an Eve) and the Harrowing of Hell. The main sources are the Old Testament and the Pseudo-Augustinian Sermon. In fact, both subject and sources are the same as those of the *Jeu d'Adam*, but there is no connexion between the two, and in the play Eve's part is given prominence. *Deu le Omnipotent* is described in two manuscripts as a Passion, and that is its subject. It relies to a large extent upon St. Bernard, and the Virgin's lament for her son on the cross has a lyric quality absent from the rest of the sermon and from its prototype. The sermon seems to have remained popular for a long time, for of the three manuscripts two may be as late as the fourteenth century. *Grant mal fist Adam* and *Deu le Omnipotent* have been edited together by the Suchiers, father and son.[1]

There were probably many more such sermons. The nationality of one called *Le Roman des Romans* is in dispute.[2] It may be continental Norman, but all the eight manuscripts (B.M. Royal B. xiv, Egerton 612; Bodleian Douce 210; Cambridge, Clare College 3. 6, Trinity College O. 2. 14; B.N. fr. 19525, 25407) in which it is extant were written in England. It has been ascribed to a writer about whom more will be said in the next chapter, Guillaume le Clerc. If it is really by him—and this seems doubtful since he elsewhere names himself—it is probably the earliest of his works, being dated about 1200. The form is decasyllabic rhyming quatrains, with a caesura. The subject is an attack on society in general and the clergy in particular, and use is made of some allegory. The keynote is contained in the line:

Bons fust li siecles, mais la gent est malvaise.   (45)

(Good might be the world, but the people are bad.)

This is perhaps a reminiscence of the first line of the *Alexis*:

Bons fut li secles al tens ancienur.

(Good was the world in the time of our fathers.)

---

[1] *Zwei altfranzösische Reimpredigten*, Bibliotheca Normannica, i (Halle-an-der-Saale). By H. Suchier, 1879, recast by W. Suchier, 1949.

[2] Ed. F. C. Tanquerey (Paris, 1922). (*Elliott Monographs*, xiv, 1923).

CATO'S *DISTICHS*

The needs of children—or, should one say, of their masters —were not overlooked. A child's first reading-book was his Psalter; 'to learn one's Psalter' was to learn to read; his second, wherein he imbibed the essence of morality simultaneously with the application of the rules of Latin grammar, was Cato's *Distichs*. The Psalter was probably the first Book of the Bible to be translated into French, and, as we have seen, several translations of it were available by the mid-twelfth century. Before the end of the century there was probably a choice of cribs to Cato in Anglo-Norman verse. There are still in existence three versions, two of them at least and probably all stemming from the same original. One, by a Benedictine, Elie de Winchester, and another, anonymous, may belong to the end of the twelfth century. The third, by a monk named Everard, possibly to be identified with Everard de Gateley, a monk of Bury, is early or mid-thirteenth century.[1]

Also thirteenth-century is the treatise of 'Trebor'[2]. The author, Robert de Ho, who signs his name both in anagram and acrostich, was probably continental, but both the surviving manuscripts are Anglo-Norman. His named sources are Cato, Solomon, Dan Statius, Dan Horace, Dan Homer, Dan Virgil, and Master Ovid. Some of these names are there for effect, and he seems to have known Cato through the medium of Elie de Winchester. Most of the poem is in octosyllabic couplets, but there are lines in couplets and in quatrains of alexandrines. At one point there is a section in over thirty stanzas tail-rhyme, which probably denotes an Anglo-Norman source.

The traditional use of 'Cato' long continued. An Edinburgh schoolmaster published an Anglo-Latin edition with grammatical annotations as late as 1709, for the use of schools, and the National Library of Scotland possesses the copy used by the ten-year-old Lord John Hope in 1714.

---

[1] For these versions and their possible relationship cf. M. D. Legge, *Anglo-Norman in the Cloisters* (Edinburgh, 1950), pp. 13–17.

[2] *Les Enseignements de Robert de Ho*, ed. M. V. Young (Paris, 1901).

THE WORKS OF SIMUND DE FREINE

Nothing mentioned so far in this chapter betrays any hint that there was such a thing as the twelfth-century renaissance, and it is possible that this intellectual movement had less effect in England than on the Continent.[1] Yet the ground for English predominance in the field of natural science in the next century was prepared in the twelfth, and occasionally traces of its influence may be seen in Anglo-Norman writers, and two of them in particular were in touch with centres of diffusion of it.

One of the great centres of learning at this period was Hereford.[2] Roger of Hereford was a well-known astronomer who compiled a set of tables for the meridian of Hereford in 1178. One of his contemporaries was the canon Simund de Freine. He belonged to a family connected with the village of Sutton (of which he farmed the tithes) from about 1131 to 1375. Part of this village is still called Sutton Freen after this family.[3] Simund's name appears in documents between 1189 and 1200, and it is known that he was dead before a period between 1124 and 1128.[4] He was a friend and supporter of Giraldus Cambrensis, whom he invited to Hereford as a congenial refugee in an elegant Latin poem, printed amongst the works of Giraldus and Simund. Some important additional lines concerning the studies at Hereford have been discovered in another manuscript, in which mention is made of geomancy—the earliest reference to this in England.[5] As in one of the poems Simund refers to his 'musa senilis', which Giraldus calls in his reply 'florida fructifera', it looks as though Simund were older than Giraldus, and writing late in life. The Latin epistles have always been

[1] I wish to thank Professor R. Southern for letting me read his unpublished paper 'The Place of England in the Twelfth-Century Renaissance' (since published in *History*, xlv, 1960, pp. 201–16).

[2] Cf. J. C. Russell, 'Hereford and Arabic Science in England', *Isis*, xviii (1932–3), pp. 14–25, and R. W. Hunt, 'English Learning in the Late Twelfth Century', *Transactions of the Royal Historical Society*, 4th Series, xix (1936), pp. 19–42.

[3] S. H. Martin, 'Sutton St. Nicholas and Sutton St. Michael, Hereford' (Herefordshire County Libraries, 1953), pp. 10–24.

[4] See Russell, loc. cit., and *Dictionary of Thirteenth-Century Writers in England* (London, 1936), pp. 149–50.

[5] R. W. Hunt, loc. cit., p. 23.

thought to have been written in 1203 and 1216 respectively, in which case they would be later than the French works, but recent research suggests that they may have been written between 1194 and 1197[1] and that the poem usually printed second is the earlier. This brings them closer to the period when he was probably writing his French works.

The order in which these were written cannot be decided, but the editor's[2] instinct in feeling that the *Roman de Philosophie* came first is probably right. This poem is based upon Boethius's *De Consolatione Philosophiae*, both the prose sections and the metres being rendered into verse. It is not, however, a mere translation, and the differences, rearrangements, and additions are clearly set out by the editor.[3] Amongst other things to note is the fact that Simund seems to be the earliest vernacular writer to combine the two ideas of taking Time by the forelock and Fortune's wheel. Some of the additions shed light on the scientific studies at Hereford. A butterfly is considered of higher value than a precious stone. A list of precious stones includes some which do not occur in lapidaries. Simund refers to clouds obscuring the sun, to disturbed water, to a grasshopper, to a spider spinning her web, all perhaps observed from nature. More remarkable is his description of an experiment with a hen's claw.[4] But there are also moralizations and allegories which are additional to those in the source. It is interesting to note that Giraldus, in one of his poems,[5] refers to Hereford as a place of joy for philosophers, where he, who so long has been a planet, has now become a fixed star. These words recall not only the existence of Roger of Hereford, but Simund's references in his Latin invitation to astronomy and the allied sciences, and to the philosophers of whom Giraldus would be the glory, and to the interest in science which led him to undertake and amplify a vulgarization of Boethius.

[1] Cf. R. W. Hunt, loc. cit., and Dorothy Humphreys, *Some Types of Social Life as shown in the Works of Gerald of Wales* (Oxford D.Phil. Thesis, 1936), which she gave me permission to consult.

[2] J. E. Matzke, *Les Œuvres de Simund de Freine* (S.A.T.F., 1909).

[3] Pp. lxvi–lxxviii, especially the tables on pp. lxxvii–lxxviii. Cf. Ch.-V. Langlois, *La Vie en France au moyen âge*, iv (Paris, 1928), pp. 293–302.

[4] M. D. Legge, ' "To Speik of Science, Craft and Sapience" in Medieval Literature', *Literature and Science* (Oxford, 1955), p. 125.

[5] *Opera*, ed. J. S. Brewer (Rolls Series), i. 378.

Simund's other Anglo-Norman poem is a *Passion of St. George*, a work of quite a different character. The occasion for it was probably the Third Crusade.[1] St. George, the patron saint of crusaders, is perhaps more in evidence in the Third than in the others. The Saracens were well acquainted with the war-cry 'St. George', and with representations of the saint on horseback, and when they killed the unfortunate Jakelin de Mailly, who wore unpainted shining armour and rode a white horse, they gave way to jubilation, under the impression that they had slain the dreaded St. George. In 1191 and 1192 the army was at Lydda, St. George's burial-place. Simund's poem may have been inspired by tales of returning crusaders, or it may have been written as part of the propaganda for the Crusade in 1188. It was then that Giraldus went on his famous preaching tour of Wales, when he moved his hearers to tears although he would preach in Latin or in French, neither of which languages was under-stood by most of his Welsh compatriots. The tour began and ended at Hereford, where he probably met Simund. A ver-nacular poem would, no doubt, have had more appeal to the local gentry than sermons in any language, but the fact that the *Passion* is derived from none of the known Latin versions and contains some episodes peculiar to itself, such as the casting of St. George into a den of lions, leopards, bears, and dragons, may mean that it is based upon fresh traditions brought back from Lydda. It seems likely that the French poems are older than the Latin ones, especially the one which refers to the 'musa senilis', but it also seems possible that the *Roman* is older than the *Passion* by several, perhaps many, years.

Both Simund's French poems are written in a very rare and tiresome metre, heptasyllabic couplets, which suggests a strong Latin influence. Apart from the awkwardness brought about by this uneven line, and a few variations from continental syllable-count caused by Anglo-Norman pro-nunciation, the editor found little to remark. He points out (p. lv) that hiatus is allowed after the fourth syllable. In other words, there are some lines which can be read as

[1] J. E. Matzke, 'The Legend of St. George', *P.M.L.A.*, xvii (1902), pp. 464–535, xviii (1903), pp. 155–6.

hexasyllables with a caesura. In other lines there is a pause after the third syllable, more rarely after the second and fourth. There is therefore more variation than appears from his analysis. It seems curious, in view of the fact that Simund de Freine can be localized and fairly closely dated, that more use has not been made of his rhymes in writings on the language of the period.

Simund cannot be condemned as a dull writer. The *Passion* is an exciting story excitingly told with no padding. In the *Roman* there was more scope for originality. Occasionally he belongs too much to his period to suit modern taste:

> Ostez *fort* de *fortune*
> Dunc verrez ke *fort* est *une*.   (59–60)[1]

At other times he shows his interest in things around him. In both poems he compares Fortune to the inconstant moon; other allusions to natural phenomena have already been mentioned. His remarks on different languages are particularly noteworthy:

> Une gent parolent griu
> E li autre lur ebriu,
> Li tierz dient lur lumbart,
> Franceis u latin li quart;
> Rien n'estendent cil d'Espaigne
> Del langage de Bretaigne;
> Li Escot e li Deneis
> Se descordent des Engleis.   (947–54)

(One people talks Greek and a second their Hebrew, a third speaks their Lombard, French or Latin a fourth; those of Spain understand nothing of the language of Britanny; the Scots [i.e. the Irish] and the Danes are quite different from the English.)

Simund signed both poems in an acrostich at the beginning of the mercifully short prologues in which he expresses the contemporary view that such vernacular works convey both pleasure and profit. The *Roman* was probably the more popular of the two. It survives in three manuscripts, two (B.M. Royal 20. B. xiv, Bodleian Douce 210) belonging

---

[1] Cf. J. Acher, 'Sur un calembour méconnu de S. de Freine', *Zeitschrift für romanische Philologie*, xxxiv (1910), pp. 211–12.

to the end of the thirteenth century and the third (B.M. Add. 46919) to the beginning of the fourteenth. *St. George* is only to be found in one manuscript (B.N. fr. 902) of the second half of the thirteenth century. All were written in England.

ADGAR'S *MIRACLES*

The other, and earlier, writer, who has a less obvious connexion with the Renaissance, is Adgar or William, who translated a collection of Mary Legends.[1] He names himself in the prologue:

> Mut volenters me numerai:
> 'Adgar' ai num; mes el i sai:
> Li plusur me apelent Willame;
> Bien le puent faire sanz blasme.
> Kar par cel nun fui primeseinet
> E puis par Adgar baptizet.
> Pur ceo par raisun m'est avis,
> Ke enz es nuns n'ai rien mespris,
> Ne cil ki Willame me claiment.
> Ore me apelgent, quei ke milz aiment. (p. 9)

(I shall name myself with pleasure. My name is Adgar, but I know another one. Most people call me William, and they may do so without blame, for by that name I was christened, and afterwards baptized Adgar. Therefore it seems to be right that I have made no mistake in my names nor have those who call me William. Now let people call me what they like best.)

Adgar's work exists in two states. The older and fuller was translated for a young man he calls Gregory, who has not been traced. The dedication appears before the epilogue. Gregory was presumably of good birth, and either knew no Latin or very little. The author calls him his friend, but describes himself as 'vostre clerc'.

> Cil ke comencier le me fist,
> E par ki jol faz en avant,
> Mult est curteis, preuz e vaillant,
> Bels bacheler e enseignie,
> De franchise forment preisie. . . .
> Ceo est mis chiers amis, Gregorie. (p. 58)

---

[1] Ed. C. Neuhaus (Altfranzösische Bibliothek, Heilbronn, 1886), and J. H. Herbert, *Romania*, xxxii (1903), pp. 394–421.

(He who made me begin it, and through whom I continue it, is very courteous, worthy and valiant, a fine and well-brought-up bachelor, much prized for his nobility. . . . It is my dear friend, Gregory.)

The use of the word 'bachelor' does not necessarily imply that Gregory was a layman. He may have been a well-born youth given ecclesiastical preferment without much book-learning. The word was used for a junior minister in a church, and Adgar uses it about Anselm the younger.

(Quidam juvenis nomine Anselmus.)

> En l'iglise out un bacheler,
> Ansealme out nun, prouz e ber;
> De bon cuer e de bon purpens
> Servi la mere Deu tuz tens. . . .
> E quant li juvencels le vit   (praefatus juvenis)
> El cuer out grant joie e delit.   (p. 18)

(In the church there was a bachelor, Anselm was his name, worthy and noble; with a pure heart and a good intention he served God's mother unceasingly. . . . And when the youth saw it, he had great joy and delight in his heart.)

It is significant, and an indication that this young man's name was really Gregory, that in one manuscript the Legends are followed by a Life of St. Gregory.

So popular did Adgar's translation become that a second and shorter version was prepared, called 'Gracial', and dedicated to ladies devoted to God's service, in the first place to the Lady Maud. As Ezio Levi deduced, this is probably the Maud, one of Henry II's natural daughters, who was abbess of Barking *c.* 1175–95.

In his prologue Adgar informs us that he found his source in the bookcase at St. Paul's, and speaks rather fulsomely of the canons there:

> S'il enquerent de l'essamplarie,
> Jo l'ai de Saint Pol de l'almarie,
> De Saint Pol, de la noble iglise,
> Ki en Lundres est bien asise.
> Tele n'ad en crestienté;
> Li clerc i sunt mut renumé.
> De clergie ne sai lur pers,
> Si sunt chanuines seculers,
> E Deu lur duint sun paraïs!   (p. 9)

(If they ask about the exemplar, I have it from the cupboard of
St. Paul's, at St. Paul's the noble church which is situated in London.
There is not another such in Christendom; the clerks there are very
renowned. I do not know their equals for learning. They are secular
canons, may God grant them his paradise!)

He repeats this at the end; and gives the name of the donor
of the book:

> Cest escrit fine, Deu merci!
> Selunc le livre Mestre Albri,
> Ke de Saint Pol oi de l'almarie. . . .
> Pur iceo ke jo començai
> Selunc le livre ke ore numai,
> Dunt Mestre Albri en est garant,
> Ki divins esteit mult vaillant,
> Selunc sun livre voil finer,
> E le surplus larai ester.   (p. 237)

(I bring to an end this writing, thanks be to God! according to the
book of Master Alberic, which I had from the cupboard of St. Paul's.
. . . Because I began it according to the book, which I then named,
of which Master Alberic is surety, who was a very worthy divine, I
desire to end according to his book, and leave the rest alone.)

For once a medieval writer seems to have been speaking the
truth about his source. Master Alberic, who is here spoken
of in the past tense, was a canon of St. Paul's who appears as
a witness to documents dated 1162 and about 1160.[1] The
book which he gave or left to St. Paul's library was, according to Professor Southern,[2] a combination of the forty legends
collected by the younger Anselm, who became abbot of Bury
in 1120, with fourteen by Prior Dominic of Evesham and
the fifty-five collected by William of Malmesbury about
1125. Both Anselm and Bury figure in the Miracles. Professor Southern raised the question whether Adgar is to be
identified with Algar the priest who with Alberic witnessed
the document no. 217 mentioned above. But Algar is a
Norse name and Adgar, a form of Edgar, is English.[3] It
seems unlikely that the misreading, for such it would be,

[1] M. Gibbs, *Early Charters of St. Paul's Cathedral* (Camden Society, 3rd Series,
lviii, 1939), nos. 217 and 245.

[2] Loc. cit., pp. 211–12, and *Mediaeval and Renaissance Studies*, iv (1958),
pp. 176–216.

[3] My colleagues Professor McIntosh and Dr. Schramm assure me that the two
are quite distinct.

should occur in all the manuscripts. But as Adgar tells us that he was generally known as William, he may have been the William who was chaplain and perpetual vicar of St. Mary Magdalene, Bread Street, between 1162 and 1200.[1] It seems likely that he held a St. Paul's living, but was not a canon, which would account for his flattery of the Cathedral Chapter.

Adgar writes agreeably in octosyllabic couplets. His material consists of a succession of short stories which hardly have time to become wearisome, however treated. The legends became popular towards the end of the twelfth century, and, as Professor Southern points out, mark a new departure, for they are the first legends of saints not connected with relics. Adgar's is the first French translation, being earlier than the famous one by Gautier de Coincy which formed the basis of the still later dramatized version. A fresh translation into Anglo-Norman of sixty of the miracles was made in the early thirteenth century, and Adgar's were modernized by Everard de Gateley, a monk of Bury, Anselm's old abbey, in the same century, but only the prologue and three of these survive.[2] Adgar's first version was probably written about 1165–70, his second 1175–80. All the manuscripts are Anglo-Norman, and there is no evidence that his work was known on the Continent or that Gautier de Coincy owed anything to it, though this would be difficult to disprove. The 'Gregory' version survives in an early thirteenth-century manuscript (B.M. Egerton 612), the 'Gracial' in one early thirteenth-century manuscript (B.M. Add. 38664) and a mid-century fragment (Dulwich, Alleyne College 13).

Adgar is no slavish translator, and occasionally indulges in a more picturesque style than his original. Thus he renders the dry statement 'Angliam autem subjectam Normannis' by

> Li reis amat mult ses Normanz;
> Les Engleis enveia as chans.   (136–7)

(The king [William I] loved his Normans much and sent the English packing.)

[1] M. Gibbs, op. cit., nos. 215, 217, 251.
[2] H. Kjellman, *La Deuxième Collection anglo-normande des Miracles de la Ste Vierge* (Paris, 1922).

These lines are sometimes quoted as evidence for the state of affairs after the Conquest. All they do is to reflect the view of it popularly held a century later, and they are worthless for any other purpose.

THE WORKS OF THE TEMPLAR OF TEMPLE BRUER

There are two writers less directly connected with the intellectual movement of the period, but who reflect the new interest in material derived from the East.

The earlier of these is the templar who wrote a series of texts for his community at Temple Bruer; the *Vitas Patrum*, as he called it, a separate *Thaïs*, a poem on Antichrist and a version of St. Paul's Descent into Hell.[1] He can no longer be identified with Henri d'Arci and must join the ranks of anonymous writers. By a curious slip in which he has been followed by everyone else,[2] Paul Meyer misread as a nominative a vocative followed by a dative. It was Miss R. J. Dean who hit upon the truth. Here is the passage again, that there may be no mistake about it:

> Henri d'Arci, frere del Temple Salemun,
> Pur amur Deu vus ai fet cest sermun.
> A vus le present e as freres de la maisun.
> Ne quer loer de vus, si bone volente nun,
> Mes ore larrai l'escrire, par le vostre congié.
>
> E si ceste translaciun vus vient rien en gré,
> Prest sui en autres choses a vostre volenté.

$$(V.P.\ 6919\text{--}23,\ 6937\text{--}8)$$

(Henri d'Arci, Brother of Solomon's Temple, for the love of God I have made you this sermon. I offer it to you and to the brethren of the house. I do not seek reward from you, save good-will. But now, by your leave, I will leave off writing. . . . And if this translation pleases you at all, I am ready to do your will in other things.)

[1] Mr. R. C. D. Perman has an edition in preparation. Individual works have been edited or epitomized as follows: *Vitas Patrum*, B. A. O'Connor (Washington, 1949), *Thaïs* and extracts from *St. Paul*, P. Meyer (*Notices et Extraits*, xxxv), *Antichrist* by L. E. Kastner (*Modern Language Review*, i, 1906, pp. 269–82) and R. Fawtier (*Romania*, xlix, 1923, pp. 331–40), *St. Paul* by L. E. Kastner (*Revue des langues romanes*, xlviii, 1905, pp. 385–95); cf. R. C. D. Perman, 'Henri d'Arci: The Shorter Works', *Studies . . . presented to A. Ewert* (Oxford, 1961), pp. 279–321.

[2] Including the present writer, *Anglo-Norman in the Cloisters*, p. 55.

Althought it is a pity to have to say good-bye to a named author, this new interpretation clears up a difficulty in dating the texts. Henri d'Arci was a person of importance between the years 1161 and 1174. Now Kastner believed that the linguistic evidence was against the poems being dated earlier than c. 1230, and in this he is followed by Mr. O'Connor. The linguistic features he lists, however, can all be found in late twelfth-century texts—the rhymes of the infinitives er : eir in Thomas and Denis Pyramus; ue (Lat. o) : e (Lat. a) in the latter; el (-alem) : el (el) in Thomas;[1] ai : ei final in Simund de Freine. Now since it is obvious that the author was a younger, perhaps a much younger, man than the respected Henri d'Arci, nothing stands in the way of dating the texts some time after 1170.

This templar was one of the most didactic and austere of all Anglo-Norman writers. Having in mind a male public of dedicated laity, he was under no obligation to make his work attractive or even palatable. The *Vitas Patrum* was usually translated into prose,[2] a better medium; however, in his defence it must be said that he writes with vigour and fluency. The Egyptian tales were no doubt thought suitable fare for templars, and it can be deduced that his translation proved so acceptable that he was encouraged to continue writing.[3]

The versification has probably suffered in transmission. One manuscript (B.N. fr. 24862) contains all four works, one other the *Vitas Patrum* and *Thaïs* (B.M. Harley 2253), two others *Antichrist* (B.M. Royal 8. E. xvii, Rylands French 6). All four are Anglo-Norman, and none is probably earlier than mid-thirteenth century. This writer may have been unknown outside England, but there he became popular outside the immediate circle for which he wrote.

THE WORKS OF CHARDRI

At the close of the century comes another writer who exploited material which derived from the East. He gives his name, Chardri, in two of his three poems, but tells us nothing

---

[1] Cf. M. K. Pope, *From Latin to Modern French* (Manchester University Press), par. 1146, 1156, 1326, 1157.

[2] P. Meyer, *Histoire littéraire de la France*, xxxiii (1906), pp. 254–327.

[3] *The Descent of St. Paul* was later reworked in octosyllables; cf. Perman, loc. cit., and D. D. R. Owen in *Romance Philology*, xii (1958), p. 39.

else about himself. Only a clerk could have produced these works, but he does not call himself Master, and no trace of a Chardri has been found in any records. The editor of his poems suggested that he wrote soon after 1200.[1] There is nothing about the language or versification which is inconsistent with this date, and as one of the manuscripts contains a chronicle which breaks off in 1216, a reasonable assumption is that this copy was made soon after that year. A passage in the *Petit Plet* praising the English and contrasting them with the French is, Koch believed, written from the point of view of a Norman domiciled in England, and probably written soon after the loss of Normandy by John in 1203. It may be added that, for reasons which will presently appear, none of these works is likely to have been composed after 1214.

Josaphaz has the following ending to the epilogue:

> Prium tuz l'omnipotent
> Ki guverne eir e mer e vent,
> Ke par la sue seinte pite
> Nus doinst itele volente
> E le poeir ke par sa grace
> Chescun de nus si ben le face,
> Ke pae en seit nostre seinnur
> E nus sauvez a chef de tur.
> Amen, amen, chescun en die!
> Ici finist la bone vie
> De Josaphaz, le duz enfant.
> A ceus ki furent escutent
> Mande Chardri saluz sanz fin,
> E au vespre e au matin. Amen.   (2941–54)

(Let us all pray to the Almighty who rules the air, the sea, and the wind, that by his holy pity he may give us the will and the power that each one of us, by his grace, may do well so that our Lord will be pleased and ourselves saved at the end, Amen, amen, let each one say! Here ends the good life of Josaphat, that sweet child. To those who were listening Chardri sends greetings without end, both in the evening and the morning. Amen.)

The *Set Dormanz* ends with a hope that his hearers will

---

[1] J. Koch, *Chardrys Josaphaz, Set Dormanz und Petit Plet* (Heilbronn, 1879), pp. xlvi–xlvii.

resist the Devil, with God's help, and keep true, and the last few lines again give the author's name:

> Ici finist Chardri sun cunte
> E dit: Doinst Deus a tricherie
> Petit honur e curte vie,
> E a tuz ceus ki l'amerunt
> E ki pur ceo me blasmerunt.
> Amen, amen dites en haut
> E jeol cunferm, se Deu me saut!   (1892–8)

(Here Chardri ends his tale, and says: May God give treachery small honour and a short life, and the same to those who love it and will therefore find fault with me. Amen, amen say aloud, and I will ratify it, if God save me!)

The third text, *Le Petit Plet* (*The Minor Dialogue*) is anonymous, but from internal evidence appears to be almost certainly by the same author as the other two.

The editor, following the manuscripts, prints the texts in what is probably the chronological order. The first is an abridged translation, the second a translation with more original treatment, and the third contains much more free composition with traces of the lyricism so often characteristic of Anglo-Norman writers.

The first text, *Josaphaz*, tells a story which became suddenly popular in the French-speaking world soon after 1200. It is a christianized version of the life of Buddha—*Josaphaz* being a corruption of 'Bhodisat.' The Christian legend was translated from Greek into Latin, and thence into vernacular languages. First in the field was French. The history of the legend has been magnificently studied by Jean Sonet in *Le Roman de Barlaam et Josaphat*.[1] Several of the French versions appeared about the same time, the 'Champenoise' before 1229, Gui de Cambrai's between 1209 and 1220, the prose gloss of Mount Athos perhaps a little earlier, and Chardri's. It is impossible to decide which came first, but of the verse translations Chardri's is probably the earliest. It is the only one which does not have Barlaam's name in the title, and is much the simplest. It differs from the others not only through the absence of any embellishments, except for

---

[1] Louvain, *Recueil de travaux d'histoire et de philologie*, 3rd series, 33rd fasc., and Namur, *Bibliothèque de la Faculté de philosophie et lettres*, fasc. 6, 1949.

a few very short reflexions, but through the pruning away of the digressions, sermons, and even the parables which may be regarded as one of the attractions of the full text. It forms, in Chardri's view, an 'exemplum', and the parables are in consequence irrelevant to his purpose. It is remarkable that M. Sonet, after studying so many texts in so many different languages, and regretting as he does the loss of the parables, can yet say of Chardri's: 'Cette composition est sans conteste une des plus intéressantes que le moyen âge nous ait laissée sur le sujet. Les auditeurs de Chardry auront certainement goûté autant de plaisir à l'écouter que nous en avons eu à la lire.'[1]

The *Set Dormanz*, which accompanies *Josaphaz*, is, strangely enough, the only treatment of the well-known story of the Seven Sleepers of Ephesus in Old French—or, at any rate, the only one which has survived. It was, however, translated several times into Old and Middle English. Chardri's exact source has not been discovered. His rendering is sometimes in accord with Gregory of Tours, sometimes with Simeon Metaphrastes, and sometimes with the Golden Legend—which was compiled later.[2] He begins with a prologue on the power of God. People have ceased to wonder at changes in the weather and other manifestations of it. It is therefore wise to contemplate one of Christ's miracles. As *Josaphaz* had been an *exemplum*, *Les Set Dormanz* is a fable. Together they form part of a sermon on the religious life, the *exemplum* and the *fabula ad idem*. The *exemplum* belongs to the class of heroic literature in which Grocheo included saints' lives and *chansons de geste*.

> . . . la folie
> Amum tant de ceste vie
> Ke plus tost orrium chanter
> De Rolant u d'Oliver;
> E les batailles des duze pers
> Orrium mut plus volenters
> Ke ne frium, si cum jeo quit,
> La passiun de Jhesu Crist.   (2931–8)

[1] Op. cit., p. 156.
[2] A. Reinbrecht, *Die Legende von der Sieben Schläfern und der A.-N. Dichter Chardri* (Göttingen, 1880). Cf. H. Varnhagen, *Zeitschrift für romanische Philologie*, v (1881), pp. 162–5.

(We love the foolishness of this life so much that we would rather hear a song about Roland and Oliver [than about Josaphat]; and we would much rather listen to the battles of the Twelve Peers than we would, as I believe, to the passion of Jesus Christ.)

Les Set Dormanz, on the other hand, belongs to romance:

> Ne voil pas en fables d'Ovide,
> Seinnurs, mettre mun estuide,
> Ne ja, sachez, ne parlerum
> Ne de Tristram ne de Galerun;
> Ne de Renart ne de Hersente
> Ne voil pas mettre m'entente;
> Mes voil de Deu e sa vertu
> Ki est pussant e tuz jurs fu
> E de ses seinz, les Set Dormanz.   (51–59)

(I do not wish to apply my study, lords, to the fables of Ovid, nor now, know it well, shall we speak of Tristram or Galeron; I will not turn my attention to Renart and Hersent, but I will to God and his power, who is and always was powerful, and to his saints the Seven Sleepers).

The introduction of the word 'fable' is significant. It was sometimes used to describe a short tale of a romantic kind, sometimes it was almost equivalent to *fabliau*, and it was also used to distinguish what we now call romance from epic.[1] What Chardri is doing in these two passages is to offer a Christian substitute for the worldly examples of all the narrative genres of the day.

The third work, *Le Petit Plet*, is the most attractive. The opening is wholly delightful:

> Beaus duz seinnurs, pur vus dedure
> Vus cunterai une enveisure
> D'un veillart e d'un enfant.   (1–3)

(Fair sweet lords, to amuse you I am going to tell you a joke about an old man and a youth.)

A youth, who was feeling melancholy for some reason, took a walk through an orchard to cheer himself up.

> Par le verger, ça e la,
> Icest vaslet itant ala
> K'il choici une funtaine
> Dunt l'ewe esteit e clere e seine,

---

[1] Cf. P. Nykrog, *Les Fabliaux* (Copenhagen, 1957), pp. 5–7.

La surce esteit e nette e bele
Ki roulout cele gravele,
Si fu la noise duce e sutive,
Si resemblout ben chose vive.
Trestut entur fu l'erbe drue,
Estencelee de flur menue,
E si esteint li arbre haut
Ke ja si grant en fust li chaut
Ke nul en fust gueres grevé
Ja si chaut ne fust l'esté.
Les oiseaus de meinte manere
S'acosteient a la rivere,
Pur la verdur e pur la flur
Mut chanteient a grant duçur.
Li vaslet de ceo mut s'esjoï,
E del duz chant ke il oï,
E mut li heita plus le liu
Ke meint riche hume sun riche fiu.   (55–76)

(Through the orchard, here and there, our squire went on until he caught sight of a fountain whose water was clean and wholesome. The spring was both clear and beautiful as it purled on the gravel, and the sound of it was sweet and soft. It might have been a thing alive. All around the grass was thick, and sparkling with tiny flowers. The trees were so high that no one, however great the heat, would be troubled by it, let the summer be never so hot. Many kinds of birds flocked to the stream, attracted by the greenness and the flowers. They sang much with great sweetness. The youth was greatly rejoiced at this and at the sweet song that he heard, and the place delighted him much more than his rich fief delights many a rich man.)

In this enchanting spot he is joined by an old man leaning on a stick, who also is sunk in melancholy, but is not, like the youth, cheered by contemplating nature. There follows a long disputation (regardless of the title) between the two. The beginning is based upon Cato's *Distichs*, but from line 313 Chardri makes use of the dialogue *De Remediis Fortuitorum* ascribed by medieval scholars and others, including the Teubner editor, F. Haase, to Seneca.[1] Chardri may have been working from a glossed copy, but some of the development is certainly his own. It is amusing to note that whereas

---

[1] Cf. ed., p. xviii; A. Mussafia, *Zeitschrift für romanische Philologie*, iii (1879), pp. 591–607, and F. Haase, *Senecae Opera* (Leipzig, 1853), III. xvi–xx.

Seneca's dialogist, in his recital of calamities, progresses from the loss of a friend to that of a wife, the medieval clerk proceeds from the loss of a 'leale amie' to that of a 'bon ami', his climax. The loss of the 'amie' enables the youth to embark upon the usual attack on women, which accords not too well with the rest of his argument. It also enables him to assert that the women as well as the knights of England are superior to those of France. Everywhere the moon shines, and even in France a few good women are to be found:

> 'Mes de cele en est flurie
> Engleterre cum bele praerie.
> Tuz les reaumes k'ore sunt
> Passe Engleterre, e savez dunt?
> De tuz deduz e de franchise,
> Se femmes i sunt de bele aprise,
> Ne devez pas esmerviller,
> Se sunt asez li chevaler,
> E tuz li autre ki sunt aprés
> Sunt pruz, gentiz e francs adés,
> (Fors sul itant ke beverie
> Empire mut lur bele vie).
> Mes tu as or perdu ta drue—
> Ben est chose aparceue—
> E vus l'avez de mut preisee,
> Leale fu, bele e enveisee.
> Or sai jeo ben par vostre dit
> Ke vus l'amiez de grant afit.
> Pur ceo dist li Engleis trop ben:
> "Tant cum l'amez, luez tun chen
> E ta femme e tun cheval."
> Kek'il eit, u ben u mal,
> Amur prise e met en haut
> Chescune ren plus k'ele ne vaut.'   (1261–84)

('But with it England is as beflowered as a fair meadow. England surpasses all the kingdoms there are, and do you know how? In all pleasures and in nobility. If the women there are well brought up you should not wonder, for so are the knights, and all the others that follow after are valiant, courteous, and noble besides (save in just this, the great harm that drink does to their fair life). But you have now lost your companion—as is well seen—and you have prized her much. She was loyal and beautiful and gay. Now I know well by what you say that you loved her with great affection. Wherefore the Englishman says very well: "As much as you love it, praise your dog, and your wife, and your horse." Whatever there is, good or bad, love esteems and rates more highly, everything more than it is worth.')

In the following section the youth explains that even if the old man had the wisdom of Solomon, he might still be deceived by his friends.

> 'Cil vus eiment e pres e loin,
> Mes il vus faudrunt au grant busoin.
> Ceo est l'amisté de main en main:
> "Tant as — tant vaus — e tant vus eim." ' (1639–42)

('These love you near and far, but they will fail you in your ultimate need. This is the friendship of cupboard love—"As much as you have, so much are you worth, and so much regard I have for you." ')

Here Chardri is quoting a famous proverb, with its untranslatable pun on *aestimare* and *amare*, which has always been attached to the story of Lear and his daughters.[1]

The work ends with a few notes of Christian exhortation by the youth, who is allowed the last word in the argument. Flowers are always in the background of his treatise:

> 'Cunfortez vus ben, si seez lé,
> Tant cum vus avra Deu destiné,
> Si cum fet iceste flur
> Ke ben veez ici entur.
> Ceo semble ke tute praerie,
> Ki pert ore si ben flurie,
> U k'ele eit joie mut parfite,
> U en sa manere se delite.'   (1757–64)

('Take comfort, and be joyful with whatever God has destined for you, as does this flower which you see here round about. It seems that every meadow, which now appears so well beflowered, either has the most perfect joy, or is rejoicing in its own way.')

The old man is to ask Mary's Son to look after his life, to bring him to a good end, and to go to join him by the right way:

> 'E vus e nus, e tut li vif
> Ki avrunt oï icest estrif.

---

[1] Cf. J. Orr, *Words and Sounds* (Oxford, 1953), pp. 114, 115, 138, 145. There are many more examples. Chardri gives the common Anglo-Norman form. I cannot agree that Wace improved upon Geoffrey of Monmouth here. To my mind Geoffrey was translating a well-known French proverb, which Wace and other early translators put back into the original tongue.

> Amen, amen, chescun die!
> Ore nus ait Seinte Marie! Amen.   (1777–80)

('Both you and us, and all those living who will have been listening to this debate: Amen, amen, let each one say! Now may St. Mary help us!')

When Chardri's works were first printed, it was said of them:[1] 'Le Petit Plet est un des morceaux les plus intéressants et les plus originaux de la littérature morale du moyen âge: l'auteur y combat directement, avec un bon sens relevé de gaieté, les sombres idées de l'ascétisme.' It is a reaction against the extreme asceticism of the twelfth century and is as yet untouched by the desire to instruct of the thirteenth. In this minor work Chardri exhibits some of the characteristics now of the later Montaigne, now of Villon, and now of Rabelais. Yet it must not be forgotten that there is more than a suspicion of irony. How seriously is it all to be taken? The Stoicism of Seneca has become a sort of Epicureanism, and the typical medieval setting has been reversed. This is the only moral dialogue in which youth is allowed to be the determiner and old age the vanquished opponent. It is called a joke, and perhaps one should beware of taking it too seriously.

The three works of Chardri are to be found together in two Anglo-Norman manuscripts, one of the early (Cotton Caligula A. ix) and the other of the mid thirteenth century (Oxford, Jesus College, 29). A third (Vatican Reg. 1659) contains the Petit Plet only, and belongs to the fourteenth century. It is quite likely that medieval people, like ourselves, preferred this work to the others. There is no evidence that this excellent writer was known on the Continent.

Chardri employs the octosyllabic couplet. Some lines are a syllable short. There is usually a caesura and anacrusis is allowed after it.

The author's hearers are addressed as 'seinnurs', and once as 'beaus duz seinnirs'. It is possible that this apostrophe had already become reduced to the level of 'Ladies and gentlemen'. Somehow Chardri does not strike one as an aristocratic writer with the nobility in mind. In his attacks on

---

[1] 'Chronique', Romania, ix (1880), p. 171.

simony and riches, and his reference to people below the rank of knights, he seems to be addressing a wider public than the earlier writers we have been considering. It is a pity that his works are not available in a more modern, attractive, and accessible form than Koch's ancient and blinding edition. Chardri is a skilful and agreeable narrator. He can be brief without being dry. It is to his credit that *Josaphaz* is 2,954, *Les Set dormanz* 1,898, and *Le Petit Plet* only 1,780 lines long. If *Le Petit Plet* is by common consent the best of his poems, its probable later popularity is in part due to the swing of interest away from narrative to moralization in the thirteenth century. Chardri, however, was a true poet, and it was here that he had the most opportunities to display his skill. He has the merit of being one of the few medieval poets who could describe a garden which owes more to nature than to Claudian. There is much to be learnt from the study of his works. It is a good thing to be reminded that there was nothing incongruous in naming Tristram and Renard in the same breath.

ROAU D'ARUNDEL'S 'LETTER OF PRESTER JOHN'

The fictitious Letter of Prester John to the Emperor Manuel of Constantinople, who died in 1180, began to circulate in the West in a Latin prose version shortly before this date. From about the middle of the thirteenth century onwards translations were made into French and Provençal prose. Only one French verse translation was made, and that is Anglo-Norman. It follows one of the Latin versions closely, but has an original prologue and epilogue.[1] The prologue is conventional, but the epilogue professes to describe the circumstances in which the translation was made. A certain Dan Gilbert le Butelier accompanied his lord, William de Ver, to the Holy Land. As a pilgrim he visited

---

[1] Ed. A. Hilka, 'Die anglo-normannische Versversion des Briefes des Presbyters Johannes', *Zeitschrift für französische Sprache und Literatur*, xliii (1915), pp. 82–112; cf. Ch.-V. Langlois, *La Vie en France au moyen âge*, iii (Paris, 1927), especially pp. 53–56; for a second manuscript see A. Gwynn, 'Some Unpublished Texts of the Black Book of Christ Church, Dublin', *Analecta Hibernica* (Dublin Stationery Office, 1946), pp. 283–337. My thanks are due to Professor Jocelyn Otway-Ruthven for further information about it. Professor E. J. Arnould has an article on it in contemplation.

Bethlehem and Jerusalem. William remained some time in
the country and was pressed to stay by the king, patriarch,
and bishops. But just as the nightingale, however young it
may be caught and however it be cherished, will always long
for the greenwood and escape thither if it can,[1] so did William
long to return to his native England, to his family and
friends. He and Gilbert returned by way of Constantinople,
where Gilbert was one of the first to obtain the Latin text of
the letter.

> Danz Guillebers fi[s]t translater
> Icest rumanz e [tut] rimer
> Par requeste e par [grant] amur
> Enz en l'ostel [de] sun seignur
> Qui[l] translata, Roau [out] nun
> Ki d'Arundel aveit surnun.
> La resun est ici finie:
> Ki plus en set, plus [vus] en die.   (1179–86)

(Dan Gilbert had this Romance version translated and rhymed
throughout by request and for great love within the household of his
lord. He who translated it had Roau as his name and was known as of
Arundel. The argument is here finished: let him who knows more of
it, tell you more of it.)

This seems clear enough, but no one has ever been able to
trace this William de Ver, or Gilbert le Butelier and Roau
d'Arundel. If any reliance can be placed on this account, it
might refer to the Crusade of Richard Cœur de Lion, from
which that king returned in 1192, having concluded a treaty
by which the Holy Places were reopened to pilgrims. If, as
seems likely, it is meant that William was welcomed by the
same king at his home-coming, the translation must have
been made before Richard's death in 1199. It would thus
have been made about twenty years after the Latin text
became known, and half a century before any other French
version. This is possible, but there is an alternative interpretation of the epilogue. William is said to have been of
high degree, which sounds plausible enough, but there follow

---

[1] The caged-bird simile goes back to Boethius, *De Consolatione*, Bk. III, metre 2.
Cf. S. de Freine, *Roman de Philosophie*, 1179–86, 1197–8, and Jean de Meung, *Roman
de la Rose*, 13941–58. The identification with the nightingale is Roau d'Arundel's
idea and is derived from the courtly lyric tradition.

two lines which M. Langlois neither mentioned nor translated in his book:

> Haut hom(e) est il, mes neporquant
> Empereür pot estre (uncore) avant.   (1167–8)

(He is a man of high rank, but nevertheless he may yet be Emperor in the future.)

This may be just absurd exaggeration, or it may indicate a lacuna in the text. Supposing the allusion is not to William de Ver, but to Henry III's brother, Richard of Cornwall. Richard's pacifying expedition to the Holy Land took place in 1240–2, and in 1257 he was elected King of the Romans. No William de Ver is recorded amongst his household by Dr. Noel Denholm-Young.[1] The date 1257 would bring the Anglo-Norman text into line with the other French versions, but it would destroy Gilbert's claim to have been one of the first to obtain a Latin copy of the letter.

Matters have been further complicated by the discovery of the second manuscript. That published by Hilka (Cheltenham 4156, temporarily inaccessible) belongs to the second half of the thirteenth century, but is probably older than the other (Black Book of Christ Church, Dublin), which was written between 1279 and 1294. The scribe had added a few lines of doggerel asking for prayers for the translator, whom he calls Johan de Arundel, and for himself, Geffrey. The epilogue of the other manuscript is here replaced by the following:

> Bien eit ke ceus vers translata
> E ki l'escrit et ki lirra.
> Kil translata Johan out anum
> Ke de Arundel ad le surnun.
> A Waltham a la sainte croyz
> Ke il le translatat par grant deduz.
> Le raisun est ici finie:
> Ki plus en set plus vus en die.

(Good befall him who translated these lines, and him who wrote it and him who will read. He who translated had the name John, who is known as of Arundel, at Waltham at Holy Cross, where he translated it with great pleasure. The argument is here finished: let him who knows more of it, tell you more of it.)

---

[1] *Richard of Cornwall* (Oxford, 1947).

The volume in which this text occurs was carried to Dublin by Henry la Warr, a Black Canon of Bristol, when he moved to Christ Church in the winter of 1300–1. Waltham Holy Cross was an Augustinian house, and other texts in the book have an Augustinian connexion. Geffrey may have been a canon of Waltham who altered the epilogue to reflect glory upon his abbey.

This text would be of greater interest than it is if the epilogue could be clarified and the facts it professes to give substantiated. A critical edition is much to be desired now a second manuscript is available. Roau is no stylist and adds little to his original. The wonders described in the latter would appeal to the same kind of person as rejoiced in the marvels of the Romance of Alexander, which have ceased to attract attention save as literary curiosities. It is important to remember that the East, here disguised as Africa, exerted a fascination over men's minds in the Middle Ages, as before and since.

MARIE DE FRANCE—*ST. PATRICK'S PURGATORY*

It is generally supposed that the *Espurgatoire S. Patrice*[1] is the latest of the known works of Marie de France. Support to this view is given by the fact that it does not belong to courtly literature and seems to have formed part of a new movement. It probably belongs to the end of the twelfth century, but it has something in common with the works to be considered in the next chapter. Here Marie de France, like Simund de Freine but unlike Chardri, is making use of a text which exhorts the hearers to penitence and was later retranslated several times for that reason. Her audience is the colourless group known as 'seignurs', but she states that she writes to help 'la simple gent' (line 46), a strange claim indeed for Marie de France! Her epilogue shows that she is addressing a wider public than in the old days when her patrons were kings and counts:

> Jo, Marie, ai mis en memoire
> Le Livre de l'Espurgatoire
> En Romanz, qu'il seit entendables
> A laie gent e covenables.

[1] Ed. K. Warnke, Bibliotheca Romanica, ix (Halle-an-der-Saale, 1938).

Or preium Deu que par sa grace
De noz pechiez mundes nus face! Amen.

(2297–302)

(I, Marie, have committed to writing the Book of the Purgatory
in Romance, so that it may be intelligible and suitable for lay folk.
Now let us pray God that by his grace he may purify us of our sins.
Amen.)

IX

THE INTERDICT AND THE FOURTH
LATERAN COUNCIL

SOON after the beginning of the thirteenth century an event occurred in Christendom which had a far-reaching effect on vernacular literature in England. This was the Fourth Lateran Council, summoned by Innocent III in 1215. Both French and English bishops[1] published statutes embodying the decrees of the Council, but the need for reform may have been felt more strongly in England, as a result of the suspension of Archbishop Stephen Langton and the recent Interdict. The Lateran Council of 1215 was followed by the important Council of Oxford in 1222.

The effect on Anglo-Norman literature was to produce a remarkable series of manuals, treatises, and encyclopedias of religious knowledge destined for the laity, or for the parish clergy who were to prepare them for confession as demanded by the clause *Utriusque sexus* of the Lateran decrees. They were also found useful in religious houses, both for monks and nuns. All sorts of people wrote these books, from an archbishop and an earl to a chaplain and a friar. Apart from the specialized works, the whole of religious and didactic literature was affected. This is why it seems unlikely that Chardri could have been writing after 1215, since his poems are entirely free from this new trend. The French were slower to act. The *Somme le Roi*, which ultimately had much influence on Middle English literature, and a work called *Miroir*, are about all Old French has to show on the Continent, and they appeared when most of the Anglo-Norman works of the kind had been written.[2]

---

[1] C. R. Cheney, *English Synodalia* (London, 1941), pp. 46–47.
[2] Ch.-V. Langlois, *La Vie en France au moyen âge*, iv (Paris, 1928), pp. 127–38.

GUILLAUME LE CLERC'S *BESTIAIRE DIVIN*

In the course of the following pages mention will be made of one writer, proud of his Norman birth and French allegiance, who lived in England and wrote for English patrons, and therefore belongs to Anglo-Norman literature rather than to French. He is known, from the descriptions he gives of himself, as Guillaume le Clerc de Normandie. The case of this man affords additional proof of the difference between England and France in their demands upon clerkly writers at the beginning of the thirteenth century. He was writing for the English market, and stands apart from his own countrymen.

The earliest work of this writer which can be dated, the *Bestiaire divin*,[1] was written under the shock of the Interdict. He was engaged upon the section on the Turtledove, he tells us, in its second or third year (some scribes have II and some III), that is, in 1210 or 1211 (lines 2707–36). In the prologue, no doubt written later, Guillaume explains that he is translating a good work on a good matter in the time of Philip of France, which was also a time of great misfortune, for England lay under an Interdict, so that no mass was said, and no body buried in consecrated ground. Having said so much, he will leave this dangerous subject. He dares not say what he thinks about treachery in 'the one and the other court', but will turn to a higher matter, the natures of the various beasts. Guillaume's main source is Hugh of St. Victor, but he may perhaps have been acquainted with the Bestiary of Philippe de Thaon, for in the epilogue he etymologizes the name of his patron Ralph, or rather Radulphus, as Philippe, years before, had etymologized the name of Queen Adeliza. This may, however, easily be mere coincidence. Ralph is too common a name for this patron to be identifiable, but since Guillaume seems to have lived in the diocese of Coventry and Lichfield, it may be asked whether he was not Ralph of Maidstone, the distinguished scholar consecrated Bishop of Hereford in 1234, who by 1215 was Treasurer of Lichfield.

Guillaume was a clerk and, if what he tells us in his

[1] Ed. R. Reinsch (Leipzig, 1890).

Besant Dieu, to be mentioned later in this chapter, is to be believed, one who had to support a wife and family by his pen. He could not, therefore, afford to neglect the tastes of his patrons, even though the loss of Normandy by the English crown in 1204 made him a French subject and aggressively aware of the fact. The other writer who refers to the Interdict was a man of quite another category.

ANGIER

Angier, canon of St. Frideswide's at Oxford, may have been obliged by the Interdict to mark time in his advance to higher orders. He seems to imply that leisure was forced upon him, and that this was why he had the time not only to translate the *Dialogues* of Gregory into French verse, but subsequently to make a fair copy (B.N. fr. 24766) of his translation, followed after an interval by the *Life* of that saint. When he finished the *Dialogues* he was a sub-deacon and had been professed for six years. As he describes himself as old in sin and young in religion, he may not have been in his first youth when he entered the priory. He was probably ordained deacon and priest as soon as the Interdict had been lifted, since he was already a priest when the *Life* was completed. He may then have been employed to serve one of the churches appropriated to St. Frideswide's, whose canons went on serving their churches after most Austin canons had abandoned the practice, but his name does not appear in any records. All that is known about Angier is derived from the remarkably full colophons to his works, but the same difficulty in dating these arises as in the case of Guillaume's *Bestiaire*. Although Angier was his own scribe, he was no safer than a professional when it came to copying Roman figures. It seems, however, most likely that he finished the *Dialogues* in 1213 and the *Life* in 1216.[1] The reference to the Interdict is added in the margin of the first colophon, as if it was of particular moment. A holograph manuscript is apt to be unique, for, as in the early days of printing, the author's draft seems to have disappeared after being copied.

[1] Cf. M. D. Legge, 'La date des écrits de Frère Angier', *Romania*, lxxix (1958), pp. 512–14. Facsimile of the first colophon in *Romania*, xii (1883, with P. Meyer's edition of the *Life*), and in the New Palaeographical Society's album.

This happened in the case of Angier, Matthew Paris, Dan Michael of Northgate, and Orm. If a work was written for a lay patron, the holograph manuscript would be lent to friends. There is no evidence that the works of Angier and Dan Michael ever circulated outside the houses where they were written. As writers, therefore, they were uninfluential. Angier was a straightforward translator with no great pretensions as a stylist. The most interesting parts of his work are the personal passages linking the *Dialogues*.[1] In view of the interest which any text preserved in a holograph manuscript is bound to possess, it seems a pity that so little of it should have been published.

Miss Pope believed that Angier was of continental birth.[2] If this is so, he differed from Guillaume in having thrown his lot in with his adopted country. But then he was a Regular, whereas Guillaume was a Vagans, and was connected by birth or education with the south-west, whereas Guillaume was a Norman and self-conscious about it.

Both these writers employed the octosyllabic rhyming couplet. This was by now the natural form in which to cast ordinary narrative. We shall see that form is of importance in considering the nature of a work.

Angier was perhaps the last writer on a religious subject of the old order. Guillaume, however, continued to write and to keep pace with the march of events. He was as a professional author never in the van, but fell in behind the great names which will be considered next.

LA PETITE PHILOSOPHIE

The effects of the new way of looking at things can be seen in various directions. The scientific treatise on the nature of the world with which the Anglo-Norman Text Society began its series of publications, the anonymous *Petite Philosophie*,[3] which does not seem a promising vehicle for the new kind of teaching, yet contrives to convey it. It is ostensibly a popularization in octosyllabic rhyming couplets of the substance of the first book of the *De Imagine Mundi*

---

[1] Ed. T. Cloran (Strasbourg, 1901).

[2] *Étude sur la langue de Frère Angier* (Paris, 1903), *passim*; cf. A. Thomas, *Romania*, xxxiii (1904), p. 441; *Anglo-Norman in the Cloisters*, p. 61.

[3] Ed. W. H. Trethewey (A.N.T.S., i, 1939).

Libri Tres, with a little additional matter. Parts of it, as might be expected from its date, have been heavily influenced by the current popularity of the *Elucidarium* of Honorius Augustodunensis. In this the unknown author resembles Peter of Peckham, who will be mentioned later in this chapter. For some of the additional passages no source has been traced. This is true of the longest of these, lines 2031–2242, which is the one which contains the most up-to-date ideas. The soul cannot attain heaven, laden as it is with sin, except by the aid of repentance, confession, and absolution. Confession is again mentioned near the end, in line 2642. The editor suggests the date 1230 for the text, on the linguistic evidence, and although this cannot be relied on with any certitude, it would fit in with the sentiments expressed in the text.

The interpolated passages are those where the writer most nearly approaches eloquence. The subject of hell is always inspiring to the poet, but the wretched condition of humanity is also found by this author to have appeal, and in this he is in a tradition of respectable antiquity in French:

> Lasse, dolente creature
> Ke Deu tant eime, tant honure
> Ke nus furme en sa figure,
> E met sur tute creature!   (2201–4)

(Alas! miserable creature, whom God so loves, so honours, that He forms us in his image, and sets us above every creature!)

'Cheitifs dolenz' is used like a refrain in lines 2217–25, and all these lamentations remind one of the refrains used by Hilarius in his plays and by the author of the *Sponsus.*

Except in a few passages of this kind, the author reproduces his source in the baldest possible way. He is a wearisome pedant, anxious to convey as much information as possible, not forgetting the Greek and Latin etymologies of many of the technical terms employed. He belongs to an age which was not afraid of dullness. The text survives in no fewer than seven manuscripts, all Anglo-Norman, all late thirteenth or early fourteenth century. One is the remarkable manuscript (B.M. Add. 45103) containing the later version of the Resurrection play, which was almost certainly bequeathed to Christ Church, Canterbury, by Prior Eastry in 1331. Another (Cambridge, St. John's College I. 11) had been given to Syon Monastery by a London priest who entered it soon after its foundation in 1414. It is a characteristic fate of a text designed for the use of the laity to find its way on to the shelves of a monastic library.

ST. EDMUND'S *MERURE*

The vernacular treatises produced in Anglo-Norman and English after 1215 have been conveniently sorted into groups by Mr. Pantin.[1] His first group has as its starting-point the earliest work of this kind, originally composed in French, but translated more than once into Latin and English. This is St. Edmund's *Merure de Seinte Eglise*. The decrees of the Lateran Council found their first echo in the diocese of Salisbury, where even before the Council of Oxford Bishop Richard Poore issued constitutions based upon them.[2] Edmund of Abingdon was at that time Treasurer of Salisbury. When, in 1238, he issued his own decrees as Archbishop of Canterbury, it is not surprising to find that Poore's are often repeated word for word. The *Merure* has inevitably much in common with them. Whether Poore or St. Edmund was the initiator of all this it is impossible to say. The *Merure* was probably compiled from sermons and treatises spread over many years, precisely as we now know the *Imitatio Christi* to have been compiled.[3] Extracts from it found in manuscripts are of two kinds: treatises, apparently independent, which were probably the raw material from which it was compiled; chapters, sometimes rearranged, used as treatises on specific points.[4]

Some idea of the popularity of this text may be gained from the fact that there are extant twenty-three manuscripts of it, complete or partial, in Anglo-Norman, twenty-eight in Latin, and twelve in English. There were at one time nine

[1] W. A. Pantin, *The English Church in the Fourteenth Century* (Cambridge, 1955), chapter x, *passim*.

[2] J. Lang in M. Gibbs and J. Lang, *Bishops and Reform 1212–1272* (London, 1934), p. 117.

[3] L. M. J. Delaissé, *Le Manuscrit autographe de Thomas à Kempis* (Paris, Brussels, Antwerp, and Amsterdam, 1956); cf. *Anglo-Norman in the Cloisters*, pp. 95–96.

[4] M. D. Legge, 'Wanted—an edition of St. Edmund's *Merure*', *Modern Language Review*, liv (1959), pp. 72–74.

Anglo-Norman manuscripts in monastic libraries. Apart from translations, there are two English works based upon it. Its indirect influence is incalculable, and many of the works now to be described are inspired by it, whether directly or indirectly. While the plan is scholastic, the treatment derives from the piety and charity of the author, and this is what makes it stand out from all similar works. Edmund was

the first master who is actually recorded to have taught the new logic in the Oxford schools and the first who is known to have taken the degree of doctor of Divinity at Oxford. But he was remembered in Oxford rather on account of the ascetic saintliness of his personal character than of any permanent contribution to the progress of thought.[1]

No more need be said to explain the nature and popularity of his *Merure*.

The aim of the work is to teach people with a vocation to the religious life how to live perfectly by means of meditation and contemplation after the fashion of Hugh of St. Victor. Eleven of its thirty or so chapters are expositions of things by number, and this was the most popular part and the most influential. The form is prose, very often rhythmical and rhymed and interspersed with prayers. The address is direct, as in a sermon or a letter. It is the only one of the works mentioned here which is still in use, and though some of it is outmoded, most of it remains helpful. Here is the real St. Edmund, whose presence is still felt in the crypt of St. Peter's in the East at Oxford and the stark nave of Pontigny, where his tawdry gilt shrine insults his memory.[2]

ROBERT OF GREATHAM'S WORKS

Only a fragment survives of a poem which presumably had the same sort of plan, apparently written for a great family by a private chaplain. This is the *Corset*[3] addressed

---

[1] H. Rashdall, *The Universities of Europe in the Middle Ages*, ed. F. M. Powicke and A. B. Emden (London, 1936), iii. 239.

[2] The *Merure* was privately printed by H. W. Robbins (Lewisburg, Minnesota, 1923). A fuller and more accessible edition would be welcome; cf. M. D. Legge, loc. cit. For the latest work on St. Edmund, cf. C. H. Lawrence, *St. Edmund of Abingdon* (Oxford, 1960).

[3] Extracts by P. Meyer in *Bulletin de la Société des Anciens Textes* (1880), pp. 62 ff.,

to a certain Alain, possibly some connexion of the Montfort family, by Robert of Greatham. The surviving part covers some of the seven sacraments—marriage, the orders, penitence, confession, and extreme unction—thus betraying the nature of the whole. It may never have achieved popularity, for it would have to compete with other works whose reputation was plainly great—the *Merure* and the *Lumere as Lais*, for instance. *Miroir* was the title of Robert of Greatham's other work, also known as the *Evangiles des Domnees*. This was written for the lady he calls Aline, the wife of his patron, to wean her from addiction to songs and fables, such as *Mainet, Sansonet, Tristran*, and *Balin* (i.e. *Basin*)—curious taste in a lady, for three of these poems were *chansons de geste*. The *Miroir* is a series of verse sermons on the Sunday Gospels, with the correct commentaries and interpretations and numerous *exempla*. It survives in seven manuscripts, of which four are more or less complete, all Anglo-Norman and all of the late thirteenth or early fourteenth century, and in an English translation, the *Mirrur*, which survives in four manuscripts.[1] It looks as though this work had been able to hold its own when the other never achieved a wide circulation, but the loss or preservation of manuscripts is sometimes a matter of pure chance.

THE *MANUEL DES PÉCHÉS*

The second group is dominated by the *Manuel des Péchés*, an aid to confession. Of this, twenty-four manuscripts are extant, and eight or nine copies were once in monastic libraries. On a statistical basis of what remains the *Manuel* might seem comparable in popularity with the *Merure*, but the figures are misleading. Its influence was much slighter and it was never translated into Latin. Robert of Brunne made a translation of it into English verse in 1303, with slight adaptations, under the quaint title of *Handlyng Synne*. Only four manuscripts of this survive. In 1350 a literal translation,

---

and *Romania*, xv (1886), p. 297; edition in preparation by Mr. W. A. Sullivan. See also *Anglo-Norman in the Cloisters*, pp. 103–4.

[1] Cf. M. Y. H. Aitken, *Étude sur le Miroir ou les Evangiles des Domnees de Robert de Gretham* (Paris, 1922); H. E. Allen, 'Two Middle-English Translations from Anglo-Norman', *Modern Philology*, xiii (1916), pp. 741–5.

so literal that sometimes French words are left in it by mistake, was made in prose. In the middle of the fifteenth century the text was exploited by Peter Idle for his *Instructions to his Son*. This is a remarkable case of survival for a work which does not seem otherwise to have exercised great influence.[1]

The *Manuel* itself was probably written about 1260. Sometimes attributed to Grosseteste, on totally inadequate grounds, it may well have come from his diocese of Lincoln. Bishop Hugh of Wells enforced many of the Lateran decrees there, notably by the Articles of Inquiry for Archdeacons in 1230. The Constitutions of Grosseteste, 1237–53, are largely based on the Lateran decrees, and he assumed that the greater numbers of the churches in the diocese would possess copies of the Oxford decrees.[2] His own contribution to vernacular literature will be discussed presently. The attribution of the *Manuel* to an otherwise unknown William of Waddington or Widdington has no sure foundation; he was probably a scribe. The actual author deliberately concealed his name, and declared that he was writing to order.

The ideas, chiefly drawn from Peraldus, are recast in a form inspired by the decrees. The medium employed is the octosyllabic rhyming couplet, and the whole work is popular in tone. Its attraction lay and lies in the skilful use of *exempla*, and it is still readable for the good stories it contains. In view of Professor Arnould's monumental work on this text it would be idle to say more about it here.

PETER OF PECKHAM'S *LUMERE AS LAIS*

In 1267 there was completed at Oxford a third work which at first sight seems to have little to do with this kind of literature. This is the *Lumere* (or *Luminere*) *as Lais*, begun at Newstead in Surrey by the Canon Peter of Peckham or Fetcham who was also known as Peter of Abernon. Its title is inspired by the *Elucidarium* of Honorius, but in another work of his, *Le Secré de Secré*, the author refers to it by the

---

[1] For the translations see E. J. Arnould, *Le Manuel des Péchés* (Paris, 1940), pp. 292–355. This book is the chief work of reference on the subject. Cf. M. W. Bloomfield, *The Seven Deadly Sins* (Michigan, 1952), pp. 143, 171–3.

[2] J. Lang, op. cit., pp. 107, 114; cf. Pantin, op. cit., p. 193.

title *Livre des Creatures*. (It will be recollected that the alternative title to the *Theologia Naturalis* of Raymond Sebonde was *Liber Creaturarum*.) The *Lumere as Lais* is a dull work written with no sense of style, but it has many points of interest. It was addressed to the laity, but makes no concessions to them except in the language used. It exploits the scholastic method to the full. It was usual in these works of popularization to attempt to convey to the unlearned the substance of clerical teaching, but quite unusual to treat the lay public as though it were a class of students. The sources provide a puzzle. Peckham began by translating the *Elucidarium*, though from the beginning he supplemented it. Gradually he came to rely more and more upon the *Sentences* of Peter Lombard, almost certainly making use of a glossed version. He twisted and developed the intention of Honorius until the last three books become nothing but a treatise of the post-1215 type, based on the system of numbers—tens, dozens, and above all, naturally, sevens. This has seemed incomprehensible to M. Yves Lefèvre, who wonders why Peter ever tried to use a book which he must have known well for a purpose for which it was unsuited, and what induced him to try to reconcile the teaching of the early twelfth century with the highly-developed scholasticism of the thirteenth. He traces the history of the 'septenaria' back to Hugh of St. Victor. Much of this is irrelevant, and is due to the unfamiliarity of a scholar used to continental ways with the state of things in thir-teenth-century England—again evidence of the greater im-portance of the decrees of the Lateran Council in England.[1] Too much initiative should not be attributed to this Austin canon. The move from Newstead to Oxford, which, accord-ing to a rubric, took place before the last two books were written, may have had something to do with the change. As stated above, the work starts out as a paraphrase of the *Elucidarium*, but the writer soon supplemented this with the *Sentences* of Peter Lombard, of which he probably used a glossed version. There are also quotations from many classical and Christian writers, who are all named, in a way

---

[1] Y. Lefèvre, *L'Elucidarium et les Lucidaires* (Bibliothèque des Écoles françaises d'Athènes et de Rome 180, Paris, 1954), pp. 315-23.

which is unusual in a vernacular work. From the second Distinction of the third Book, where he begins to enumerate the different kinds of sins, followed by a list of virtues, works of mercy, commandments, articles of the faith, sacraments, joys of the spirit, and so on, the work becomes another of the type which we are considering. It must remain a puzzle why Peter ever embarked upon a translation of the *Elucidarium*, but in its English context it is no surprise that he should have wanted to write this kind of *Summa*.

The *Lumere*, like the other texts, was popular for a time. It is extant in eleven complete and two fragmentary manuscripts, and one or two may still be lurking in private libraries. They vary very much in character, ranging from a sumptuous specimen of East Anglian art (B.M. Royal 15. D. ii), with text of a size suitable for a lectern, and beautiful miniatures, bound up with an Apocalypse, to plain portions of small volumes of devotional works, with no ornamentation but rubrication, which religious carried about with them. About half a dozen copies were in monastic libraries. The two Benedictine houses at Canterbury had two copies each. The work seems never to have been translated into either Latin or English, and no trace of its influence has been detected in any other text. Yet, apart from its own popularity, its writer enjoyed a certain vogue, since he afterwards wrote the *Secré de Secré*, and was later invited by a canon of Chichester to write the *Life* of their bishop, St. Richard, for the benefit of Isabelle, Countess of Arundel.

Except for the Latin versions of St. Edmund's *Merure*, none of these works seems to have circulated on the Continent. They were produced to suit local conditions, and, quite apart from the fact that by the mid-thirteenth century there was less likelihood of Anglo-Norman works being imported into France, the need for such things was not felt there. It was not until 1279 that Lorens of Orleans, the Dominican confessor of Philip III, and prior of St. Jacques, wrote his *Somme le Roi*.

HENRY OF LANCASTER'S *SEYNTZ MEDICINES*

The numerical system did not die with the thirteenth century, and in England there are two belated works which employ it written in French in the mid and late fourteenth century. The earlier of these only came to light in recent years. *Les Seyntz Medicines*[1] is a long prose treatise written in 1352 by Henry, last Earl and first Duke of Lancaster, the father of Chaucer's Duchess Blanche and the predecessor of John of Gaunt, the first Royal Duke of Lancaster. Duke Henry was born at the beginning of the century and died of the plague, as his daughter was to do, in 1361. His will is drafted in French, the ordinary business language of the day, and still much used by the gentry and the civil service. John of Gaunt's Register was kept in that language, and it remained customary to use it for polite letter-writing for more than a century to come. At the end of his book the duke apologizes for his shortcomings:

L'une est qe jeo n'ai pas le sen de moy entremettre de haut chose; l'autre si est, si le franceis ne soit pas bon, jeo doie estre escusee, pur ceo que jeo sui engleis et n'ai pas moelt hauntee le franceis; la tierce chose est qe jeo ne sui pas bon escryvene, car unqes ne l'apris forsqe tard, de moy meismes. Si qe par ces trois chosez il me semble qe jeo puisse escuser les defautez de cest livre et moy.

(The first is that I have not sufficient wisdom to employ myself on a high matter; the second is, if the French does not happen to be good, I ought to be excused because I am English and have not much experience of the French of France; the third thing is that I am no great scribe, because I only learned to write late, and by myself. So that it seems to me that on account of these three things I may excuse the defects of my book and myself.)

These excuses need careful analysing. The first is a protest that he is unworthy to undertake a task which, in fact, he had just brought to a conclusion. It is not, therefore, to be taken too seriously and is a conventional piece of mock modesty. The next is an apology for any possible shortcomings in his French, which may not measure up to continental standards. Too much stress has been laid on this. It is, like the first, conventional, and his French has little need of any excuse. The last is an explanation that he is not a good writer because he is self-taught and only began to learn after he was grown up. Although all knights could

[1] E. J. Arnould, *Le Livre de Seyntz Medicines* (A.N.T.S., 1940), and *Étude sur le Livre des Saintes Médecines* (Paris, 1948).

read by this date, not all could do much more than sign their own names. The great Talbot, when Governor of Normandy in the reign of Henry VI, scrawled his as though he was using the point of his sword. Warwick the Kingmaker, on the other hand, had an almost elegant signature. Holograph letters are rare, but are usually, when they occur, in a hand composed of pothooks quite unlike the various types of hand cultivated by the professional clerk or scribe. *Les Seyntz Medicines* is a very long book, and if this statement means that it was hand-written and not dictated, this makes it a feat. The autograph which presumably existed has disappeared, but one of the two extant copies (at Stonyhurst and Cambridge, Corpus Christi 218) is particularly interesting. The Stonyhurst copy is probably not very much later than the text itself and is ornamented with coats of arms. Lancaster's own arms are blazoned within the first initial. It was given by Lord Carew to Duke Humphrey, whose autograph *ex-libris* it bears.

Although this manuscript may be very close to the original, it is professional work on which no expense has been spared. Consequently, nothing can be deduced from it about the author's language except for his syntax and style, and there is little there to distinguish it from contemporary French. His sentences are sometimes involved, and he was evidently in the habit of reading books in which the love for subordinate clauses was beginning to be apparent and which foreshadowed the prose of the Grands Rhétoriqueurs.

The idea that sin is a disease which needs medical treatment is not original, in fact it was universally assumed; but it is rare to see it treated with such a wealth of detail. The framework, the enumeration of sins, had been a commonplace since the days of St. Edmund. The conversational prayers addressed to our Lord, which struck Mr. Pantin as remarkable,[1] recall those in the *Merure* and in the Sermon of Thomas of Hales. It seems likely that the oral tradition of sermons may account for some at least of the resemblances between this text and so many others. What would explain the peculiar quality of the *Seyntz Medicines* is the influence of the duke's confessor. It is not known who Lancaster's

[1] Loc. cit., p. 231.

confessors were, but at this date it was customary for royalty and the nobility to employ friars for this purpose—John of Gaunt had two friars in succession. The duke's frank confession of his worldliness and addiction to tournaments, which was not combined with a renunciation of any of the faults he acknowledges, could be explained if the book is regarded as a sort of 'imposition'. Not that he was at all a wicked man. He merely lived the life of a great lord of his time, and did all the right things, including the foundation of the Newarke or College of the Annunciation for secular canons at Leicester, where he is buried.

The book is a series of allegories. The seven deadly sins are seven wounds, for which there are seven remedies. But this is not all. It abounds in illustrations, each of which is also allegorized. There are many resemblances to the *Contes* of the Franciscan, Nicole Bozon. The illustrations contain much information about the social life of the times. The duke seems to have had expert knowledge of the remedies, medicinal and culinary, which he describes. He waxes enthusiastic over the destruction of foxes. There are three ways of doing this: by stopping the earths and catching the foxes with hounds, by smoking them out, and by sending down a terrier. The terrier is his conscience and the huntsman his confessor. Here the source is undoubtedly personal observation, whereas other comparisons—to a castle, for instance, and a ship—are commonplaces. The comparison of his heart to a fair recalls a passage in the Franciscan *Fasciculus Morum* of about 1317–23, where the world is imagined to be like a fair.[1] Lancaster may, as Professor Arnould suggests, have been thinking of his own fair at Leicester, but it would be unprofitable to spend time seeking analogies to Vanity Fair. It is a tradition in English literature and speech—'going like a fair', 'too late for the fair'; in such phrases an aspect of medieval life which provides preachers with a useful *exemplum* lives again.

One of the strangest features of Lancaster's writing is his extensive use of the figure *annominatio*. Professor Arnould describes this as 'euphuisme avant la lettre', and seeks to explain it by the influence of alliteration in English. It is not,

[1] A. G. Little, *Studies in English Franciscan History* (Manchester, 1917), p. 148.

he says, characteristic of Anglo-Norman.[1] All this seems a little far-fetched. Paronomasia is a much wider thing than alliteration, and it does occur in Anglo-Norman. Gower, as is to be expected, was fond of it. It was probably Thomas who introduced the triple pun on 'amer' into vernacular literature, and Cordelia's punning reply to her father occurs outside Wace. The author of the *Donnei des Amants* thoroughly enjoyed deriving 'gelus' from 'geler'. English writers also used it in Latin, the language in which it properly belongs.[2] The only puzzle is how a man who took to penmanship only late in life came to be so well versed in the rules of rhetoric. Was it due to early drilling by a tutor, to constant reading, to sermons, or has the last word not been said about his written sources?

This work undoubtedly enjoyed a more restricted circulation than those mentioned above. There are, as has been said, two extant manuscripts. Two medieval references to manuscripts, one in the catalogue of Tichfield Abbey and the other in a bequest to a niece of the duke, may indicate the former existence of two more. Biographers of the duke were aware of it. Thomas of Otterburne (*c.* 1420) calls it *Mercy et Grantmercy*, and Capgrave, a century later, *Mercy Gramercy*, from words which occur in the prologue. The fame of the author must have given it a certain prestige, and his relations must have felt obliged to have a copy on their shelves, even if they never opened it.

The late Professor Tanquerey did not hesitate to say that 'ce traité pourrait facilement passer pour le chef-d'œuvre de la prose française en Angleterre au XIVᵉ siècle'[3]—a claim which is not very difficult to sustain. It is a useful corrective to the prevailing view of Anglo-Norman based on the study of Bozon's *Contes*. Yet the great interest of the work is, as Mr. Pantin points out, that it comes from the pen of an amateur, a devout layman, and this is something new.

GOWER'S *MIROUR DE L'OMME*

The swan-song of Anglo-Norman literature exploits this same numerical technique. This is the *Mirour de l'Omme* by

---

[1] *Études*, pp. ccv–ccvii.

[2] Cf. R. Vaughan, *Matthew Paris* (Cambridge, 1958), pp. 33, 127.

[3] *Medium Ævum*, x (1941), p. 116.

John Gower, written, according to its editor, about 1376–9, and probably his first book.[1] It was a poem of over 30,000 lines in octosyllabic couplets. The unique manuscript (Cambridge Univ. Lib. Add. 3035), which unluckily has lost its last folios, has 29,945. The poem is divided into ten parts. The first deals with vices and the second with virtues, and it is these two sections which are in the tradition of St. Edmund and chiefly concern us here. Each sin has five daughters, an allegory which recalls the idea of the Four Daughters of God, exploited by Grosseteste amongst others, and the Marriage of the Devil's Nine Daughters. The division of each sin into five is unusual, but Gower repeats it in his English work, the *Confessio Amantis*, though there the sins have ministers instead of daughters. Although the sections on the vices and virtues appear to occupy only a fifth of the work, in point of fact it takes 18,420 lines to dispose of them. The next six parts deal with the different orders of the upper and middle classes—prelates, religious, princes, knights, magistrates, merchants, and artificers. Here there is some affinity with Gower's Latin work, the *Vox Clamantis*. The pedigree of this attack on society goes back in the vernacular to the *Fables* of Marie de France, by way of the *Bible* of Guiot de Provins and other thirteenth-century works. The development went on during the fifteenth century, to reach new heights with the *Satire of the Thrie Estaits*. The part played by Fortune in all this shows the increasing importance of the notion of peripeteia. This again has its starting-point in the twelfth century with Simund de Freine, and its development can be traced through the Three Living and the Three Dead on the church walls to the Dance of Death, through the Fall of Princes, to the Mirror for Magistrates and sixteenth-century tragedy. The ninth part tells how man's sin is the cause and not the result of the corruption of the world. The tenth explains how the sinner may be reformed by the help of God and the Virgin, and includes a life of Mary, with prayers addressed to her.

The whole work is full of allegorical allusions, comparisons drawn from natural history, quotations, proverbs, and exemplary stories. The review of society naturally gives

[1] G. C. Macaulay, *The Works of John Gower* (Oxford, 1899), I. xliii.

opportunities for fascinating glimpses of the life of the time.
The editor, in his introduction, has done full justice to the
interesting aspects of the poem. It is, in fact, not only the
most complex but the most sophisticated of all vernacular
treatises. Gower was the last considerable English writer in
French, and his language and versification are influenced
by continental usage. Nevertheless, Anglo-Norman was not
quite dead at the time when he was writing, and he is not
just a foreigner writing in French.

THE FRANCISCANS

The arrival of the friars coincided with the carrying out
of the decrees of the Lateran Council. The Dominicans
reached England in 1221 and the Franciscans followed in
1224. It was the Franciscans who left their mark on Anglo-
Norman literature. Both Orders, and the later Orders of
friars, supplied royalty and the nobility with confessors, and
there may have been more indirect influence than can be
measured. Friars also preached and held missions wherever
the bishops allowed, and during their first few years drew
recruits from monasteries.

ROBERT GROSSETESTE

The name of Grosseteste has already been mentioned in
connexion with the question of the authorship of *Le Manuel
des Péchés*. He was never himself a friar, but he was the first
lecturer to the Franciscans at Oxford. A list of his Anglo-
Norman works is given by Professor Harrison Thomson,[1]
and it is a matter for regret that they were not included in
the volume commemorating his seventh centenary. Besides
a prayer to St. Margaret, a grace after meals, and the treatise
on husbandry written for the Countess of Lincoln, there are
three short pieces in prose which are relevant here. The first
is a form of confession relating to the Seven Deadly Sins,
which are used to supply the plan; the second an injunction
to the penitent after he had made his confession, which was
apparently expected to be in French; the third describes the

---

[1] S. Harrison Thomson, *The Writings of Robert Grosseteste* (Cambridge, 1940),
pp. 152–9; *Robert Grosseteste*, ed. D. A. Callus (Oxford, 1935).

pains of purgatory. The second forms a sequel to a Latin treatise, and the third exists also in a Latin version. In view of Grosseteste's express desire that the laity should be allowed to use a vernacular, sometimes specified as French, it seems likely that it was he himself who was responsible for giving help to his clergy by supplying them with forms and treatises in French. He also addressed the laity direct, using for this purpose allegory in verse. The *Chasteau d'Amour* is well known and exerted wide influence. It was translated into Latin and several times into English. It has, however, faults, and appears to be a compilation from various sources hastily put together, perhaps for noble youths such as De Montfort's sons who were being brought up in his household. The name by which it is generally known indicates its aristocratic and feudal tone,[1] and it really belongs to courtly literature. Yet it is unmistakably part of the thirteenth-century movement. The castle has four towers, which are the Four Virtues, and seven barbicans which repel the Seven Deadly Sins. It represents the Virgin, and interest in the Virgin increased during the century. In it the Son takes refuge from three foes, the World, the Flesh, and the Devil. Included is a further allegory of God's Four Daughters. This is probably not Grosseteste's own invention, though it is Anglo-Norman in origin. It became popular on the Continent, where it became the subject of four different versions, and it was incorporated into the *Gesta Romanorum*. Grosseteste's prestige may have helped to generalize it.[2] So far the poem does not sound very exciting, but it has a claim to originality which has been overlooked from that day to this, and which demonstrates more clearly than anything else that the attribution to Grosseteste is correct. For in his description of the castle he applies his scientific theories to theology. The outside of the castle has all the colours of the rainbow, while the inside is pure white. This has to be related to Grosseteste's work on optics and the theories he expounded in treatises on light, colour, and the rainbow. The colours of the prism when blended produce light, which to Grosseteste was white.

[1] For Grosseteste and politics see W. A. Pantin in *Robert Grosseteste*, pp. 205-6.
[2] A. Långfors, 'Les Quatre Filles de Dieu', *Notices et Extraits*, xlii (1933), pp. 139-288.

Light was energy, and the energy which created and moved the world was love. Hence the sub-title, *Carmen de Creacione Mundi*.[1] All this is so far above the heads of the readers for whom it was intended that it has escaped notice.

A second, slighter poem is the allegory of the Marriage of the Devil's Nine Daughters—nine vices appropriately paired off to nine sorts and conditions of men. In the prologue (the first twelve lines of which occur also in that to Rauf de Lenham's *Calendar*, written in 1256—a work too technical to find a place in this book) it is stated that 'St. Robert' translated it from the Latin. The idea was current at the time and preachers were fond of it. Grosseteste's source is unknown, and it seems likely that he made use of a lost Latin treatise on the subject, variants of which were at the disposal of the continental preachers.

For both poems Grosseteste employed the octosyllabic couplet. The *Chasteau* is 1,168 lines long, the 'Marriage' only 566.

WILLIAM LE CLERC'S *VIE DE TOBIE*

The 'Four Daughters of God' was, it is curious to note, used as an introduction to the story of Tobias and the Angel by Guillaume le Clerc. To this it does not appear to be particularly relevant, and it was formerly suggested that it was an interpolation. It is now known that it formed an integral part of the work. The *Vie de Tobie* was written for William, prior of Kenilworth in Arden, an Augustinian house in the diocese of Coventry and Lichfield. This was presumably W., formerly sub-prior of Oseney, who was prior of Kenilworth 1214–27. These dates seem to have been unknown to Professor Harrison Thomson, and the question whether Guillaume followed or preceded Grosseteste is more open than it appeared when he was writing.[2]

The allegorical use of daughters had been a commonplace for many years. The timing of these two poems belong-

---

[1] Cf. M. D. Legge, ' "To Speik of Science, Craft and Sapience" in Medieval Literature', *Literature and Science* (Oxford, 1955), p. 125.

[2] Cf. R. Reinsch in Herrig's *Archiv*, lxii (1879), pp. 375 ff.; R. J. Dean, 'A missing chapter of the "Vie de Tobie" ', *Modern Philology*, xxxiii (1935–6), pp. 13–19; J. C. Russell, *Dictionary of Writers of Thirteenth-Century England* (London, 1936), p. 208.

ing to a thirteenth-century movement must not obscure the fact that an old idea was being put to a more general use than in the past. It is said that Fulk de Neuilly, the revivalist preacher, blamed Richard I for the wickedness of his daughters, and when the king denied their existence, named them as Pride, Avarice, and Lust. Richard, however, gave as good as he got, and declared that he had given the first in marriage to the Templars, the second to the Cistercians, and the third to the prelates.[1] The thirteenth century invented little in this direction, but made use for its own purposes of what lay ready to hand.

JOHN PECHAM'S *JERARCHIE*

The only known theological work in French to come from the hand of John Pecham, the Franciscan Archbishop of Canterbury, is the *Jerarchie* written, apparently, at the request of Eleanor of Castile, queen of Edward I. This seems strange, in view of the part he played in disseminating the results of the Lateran Council, and it is a pity, for he was an excellent writer. His language and style, and the terms he was on with the Royal Family, are described by Tanquerey.[2] The *Jerarchie* is cast in the form of a private letter, but it obviously circulated amongst Franciscans, if not more widely. The surviving manuscript has an excellent pedigree. Written in 1297, five years after Pecham's death and seven after that of the queen, it was resigned to the Friars Minor of Southampton by Friar Jordan de Kyngestone of that house by permission of the minister, William of Nottingham, in 1317. Unluckily, it has a lacuna, two chapters having been telescoped. While merely a copy, and a defective one at that, it is close enough in time to the original to inspire confidence in the attribution attached to it. The treatise is based on the *Heavenly Hierarchy* of the Pseudo-Dionysius, but incorporates ideas from elsewhere, notably from Isidore of Seville. The hierarchy of heaven is compared to an earthly one, the court of heaven to a royal court. This comparison is also to

---

[1] Roger of Hoveden, ed. W. Stubbs (R.S.), iv. 76–77. Cf. Giraldus Cambrensis, *Itinerarium Kambriae*, ed. J. F. Dimock, *Opera*, vi (R.S.), p. 44. Walter of Hemingburgh tells the story, with much less probability, of Walter of Coutances at Richard's death-bed.

[2] *Recueil de lettres anglo-françaises* (Paris, 1916), pp. xiv–xvii.

be found in the *Golden Legend*, in the chapter for Michaelmas. Though this could have been Pecham's source, it seems more likely that both are based upon some lost Latin commentary. Pecham's earthly hierarchy and royal court are English ones, those in the *Golden Legend* are continental. Some credit for originality must therefore be allowed to the archbishop.[1]

ADAM OF EXETER

The Oxford Master, Adam of Exeter, 'renowned throughout the whole world' as Thomas of Eccleston said, who became a Franciscan in 1227 and died in 1231 in Italy on his way to conduct a mission to the Saracens, wrote a little treatise expounding the Pater Noster petition by petition. Two manuscripts survive: one (Cambridge, Pembroke College 112) addressed to 'ma chere mere', in which these words have been later altered to 'beau sire', and a more recent one (B.N. fr. 19525), anonymous, addressed to 'mun chier frere'. The probability is that it was composed for some abbess or prioress, and later adapted for men religious. The earlier copy presumably came into the hands of some layman, though at one time it was in a monastery. It is probable, though it cannot be proved, that this little work was written after Adam of Exeter became a friar and before his departure, that is, between 1227 and 1230.[2]

Many other tracts of this kind exist—paraphrases of the Creed and the Pater Noster, manuals for confession, on the deadly sins, the gifts of the spirit, on penitence and so on—which it would be tedious to enumerate.[3] They are all anonymous. Some are in verse, but most in prose. They represent the efforts of innumerable friars and confessors to instruct the laity, and should not be forgotten when the longer and more popular works are considered. Some, indeed, may be due to men of famous names, since it is sometimes only by accident that the ascription to the author of a tract

---

[1] Cf. A. Rosin, 'Die "Hierarchie" des John Peckham', *Zeitschrift für Romanische Philologie*, lii (1932), pp. 583–614, especially p. 611. I was unaware of this article when I published the text with greater accuracy in *Medium Ævum*, xi (1942), pp. 77–84. Cf. *Anglo-Norman in the Cloisters*, pp. 81–82.

[2] Cf. *Anglo-Norman in the Cloisters*, pp. 82–84.

[3] There is an extensive bibliography in J. Vising, *Anglo-Norman Language and Literature* (London, 1923), pp. 57–58.

has been preserved by a scribe. This case of Adam of Exeter is exemplary. Only the anonymous copy might so easily have survived. To give another example, an extract from St. Edmund's *Merure*, which appears twice in the Fitzwilliam Museum MS. McClean 123, is catalogued as an anonymous treatise on the Pater Noster.[1]

THOMAS OF HALES

How much preaching took place in French it is difficult to say, since notes of sermons were often made in Latin regardless of the language actually used. In fact, the same sermon may have been preached in more than one language according to the circumstances. It seems likely that sermons to nuns and the laity were often preached in French. One sermon preserved in Anglo-Norman is ascribed to one of the most famous of the early English Franciscans, Thomas of Hales. This is especially interesting since he was a considerable writer in Latin, especially of saints' Lives, and an English poet. His beautiful poem, the *Luve Ron*, was written for a nun, and it may well be supposed that his sermon was preached in a convent. This would account for the emphasis placed on the part played by Mary and any other 'dames' mentioned in the Gospels, and also for the reference to St. Helen, of whom he had written a Life in Latin. As in the case of the *Jerarchie*, the pedigree of the unique manuscript (Oxford, St. John's College 190) of the sermon inspires confidence in the ascription. It was procured from some vicar named William de Felton for Westminster Abbey by William of Haseley, who was dead by 1283. Thomas of Hales was a contemporary, probably a younger contemporary, of Adam de Marisco, who died before his time, worn out by his exertions, in 1258. This suggests that the manuscript is not very much later than the date of the text.

The sermon has the quality to be expected of the poet of the *Luve Ron*. It lacks its text and any allusion to the occasion or season for which it was composed, and opens with a quotation from St. Bernard on the love and knowledge of Christ. It is a meditation in the form of a figurative Kissing of Christ's feet. It is divided into ten, the divisions corresponding to the

---

[1] Cf. M. D. Legge, *Modern Language Review*, liv (1959), pp. 73–74.

ten talents of Matthew xxv. 14–30, and so conforms in some
degree with the numerical tradition. Each division opens with
a prayer in French and closes with another in Latin.[1] It is
instructive to compare the grace of Thomas of Hales with
the dry, matter-of-fact approach to his subject of Maurice
de Sully in the previous century.

GUILLAUME LE CLERC'S *BESANT DIEU*

The theme of the talents is also used by Guillaume le Clerc
in his poem *Le Besant Dieu*.[2] This must have been finished
soon after 1226–7, since a passage in the prologue, lines
159 ff., refers to Louis VI's campaigns in the south of France
and to his death. It is therefore puzzling that he should imply
that he had undergone a midnight conversion and that this
was his first serious work, his previous writings having been
fables and songs, for there seems little doubt that this is the
same Guillaume who wrote the *Bestiary*. Though it is just
possible that he counted this as fables, the whole passage has
the air of a literary convention and should not perhaps be
taken absolutely literally. The *Besant*'s main subject is sin,
and it is inspired by the *De Miseria Conditionis Humanae* of
Innocent III, who is mentioned in lines 1251 ff. and 3299 ff.
Besides the parable of the Talents, many others are quoted as
exempla and the name of Maurice de Sully is mentioned in
connexion with the parable of the labourers in the vineyard.
Maurice deals with this in his sixth sermon, and with the
talents in his sixty-third. Since he there translated 'talent' by
'mars d'argent', it is possible that Guillaume made use of a
collection in Latin, though an important family of manuscripts of the French version is Anglo-Norman.[3] When the
Besant was finished Alexander of Stavensby, Bishop of
Coventry and Lichfield 1224–38, seems to have pointed out
that he had omitted a section, which he then made the subject
of his shorter poem, *Les Treis Moz*.[4] The bishop issued
an important set of decrees, not dated, but probably composed soon after his consecration, which followed on the

---

[1] Cf. *Anglo-Norman in the Cloisters*, pp. 84–85.
[2] Ed. E. Martin (Halle, 1869).
[3] The French sermons are edited by C. A. Robson (Oxford, 1952).
[4] Ed. R. Reinsch, *Zeitschrift für Romanische Philologie*, iii (1879), pp. 200–31.

Council of Oxford. He included a homily for the use of parish priests, in Latin, but with the important words translated into English or French.[1]

NICOLE BOZON'S WORKS

Grosseteste, Pecham, Adam of Exeter, and Thomas of Hales represent the universities of Oxford and Paris at their best. There was nothing common about them; even when they approached the laity they never made use of anything mean. The same is not true of a later Franciscan who may have acquired the title of Master at Oxford, Nicole Bozon. Bozon was not as vulgar as preaching friars were later to become, but he was of coarser fibre than his predecessors. It is possible that he was a townsman, whereas Grosseteste at least was country bred.

Bozon's name has never been recovered from any records, which seems strange when it is obvious that he must have been a well-known figure. It is now almost certain that he belonged to the Nottingham friary,[2] which belonged to the Oxford custody. His output is truly astonishing. The best list of works attributed to him is that compiled by Antoine Thomas.[3] One of the most interesting points about it is the variety of forms employed, which has sometimes caused doubt to be cast upon the attribution of the works. The list which follows is broken up according to genre, and it will be seen how Bozon was concerned to fit style to subject. Works attributed to Bozon either by the author himself or a scribe are marked by an asterisk. The others have been assigned to him on internal evidence.

Allegory. In quatrains of alexandrines Bozon wrote two substantial allegories. *The *Char d'Orgueil* is about 500 lines long. Pride, a daughter of Lucifer, has a carriage constructed out of the various vices, the description of which enables the author to attack the evils of contemporary society. The image of the carriage may be original, the rest comes out of the

---

[1] M. Gibbs and J. Lang, op. cit., pp. 108–9.

[2] M. Amelia Klenke, *Three Saints' Lives by Nicholas Bozon* (New York, 1947), especially pp. xxvii–xxix.

[3] *Histoire Littéraire*, xxxvi. 400–24. Supplemented by M. A. Klenke, op. cit., pp. xxxv–xl.

common stock, and its affinities are obvious. The *Passion* is
a kind of topsy-turvy *Lancelot*. The 'Amie' (mankind) of a
king (Our Lord) is abducted. The king borrows the arms of
his squire (Adam) and is equipped (the Incarnation) by a
maiden (the Virgin). He attacks Belial on a mountain
(Calvary) and receives five wounds (the Five Wounds of the
Crucifixion). He recovers his 'Amie', pardons and marries
her (the Redemption). Two similar stories are told by the
Dominican Gui d'Évreux and the Franciscan Albert de
Metz, at the end of the thirteenth century and the beginning
of the next. The idea seems to have been a commonplace of
the time, but its starting-point is unknown. The same metre
is employed for the shorter *Comment le fiz Deu fu armé en la
Croyz*. The *Lettre de l'Empereur Orgueil*, which bears no
relationship to the *Char d'Orgueil*, is in octosyllabic couplets.
A Debate between Winter and Summer is in varied form.
Winter uses the octosyllabic couplet, Summer a six-line
stanza. Another between the Body and the Soul is in six-line
stanzas in tail-rhyme. The lovely *Plainte d'Amour* is in six-
line stanzas without tail-rhyme. It is a social satire, attacking
not only the world in general for its moral decay, but the
Roman Curia. Amongst the satires are two poems on the
subject of women. A short poem in tail-rhyme is devoted
to an unflattering comparison of Woman to the Magpie.
Another poem, however, in the same metre, rallies to the
defence of women. It is thirty-nine stanzas long, but appears
to be incomplete. Apparently a woman, not a 'dame' but a
'femme', had taken offence at some anti-feminist remarks in
the *Char d'Orgueil*, and Bozon had felt obliged to make some
sort of apology. Anti-feminism in preachers is nothing new,
but amends are rare.

  Poems on the Virgin. Bozon wrote several poems commemorating the Virgin. One on the *Annunciation and a
*prayer to the Virgin are both in tail-rhyme. The *Ave Maria
is paraphrased in quatrains, the words of the prayer being
used for the rhyme. A shortened translation of St. Bernard's
Planctus is in alexandrine quatrains.

  Saints' Lives. There are eleven of these, only two of which
are lives of men. They are all very short, varying from 440
lines down to 200, and are dryly told in octosyllabic couplets.

They were perhaps designed for meal-time reading in some convent.

Proverbs and Sermons. The *Proverbes de Bon Enseignement* is a collection of moral sentences from the Bible and the philosophers. Each saying is given in Latin and accompanied by the French paraphrase written in a four-line stanza of seven or eight syllables rhyming in couplets. *Denaturesse* is a treatise on the lack of natural affection, written in octosyllabic rhyming couplets. The same metre is employed in the popular poem on the love of God, usually opening with the words 'Seint Pol li apostre dist', which has only recently been added to the Bozon canon by Miss Klenke.[1] The seven short sermons in verse are all in octosyllabic couplets except one, which is in six-line stanzas. In two of these the name of the author appears.

Doubt has been cast on some of the attributions, precisely because of the differences in style, but it is plain from the above analysis that there was method in Bozon's madness. For reflective poems he thought long lines, grouped in stanzas, most suitable; for narrative, the octosyllabic couplet with no frills; for sayings, prayers, and anything vaguely lyrical, stanzas of short lines, nearly always in tail-rhyme. Bozon gains in stature as a writer if all this is taken into consideration.

When all is said, Bozon's fame is bound to rest on the work known as the *Contes.* These are not exactly a preaching manual, but rather the material for the illustration of sermons after the fashion of the Franciscans.[2] Bozon does not slavishly follow a pattern, but his intention is to state a fact of natural history, or describe some natural phenomenon, to 'moralize' it with the aid of scriptural quotations, and then to reinforce the lesson with an anecdote. This may be an animal fable, or a 'narratio'. For the fables, he drew on a collection akin to the source of Marie de France. The narrations are sometimes of contemporary events, which naturally have a particular interest today. He does not always give a story in full, if he thinks it is well known, but contents himself

---

[1] *Seven More Poems by Nicholas Bozon* (St. Bonaventure and Louvain, 1951).

[2] Cf. J. S. Brewer, *Monumenta Franciscana* (Rolls Series), i, p. li; M. Deanesly, *A History of the Medieval Church* (8th ed., London, 1954), p. 160.

with a mere indication of it. In many cases, especially in the fables, Bozon seems to have been using a source which was in verse, but in some instances he may have used rhyme as an ornament.[1] He was fond of proverbs, and often quotes pithy sayings in English. This does not mean that he habitually preached in English, any more than the fact that his scriptural texts are in Latin means that he preached in that language. The *Contes*, it is interesting to note, were given wider circulation by being translated into Latin, but were never translated into English until recent times.[2]

The poems seem to have preceded the prose book. Bozon is unlikely to have begun writing before 1280, and, from internal evidence, the *Contes* cannot be earlier than 1320. Thus they were written more than thirty years before the *Seyntz Medicines*. Though they lack the elegance of that work, the apparent badness of the language is often due to the false impression created by wild spelling. Bozon is never obscure, and has a certain refreshing directness. He was an excellent narrator. The story related by John of Alderby, Bishop of Lincoln, to the abbot of Eynsham, about the miser who had buried his money under the only chair in the house, once read, can never be forgotten. 'Huyt mille liverez! huyt mille liverez, sire abbé, en tresorie avoyt, e unqes un bon repast manger ne poeit!' Such was Anglo-Norman table-talk at the beginning of the fourteenth century.

Bozon was a very popular writer. Many of his works exist in several manuscripts, the *Proverbes* holding the record with nine, while the *Contes* are in only two (B.M. Add. 46919 and Gray's Inn 768) besides the Latin translation. It is sad to reflect that only fifty years later Gower was joining in the chorus of abuse of the corruption of the Mendicant Orders. Their work was already done.

JOHN OF HOVEDEN'S *ROSSIGNOS*

A poet who was a secular, but was clearly influenced by the Franciscans, is John of Hoveden, or more correctly of

---

[1] Cf. for the trick of breaking into rhyme in English and Latin, Pantin, loc. cit., p. 141.

[2] The *Contes* were magnificently edited by Lucy Toulmin Smith and Paul Meyer for the Société des Anciens Textes in 1889.

Howden. A clerk in the service of Edward I and of his mother, Eleanor of Provence, he was rewarded by ecclesiastical preferments, amongst others the prebend from which he got his name. He seems to have been a Londoner. Most of his poetry is in Latin. He has been compared to the seventeenth-century metaphysical poets and to the Franciscan Archbishop Pecham.[1] His work was known to Charles of Orleans, who was much influenced by the London Grey Friars in the days of his captivity, and it is one of the sources of his Latin poem *Canticum Amoris*.[2] The best known of his poems is *Philomena*, 'which has been described as an epical-lyrical representation of the life and passion of Jesus'—with, it may be added, his characteristic emphasis on the life and death of the Virgin.

For Queen Eleanor Hoveden wrote a similar poem in Anglo-Norman with the same title, *Rossignos*.[3] It is not a translation but a recasting of the Latin in a form suitable for the laity. Probably the queen had demanded for her own use a vernacular version of a poem which was causing some stir. The Latin is in quatrains, the French in stanzas of eight lines made up of two rhyming quatrains in sequence. The ground covered is the same, but there are developments of a mystical nature which recall the additions made by the nun of Barking to her translation of the *Life of Edward the Confessor*.[4] The *Rossignos* must have been written in the spring of 1274, when Edward had already succeeded to the throne but had not returned from his crusade.

A prose headnote explains the dedication and the title:

Ci comence la pensee Johan de Houeden, clerc la reine d'Engleterre, mere le roi Edward, de la naissance et de la mort et du relievement et de l'ascencion Jhesu Crist et de l'assumpcion Nostre Dame. Et a non ceste pensee: *Rossignos*, pur ce ke si come li rossignos feit de diverses notes une melodie, auci feit ceste livres de diverses matires une acordaunce. Et pur ce enkores a il non: *Rossignos*, que il estoit fez et trové

---

[1] F. J. E. Raby, *A History of Christian Latin Poetry* (Oxford, 1927), pp. 389–95; cf. his introduction to *Poems of John of Hoveden* (Surtees Society, cliv, 1939).

[2] G. Ouy, 'Un poème mystique de Charles d'Orléans', *Studi Francesi*, iii (1959), pp. 64–84.

[3] L. W. Stone, 'Jean de Howden, poète anglo-normand du xiiie siècle', *Romania*, lxix (1946–7), pp. 496–519.

[4] Cf. above, pp. 65–66.

en un beau verger flori ou rossignol adés chauntoient. Et pur ce fu il faiz que li quor celi qui le lira soit esprys en l'amour Nostre Seignour. Benoit soit qui le lyra.

(Here begins the meditation of John of Hoveden, clerk to the queen of England, mother to King Edward, about the birth, the death, the resurrection and the ascension of Jesus Christ and about the assumption of Our Lady. And this meditation is called *Nightingale*, because as the nightingale makes out of diverse notes one melody, so does this book make out of diverse matters one harmony. And for this further reason is it called *Nightingale*, that it was made and contrived in a fair orchard in flower where nightingales were just then singing. And it was made in order that the heart of him who will read it should catch fire with the love of Our Lord. May he be blest who reads it.)

A long development composed of curious comparisons to things is followed by another listing heroes and crusaders; in this, amongst many others, Roland, Robert Curthose, Gawain, Yvain, Perceval, the Young King, Arthur, and Edward I occur, in that order.

The last two stanzas contain an address to Our Lord, couched in courtly terms, and an envoy to the queen:

> Jhesu, des sainz joie enterine,
> Ma chanzounete qui termine
> T'envoie un salu d'amor fine;
> Preng la, doz ami, et l'affine.
> Et quant mort me ferra finer,
> Facet amours por moi finer
> Et me voillez si affiner
> Que soie o toi sanz diffiner.
>
> A toi soit honor, roi de gloire,
> Fine joie, nient transitorie,
> Loange, vertu et victoire!
> Einsi termine cest estoire.
> A la roïne, l'esmeree,
> Mere au roi Edward, la senee,
> Va, chanzon, et se li agree,
> Li soiez leue et recordee.

(Jesus, the perfect joy of the saints, my sonnet which is coming to an end I send thee, a salutation of true love; take it, sweet friend, and refine it. And when death causes my end, cause love to make a fine for me, and refine me so that I may be with thee without end.

To thee be honour, King of Glory, true joy, not transitory, praise, virtue, and victory. Thus ends this story. To the queen, the pure, mother to King Edward, the wise, go, song, and if it pleases her, be read and repeated to her.)

Even from these few remarks and quotations, it will be seen that Hoveden is inclined to rhetoric and is a facile rather than an inspired poet, in French if not in Latin. His use of grammatical rhymes cannot be reproduced in translation.

It is quite in the Franciscan tradition that Hoveden should have undertaken this task for Queen Eleanor, just as Archbishop Pecham made his French prose *Hierarchy* for her daughter-in-law, Eleanor of Castile.

The *Rossignos* survives in only one manuscript (Cambridge, Corpus Christi 471), which was copied in the second half of the fourteenth century. Presumably there was once a presentation copy.

SERMON ON ANTICHRIST

A sermon in which reference is made to Antichrist, the Fall of Man, and the wickedness of the world, long known only by an extract a few lines long, has now been published in full.[1] It is 948 lines long, in octosyllabic rhyming couplets. It survives in only one manuscript (Bodleian Rawl. Poetry 241), which perhaps is incomplete. The author makes some interesting comments on the translation and its purpose. As usual, his protestations of inadequacy are not to be taken seriously, and it may well be that he was calling attention to the excellence of his French, although he had not had the benefit of a French education.

> Seignurs, pur Dieux, ceo qe ai dist
> Ne le aietz pas en despit.
> Car tut soit le romaunce ci petit,
> En latyn est mult grant escrit.
> Jeo ne sai guers romanz faire
> Ne de latyn ma sermon traire,
> Car jeo ne fu unques a Parys
> Ne al Abbaye de Saint Denys.
> Pur ceo nul homme ne me doit blamer
> Si jeo ne sai mye bien romauncer;

[1] Ed. M. E. Porter, *Symposium*, vi (1952), pp. 88–99. (Attributed to Henri d'Arci through a mistake in Vising's *Manuel*.)

Mes nepurquant voil amender
La laie gent et ensencer
Que ne sevent pas tut la escripture,
Que assetz est grant et obscure
A ceux qe ne entendunt de letrure,
Ne que as teles choses ne ount mys lour cure;
En latyn est il meuth escrit
Ceo qe ai en romaunz dist.   (59–76)

(Lords, for Heaven's sake do not despise what I have said. For although it may be so little in French, it is a very great writing in Latin. I hardly know how to do the French, or to take my sermon from Latin, for I never was at Paris, nor at the Abbey of St. Denis. Therefore no man should blame me if I am not good at writing in French. But nevertheless I wish to improve the lay folk, and make wise those who do not know the whole of this writing, for it is very great and obscure to those who are not lettered, and are not concerned about such things. It is better written in Latin, what I have said in French.)

Again and again, these thirteenth-century writers make it plain that French was a suitable medium for the instruction of the laity at large, that it was universally understood, and that they found difficulty in putting into any vernacular the kind of thing which to them seemed more easily expressed in Latin. They do not mean that they would have found it any easier to translate from Latin into English. In view of the kind of education that they had had, it would obviously have been even harder for them.

THE APOCALYPSE

Before quitting the subject of the impact of the Fourth Lateran Council on Anglo-Norman literature, it is necessary to say a few words about a subject which at first sight may seem irrelevant—the translations of the Apocalypse. Dr. M. R. James has traced the history of the illustrations to this book of the Bible, which were more important than the text, from Italian mosaics and frescoes to the Angers tapestries. The best of the books were produced in England. He remarks:[1] 'With the thirteenth century we encounter a sudden expansion of our material. Illustrated Apocalypses in book form now appear in considerable numbers.' He does

---

[1] Introduction to the *Trinity College Apocalypse* (Roxburghe Club, 1909), p. 9.

not investigate the causes for this, but various attempts to do so have since been made.[1] The sudden popularity of this book is partly due to the mention in it of penitence and preachers, both words which had specific meanings at the beginning of the thirteenth century. The fact that it lent itself to illustration in incomparable fashion did the rest. The laity loved it, for it was treated as an episode in the life of St. John, whose part as hero of romance is compared by Dr. Freyhan to that of Alexander. At first only the very rich could afford such books, but by the fourteenth century a rather cheaper range, expensive still but not in the same class, was being produced.

The Apocalypse in book form seems to have begun with pictures only. The next stage was to add explanatory legends, the third to place the pictures at the top of the page, with a full text and commentary below. This is the layout employed by Matthew Paris for his saints' Lives, to be described in the next chapter. Many of this type have the text in French only, others have both French and Latin. All are in prose. The best examples are Anglo-Norman, including the 'Charles V' copy, which passed into the French Royal Library (B.N. fr. 403), and they are superb. Some, including the Trinity College manuscript (R. 17. 1), were executed at St. Albans, and others, including the Douce Apocalypse,[2] have been assigned to Canterbury on slender grounds. The lovely British Museum Royal XV D. ii, which also contains the *Lumere as Lais*, is East Anglian and belongs to the Queen Mary Psalter group.[3]

The verse Apocalypses might seem to have the most claim to be considered as literature, but alas, their literary value is slight. The explanation of their defective versification seems to be that they were based on the prose version, and the versifiers took no pains to do more than divide the prose they

[1] e.g. by F. D. Klingender and R. Freyhan, *Journal of the Warburg and Courtauld Institutes*, xvi (1953), pp. 13–23; xviii (1955), pp. 211–44.

[2] Ed. M. R. James (Roxburghe Club, 1922). Cf. A. G. and W. O. Hassall, *The Douce Apocalypse* (London, 1961).

[3] Traditionally said to have been passed to Greenfield nunnery, Lincs.; cf. P. Brieger, *Oxford History of English Art 1216–1307* (Oxford, 1957), pp. 217–18, but probably made for the Welles family, from whom it passed to the King's library, perhaps in 1507; cf. D. D. Egbert, 'The So-called "Greenfield" *La Lumiere as Lais* and *Apocalypse*', *Speculum*, xi (1936), pp. 446–52.

were following into lines of roughly equal length rhyming in couplets. It has to be remembered that the text was originally only an accompaniment to the pictures. The earliest of the three different versions of this class exists in nine manuscripts, two of which are closely allied. Four seem to have made their way into monastic houses, but they were all made for lay patrons, or perhaps prelates. For instance, a copy which was at St. Augustine's, Canterbury, had belonged to Isabella de Leybourne, Countess of Huntingdon, who married the Earl of Huntingdon in 1337 and died in 1354. The illustrations may derive from the St. Albans school. The manuscripts of this version show considerable variation in the text.[1] An independent version[2] of about the same date, 1291–1302, is preserved in only one manuscript (now in the Bodleian). This is the only case of the commentary being versified as well as the text. It is the work of the chaplain to Shaftesbury Abbey, William Giffard, who was presumably a kinsman of the Abbess Mabel Giffard, sister of Walter Archbishop of York and Godfrey Bishop of Worcester. The nepotism of this family was notorious, even for those days. The manuscript is a copy probably made soon after the author's death, since the epilogue speaks of him in the past tense and prays for his soul. The first leaf is lost and it is only thanks to this epilogue that the name of the author and the occasion of the composition of the text are known. There are no miniatures, unless there was one on the missing first folio, and Sir John Fox's surmise that this copy once belonged to the abbey may be correct. He was, however, mistaken in thinking that the nuns were meant to learn the poem by heart; the word 'memoire' (line 88) means 'mind', not 'memory'. The purpose of the study of the Apocalypse at this date is underlined by the addition of a treatise on the Seven Deadly Sins at the end of the manuscript. Giffard aimed at octosyllabic couplets, but was more concerned with keeping closely to his source than with style, and the result is even worse than in the case of the common verse translation. Some curious word-order to which attention is called

---

[1] Ed. P. Meyer, *Romania*, xxv (1896), pp. 174–257. Cf. for additional manuscripts M. R. James, *The Apocalypse in Latin* (Oxford, 1927), p. 30.

[2] Ed. Olwen Rhys and Sir John Fox, A.N.T.S. vi (1946).

in the Introduction is due to the difficulty the author had in ending his lines with rhyme-words, while sticking to his text. The vocabulary is interesting, and contains an example of the word 'surunder', apparently in the sense of 'surround', about three centuries before the first English example recorded in the *O.E.D.* The commentary, versified here along with the text, was probably Norman in origin, but was adopted on both sides of the Channel. The third of the verse Apocalypses is also preserved in a unique copy, the 'Kerr manuscript'.[1] This is probably a little later than the other two. The manuscript is continental, but the curious mixture of metres raises the question whether the original was not Anglo-Norman. It begins with twenty-six stanzas of octosyllables in tail-rhyme, followed by eleven in which the lines have only seven syllables. Next come eighty-eight stanzas rhyming abba of octosyllables and finally a long series of stanzas rhyming ababbaba, in which the lines have sometimes eight and sometimes seven syllables. There is more conscious attempt to write verse than in the other two versions. This manuscript boasts only one miniature.

At the end of the twelfth century the Apocalypse had been used to drive home the dangers of the followers of Antichrist at large in the world, and the general state of wickedness on the earth at that time.[2] Here again Richard I comes into the story, for he discussed the subject with Joachim de Floris in person.[3] Its general use, however, for the instruction and incidentally the delight of the laity is a thirteenth-century development, and one which lasted for a very long time.

ST. PATRICK'S PURGATORY

The Apocalypse was not the only book to take on a new lease of life with the opening of the thirteenth century. The influence of new ideas can be traced in other works which could be adapted for special purposes. Such was *St. Patrick's Purgatory*. Henry of Saltrey's Latin account is thought to

---

[1] H. A. Todd, 'Old French Versified Apocalypse', *P.M.L.A.*, xviii (1903), pp. 535–77.

[2] Cf. for a useful summary Sir John Fox's introduction to the *Anglo-Norman Rhymed Apocalypse*, pp. xxxii–xxxvi.

[3] Roger of Hoveden, iii, ed. W. Stubbs (R.S.), p. 78; cf. Benedict of Peterborough, ii (ibid.), pp. 151–5.

have been written about 1185, and the first French transla-
tion, as has already been mentioned, was made soon after by
Marie de France. As in the case of her Fables, this work is
simple and straightforward. In the course of the thirteenth
century no fewer than five fresh versions were made in
Anglo-Norman, of which the most important is by a certain
Béroul.[1] This is at once an abridged and enlarged version.
The expansions consist of moralizations, a description of Ireland, and, most important, an account of the sins of Owen.
An original epilogue is an invitation to confession and penitence. The text naturally lent itself to a development of this
kind. Béroul's poem is not in the octosyllabic couplet which
might have been expected, but in four-line stanzas in mono-
rhyme. It was known on the Continent, for of the two manuscripts extant a late thirteenth-century one is Anglo-Norman
(Cheltenham 4156, temporarily inaccessible), but the other,
fourteenth-century (Tours 948), is written by a scribe from
the south-east of France, who has not entirely succeeded in
obliterating the spelling of his original.

THE HOLKHAM BIBLE PICTURE BOOK

As an appendix to this brief account of the illustrated
Apocalypses mention must be made of a book which is in a
class by itself, the Holkham Bible Picture Book (B.M. Add.
47680).[2] This seems to have been planned and ordered by
a Dominican for wealthy, though not aristocratic, patrons,
probably about 1326. Possibly the friar was confessor to
some merchant or even guild. The book was probably made
in London, and this would, perhaps, account for the choice
of French rather than English for the captions. French was
kept up better in sea-ports than in other towns. English
might well have been used, for the caption-writer makes use
of it for the shepherds' speech, and this English appears to
be in the London dialect. Another fact that suggests that the
book was made in a port is that the artist could draw station-
ary ships to perfection, but made a sad muddle when he
wished to depict them in full sail. Obviously he was familiar
with ships at anchor, but had never seen them at sea.

[1] *Le Purgatoire de Saint Patrice par Berol,* ed. M. Mörner (Lund, 1917).
[2] Edited with facsimile by W. O. Hassall (London, 1954).

The book, which is not a Bible Historiale, is a sort of triptych. The first part tells the Old Testament story from Genesis to Noah, the second is a Gospel harmony, and the third treats of the last things. The theme of the book is comparison between the Three Trees—the Tree of Life, the Tree of Jesse, and the Tree of Calvary. Not only the plan, but the kind of illustration, is unique. Much of it is just tinted drawing. It has certain affinities with the St. Albans style, but strikes out a line of its own.

The text is nothing but captions to the pictures. It is in rough octosyllabic couplets. The writer seems to have been allowed a free hand, for his description of the pictures does not always tally with the artist's intentions, but is his own interpretation of what he thought he saw. This is a strange and beautiful thing. The effect of the conception is only heightened by imperfections of technique. It may not have the excellence of the best St. Albans or East Anglian illustrated books, but its emotional quality is unsurpassed.

Paul Meyer had some very harsh things to say about the style and versification of the verse Apocalypse which he edited, and also about the literary taste of the day, particularly in England. He does, however, recognize that it is unfair to judge the past by the present, and this point was taken up by Mr. Todd when he edited the 'Kerr manuscript'. It is hoped that the present chapter has done something to clear away a misconception of the religious texts, including the Apocalypse, of the thirteenth and fourteenth centuries. They were intended to be useful, and there is little evidence that they were thought of as belonging to the realm of belles-lettres. The interest in romances continued.[1] The complaints made by serious writers that people preferred to hear about Charlemagne, Arthur, and Tristram instead of the saints become stereotyped, but always had a basis of truth. This is why Froissart wrote his deadly dull *Meliador*, and why later on Malory conferred immortality upon the prose romances. Those who could afford them went in for sumptuously illustrated books: allegories, histories, and travels, historiated

[1] Cf. L. Delisle, *Recherches sur la librairie de Charles V* (Paris, 1907), i. 40–41; M. V. Clarke, *Fourteenth-Century Studies* (Oxford, 1937), pp. 120–2.

Bibles and Apocalypses. Paul Meyer would not have condemned the text of the *Roman de la Rose*, but it was largely owing to its suitability for illustration, and not to its literary merits, that over three hundred manuscripts of it survive. The preservation of so many religious tracts is partly due to the fact that they were apt to find their way into religious houses, although they were aimed at the parish priest and the layman. There is much more in this question than mere fashion and taste.

The efforts made by the writers studied in this context bore fruit. It is indeed striking that a powerful noble like the Duke of Lancaster should himself have been moved to write a book out of his religious experiences. Ladies liked even more than lords to have illuminated Psalters and Books of Hours in which to follow services. Innumerable prayers in verse and prose, hymns and paraphrases, were made in French for the benefit of the laity. The production of all these things, from a trickle in the twelfth century, became a flood in the thirteenth. The devout occupied the periods of silence at Mass with private prayers in French, and said more prayers before retiring. Suitable prayers and hymns are often found scattered in Latin books, and copied on blank spaces or fly-leaves if they are not part of a deliberate plan.[1] Obviously it was becoming usual for great ladies to be able to read with ease.

In this chapter an attempt has been made to separate works which may be said to be directly due to the decrees of the Fourth Lateran Council and the Council of Oxford. The claim is made that, though the laity were instructed and interested before these assemblies took place, a tremendous impetus was given to writers at that period. In the next chapter, too, it will be seen how a line can be drawn soon after the beginning of the thirteenth century.

[1] For descriptions of how great ladies were supposed to pass the day, cf. Pantin, loc. cit., pp. 254, 256.

X

THE DEVELOPMENT OF THE LEGENDS
OF THE SAINTS

FOR Johannes de Grocheo, writing about 1300, the term *cantus gestualis* included not only what we call *chansons de geste* but saints' Lives.[1] Together they formed heroic poetry of an exemplary nature. The French saints' Lives seem to have begun as translations of the legend versified to fit the tune of the proper sequence, which could be sung in church or outside it for the benefit of the illiterate. This explains the peculiar forms of the *Eulalia*, the *Passion*, *St. Leger*, and *St. Alexis*. Probably in 1115, certainly before 1119, an altar or chapel to St. Alexis was consecrated at St. Albans by Rannulf Flambard, and it seems probable that the *Life of St. Alexis* was sung in connexion with the ceremonies on that occasion. Soon afterwards the oldest extant copy of it was made for a book written and illustrated at the abbey and given to the anchoress Christina de Markyate. She herself is reputed to have played a similar part to that of St. Alexis, when first of all Flambard had tried to seduce her and had then forced her into matrimony with one of his followers. By a coincidence this earliest copy of the translation of a legend from Constantinople shows marked Byzantine influence on the illustrations. St. Alexis was never a popular saint in England, and today there is not a single church dedicated to him anywhere in the country, though this Life was copied there more than once. The connexion with St. Albans was probably inherited from Bec.[2]

Even if it was written in England the actual poem on

---

[1] *Die Musiklehre des Johannes de Grocheo*, ed. Johannes Wolf (Sammelbände der internationalen Musik-Gesellschaft, i, 1899), p. 90.

[2] M. D. Legge, 'Archaism and the Conquest', *Modern Language Review*, li (1956), p. 228; C. Horstman, *Nova Legenda Angliae* (Oxford, 1901), ii. 533–4; T. S. R. Boase, *English Art 1100–1216* (Oxford, 1953), pp. 101–10; O. Pächt, C. R. Dodwell, and F. Wormald, *The St. Albans Psalter* (London, 1960), *passim*; C. H. Talbot, *The Life of Christina of Markyate* (Oxford, 1959), *passim*.

St. Alexis is probably by a Norman. In the twelfth century the verse saint's Life flourished particularly in the Duchy of Normandy and the linked Kingdom of England. It may have been before *St. Alexis* found its way to St. Albans that *St. Brendan's Voyage*, one of the earliest Anglo-Norman texts and perhaps the earliest extant, was written.[1] The poem's peculiar system of versification may be due to the fact that it had been composed, like its predecessors, to a hymn-tune. It fits perfectly the rhythm of an Irish hymn commemorating St. Brendan, the music to which unfortunately does not survive. If that is the case, it is in process of freeing itself from the pattern of the music, for the hymn is in quatrains, but the poem is perhaps the earliest example in French of the octosyllabic couplet being used for narrative in a continuous flow, unimpeded by grouping into stanzas as in the *Passion* and *St. Leger*. Thus, in form and matter, *St. Brendan* is one of the parents of the courtly romance.

St. Brendan's Voyage is not a complete Life, but the history of an episode, and though the subject, drawn from Celtic traditions, is very different it has therefore something in common with what seems to be the primitive form of legend, the *Passio*. Only martyrs have Passions, but the case of a martyr lends itself to exemplification and therefore martyrs are more commonly to be met with in literature than more fortunate saints. Here again the saint's Life has something in common with the *chansons de geste*. 'Enfances' were added, more and more detail, however irrelevant, was inserted into the Life; similarly, later on, the Passion play turned into a complete Life of Christ. In the case of post-Biblical persons, an account of posthumous miracles, collected as evidence for sanctification, was added as an appendix.

THE *PASSION OF ST. EDMUND*

St. Eulalia, the oldest French poem, is at the same time the earliest example of a Passion in French. The type is represented in Anglo-Norman by two examples from the twelfth century, Simund de Freine's *Passion of St. George*[2] and an anonymous *Passion of St. Edmund*.[3] The latter is based

---

[1] Cf. above, pp. 8–18.   [2] Cf. above, pp. 185–7.
[3] Ed. A. Nabert (Greifswald, 1915).

on the *Passio* of Abbo of Fleury, with very little additional matter or editing. Abbo was the first to write a legend of St. Edmund, and he did it at the request of the monks of Ramsey, where he spent two years as teacher. He sent a dedicatory copy to Dunstan, for, except for the final miracle, all the substance, including the story of the lost head, was derived from Dunstan's conversation, and Dunstan had talked to Edmund's own squire in his old age at Athelstan's court. Abbo was at Ramsey in 985-7, and Dunstan died in 988.[1] It seems likely that the translation was also made at Ramsey. The poem ends with a pious exhortation which opens with a prayer for help to St. Edmund:

> Seint Edmund, fort reis curuned,
> Devant le rei de maïsted
> Pur nus seiez cum avued
> A lui ki nus ad tuz furmed. (1673-6)

(St. Edmund, strong king crowned, be as our advocate before the King of Majesty, to him who has created us all.)

This might suggest that the translation was made at Bury, but the writer made no use of Herman's *Miracles* (1065-97) or the *De Infantia* of Galfredus de Fontibus (1148-56), which was written as an introduction to Abbo. While it is not impossible that a Bury writer should have ignored these works, it is unnatural. As the cult of St. Edmund extended over the whole kingdom the poem might have been written anywhere, but Ramsey is the most reasonable suggestion.

The form of the poem is primitive, reminiscent of that of the *Passion*. It is in stanzas of four octosyllables in mono-rhyme, except for the first, which for convenience is in couplets. There is a medial caesura, and a very small pro-portion of lines has more or less than eight syllables. It has to be remembered that the manuscript (Gonville and Caius 435) is thirteenth-century, possibly written a whole century after the text. The scribe has been careful to reproduce some archaic features, such as final *d* after a vowel—Latin *t*. The poem has an air of greater antiquity than the religious poems of Wace, which may be as early as 1135-55. This may, how-ever, be due to its insular origin, and appearances are often

---

[1] Ed. in T Arnold, *Memorials of St. Edmund's Abbey* (Rolls Series), i.

deceitful. The editor's date of the second half of the twelfth century may, nevertheless, be underestimating its age.

DENIS PYRAMUS

The *Life and Miracles of St. Edmund* by Denis Pyramus[1] seems to be quite independent of the *Passion*, though one of the principal sources is Abbo. Denis carried out Galfridus de Fontibus's intention, by inserting the *De Infantia* into the *Passio* at the appropriate place. For the *Miracles* he used the collection made by Herman the Archdeacon, but not the revision of it made by Abbot Sampson. He also made use of Gaimar. This Life was written at the behest of the 'elders' of St. Edmund's by a monk, whether Dionysius the Cellarer or another of the same name, who deliberately sets out to rival the courtly romance. It is to be supposed that it was written for some Gaudy for the benefit of laity present, and belongs to a group of texts written as propaganda for some religious house. In form this Life has long outgrown any association with the liturgy, and appears to be more suited to the abbot's lodgings than to the church building. It most probably belongs in time to the end of the twelfth century.

THE BARKING *EDWARD THE CONFESSOR*

The full-dress Life and Miracles was by then established as a genre. The earliest example of it is probably Wace's *St. Nicholas*, considered to be the latest in date of his religious poems.[2] This was, however, a comparatively minor affair, written for a member of a Norman family well known at Caen and Bayeux, and not for a royal personage. The two parts are continuous and not separated by a break. The next in date is most likely the *Life of Edward the Confessor* by a nun of Barking, written perhaps soon after 1163. This is a much more ambitious effort, and, speaking from a purely historical point of view, more important. The two parts are clearly distinguished. Each opens with a prologue and closes with an epilogue: this was to become the standard form. It

---

[1] See above, pp. 81–85.
[2] *La Vie de S. Nicolas par Wace*, ed. E. Ronsjö (Lund and Copenhagen, 1942), pp. 21–26.

was something quite new in hagiography. The Latin source was the Life by Ailred, who had been brought up at the court of David I, great-grandnephew of the Confessor, and the translation was made for Henry II and his queen, the king being David's great-nephew. It had a personal interest, and dealt with the immediate past. It was propaganda of a different kind from the monastic, although it was produced in a convent, and its object is more political than pious.[1] It may seem strange that this work should have become well known on the Continent, but it had a double claim to general interest: it was regarded as a historical source, and so found its way into a copy of Wace; it was also the legend of a virgin saint, and so was accounted worthy of a modern edition, in prose.

A LOST *EDWARD THE CONFESSOR*

It is possible that there was once another translation of Ailred into Anglo-Norman. Amongst the posthumous miracles, he recounts the attempted deposition of Wulfstan from the see of Worcester. Wulfstan refused to yield his crosier save to St. Edward, and dropped it on his shrine. There it was gripped with such force that it was only released to Wulfstan himself after his reinstatement. This is translated by the nun of Barking, lines 5670–5949. An independent version is to be found, the *Livere de Reis de Engletere*.[2] This rather dull compilation is precious because amongst its sources were works, chiefly chronicles, in verse, and scattered about in the prose are snatches of the original verse. The longest consecutive passage (pp. 148–50) is of fifty-one lines, pieced together with prose, from some poem in which this miracle occurred. It is impossible to date this fragment: the author of the *Livere* has done his work too well. The form was couplets of alexandrines rhyming in pairs. Most of the lines scan after a fashion, but a few have been hopelessly altered. Rhyming groups of three or four lines at a time occur. This is characteristic of Anglo-Norman, but here it may be due to omissions by the writer. The translation is faithful, but parts of the original are missing, and this may

---

[1] Cf. above, pp. 60–66.
[2] Ed. J. Glover (Rolls Series). Cf. below, pp. 278, 291.

be due to abridgement, especially as the beginnings of passages are represented; it is the middle or, more often, the end which is not there. There is no knowing whether this is a fragment of a complete Life of the Confessor, or of St. Wulfstan, or of a chronicle, but the first of these alternatives is most likely. It is regrettable that there is no more of it, but it is something that even this has been accidentally preserved.

KING EDWARD'S RING

The miracle of the ring of Edward the Confessor[1] is the subject of an episodic poem in alexandrines, like the fragment just mentioned, but as its source is an interpolation into the *Life of St. Edward* by Osbert of Clare, it is probably not an extract from the same poem. As the editor remarked: 'This poem is noteworthy for the fact that it is written in Alexandrines, whereas the majority of saints' lives are written in octosyllables.' He was not aware of the fragment relating to the miracle of Wulfstan's crosier, or he might have added that it is a curious coincidence that two poems relating to the same saint are in this exceptional form. The most outstanding example of a saint's Life in alexandrines is the *Life of St. Alban* by Matthew Paris, which will be mentioned presently.

King Edward's Ring is preserved in only one manuscript (Cambridge Univ. Lib. Add. 3392 C), which otherwise contains nothing but pieces in Latin.

LIVES OF THOMAS BECKET

In 1170 there occurred an event which carried the immediacy of sanctity a step further. This was the murder of Becket. Lives of him were written even before his canonization, which took place only three years after his death. First in the field was Edward Grim, whose Life appeared within two years of the martyrdom and one year before the canonization. It was followed by three more in Latin within the following two years. These, however, had been preceded by a translation of Grim into French. In view of the emotion

---

[1] Ed. H. J. Chaytor, *Miscellany of Studies . . . presented to L. E. Kastner* (Cambridge, 1932), pp. 124–7.

caused, and the international complications of the quarrel between Henry II and Becket, it is not surprising that the Latin Lives should have been read in France almost as soon as they were written. A copy of Grim must have been circulating forthwith in the north of France, where it fired the imagination of a *vagans* named Guernes de Pont-Sainte-Maxence, with the result that he translated it into French verse. Dissatisfied with this, according to his own account, or perhaps in search of a more generous audience, he crossed the Channel and visited Canterbury, where he was able to make corrections and additions with the aid of eyewitnesses of the murder. The improvements made proved successful, and he was well rewarded by both Prior Odo of Canterbury and the abbess Mary of Barking, who was Becket's sister. Meanwhile the first version, to his disgust, had been pirated, and rich men were paying for copies which brought him in nothing. This has been presumed lost, but what appear to be fragments of it, in an early thirteenth-century Anglo-Norman copy, have recently been discovered by Professor Francis Wormald.[1] Some lines coincide with the later version, and some are slightly different or occur in different order, but it sticks closer to Grim and is noticeably kinder to Henry II, which is just what is to be expected given the history of the later version. This survives in six manuscripts, all Anglo-Norman, three of which belong to the first half of the thirteenth century. It is worthy of note that Guernes's French, in spite of its boasted purity, shows traces of Anglo-Norman influence.[2]

Both versions are in the same form, five-lined mono-rhymed stanzas of alexandrines. Except that alexandrines have been substituted for decasyllables, this, it is interesting to observe, is the form used for *St. Alexis*. A five-line stanza is common in Latin hymns.

Although Guernes belonged to the Île de France, and was proud of it, there is no evidence that his Lives of Becket became popular on the Continent, or indeed that the second version was known there at all. Obviously the English would

---

[1] I am most grateful to Professor Wormald for lending me his photostats and notes on these fragments.

[2] Editions by E. Walberg (Lund, 1922), and C.F.M.A. (Paris, 1936).

provide a readier market for the sales of this work. As in the
case of Guillaume le Clerc, his poems are part of Anglo-
Norman literature, whatever the dialect in which they were
written. Before the century was out a second writer had produced a *Life of Becket*,[1] and about his nationality there is no
room for doubt.

Beneit was a monk of St. Albans, writing between 1183
and 1189, probably in 1184. The great merit of his work is
that it is based, as Professor Walberg discovered, on the lost
Life by Robert of Cricklade, prior of St. Frideswide's from
about 1140 to 1177, the only prior of this house undistinguished for scholarship who was a Master. The same source
was used for the *Thomas Saga Erkibyskups*.

Like the Life by Guernes, this is in a form which is really
lyrical, this time in six-line stanzas of tail-rhyme. This is even
less suitable for narrative than the other, and the 354 stanzas
contain many clichés in the tail-line, which could often be
amputated without making any difference to the sense. The
use of this particular form for narrative appears to be confined to England. It is noticeable that some kind of stanza
is often employed in Middle English romances.[2] The group
known as the Tail-rhyme Romances is localized in East
Anglia. The extant examples are all later than the *Life of
St. Thomas*, and show a curious development in combining
Old English alliterative verse with a stanza form of Romance
origin.[3] The result is even more awkward than in Beneit's
case, and was pilloried by Chaucer in *Sir Thopas*. Beneit's use
of the stanza bears all the marks of a long history behind it,
and its adoption in English long before the extant examples
is to be suspected.[4]

Martyrdom, renunciation, virginity: these were the favourite themes in the twelfth century. The thirteenth added to
these an interest in penitence. Saints' Lives lend themselves
to propaganda: at first for the faith, then for the Christian
way of life, and lastly for less worthy ends, the aggrandizement

[1] B. Schlyter, *La Vie de Thomas Becket par Beneit* (Lund and Copenhagen,
1941); cf. *Anglo-Norman in the Cloisters*, pp. 19, 20, 139.

[2] e.g. for *Amis and Amiloun*; cf. above, pp. 115–21.

[3] Cf. A. McI. Trounce, 'English Tail-rhyme Romances', *Medium Ævum*, i
(1932), pp. 87 ff., 168 ff., ii (1933), pp. 34 ff., 189 ff., iii (1934), pp. 30 ff.

[4] Cf. *Anglo-Norman in the Cloisters*, p. 139.

of a religious house or even politics. Saints' legends now become too numerous to treat in detail, and some selection
is necessary.

ST. LAWRENCE

Of martyrs, one of the most typical examples is St. Lawrence, commemorated in Northern French only by an Anglo-
Norman Life[1] of the twelfth century, a fourteenth-century
prose version, and a fifteenth-century mystery play. The
verse Life was written

> Por une ancele Saint Lorenz
> Qui sa passion e s'estoire
> Veut por lui aveir en memoire. (76–78)

(For a handmaid of St. Lawrence who wishes to have in mind his
passion and his story for herself.)

The word 'ancele' was used, like 'ancilla', for nun as well as
servant. (The Nun of Barking called herself, in line 530, 'une
ancele al dulz Jhesu Crist'.) And this suggests that the
patroness was a nun, probably an abbess or prioress, of a
convent dedicated to St. Lawrence. There were only two
of these—Rosedale or Russedale, Yorkshire, dedicated to
St. Mary and St. Lawrence in the time of Richard I by Robert,
son of Nicholas de Stutevile; and Oldbury, Warwickshire,
a cell of St. Mary's Priory at Pollesworth. The latter had
a legendary history. According to one account it was founded
for the benefit of St. Modwenna after she had healed King
Egbert's son Arnulph of leprosy. One of the nuns there was
St. Osyth. The list of prioresses is incomplete, but it may be
possible that one of the twelfth-century prioresses was a
patroness of literature, and caused to be written not only the
Life of St. Lawrence but those of St. Modwenna and
St. Osyth also.[2]

The literary value of *St. Lawrence* is slight. The language
has some archaic features and the translator has often left
Latin words and phrases, a sign of antiquity. The prologue
is based on that to Philippe de Thaon's *Cumpoz*, the first

---

[1] W. Söderhjelm, *De Saint Laurent* (Paris, 1888).
[2] For these houses, cf. Dugdale, *Monasticon*, iv. 316 ff., ii. 364 ff.; *V.C.H. Warwickshire*, ii. 62 ff.

three lines being practically identical. The tone is senten-
tious:

> E Deus! qu'est ore devenu
> Le grant sen Aristotilis,
> La richeise dan Cesaris,
> Le pris et la force Sanson,
> E la grant beulté Apsalon? (38–42)

(Ah God! What has now become of the great wisdom of Aristotle,
the riches of Dan Cesar (i.e. Octavian), the worth and the strength of
Samson and the great beauty of Absalom?)

The jests of St. Lawrence on the gridiron, like the wit of St.
Catherine, no longer appeal to a sense of humour less robust
than that of the Middle Ages, and merely appear to be in
doubtful taste. A long passage (lines 495–511) contrasting
the Forbidden Tree and the Cross is signalized by the editor:
'Le jeu de mots avec les deux arbres . . . est, s'il est de
l'invention de l'auteur, ce que je ne peux pas résoudre, le
seul endroit où il ait lâché un peu la bride à son imagination
poétique' (p. 36). In fact, his imagination was not great, for
the passage in question is a scholastic variation on the theme
of the True Cross, developed with far more grace in the
famous hymn of Venantius Fortunatus, 'Pange lingua
gloriosi'. Both manuscripts of this text (Egerton 2710 and
B.N. fr. 19525) are Anglo-Norman, and are of mid-thirteenth-century date.

POPE CLEMENT

Pope Clement had three claims to fame; he was a martyr,
he was one of the patrons of sailors, and, perhaps most important of all, he was the author of two Epistles on Virginity
often appealed to in the Middle Ages. Yet there is only one
Life of him in French, and that is an anonymous Anglo-
Norman work. This poem is incomplete in its unique copy
(Cambridge, Trinity College R. 3. 46), but even so it runs
to 15,000 octosyllables. It has little or no stylistic merit, but
one peculiarity of versification. At the beginning many of the
lines have only seven syllables, and a few have nine. In the
middle the proportion of eight-syllable lines begins to increase, until by the end they are practically universal. Vising

says: 'This no doubt means that he has learnt versification in the course of writing his long poem of 15,000 lines.'[1] This explanation seems a little difficult to swallow. One would like to be able to check the date by reference to other manuscripts, but unfortunately there are none. The surviving copy is mid-thirteenth-century, the text itself probably belongs to the beginning of that century.

From the point of view of sources the poem is interesting. Several are combined. To a certain extent this combination is to be found in a fifteenth-century mystery play from Briançon.

A critical edition of this Life would be a useful piece of work. For the moment, there are available in print a description, analysis of sources, and copious extracts by Paul Meyer.[2]

MARY OF EGYPT—EUSTACE

For this theme of renunciation the writers drew their material chiefly from Eastern sources. St. Alexis was the first Life exploiting it known in Post-Conquest England. The Templar who made use of the *Vitas Patrum*, and Chardri with his early version of *Josaphaz*, had followers: Adgar added a *Life of Mary of Egypt* to his *Miracles*, and there is at least one thirteenth-century Life of the same saint. Two of the *Lives of St. Eustace* are Anglo-Norman; one of these is in tail-rhyme.[3]

JOHN THE ALMSGIVER

The only *Life of St. John the Almsgiver* is Anglo-Norman. It occurs in the same manuscript as the *Life of Pope Clement*, and it has been suggested that it is by the same writer. This, however, is unlikely. Its versification is orthodox, and the source is, quite simply, the Latin translation of the Life by Leontius of Neapolis. There are, therefore, reasons for assigning it to another author. Moreover, it has very likely been post-dated. The prologue begins with a lamentation

---

[1] *Anglo-Norman Language and Literature*, p. 81.

[2] *Notices et Extraits*, xxxviii (1903), pp. 308 ff.; there is an unpublished D.Phil. thesis on it (Cambridge, 1952), by N. K. Wilkinson.

[3] For *St. Eustace* see M. Esposito, *Textes et Études de littérature ancienne et médiévale* (Florence, 1921), pp. 29–61.

over the state of the world, which is going from bad to worse, in a fashion which is more in keeping with the twelfth century than the thirteenth. Almsgiving provides a way of salvation; there is not a word about penitence. There are, it is to be noted, few feminine lines in the 77,000 octosyllables of the poem, and this is a sign of antiquity. The work is unpublished, but there is a description, with extracts, by Paul Meyer, which immediately precedes that of the *Life of Clement*.[1]

ST. GILES

A curious place in this story is occupied by the *Life of St. Giles* by Guillaume de Berneville.[2] On linguistic grounds, the mixture of archaism and precocity, it has been assigned to the end of the twelfth century and to England. The author may have taken his name from Barnwell Priory, Cambridge, where there were two canons named William at the end of the century. The priory was founded in connexion with St. Giles's church, and moved to St. Andrew's hermitage at Barnwell in 1112. In 1190 a new church was dedicated there to St. Giles and St. Andrew, and the poem may have been written as part of the celebrations on that occasion.

According to the prologue, which has nothing pedantic about it, this is the story of a rich nobleman who gave up everything for the love of God and his neighbour, fled by night and dwelt among wild beasts, sustaining himself on raw herbs. So far, it sounds like another *St. Alexis* or *Josaphaz*, but what follows is an intriguing adventure story. Giles was born of Greek parents, and as a child was as beautiful as any hero of romance—or heroine either.

> Plus bele ren ne fist nature. (66)

(Nature never fashioned a more beautiful creature.)

After the death of his parents he escaped from his house and attendants by night and took ship, arriving at Marseilles, a Greek colony, after an exciting voyage lovingly described. In Provence he retreated to a hermitage, where during a hunt by King Flovent he was wounded by an arrow intended for

---

[1] Cf. above, pp. 252–3.

[2] Ed. G. Paris and A. Bos (S.A.T.F., 1881). Cf. *Anglo-Norman in the Cloisters*, pp. 57–61. For the source, cf. E. C. Jones, *Saint Gille* (Paris, 1914).

the heaven-sent hind who was nourishing him. To the poet's great regret, there is no further reference in his source to this kindly beast. The fame of St. Giles reached Charlemagne, who sent for him to Orleans. It was there, according to this version of the story, that the revelation of the king's unconfessed sin took place. There is, as is well known, a possible reference to this mysterious happening in the *Chanson de Roland*, lines 2096–7. It is interesting to note that Guillaume de Berneville, far from scolding his audience for being attracted by worldly epics, seems to have been inspired by the very words of the *Roland*, as Gaston Paris pointed out.[1]

> La vus mustra il grant amur
> Quant pur vus fist de noit le jur
> En Rencesvals as porz passant
> Pur venger la mort de Rollant.   (2891–4)

(There he showed you great love, when for you he turned night into day, in Roncesvalles at the crossing of the passes, to avenge Roland's death.)

Moreover, in the *Roland*, the saint is 'li ber Gilie' (line 2096), and Guillaume speaks of him as 'le bon barun' (line 3770). This word is rarely used of a saint, though its use is permissible and not unknown. After this episode St. Giles, realizing that he had not long to live, travelled to Rome to obtain privileges for his abbey in Provence, and was received by the Pope. Soon after his return to the abbey he passed away as he had foretold. There is a sort of double epilogue. The first part names the poet for the second time; the second refers to the pains of hell:

> Deus nus desfent ke nus n'entrum!
> *Amen* dites tut envirun.   (3794–5)

(God keep us from entering it! Amen, say those all around.)

This appeal to the auditors has a parallel in the anonymous *Barlaam et Josaphat*:[2]

> Amen respondés anviron,
> E puis Pater Noster dirom.   (1223–4)

(Amen, reply those around, and then we shall say the Pater Noster.)

[1] Op. cit., pp. xliv–xlv.
[2] Ed. Jean Sonet, *Le Roman de Barlaam et Josaphat*, ii (Louvain and Namur, 1949).

This Life is in the usual narrative form of octosyllabic couplets. There are a certain number of conversations. A passage in the interview between St. Giles and Charlemagne is worthy of comparison with scenes from the *Adam*:

'Ço ne poz tu faire vers mei.'
'Vers vus? Si puis.' 'Nenal par fei.'
'Ne puis? Pur quei?' 'Car jol sai ben.'
'Ço ne sout unkes crestien.'
'Jo sui crestiens e sil sai.'
'Ne l'os creire.' 'Jol musterai.'
'Vus comment le poez saveir?'
'Ço guarde tu.' 'Nel puis veer.'
'Pur quant jol sai.' 'E vus coment?'
'Il m'est tut dit.' 'N'en quid neent.'
'Nel quides tu?' 'Jo nun, par fei.'
'Tant est maiur folie.' 'En quei?'
'Pur ço ke te covent gehir.'
'Ço ne serrad trés k'al murir.'
'Dunc ert trop tart.' 'Jo ne puis meis.'
'Si poz.' 'Coment?' 'Fai tei confés.'
'Certes nu frai a mun vivant.'   (3115–31)

('Thou canst not do this to me.' 'To you? I can.' 'No, no, in faith.' 'I cannot? Why not?' 'For I know it well.' 'No Christian ever knew it.' 'I am a Christian and I know it.' 'I dare not believe it.' 'I will prove it.' 'How can you know it?' 'Look!' 'I cannot see it.' 'Yet I know it.' 'But how can you?' 'It is all told me.' 'I believe none of it.' 'Thou dost not believe it?' 'Certainly not, in faith.' 'It is so much the greater folly.' 'How so?' 'Because thou wilt have to confess.' 'That will not be before the moment of death.' 'Then it will be too late.' 'I cannot do more.' 'Thou canst.' 'How?' 'Make thy confession.' 'Indeed, I shall not while I live.')

The emphasis on confession and penitence was bound to make this Life popular in the next century and later. The manuscript (Florence, Laurentian Conv. Sopp. 99) from which the edition was made is early thirteenth-century. Afterwards the late Professor Brandin discovered a fragment from a fourteenth-century manuscript (B.M., Harley 912) which has a common error with the complete copy, but contains some additional couplets. Both manuscripts are Anglo-Norman. It is curious that the later fragment comes from the passage where the angel descends with the 'bref petit' describing Charlemagne's sin, and St. Giles prays to ask what penance he should impose for the unconfessed transgression.[1]

Lydgate made use of our text as one of the sources for his short *Life of St. Giles* in Middle English. He keeps the same form.

Guillaume's Life is as readable as many of the contemporary romances. It has a classical economy of narration, with no irrelevancy and little moralizing, with charm and at times liveliness. It has a full and interesting vocabulary. Compared with some Lives of the next century, it is of a moderate length, under four thousand lines.

The theme of virginity, one of the main topics of the twelfth century, continued to be elaborated in the thirteenth, in both religious and romantic literature. Its importance has been sympathetically treated by the late Professor R. L. G. Ritchie.[2]

The Lives of virgin saints, both men and women, were amongst the most popular. The earliest in France include the Sequence of St. Eulalia and the Life of St. Alexis. From one point of view, the Barking *Life of Edward the Confessor* may be included in the list, which continues with the other Barking Life, Clemence's *Life of St. Catherine*.[3] This is the only French translation of the Life of this popular saint.

ST. FAITH

Also unique in northern French is the *Life of St. Faith*[4] written a little before 1216 at Bury by a monk named Simon of Walsingham, who had been born on St. Faith's Day. The sources appear to be the Latin *Passions* in verse and prose and the *Liber Miraculorum Sancte Fidis*. The actual piecing together may not be his own work, since he declares that he is translating a book sent him by a certain Dan Benjamin, which may have been a Latin compilation. The translation was made at the request of another of the monks, perhaps the

---

[1] Description and text of fragment, *Romania*, xxxiii (1904), pp. 94–98.

[2] *The Normans in Scotland* (E.U.P., 1954), pp. 354–7, 361, 416–17.

[3] Cf. above, pp. 60–66 and 66–72.

[4] Ed. A. T. Baker, *Romania*, lxvi (1940–1), pp. 49–84; cf. *Anglo-Norman in the Cloisters*, pp. 9–12.

better-known Thomas of Walsingham (not the chronicler). There was a chapel dedicated to St. Faith at Bury, and, as Simon says, he had a special reason for his devotion to the saint. He was no stylist and this text cannot compare with the Provençal *St. Faith*. The form used is the octosyllabic rhyming couplet, and the verse is not incorrect by insular standards. The editor points out some interesting words used, and many examples of words earlier than those recorded by Godefroy. The only known copy is in the Campsey collection (Welbeck 1 C. 1).

ST. MARGARET

There are several Lives of St. Margaret. One of the twelfth century may be continental, though it exists only in an Anglo-Norman manuscript. The fact that it is in six-line stanzas tells in favour of its being Anglo-Norman. Others are of the thirteenth century. One is in four-line stanzas, another in *laisses*, usually of six lines, and three are in octosyllabic couplets. One of these is by Bozon.[1] In view of the fact that copies of the *Life of St. Margaret* were placed on the breast of women in childbirth to act as a charm, the demand for vernacular translations in such numbers is easily understood.

ST. FRANCIS

The thirteenth century, however, has a saint of its own to celebrate—St. Francis. One of the Anglo-Norman Lives was edited, but not, unfortunately, published, by Marcel Thomas for his thesis at the École des Chartes.[2] The source, which is named, is the *Legenda Major* by St. Bonaventure, with some additions from the *Legenda Minor*. It was probably made not long after Bonaventure's death in 1374. The translator was very likely a Franciscan, but, more modest than Bozon, he deliberately concealed his name:

> Pur ly pryez ke se entremyst
> De translater en frounceys
> Ceste vie de Seynt Frounceys,

---

[1] For the bibliography, see Vising, nos. 18, 117–21.
[2] I wish to thank M. Thomas for kindly lending me a copy of his thesis.

Ke de ses pechez ayt pardun.
Suffist ke Deu ben set sun nun.
Explicyt.   (B.N. fr. 13505, f. 46c)

(Pray for him who undertook the translation into French of this
life of St. Francis, that he may have pardon for his sins. It is sufficient
that his name is known unto God. The End.)

The versification is fairly correct as regards syllabic count;
enjambement is frequently and skilfully used. The vocabulary is interesting. The unique manuscript (B.N. fr. 13505),
which is incomplete at the end, must be nearly contemporary
with the text. The publication of the Life is to be desired.

A few fragments of a collection of *exempla* drawn from
St. Bonaventure and Thomas of Celano also survive. This
may have been made by Bozon.[1]

More interesting from the point of view of subject-matter
are three Lives of native virgin saints. It is important to note
that these are not due to any altruistic interest in Pre-
Conquest history. All these saints were foundresses and
patrons of religious houses.

ST. OSYTH

The earliest is probably the *Life of St. Osyth*.[2] It tells the
story of an Anglo-Saxon Princess, married to Siher, King of
the East Saxons, who managed to preserve her virginity.
After leaving her husband she founded a nunnery at Chich,
Essex, later replaced by a House of Canons. There she was
martyred by the Danes, and, like St. Denys, carried her own
head into the church. Long after, pilgrims were able to ad-
mire the imprint of her bloody hands on the doors, as well
as the shrine within. The Life proper occupies 806 octosyllables rhyming in couplets followed by a section on
Miracles of almost equal length.

The real interest of this Life is in its connexions with
romantic literature. The saint's resistance to her husband is
treated with less detail and more delicacy than the resistance
of Félice to Alys in *Cligés*, but the hagiographer has perhaps
watered down this popular theme of the deluded husband.

[1] Ed. L. W. Stone, *Archivum Franciscanum Historicum*, xxxi (1938), pp. 48–58.
[2] A. T. Baker, 'An Anglo-French Life of St. Osith', *Modern Language Review*,
vi (1911), pp. 476–502; cf. *Anglo-Norman in the Cloisters*, pp. 74–75.

The final chance of escape is given by the sudden appearance of a white hart, in chase of which the whole court goes rushing off. This hunt is again a commonplace, and is represented in Arthurian literature, notably in *Erec* and *Fergus*,[1] while the tradition survived in Cheshire to furnish Joan of Kent and her elder son with a white hind as badge, and Richard II with the famous white hart livery, worn by the Cheshire Guard, and, to our ideas with less congruity, by the angels in the Wilton Diptych.[2]

The *Life and Miracles* are based upon a Latin Life; how faithfully cannot be judged without a critical edition of the original. There are two important additions which seem to have no known source. One comes at the end; the other is an interpolation. Professor Baker dated the main part of the poem late twelfth-century, basing his conclusions upon linguistic evidence. The end part cannot be earlier than 1198, the year that Bishop Richard Fitz-Neal died, since it tells of his death. The interpolation is so different in language and versification that it clearly belongs to the latter half of the thirteenth century.

The addition, if addition it be, tells a story against the bishop. There is other evidence for his desire, prevented by his death, to retire to the priory at Chich which had succeeded the nunnery; but none for the previous efforts to oust the canons in order to secure the revenues of the place for himself, or for his consequent attack of paralysis, cured by the saint after he had signalized his repentance by the offer of a ring. This disgraceful story is told as an example for the benefit of the 'Seigniurs freres'. The interpolation tells of the mythical association of St. Osyth with St. Modwenna. The identification of the maiden Osid, who figures in the Legend of St. Modwenna, with the martyr is perhaps due to Albericus Verus, canon of Chich, who composed a Life dated 1250, and if this is true it supplies a *terminus post quem* for the interpolation.

Everything suggests that this *Life of St. Osyth* was written

---

[1] Cf. R. S. Loomis, *Arthurian Tradition and Chrétien de Troyes* (New York, 1949), pp. 68–70; R. Harris, 'The White Stag in Chrétien's "Erec et Enide"', *French Studies*, x (1956), pp. 55–61.

[2] Cf. especially Anthony Steel, *Richard II* (Cambridge, 1941), pp. 233; M. V. Clarke, *Fourteenth-Century Studies* (Oxford, 1937), pp. 276–8.

and rewritten at Chich by one of the canons. The original author saw nothing strange in delivering an attack, enhanced by a subtle use of rhetoric, on the frail nature of woman (lines 1328–1336) in a work devoted to the praise of one of the species. Yet it is just possible that it belonged or passed to Pollesworth, and that the interpolation was made there. The only surviving manuscript is in the Campsey volume (Welbeck 1 C. 1). The nuns there had to endure being addressed as 'seigniurs' at meal-times.

ST. MODWENNA

St. Modwenna herself, a virgin but no martyr, is commemorated by a Life[1] which has several distinctive features. This has been dated 1230, but is either earlier or is modernized from a late twelfth-century text. The language and versification seem early, and trestle tables are said to be still in use (line 4205).

The main source is Geoffrey of Burton's Life, which is itself based upon the Life by the Irishman Conchubranus. Geoffrey was abbot of Burton 1114–51. The French Life contains two additional miracles the sources for which are unknown, though both are recorded elsewhere. St. Modwenna is a conflation of two, if not three, persons. The Abbey of Burton seems to have annexed the story of an Irish saint to give prestige to a local saint of its own; it is uncertain when this took place and whether it is due to the enterprise of Abbot Geoffrey. Most of the Life represented by the translation is therefore of Irish origin, and it has something in common with *St. Brendan's Voyage*. Posthumous miracles are added at the end, in the regular manner, but the whole of St. Modwenna's life was marked by miracles. Many of these, as befits an Irish legend, have to do with domestic animals, pigs and calves, and their attendant herds. The sea is never far away. A silver cup presented to St. Modwenna and which she had 'lost' in order not to embarrass the donor by a refusal was wafted to her on the sea after being confided to the Liffey for return. A full wine-jar, dropped by mistake into the sea, surfaced and was recovered without a drop being

[1] Ed. A. T. Baker and A. Bell (A.N.T.S., vii, 1947).

spilt. Modwenna went on several sea voyages, between Ireland and England and to Rome. She herself is rather a
colourless person. No one tried to prevent her from becoming
a nun, she did not have to run away and hide from a husband
forced upon her. St. Patrick himself gave her the habit. Her
chosen path through life was smooth. Any difficulty such as
robbery or shortage of food, drink, and clothing was easily
disposed of by a miracle. Fairy-tale after fairy-tale comes to
mind as one reads. Even her death occurred after a warning,
and as the result of a short and apparently painless indisposi-
tion. She could not be held up as an example, but can only
be represented as a sort of kindly magician, always ready to
help when invoked, whether alive or dead. St. Alexis and
St. Eulalia seem very far away.

The poem is 2173 lines long and divided into mono-
rhymed quatrains. (There is one stanza of five lines which
appears to be original.) The lines are roughly octosyllables,
with a caesura, and, as Mr. C. A. Robson pointed out in an
important if unnecessarily severe review,[1] each stanza is
usually composed of thirty syllables, however these may be
divided up amongst the lines. He compares this to a system
used in Middle English, but both the French and English
stanza probably go back to a common ancestor, a Latin hymn
tune. *St. Modwenna* could have been written to be sung to
the tune of one of the 'alphabetical' hymns published by
Dr. Esposito.[2] The stanzas of this hymn are of eight lines,
which can be regarded as double quatrains. Except for the
introductory stanza, each has a two-line refrain in the same
metre as the rest, but rhyming with the A-stanza. This has
obscured the issue. Metrically and musically this is not to be
counted as a refrain. It is an integral part of the whole. Like
the *Brendan*, this poem looks back to the sung Life of the
St. Leger type, and forward to the read Life in octosyllabic
couplets. The question whether *St. Brendan* and *St. Modwenna* were ever sung must remain an open one, but at any
rate it can be stated that they are written in a form which is
singable. In *St. Modwenna* there is often enjambement
between the stanzas, but this is not an incontrovertible

[1] *Medium Ævum*, xviii (1949), pp. 49–60.
[2] *Proceedings of the Royal Irish Academy*, xxviii, C. xii (1910), pp. 239–42.

argument that it was read. This long poem is divided by
the translator into a series of fits convenient for chanting or
reciting at a sitting, each with an epilogue announcing the
subject of the next. The length of these provides evidence
of how other works, including the romances of Crestien,
were probably divided. When they were performed by a
jongleur the hat could be passed round at the end of each
section.[1]

The style is rhetorical, and the poet is particularly fond of
rhetorical questions, often involving the repetition of a key
word, thus:

> Ne sai cument, par quel veisdie,
> Nes ad Nature en seignurie.
> > Nature? Nun! Oez pur quei. (47–49)

(I do not know how, by what cunning, Nature has them not in her
lordship. / Nature? No! Listen why.)

> Li saives hom mult veir se dit
> En sun proverbe, ke il escrit,
> Ke le povre par tuit se git.
> > Git? Oil, pur veir! Rien n'i mesprit. (2097–100)

(The sage[2] says this very truly in the saw which he wrote, that the
poor man is everywhere despised. Despised? Ay, indeed. He was not
mistaken there.)

The translator has many reflections on the world's in-
stability. Fortune's wheel turns up and down, Alexander the
Conqueror himself could not escape death. Very occasionally
there are flashes of poetry, as in the description of the willow-
tree that bore apple-blossom (lines 4565 ff.). The language
is often Biblical, the vocabulary rich and unusual.

The audience is often apostrophized as 'seignurs'. It is
worthy of note that the maiden Osith is not here identified
with the saint of that name. The translation was almost certainly made for patrons or guests of Burton.

Two manuscripts (Bodleian Digby 34 and Welbeck 1 C. 1)
survive, both Anglo-Norman. The first-named may be early
thirteenth-century.

---

[1] I cannot follow Mr. Robson's argument that the Life is a stringing together
of what he calls the Twelve Lays.

[2] i.e. Ovid. 'Pauper ubique jacet' (*Fasti* I. 218) has remained a tag.

ST. AUDREY

The last of the native virgin saints commemorated is St. Etheldreda, better known as St. Audrey. The Anglo-Norman Life[1] is by a certain Marie, who does not tell us anything about herself. She was probably a nun, but the present writer's suggestion[2] that she may have belonged to Canonsleigh, the sole example of a convent with a dedication to St. Audrey, cannot be sustained; the language of the text, now available for examination, is clearly earlier than 1285, the date of the dedication. Marie may have been a nun of St. Mary's Abbey of Chatteris, Cambridgeshire, an Anglo-Saxon foundation connected with Ramsey, which was given by Henry I to Ely Cathedral in the time of Bishop Harvey (d. 1131). Of the four post-Conquest abbesses before 1265 whose names have been recorded, the last was called Mary de St. Clare.[3] Perhaps in some earlier and humbler capacity she had composed the Life in honour of the virgin patroness of Ely.

Marie's named source is Bede, but this is a mere quotation from the work which she was translating, sections of the *History of Ely* compiled by the monk Thomas, who had been cured of a great sickness by the intervention of the saint. The date when he was at work is not very clear, but the miracles related by Marie include one of the time of Bishop Geoffrey Ridel, who died in 1189. This may be an interpolation into the *History* of Thomas, whose main work is believed to be earlier, but it proves that Marie cannot have been writing earlier than 1190, and most probably belonged to the first half of the thirteenth century.

The poem is bald. After sixteen lines of prologue, an exhortation to spend one's life wisely, the writer proceeds to hold up St. Audrey as an example. The next 4,048 lines recount her life and miracles. As Dr. Södergård has pointed out, Marie has done her best to impart a sense of liveliness to the dull narrative of her source, but she still gives an impression

---

[1] An edition, left unfinished by J. A. Malone, who joined the Army in 1916 and lost his life, is extant at Sheffield University. The text is now available in print, *La Vie Sainte Audrée*, ed. O. Södergård (Uppsala, 1955).

[2] *Anglo-Norman in the Cloisters*, p. 75.   [3] *V.C H. Cambridge and Ely*, ii. 220–3.

of dryness. Thomas was writing history, and the Life is overloaded with genealogical details, which hold up the action. St. Audrey was the daughter of Anna, King of East Anglia. She was twice married, first to a local magnate named Tonbert, who gave her the Isle of Ely as a morning-gift, and after his death to Egfrid, son of King Oswy of Northumbria, from whom she obtained Hexham. In each case she contrived to preserve her virginity, with less trouble in the first than in the second. Egfrid had a powerful ally in St. Wilfrid of York. However, St. Audrey pursued her chosen course, overcoming all opposition. For this she has been much blamed in the nineteenth century, but her behaviour was in keeping with the ideas of the time and she had been married against her will. The conduct of Edward the Confessor, who, as Gibbon said of Basil II, 'preferred his private chastity to the public interest', was equally reprehensible, from this point of view. St. Audrey used her dower-lands to found the abbeys of Hexham and Ely. At one point she herself retired to her Aunt Ebba's priory of Coldingham, but left it for her mixed foundation of Ely, where she died, no martyr, but the victim of a painful affliction of the throat which she had formerly loved to adorn with jewels—a fate which was commemorated by the sale of 'tawdry necklaces' at Ely Fair. Later her nuns were all massacred by the Danes, so that they at least were martyrs. Posthumous miracles were many, and Marie recounts some thirty of them. The last thirty lines are epilogue, and the last two give her name:

> Ici escris mon non MARIE,
> Pur ce ke soie remembree. (4619–20)

(Here I inscribe my name MARIE, so that I may be kept in mind.)

Marie's language is remarkably free from provincialism and her versification comparatively correct by continental standards. The form employed is the octosyllabic couplet, but, as so often in Norman and Anglo-Norman texts, the same rhyme is sometimes repeated. Feminine rhymes are not rare. Enjambement occurs, but the verse has a regularity which is monotonous by comparison with some other Anglo-Norman texts. Rare are passages such as this:

'Pastor sui. As bestes entent
Garder. Ceo est ma femme ici.
Tele vie mein com jeo vous di.'   (434–6)

('I am a shepherd. My business is to look after these beasts. Here is my wife. I lead the life I describe to you.')

This lack of style is partly due to the nature of the text which she was translating. Her object was to tell a plain tale plainly. There is no evidence that she was French or had been abroad, but she was probably of good birth and accustomed to speak French from infancy. The late A. T. Baker's statement, that in *St. Audrey* the 'authoress names three continental convents to which English girls were sent to perfect their French',[1] is due to a lapse of memory. It is Bede who said that Anglo-Saxon princesses were sent to continental nunneries, to learn not the French language (which they may have picked up in the process) but French ways, and this is naturally repeated by Thomas of Ely and by Marie after him. The three houses named were Chelles, Brie, and Les Andelys. For the last of them Marie has substituted 'alliors' for convenience of rhyme.

The text is preserved in only one manuscript, the Campsey collection (Welbeck 1 C. 1), which can be dated about three-quarters of a century later. The scribe has made a number of changes in the language which are for the worse, but are mainly superficial and easily corrected.

ST. MELOR

Professor Diverres has in preparation an edition of the Life of St. Melor, taken apparently from a Breton, not a Welsh, source.

MARY MAGDALEN

The thirteenth-century emphasis on confession and penitence naturally fostered an interest in the story of the Magdalen. It is in the course of this century that the sorry affair of the rape of the relics at Vezelay reached its climax and its end. English interest may have been aroused when Richard Cœur de Lion took the cross at Vezelay in 1190. No

[1] 'Saints' Lives written in Anglo-French', Royal Society of Literature, *Essays by Divers Hands*, iv (London, 1924), p. 145.

less than four Lives written in England are known: a fragment of forty-two lines in the stanza used by Guernes de Pont-Sainte-Maxence, another in tail-rhyme stanzas, a Life by Bozon in octosyllabic couplets, and another in the same metre by Guillaume le Clerc, swimming as usual with the tide of events.[1]

THE VIRGIN MARY

Interest in the Virgin Mary also increased. The proclamation of the doctrine of the Immaculate Conception in the twelfth century led to Wace's poem *La Conception Nostre Dame* and to Adgar's *Miracles*, the first work of the kind not associated with the cult of relics.[2] These were rewritten in the thirteenth century by Everard de Gateley, a monk of Bury. Only three of his miracles survive.[3] An entirely fresh translation was also made by an anonymous writer,[4] in which much is made of confession, prayer, and penitence. The eighth miracle, illustrating the value of confession, occurs only in this place. The editor rightly calls attention to this, and ascribes the authorship to some preacher anxious to encourage his flock in spiritual exercises. It may be the work of some chaplain or confessor.

An Anglo-Norman version of the 'elemental cycle' of miracles of the Virgin was made in the thirteenth century, and is preserved in one manuscript (Royal 20 B. xiv) of the end of that century or the extreme beginning of the next. They are: Fire—the little Jew boy (in which the poet makes it clear that he was writing in England); Air—Theophilus; Water—the drowning woman; Earth—Julian the Apostate. The *Miracle of Theophilus*[5] contains four lines which are inspired by the story of Tristan:

> Ceo est de Theophele le dolerus,
> Le perdu, le maleurus.
> Pur le peché de la neire mort,
> E coment il en aveit confort.   (33–36)

---

[1] For the bibliography see Vising, nos. 135, 136, and R. Reinsch, *Archiv*, lxiv (1880), pp. 85–91.

[2] See above, pp. 187–91.   [3] P. Meyer, *Romania*, xxix (1900), pp. 27–47.

[4] H. Kjellman, *La Deuxième Collection anglo-normande des miracles de la Sainte Vierge* (Paris and Uppsala, 1922).

[5] Ed. H. Kjellman, *Studier i Modern Språkvetenskap*, v (Uppsala, 1914), pp. 185–227.

(This is about Theophilus the dolorous, the lost, the unhappy, on account of the sin which brings dark death, and how he was relieved of it.)

This is an echo, conscious or not, of Thomas.

There are also other poems devoted to the Virgin, in lyric form—three versions of the Annunciation, seven on the Joys of Mary, of which one is by Martin, another Bury monk, and a version of them in prose, and two Laments, one of which is by Bozon. Guillaume le Clerc contributed yet another *Joys of Mary*, thus once again conforming to the fashion of the moment.[1]

THE *LIVES* BY MATTHEW PARIS

Anglo-Norman hagiography took its rise in court patronage. In the thirteenth century the extension of literacy and the rise of a middle class broke the monopoly of court circles, but this century did see one remarkable survival of courtly patronage in this field. The man who did most to supply the wants of great ladies in this regard was the chronicler Matthew Paris, a fact that was formerly received with incredulity but is now acknowledged to be without doubt.[2] He seems to have become involved in this undertaking through the illustrated French *Life of St. Alban* (T.C.D., E. 1. 40) which he produced. Except for the rubrics, which are in octosyllabic couplets, this is written in *laisses* of alexandrines. There is a faint possibility that the actual poem is by an earlier writer, and that Matthew Paris merely supplied the drawings and the rubrics, but this must remain a speculation. The epic form, however, suggests that it was designed for a masculine audience, though hardly, as Dr. Vaughan thinks, for the monks themselves. The manuscript did remain at St. Albans, whose press-mark it still bears. It may have been designed for some great Gaudy. The fly-leaves were used by Matthew Paris as a notebook, and the jottings on them shed light on the fortunes of the later Lives. The next was either *St. Edward the Confessor* or *St. Thomas*, which were once in

[1] For the bibliography see Vising, nos. 84–96; R. Reinsch, *Zeitschrift für Romanische Philologie*, iii (1879), pp. 200–31.

[2] *Anglo-Norman in the Cloisters*, pp. 20–31; cf. R. Vaughan, *Matthew Paris* (Cambridge, 1958), pp. 168–81.

the same manuscript, but survive in separate copies, *St. Thomas* being in fragments. *St. Edward* was a translation of Ailred's Life made for the queen, Eleanor of Provence. One of the fly-leaf notes states that Isabelle, Countess of Arundel, is to return the copy of the *Lives of St. Thomas and St. Edward* in order that it may be lent to the Countess of Cornwall. It is to this Countess of Arundel that the latest of the Lives is dedicated, that of St. Edmund of Abingdon. This was written about ten years after the others, after 1250. This work is especially interesting, because it is the only one in which the author names himself, 'ge Maheu', and because the Latin source translated is by Matthew himself.

All these books are 'picture books', though *St. Edmund* survives only in a copy without pictures. The plans for yet another, of a slightly different type, exist on the *St. Alban* fly-leaves. It is not known whether this book was ever made. The arrangement of the illustrated manuscripts is almost exactly the same as for the St. Albans type of Apocalypse, with the pictures occupying the top of the page.

The style and versification of the texts are careless, and it is interesting to note that it has now been revealed that Matthew Paris was also careless and inaccurate when writing in Latin, which was formerly thought not to be the case, and appeared to be an argument against the attribution of the French Lives to the great chronicler.[1]

Dr. Vaughan's amusing statement that Matthew Paris 'ran a kind of circulating library among his aristocratic friends' must be taken with a grain of salt. It is doubtful whether queens and countesses would have considered him in the light of a friend, and the lending of books was nothing new. How a copy of Geoffrey of Monmouth was lent by Robert of Gloucester himself to Walter Espec, and by Walter to Ralph FitzGilbert, and by him to his wife, and by her to Gaimar, must be remembered. Monastery libraries were naturally asked for loans: King John borrowed a quantity of theological books from Reading.[2] The practice was probably commoner than has been supposed.

[1] Cf. *Anglo-Norman in the Cloisters*, pp. 30, 31; *Matthew Paris*, pp. 130–1.
[2] M. R. James, *The Ancient Libraries of Canterbury and Dover* (Cambridge, 1903), pp. xlv–xlvi; and above, p. 108.

PETER OF PECKHAM'S *RICHARD OF CHICHESTER*

In or about 1259 Matthew Paris died, and his mantle as translator fell upon less distinguished shoulders. When writing about Richard de Wyche, Bishop of Chichester, Matthew Paris had drawn upon the reminiscences of Ralph Bocking, the bishop's Dominican confessor. In 1262 Richard was canonized, and just before his death in 1270 Ralph Bocking wrote, at the request of Archbishop Kilwardby, himself a Dominican, the Latin *Life and Miracles* of the new saint. This was dedicated to Isabelle, Countess of Arundel, then recently widowed, for whom Matthew Paris had translated his *Life of St. Edmund*. One of the canons of Chichester sent the Latin *Life* with a request for a French translation to a man who already had a certain reputation as translator and adaptor, Peter of Peckham or Fetcham,[1] who names himself in the epilogue, and gives an account in the prologue of the circumstances which led to his undertaking the task. The translation was dedicated to his 'Patron', John of Abernon, probably a kinsman. The *Life*, but not the *Miracles*, was edited by Professor A. T. Baker.[2]

Many chapters of the *Life* are missing from the unique copy which survives (Welbeck 1 C. 1), and it must once have been about twice as long as it is now. At present it is 1,696 lines long, and the *Miracles* occupy another 1,310. Peter seems to have followed his source literally, but he must have known a manuscript of Bocking which differed from the one extant, for he appears to be following at times the shorter version which was used later by John Capgrave. Peter's work occurs only in the 'Campsey collection'.

The *Life of St. Richard* has much to recommend it. As a young man he had rejected an offer of a rich marriage and his elder brother's estate in order to go to Oxford. He was so poor during his sojourn there that he is reputed to have shared a gown and tunic with his chamber-fellow, with whom he played Box and Cox when attending lectures. Later on he became Chancellor of the University. In between he went to

---

[1] Cf. above, pp. 214–16.
[2] *Revue des Langues Romanes*, liii (1910), pp. 245–396. A transcript of the *Miracles* promised by O. A. Beckerlegge has never appeared.

Orléans to study theology, and it was there that he acquired his admiration of the Dominicans, whom he encouraged when he became bishop. St. Edmund made him Chancellor of Canterbury, and he accompanied the archbishop on his last journey and was with him when he died at Soisy. He himself was taken ill and died at Dover on his way to consecrate a new church dedicated to St. Edmund. His career explains the interest taken in it by Robert Kilwardby the Dominican and the Countess of Arundel, who belonged to his diocese and already possessed the *Life of St. Edmund*.

It is noticeable that Peter's verse is more halting in the parts where he is translating than in the parts which he composed himself. This is a phenomenon which can be observed elsewhere. Like William Giffard and the translators of the Apocalypse, he appears to be making a compromise between a verse and prose translation. As in his other works, a caesura is often employed and enjambement is fairly frequent. Peter conforms to a pattern of versification which is representative of Anglo-Norman, but he was no poet. The utilitarian nature of so much Anglo-Norman verse is a factor to be taken into account when assessing its qualities.

THE *LIVES* BY NICOLE BOZON

At the end of the thirteenth century and the beginning of the fourteenth that prolific Franciscan, Nicole Bozon, treated all the old themes in a new way. He has left a series of eleven saints' Lives[1] which are to the normal kind what the lay is to the romance. All but two are of women saints, and nearly all are based on the Golden Legend. It has been suggested that they were made for some convent. That may be, but it is far more likely that they were made for some laywoman or laywomen, or parishioners to whom Bozon acted as confessor. It is to be noted that the *Life of St. Martha*, which might be thought suitable for a woman reader, is addressed to 'Beu segnours', a form of address which, as has been said before, is equivalent to our 'Ladies and gentlemen' but was sometimes used for fellow monks. The emphasis on penitence and salvation in the epilogues to these Lives is characteristic of

---

[1] Cf. above, pp. 226–32.

the Franciscans, who supplied so many confessors. Bozon himself belonged to a community which had powers normally reserved to the Ordinary. The eleven Lives are usually listed in alphabetical order, as though the names had been drawn out of a hat, but they were in fact carefully chosen and may be conveniently distributed as follows:

Virgin martyrs: Agatha, Agnes, Christina, Juliana, Lucy, Margaret.

Penitents: Mary Magdalen (identified with Mary of Bethany), Martha (supposed therefore to be her sister).

Ascetics: Elizabeth of Hungary (the only modern saint— a patroness of Franciscans and ultimately a Tertiary of the Order), Abbot Paphnutius (the 'Buffalo'), Paul the Hermit (these last the only two male saints).

Viewed thus the list makes some sort of sense.

The legends are told in very summary form, and the appalling tortures of the martyrs, over which miniaturists and stage-managers so often gloated, are mercifully passed over with great rapidity, otherwise the gallery of virgin martyrs would have been a mere Chamber of Horrors, the literary counterpart of S. Stefano Rotondo. Bozon set out to be austere, and made no concessions to the thirst for romance or excitement on the part of his readers. As was pointed out above, his style here is plain compared with that of the reflective poems.

SETH

Apart from actual Lives of saints and poems connected with the Virgin, all sorts of apocryphal books were used as sources. The Gospel of Nicodemus was particularly popular. *Seth*, or the *Legend of the Holy Rood*, is the subject of an interesting poem in octosyllables.[1] It is the only poem in Old French entirely devoted to this story. The manuscript (Cambridge, Corpus Christi 66) is of about 1243–54. The introduction to the critical edition is important for the history of the legend.

---

[1] Printed, without critical apparatus, by H. H. Hilton, *University of North Carolina Studies in the Romance Languages and Literatures*, ii (Chapel Hill, 1941), pp. 41–61. Critical edition by M. Lazar, 'La légende de "l'Arbre de Paradis" ou "Bois de la Croix" ', *Zeitschrift für Romanische Philologie*, lxxvi (1960), pp. 34–63.

THE PASSION OF JUDAS

Also unique in Old French is the Anglo-Norman *Passion of Judas*. The starting-point of this poem is the encounter with Judas imprisoned on his island of ice (Jan Mayen) described in *St. Brendan's Voyage*. After alluding to this punishment the writer relates the betrayal and passion of Jesus, and proceeds to draw a moral. The body will die, but the wicked soul will go to hell, the good to purgatory. The versification of this text is peculiar, and has obviously suffered in transmission. Unfortunately it survives in only one manuscript (Bodleian Laud Misc. 471). The beginning and end are in octosyllabic couplets, but in between there are passages in decasyllables and alexandrines. The number of syllables in all classes of line is only approximate in the state in which this text is preserved, but many lines can easily be corrected by the addition or omission of a monosyllabic word, which suggests that much of the weakness in the versification is due to scribes. The longer lines often rhyme in quatrains, and just before the end the octosyllables also rhyme in fours. As we have it now the text has the appearance of one of those accompaniments to picture books already described,[1] but the poem is cast in the form of a verse sermon and seems to have been recited to a large audience. It begins:

> Seignurs, pur Deu ça escutez,
> Vos ki estez ci assemblez,
> Coment fut traÿ nostre seignur.

(Lords, for the sake of God listen to this, you who are assembled here; hear how our Lord was betrayed.)

Later, the audience or congregation is addressed as 'bone gent'—'good people', which suggests that they were not gentlefolk. There is a suggestion that the reciter was able to point to some pictorial representation of heaven:

> Kar quicunkes vult a Deu venir
> E ses pechez vult espenir
> Il ne deit unkes cessir
> Ne ne deit jamés finir
> Ne par nut ne par jur
> De requere sun sauveor,

[1] Cf. above, pp. 136–40.

Ki meint lasus en icele tur,
Ki del ciel est creatur,
Ke il eit merci de noz pechez.

(For whosoever will come to God and expiate his sins, must never cease nor finish, either by night or day, requesting his Saviour, who dwells above in that tower, who is creator of heaven, to have mercy on our sins.)[1]

VISITS TO THE OTHERWORLD

Interest in the Otherworld inspired, besides Lives of saints, several poems of the twelfth and thirteenth centuries, remote ancestors of the *Divine Comedy*. There are three versions of *St. Paul's Descent to Hell*, one by the Templar of Temple Bruer,[2] another by Adam de Ros,[3] perhaps an Irish Cistercian, while a third is anonymous.[4] These last two are in octosyllabic couplets, and the third is a modernization of the Temple Bruer version.[5] There are, as has been mentioned, the five versions in Anglo-Norman of *St. Patrick's Purgatory*, and the earlier one of Marie de France had, of course, been made for the English market. There is also a version, in *laisses* of alexandrines, of another Irish legend, the *Vision of Tondale*.[6] The author says that he is translating from the Latin

En fraunceis pur lez unes qi ne seivent de clergie.

(Into French for those who have no learning.)

It is doubtful whether he was talking about men, women, or both.

These visions are semi-allegorical, and are a branch of the dream-literature, inspired by the *Somnium Scipionis* and the *Consolatio Philosophiae*, so popular in the Middle Ages. Interest in the Otherworld was, however, transmitted to them by the Irish, and it would not be surprising, therefore, to find that some of the writers on this theme in French

---

[1] Extract by P. Meyer, *Documents manuscrits de l'ancienne littérature de la France* (Paris, 1871), pp. 242–3; text printed without critical apparatus and with no attention paid to the versification by N. Iseley, *University of North Carolina Studies in the Romance Languages and Literatures*, ii (Chapel Hill, 1941), pp. 29–40.

[2] Cf. above, pp. 191–2.　　　　[3] Cf. *Anglo-Norman in the Cloisters*, p. 53.

[4] P. Meyer, *Romania*, xxiv (1895), pp. 357–75.

[5] Cf. D. D. R. Owen, 'The Vision of St. Paul: The French and Provençal Versions and their Sources', *Romance Philology*, xii (1958), pp. 33–41, and R. C. D. Perman, 'Henri d'Arci', *Studies . . . Presented to A. Ewert* (Oxford, 1961), pp. 308–21.　　　　[6] Ed. V. H. Friedel and Kuno Meyer (Paris, 1907).

dwelt in Ireland, as has been suggested in the case of Adam de Ros.[1]

It is apparent that the verse Saint's Legend is one of the most remarkable characteristics of Anglo-Norman literature. The love of this form persisted in England at a time when it was being replaced by prose on the Continent, and when a decline in poetical inspiration is to be noted in the translators. The tradition in England of the verse Life seems to have been too strong for the writers to follow their natural inclination, and the result is a decline in quality though not in quantity. While the octosyllabic rhyming couplet is the commonest metre employed, the *laisse* of longer lines is not unknown. The number of Lives in stanzas, often of tail-rhyme, occasionally of alexandrines, but often of octosyllables, is noteworthy, and shows the conservatism characteristic of Anglo-Norman. The lyric form out of which the Saint's Legend developed was kept longer than on the Continent, and was kept alive partly, perhaps, by what seems to have been a natural love of stanza-form in English, where it was used not only in Saints' Lives, but in Romances. The point has to be made, since it is often overlooked, that these legends, whoever wrote them, were as a rule produced for layfolk. Often they were written by religious, but this was for the benefit of patrons and guests and for the purpose of attracting gifts of favour. They may have been used for relaxation by monks and nuns themselves on solemn feasts or patronal festivals, but they were not composed for meal-time reading, though they may occasionally have been used for that purpose, as was a collection bequeathed by a lay-woman at Campsey. There is extraordinary variety in the Legends. Some are quite as well worth reading as any romance. Some verge on history, some borrow from native traditions, not because of any enthusiasm in the Normans for their new country, but because local history was of importance for ancient foundations. Here, as in history and romance, the terror of the Danes was kept alive. France and Spain had their Saracens to contend with, but England and Normandy had a closer acquaintance with the Vikings, predatory and pagan.

[1] For Ireland cf. W. W. Heist, *The Fifteen Signs before Doomsday* (Michigan, 1952), pp. 101, 202–3.

XI

HISTORY AND CHRONICLES

BOTH the Anglo-Saxons and the Normans seem to have been more interested in history than other peoples were, and after the Conquest Anglo-Norman writers turned their attention to the history of Britain and England. They exploited it for political purposes on a national scale, just as the royal and noble families exploited local traditions and invented ancestors for themselves for reasons of prestige, and ancient religious foundations fostered an interest in native saints.[1]

In view of all this it is perhaps unfortunate that Professor R. R. Darlington in his Inaugural Lecture entitled *Anglo-Norman Historians*[2] should mention only Gaimar, and him only as a translator of the Anglo-Saxon Chronicle. While the lecture admittedly covers only the century after 1066, and no one will dispute his conclusion that 'the disappearance of English historical prose was really due to the writing of the Latin histories of Malmesbury and his contemporaries', it is a pity that the impression should be left that there was nothing of interest or value ever written in Anglo-Norman. The following chapter should help to clear up this misconception, sometimes prevalent amongst people who should know better; but, it is hoped, no exaggerated claims will be made.

Although much genuine history and biography was written in Anglo-Norman, and in French for Anglo-Norman patrons, the desire for vernacular history was due mainly to the appearance of a romantic and readable book in Latin—the *History of the Britons* by Geoffrey of Monmouth. While the mythical part of this was perpetuated and almost believed in, it led to continuations based on reliable sources such as Bede and the Anglo-Saxon Chronicle, ending up with accounts of contemporary history wdich are sometimes first-hand.

---

[1] Cf. above, pp. 139–75 and pp. 259–66.
[2] Birkbeck College, University of London (1947), pp. 5–6.

To all intents and purposes the earliest chronicle in any French dialect is Gaimar's. We have no means of knowing what David's song about Henry I (to which he refers) was like, nor even what language it was written in. Although Gaimar had probably begun his chronicle before he had access to a copy of Geoffrey of Monmouth, which was then brand-new and difficult to obtain,[1] it was perhaps his meeting with that book which caused him to conceive of his tripartite plan—a History of the Britons, a History of the English, and a History of His Own Times. Only the middle survives in its entirety, but the plan was followed, generation after generation, and Gaimar set, before the middle of the twelfth century, a pattern which was copied for three or four centuries. The chief interest of Gaimar today lies in four directions: his knowledge and use of legends about the Danes, including a mythical series of Danish kings and the story of Havelok; his preservation of gossip about recent events, in particular the death of Rufus; his use of sources in three languages; the chain of borrowings which was necessary to enable him to read Geoffrey of Monmouth. A point which is not made by Professor Darlington is that any layman who could read would prefer his history in Latin, but women preferred to listen to French verse. Gaimar's patron was a lady. Her husband had borrowed Geoffrey of Monmouth apparently for his own use, and from him it was borrowed for Gaimar.[2]

The tripartite pattern was next employed by Wace, whose *Brut* caused the disappearance of Gaimar's *History of the Britons*. For the *History of the English* his plan comprised the *Rou*, a history of the Dukes of Normandy. This, however, he left unfinished, finding himself superseded in favour of Benoit. Benoit in turn left his work unfinished, so that Wace's intentions remained unfulfilled.[3]

Anonymous writers added to Wace's *Brut*. These con-

---

[1] Cf. A. Bell, 'The Epilogue to Gaimar's "Estoire des Engleis" ', *Modern Language Review*, xxv (1930), p. 55.

[2] Cf. above, pp. 28–32.

[3] Cf. above, p. 75, and M. D. Legge, 'Patronage and Old French Literature', *Stil- und Formprobleme* (Heidelberg, 1959). Whether Wace knew Gaimar or not is an open question. A. Bell hesitates about it, but no conclusion is possible. Gaimar's *Estoire des Engleis* (A.N.T.S., 1960), pp. lxxiv-lxxv.

tinuations are always in the octosyllabic couplet. They also provided the introductory *Des Grantz Geanz*.[1]

PETER OF ICKHAM

In the thirteenth century a prose epitome of various chronicles was made, which has been ascribed to Peter of Ickham, though he was probably only the donor of a manuscript of it to Canterbury. One of its merits is that it preserves quotations from verse chronicles. Some come from Wace (or possibly Gaimar), others are unidentifiable. A substantial extract from a probable translation of Ailred's *Life* of Edward the Confessor is included.[2] Although this work is such a hotch-potch, the compiler is sometimes inspired, and his translation of Henry of Huntingdon's account of the death of Siward could not be bettered:

E donc dist il: 'Honte est a mei ki unkes ne poei murir a tant de batailles com jeo ai esté, estre ore mort a fer de vache. E pur ceo metez moy moun hauberc, e ceignez moi de m'espee, e metez la hache dorree en ma mein ke jeo pusse morir a feor de chivaler.' E issi rendi le esperit armæ.

(And then he said: 'Shame on me that I, who could never die in the many battles where I have been, should now be dead in the manner of a cow! Wherefore put upon me my hauberk, and gird me with my sword, and place my gilded axe in my hand, that I may die in the manner of a knight.' And thus, fully armed, he gave up the ghost.)[3]

LANGTOFT

In the fourteenth century an imitation of Gaimar on a large scale was made by the canon of Bridlington, Peter of Langtoft, in *laisses* of alexandrines.[4] The prologue (not in the printed edition) is a rewriting of the prologue of Wace (or Gaimar) in the longer line. Much of this chronicle is valueless as history, being derived from well-known sources, but occasionally Langtoft gives a glimpse of traditions current in his day, as in the case of Guy of Warwick quoted above.[5] The last and contemporary part, the Reign of Edward I, is often

[1] Ed. G. E. Brereton (Oxford, 1937).
[2] Cf. *Anglo-Norman in the Cloisters*, p. 45, and above, pp. 147–8.
[3] *Le Liver de Reis de Brittanic*, edited by J. Glover (R.S.), p. 124. Cf. M. D. Legge, 'In fere of werre',*The Scottish Historical Review*, xxxv (1956), p. 22.
[4] Ed. T. Wright (R.S.).   [5] Page 68.

first-hand and authoritative. Some of the material seems to have been obtained from the entourage of Anthony Bek, Bishop of Durham, a prominent statesman. Langtoft's patron bore a north-country name, Scaffeld. Nothing whatever has transpired about this man, but it may have been he who was connected with Bek. One of the interesting points about this part of the work is the quantity of satirical songs, some of them in English, which are preserved in it. Such songs were often made in the two languages, and it is not necessary to suppose that the French songs, and parts of songs, are all translations from English made by Langtoft.[1]

This chronicle originally terminated before the end of Edward I's reign. Langtoft was animated by a dread and hatred of his neighbours, the Scots, and his first version ends on a note of triumph when, with the betrayal of Sir William Wallace, the three kingdoms of Logres, Kambria, and Albany seemed to have been reunited under a new Brutus. This state of affairs did not last, and the end was revised several times, probably by Langtoft himself, on a bitterer and bitterer note, until the final version terminates with the expression of misgiving, only too well founded, about the future when Edward II came to the throne.

Langtoft's chronicle was very popular, especially in the north of England, where several religious houses possessed copies of it. It was translated into English by the Gilbertine Robert of Brunne, canon of Sixhill, a Lincolnshire neighbour. He, however, substituted for the first part a translation of Wace's *Brut*, proving the lasting popularity of the work which had already caused the disappearance of Gaimar's first part. The result is curious, for the translator used a short line for Wace and a longer one for Langtoft, so that the whole work lacks unity.

The vitality of Anglo-Norman at the end of the thirteenth century and the beginning of the fourteenth is perhaps more clearly demonstrated by the demand for and popularity of a work of this nature, written at this date in Yorkshire, than by the facts that the court was still French-speaking by preference and that French was still the language of Parliament, the Law, and trade, and the vernacular of the Church.

[1] Cf. below, pp. 351-4.

Although, as has just been remarked, this work was naturally popular in the north of England, it had a wider circulation, for it is the source for the reign of Edward I in all the prose *Brut* chronicles, whether French, Latin, or English.[1]

BRUTS

Although the prose Saint's Legend, as has been remarked in the previous chapter, never ousted the verse form in England, this was not because Anglo-Norman was dying out when prose came into favour, as has been suggested, but because of the strong tradition of the verse *Life*. The same is not true of the chronicle. The *Brut* was turned into prose several times in the fourteenth century, sometimes in fuller and sometimes in shorter versions, and continually brought up to date. In default of a recent investigation of these versions—Vising lists five of them, and his tale of manuscripts is not complete —it would be idle to attempt to describe them here.[2]

LE BRUTE ABRÉGÉ

A prose chronicle of the fourteenth century bears the title of *Le Brute d'Engletere abrégé*. It has been held that this is a shortened prose translation of an English poem, but this seems improbable. The English bears every mark of having itself been translated from a French octosyllabic poem, and it is more likely that the extant French version is derived from the lost source of the English chronicle.[3]

LE PETIT BRUIT

There stands out from the general run of prose *Bruts* a mysterious work called *Le Petit Bruit*, the occasion for which is thus set forth in the prologue:

Cy comence *Le Bruit d'Engleterre*, que vous dirra de Roy en autre, payne e chrestien, jekes Roy Edward de Carnarvan qe ore est, solome

---

[1] For Langtoft's life and work, cf. *Anglo-Norman in the Cloisters*, pp. 70–74. My colleague, Professor Angus McIntosh, informs me that one manuscript was probably written in Ireland (Cambridge Univ. Lib. Gg. I. 1).

[2] Cf. especially F. W. D. Brie, *Geschichte und Quellen der mittelenglischen Prosachronik The Brute of England* (Marburg, 1905), pp. 17 ff., 33; G. E. Brereton, op. cit., pp. vi ff.; M. D. Legge and G. E. Brereton, 'Three Hitherto Unlisted MSS. of the French Prose *Brute Chronicle*', *Medium Ævum*, vii (1938), pp. 113–17.

[3] E. Zettl, *A Short English Metrical Chronicle* (E.E.T.S., o.s., 196, 1935): M. D. Legge, 'The *Brut Abridged*, a Query', *Medium Ævum*, xvi (1947), pp. 32–33.

la ordinaunce Meistre Rauf de Boun, qe a la requeste Monseignur
Henry de Lacy, Count de Nichole, ceste chose ad novelment abbregge
hors du *Grant Bruit*, en l'an du reigne nostre seignur le Roy Edward
de Carnarvan le tiers en entraunt. Kar vous entendrez qe ceste chose
fuit faict par encheson du darrain Edward, piere cely Roy qe ore est,
de quy vous troverez playne proces de tout sa vie, jekis a jour q'il
morust.

(Here begins *The Brut of England*, which will tell you from King
to King, pagan and Christian, down to King Edward of Carnarvon
who now is, according to the ordinance of Master Ralph de Bohun,
who, at the request of My Lord Henry de Lacy, Earl of Lincoln, this
thing has abridged anew from the *Great Brut*, in the year of the reign
of our lord the King Edward of Carnarvon the third at the beginning
[1310]. For you shall understand that this thing was made on account
of the last Edward, father of this King who now is, of whom you will
find full record of his whole life, down to the day of his death.)

What was this *Great Brut* which Ralph de Bohun claimed
to abridge? Vising (no. 375) says that it is *Le Livere de Reis
de Brittanie et Le Livere de Reis de Engleterre*, but this is not
so, though it is true that some of the names of the kings have
a certain resemblance to those in that work. 'Brut' might
mean Geoffrey of Monmouth's *Historia*, Wace, or any later
Brut chronicle. But the fact is that *Le Petit Bruit* appears to
be independent of all these, and some of the facts reported
cannot be explained as misunderstandings or re-formations
of the *Brut* as generally conceived. From the form of the
proper names one would suppose the source to have been in
Latin.

Brutus is here, as the title implies, but his wife is called
Galiene, and their three sons are called Silu II, who was to
inherit England; Log'us, who received the land of Log'ene,
now called Scotland after Schotus fitz Patrik, and formerly
known as Wastilde; and Walstanus, allotted Walslande—
formerly known as Brutayne le Greindre to distinguish it
from Brutayne le Maindre—which is now England. It is
difficult to see how this is to be explained as due to a succession of scribal errors. The name Silvius occurs in Geoffrey
several times, once as the name of the father of Brutus. It has
always been the correct thing to name the eldest son in a
family after his grandfather, and on the face of it the *Petit*

Bruit is more logical than Geoffrey. But it is only when one comes to read it that one realizes that Geoffrey's names for the three sons of Brutus have become, if not part of English history, at least part of English literature. Any difference in them arouses the sort of resentment which would be caused by a tampering with the names of Lear's three daughters— who, by the way, are not mentioned at all in the *Petit Bruit*, a significant fact, since this story appears to be pure invention on the part of Geoffrey. The reader will receive further shocks. The 'Chastel de Pucelis' is in Scotland all right, but the 'Chastel Sidemound Dolorous' is now known as Notyngham—a key point, especially in Stephen's time. Bath was built not by Bladud but by Baconus, and Leicester not by Lear but by Leirius, who was poisoned with the connivance of his son Belyn and is buried on the spot where Athelstan afterwards founded the Hospital of St. Cross for the repose of the soul of Guy of Warwick, who, it will be remembered, fought Colbrand at Winchester. Some of this, but by no means all, might be due to telescoping Geoffrey's account. There is the possibility that Ralph de Bohun made deliberate alterations to please his patron, but as the early part was intended to serve as introduction to the reign of Edward I, it is difficult to see why the son who inherited Scotland was moved up from third to second place. The feeling of bewilderment induced by reading the *Petit Bruit* lessens as the reader proceeds. William Bastard, called William the Conqueror, does nothing out of the way, and King Edward died at 'Burgh sus Sablouns, si gist a Westmoustre'.

The only parts of this work in print are an extract by Paul Meyer in his description of the manuscript (Harley 902) in the *Bulletin de la Société des Anciens Textes* (1878), pp. 110–13, and by Sir F. Madden in *Havelok the Dane* (Roxburghe Club, 1828), which has often been quoted since. Here attention is called to the fact that the *Estorie de Grimesby* quoted by Ralph de Bohun is the English romance of Havelok, a statement which has been queried by Skeat in *Havelok the Dane* (E.E.T.S., o.s., 4, 1868). Madden also pointed out that the chronicler Henry Knighton seems to have used the *Petit Bruit* as one of his sources.

All things considered, it is remarkable that no one has

so far troubled to edit this puzzling text, but this may be accounted for in part by the unfortunate fact that it survives only in a seventeenth-century copy (B.M. Harley 902). A university student in search of a subject for a thesis might well fight shy of it, but some mature scholar would find entertainment in trying to get behind the obvious misreadings of the original in many places. It is, however, impossible to avoid the feeling of suspicion that the *Petit Bruit* has been so neglected because it strikes out a line of its own, and it is more convenient to pretend that all *Brut* material is founded on Geoffrey's *Historia* than to share with medieval writers the belief that there were other books in the ancient British tongue.

Efforts to trace Ralph de Bohun have failed, but his patron, Henry de Lacy, Earl of Lincoln, was a very well-known soldier and statesman, who was Guardian of the Kingdom just after the accession of Edward I until his return from the Crusade, and later one of the Lords Ordainers. This suggests that Ralph may have been a member of the de Bohun family, Earls of Hereford and Essex and Constables of England, who must often have been associated with de Lacy. He may have been some kind of cousin, who had perhaps taken orders. De Lacy himself will be mentioned in a later chapter as one of the protagonists in the *tençon* of Walter de Bibbesworth, knight, crusader, and grammarian. There was evidently a lingering tradition of the aristocratic troubadour in English court circles at this time.

THE *SCALACRONICA*

The last half of the fourteenth century saw the swan-song of the *Brut* tradition in Anglo-Norman, and it is a masterpiece. It is a relief to turn from the later prose continuations of the *Brut*, slung together for information without any sense of style, to the *Scalacronica* of Sir Thomas Gray of Heton.[1] Gray was taken prisoner by the Scots in August 1355, and confined in Edinburgh Castle. Either he found there a considerable library, or he bought or borrowed quantities of books, for he devoured all the best-known chronicles, whether in Latin, French, or English, and took it into his head to pass

[1] Partly edited by J. Stevenson (Maitland Club, 1836).

the time 'a treter et a translater en plus court sentence lez cronicles del Graunt Bretaigne et lez gestez dez Englessez'. Here one thinks instinctively of Malory drawing out of his French books. Now Malory was in prison eight times, once for two and a half years. Gray could have been released at once, but the ransom demanded for him was too heavy for him to pay without assistance. Before November 1356 he appealed to the king for help, and he was released by August 1357. He had, therefore, about two years in which to write his chronicle, and it is just possible that most of it was accomplished in the time. It begins with the Fall of Lucifer and ends in 1362. Gray died in 1369. Stevenson printed only the part from 1066 onwards, and even so his edition occupies 203 quarto pages, which gives some idea of Gray's industry, and of what he meant by an abridgement.

The prologue is allegorical, and belongs to the dream tradition. The Sibyl appears to the author and shows him a ladder (the Gray family bore a scaling-ladder in their arms), each rung of which represents a different source. Beneath the ladder are the Bible and 'La gest de Troy'. The first rung gives access to 'Gauter erchedecen de Excestre', the second to Bede, the third to Higden, interpreter to Malmesbury, Huntingdon, Hoveden, and Marianus Scotus, the fourth to John of Tynmouth. The fifth rung gives access to the future, and cannot be climbed. The ladder is held up by the Franciscan Otterbourne, whose chronicle is not extant. In Stevenson's introduction he points out that Gray had access to other books, some of which he mentions as he goes along, and sources which cannot be precisely identified.

Tribute must be paid to Gray for this effort at synthesis, but the only really valuable part of his immense work is the period covered by his father's lifetime and his own. Both spent their lives fighting and garrisoning the north of England, and both were at various times taken prisoner. The father was captured, amongst other occasions, at Bannockburn. When Henry de Beaumont proposed to give ground a little, to entice the Scots forward, Gray objected that they might retreat too far.

'Voir,' fesoit le dit Henry, 'si tu eiez poour, fuez.' 'Sire,' fesoit le dit Thomas, 'pur poour ne fueray jeo huy.' Si fery cheval des esperouns. Entre ly et Willam Dayncourt, chevaler, assemblerent en my lieu dez enemys; Willam fust mort, Thomas fust pris, soun cheval tué dez launces.

('Indeed,' said the aforesaid Henry, 'if you are afraid, flee.' 'Sir,' replied the aforesaid Thomas, 'for fear I shall not flee this day.' And he struck spurs to his horse, and he and William Dayncourt, knight, went together into the midst of the enemy. William was killed, Thomas taken, his horse killed with the lances.)

This was at the beginning of the battle. It was at the end, as readers of Scott will remember, that Sir Giles de Argentine led the king from the field.

'Sire, votre reyne me fust baillez, ore estez a sauveté, veiz cy vostre chastel ou vostre corps purra estre savé. Jeo n'ay pas esté acoustomé a fuyre, ne plus avaunt ne voil jeo faire. A Dieux vous comaunde.' Si fery cheval dez esperouns, si reenala asembler, ou fust mort.

('Sire, your rein was entrusted to me, now you are in safety. There is your castle where your person may be saved. It has not been my custom to flee, so I will go no farther. I bid you adieu.' And he struck spurs to his horse, and went back to the attack, where he was killed.)

It is to be imagined that such fighters as the Grays had no use for the bastard chivalry of the day. When Sir William Marmion was presented by his lady with a gilt-crested helmet, with orders to take it to the most perilous place in Great Britain, and there make it known, he went off to Norham, where the Scots were besieging the Constable, Gray's father. When Gray saw the silly young fop arrive on foot, all glittering with gold and silver, and the ridiculous helm on his head, he called out to him:

'Sire chevaler, vous y estez venuz chevaler erraunt pur faire cel healme estre conuz, et si est meutz seaunt choz qe chevalery en soit fait a cheval qe a pee, ou covenablement ceo purra faire. Mountez vostre cheval, veez la voz enemys. Si ferrez cheval dez esperouns, va assemblere en mylieu dez eaux. Si renay jeo Dieu si jeo ne rescovroi toun corps, vive ou mort, ou jeo murreray.'

('Sir knight, you have come here as a knight errant to make this helm known, and it is more fitting that knightly deeds should be performed on horseback than on foot, wherever this can conveniently be done. Mount your horse, there are your enemies yonder. Strike spurs to your horse and go and attack them in the midst. Damn me,[1] but I'll rescue thee, dead or alive, or die for it.')

Marmion had more luck than he deserved. He charged, was wounded in the face and dragged from his saddle, and rescued as promised by Sir Thomas Gray.

Border warfare was rarely conducted by pitched battle, which is why Bannockburn and Flodden are so conspicuous. It was an affair of sieges, surprise night-attacks, and the firing of tents and billets, skirmishes and ambushes. The ease with which knights were taken prisoner, and the speed with which, as a rule, they were ransomed are remarkable. But then Gray takes for granted what Froissart found surprising, that Scots and English were always on the best of terms the minute they had decided to break off fighting. What Froissart learned by assiduously interviewing helpful persons, Gray knew by experience. The amazing thing is that he was able to get it down on paper, and we have reason to be grateful to the ambush at Nesbit where he was taken prisoner.

It is fitting that this remarkable narrative should end on a Chaucerian note:

Et cest riot pur le temps ensi enmesez, le dit David prist en espouse Dame Margaret de Logy, un dame q'autre foitz avoit esté marié, qe ove ly avoit devaunt demurrez; cest matrimoigne fust fait soulement per force d'amours, qe toutz veint.

(And this quarrel having been appeased for the time being, the said David took to wife Lady Margaret Logie, a lady who had been married before, and had previously lived with him. This marriage was made by force of true love alone, which conquers all things.)

The early part deserves more attention than has hitherto been paid to it. Gray had a mind trained in military administration, and discrepancies worried him. For instance, when he relates the story of Havelok, he does not try, as Gaimar did, to fit Havelok into the list of English kings. He explains that Athelbright and Edelsy, kings of Norfolk and Suffolk and of Lincoln respectively, are not mentioned in chronicles

---

[1] This alarming-looking blasphemy was merely a common imprecation. Even in a softened form it was obsolete in Cotgrave's day. '*Jarnigoy*, as much as, *Je renie Dieu*; (an old, and rusticall blasphemie)'; cf. Littré, s.v. *jarnidieu*, Henri IV's favourite oath.

of the Saxon kings because in those days there were many
petty kings, and only principal kings were thought worth
noticing. Athelbright's daughter is given both the names
under which she was known in the different versions, with
the explanation that Argentile is British and Goldesburgh is
Saxon. Havelok, after recovering her heritage, retired to his
native Denmark; hence he never became King of England.
Bede was ignorant of British history because his sources did
not deal with it, and moreover Bede did not know the language in which histories of the Britons were written.

The *Scalacronica* survives in a solitary manuscript, Cambridge, Corpus Christi 133. An abstract in English made by
Leland shows that near the end about two folios are missing.
It is not known whether Leland was using this manuscript;
if he was, these folios have disappeared since his day. Leland's text is given in an appendix by Stevenson in his edition, and was used by Sir Frederic Madden in his introduction
to *Havelok the Dane*.[1]

The uncouth aspect of Gray's language is the spelling.
Many of what appear to be false concords of number and
gender are nothing more or less than spelling mistakes. On
the whole, Gray's Anglo-Norman is easier to read than
Froissart's Hainault. It is a pity that Stevenson did not make
the reader's task lighter by distinguishing *i* from *j* and *u* from
v, by supplying accents and apostrophes, and abandoning
the long *s*. If this had been done less recourse would have
to be made to translations made by people who are not
familiar with Old French.

It is impossible not to regard the *Scalacronica* as a *tour
de force*, but the venture into literature of this middle-aged
warrior is amply justified, and the months he spent immured
in 'le opidoun Mount Agneth, jadys Chastel de Pucelis, ore
Edynburgh', were not wasted.

MERLIN'S PROPHECIES

The *Brut* chronicles naturally contain the prophecies
of Merlin. These sometimes appear by themselves. Langtoft's version of them is found as an extract, and there is a

---

[1] Roxburghe Club (1828), pp. xxxiv–xxxv.

translation into octosyllabic couplets of Geoffrey of Monmouth's account of Merlin in the *Historia*. Unfortunately, only a fragment of it survives, breaking off in the middle of the prophecies to Vortigern.[1]

The prologue explains the reasons for translating this work, and describes the difficulties of the translator:

> Kar tote gent ne entendunt mye
> Lettre en Latyn ne clergie,
> Et pur ço l'ai jo feet en romaunz,
> Ke tuz entendunt, petiz et grauns. (27–30)

(For everybody does not understand Latin literature, or learning, and therefore I have done it into Romance, that everyone, small and great, understands.)

Apparently the later prophecies, which have not survived, were in prose, and only the life of Merlin was in rhyme, for, the translator explains, the prophecies are too important to be reproduced inaccurately, and yet they are very obscurely put. He has not, therefore, rhymed them:

> Kar cil ky voudra rimer
> Ne put mye tut dis le dreyt aler;
> Hors de estorie ly covent trere
> Sovent, e menter pur rime fere. (35–38)

(For he who wishes to rhyme cannot always follow straight; he is obliged often to stray from his text, and misrepresent it in order to get his rhymes.)

The later prophecies about the reigns of the kings subsequent to John are extant in various copies.[2]

The generalization 'The monastic chronicler addressed his work to a clerical public, and he wrote exclusively in Latin'[3] needs a little qualification. Monastic chroniclers did sometimes address a lay public, and they did sometimes write in French, not only for the laity but for themselves.

THE *ANONIMALLE CHRONICLE*

French chronicles designed for home consumption seem to have been due to the accident that in the fourteenth

---

[1] Ed. J. Koch, *Zeitschrift für romanische Philologie*, liv (1934), pp. 22–42.
[2] Cf. H. L. D. Ward, *Catalogue of Romances* (London, 1883), i. 300, 308.
[3] D. Hay, *The Anglica Historia of Polydore Vergil* (Camden Series, lxxix, 1950), p. xxiv.

century monasteries were apt to possess copies of the *Brut* in French, which they then proceeded to keep up to date in the same language.

The most famous and historically important of the *Brut* continuations is the *Anonimalle Chronicle* of St. Mary's, York.[1] The manuscript (at Ripley Castle), copied in that house, contains some miscellaneous entries about the see of Carlisle derived from the *Lanercost Chronicle*, a short Latin chronicle to 1369, and a list of the abbots of St. Mary's, then a French prose *Brut* chronicle (Vising's no. 3781 as far as 1307, and thereafter independent down to Halidon Hill, 1333), followed by the *Anonimalle Chronicle*. This is in three hands and two parts. There may have been a gap of twenty years between the copying of the period 1334–56 and the period 1356–82.

The first part is based on the source or another version of what survives as the *Lanercost Chronicle*. We thus have the spectacle of Benedictines making use of a Franciscan source. Only two of the official documents interpolated into the *Lanercost Chronicle* are represented, but there is some additional matter about Crécy and Neville's Cross. From 1338 onwards the *Anonimalle* has preserved a text in a less confused state than *Lanercost*. The remainder is derived from unidentified sources, but is always a translation or revision of an earlier work. This leads to a curious state of affairs. The writer suddenly evinces an interest in foreign affairs, or speaks in the first person as eyewitness of some event at which he could not possibly have been present, and thinks nothing of presenting opposite views of a man's character and actions on successive pages. Sometimes he was able to paraphrase official documents. He loved to record *minutiae*. His account of the coronation of Richard II finds room for the loss of one of St. Edmund's sandals 'a cause q'il fust trop graunt et rude' (a detail known from other sources), and the fact that the crown had to be held on his head during the banquet 'a cause q'il fuist si pessaunt et ponderaunt q'il mesmes ne purroit porter pur sa juvence'. The convalescence of Edward III was hastened by a diet of old-fashioned nursery prescription—broth and bread-and-milk—the best white

[1] Ed. V. H. Galbraith (Manchester, 1927).

bread soaked in warm goat's-milk. A contemporary of
Sir Thomas Gray and Froissart was bound to include a few
picturesque episodes. The account of the death of Sir Robert
de Boynton at Berwick is even an improvement on Froissart.
According to the *Anonimalle* the Scots did not scale the ram-
parts in the orthodox way, but broke into the cellars and
caroused until everybody had gone to bed. The Captain,
when roused, rushed into the courtyard barefoot and in his
dressing-gown, and with his naked sword in his hand. There
he died fighting with his back to the wall. Straight from a
pantomime comes the story of Sir John Harpeden's victory
over the two Ethiops from India, who were 'freres jermains et
twynlynges' and always fought as one man.

For some occurrences, such as the Good Parliament, the
Parliament of Worcester, and the Rising of 1381, the *Chronicle* is a valuable source. Like the Cistercian who compiled
the *Dieulacres Chronicle*,[1] the writers were 'trying, not unsuc-
cessfully, to combine local with general history'. Occasionally local patriotism got the better of them. The character of
Sir Robert Knowles is blackened, and he is accused of having deserted his men during the Breton expedition of 1370,
merely because he had secured the grant of a manor belonging
to St. Mary's. The destruction of the nave and cloisters of the
abbey by a fire when the building was struck by lightning,
and the stranding of a school of porpoises off Cleveland, to
the great benefit of the nobility and clergy of the neighbourhood, are given the same prominence as events of world-wide
importance. Yet these details have their own value. It is impossible to speak of a style, since this varied according to the
nature of the source translated or paraphrased, but the pages
are enlivened by plenty of dialogue. It must be confessed, however, that the monks had a pedantic love of the cliché.

This *Chronicle* was edited by an acknowledged authority
on the period, because, with all its drawbacks, it is an in-
dispensable source of information about the fourteenth
century. As a specimen of what the Anglo-Norman dialect
was capable of at that late date, it has an additional importance.

---

[1] M. V. Clarke (with V. H. Galbraith), in *Fourteenth-Century Studies* (Oxford,
1937), p. 55.

LE LIVERE DE REIS

Le Livere de Reis de Brittanie e Le Livere de Reis de Engleterre[1] may have been begun at Canterbury, but it was continued in two other religious houses. The '*Wroxham*' *Continuation* (Cambridge, Trinity College R. 14. 7), down to 1306, is now known to have been made at Norwich. The book bears the Cathedral Priory press-mark, and the name of Geoffrey of Wroxham, who died in 1322.[2] It is quite colourless, and may be a mere copy. The *Sempringham Continuation* (Vatican MS.), on the other hand, was made at the Gilbertine Priory there, and has the same qualities as the *Dieulacres* and *Anonimalle Chronicles*. Here and there, amidst the recital of events of national importance, are references to local history. For instance, in 1312 an attack was made on the Priory, in 1317–18 there was a plague of long-tailed water-mice, bigger than rats, in 1319 a number of new nuns were blessed, in 1322 the sky one evening was blood-red, and in 1324 Joan de Mortimer took the veil. Names of representatives of the priory are given. It does not amount to very much, but proves without any doubt the origin of the chronicle. There are other continuations of less importance and impossible to identify.

POLISTORIE

John, a monk of Christchurch, Canterbury, wrote for another John, presumably one of his seniors, an enormous work with the grandiloquent title of the *Polistorie*[3] which he describes, erroneously, as 'ceste compilatiun breve'. Like the *Scalacronica*, it begins with the Creation and soon becomes a *Brut*, with the characteristic prologue. It is continued until 1313. French is employed 'pur ceo ke comunement la gent cel langage entendent'. The sources, carefully named in the margins, are the usual ones, Geoffrey of Monmouth, Bede, Marianus Scotus, various saints' Lives, and so on. The continuation has the features characteristic of this class, and its

---

[1] Cf. above, pp. 247–8 and p. 281.

[2] N. R. Ker, *Transactions of the Cambridge Bibliographical Society*, i (1953), pp. 7, 15.

[3] Unpublished, contained in Harley 636. Three other manuscripts are wrongly listed by Vising. Owing to the War, I was unable to see this chronicle before *Anglo-Norman in the Cloisters* went to press; see p. 45 of that book.

historical value resides in the local information it contains. The author's real purpose was to extol

l'Eglise de Caunterbire, mere de tote Engletere: quele digneté sur l'eglise eyt de Everwik et de tuz autres du reaume avaunt la venue des Normauns, et aprés euwe et usee.

(the church of Canterbury, Mother of All England: what dignity it has above the church of York and all others in the kingdom before the coming of the Normans, and since had and enjoyed.)

Anyone who knows the ecclesiastical history of medieval England will see at once what is afoot. The concern of the author of this weighty tome (B.M. Harley 636) is the great struggle for supremacy between the two primates, and, even more, the perpetual squabble with the monastery of St. Augustine's. The trickery of the latter in retaining the duplicate of a privilege obtained on false pretences and condemned to be publicly burnt is described with much indignation, and the intervention of 'Deu ke tut voyt, et tens passé et avenir' on the side of the innocent is noted with satisfaction. The impudent (but well-founded) claim of St. Augustine's to seniority is refuted, with the consequent outrageous reading, singing, and ringing of bells 'avant ke soné fust en la Mere Eglise'. This ringing of bells first in the morning was a matter of prestige, and was important before the days of striking clocks. The clock-tower of Christchurch was erected only in 1292, and it was one of the earliest in the country, perhaps being second only to the famous Westminster tower said to have been built out of the proceeds of Hengham's fine. In London the signal was given by St. Martin's-le-Grand until Edward III's reign, when the proverbial Bow Bells were substituted.[1] For the quarrel between the two Canterbury churches we are fortunate in having the opposite view presented by William Thorne (1380–1400), who was 'working over an elusive predecessor, Sprot'.[2]

The *Polistorie* was presumably written, like some other monastic chronicles in French, to be mentioned next, to enlist the sympathy of powerful laymen. In order to prove

[1] Cf. U. T. Holmes, *Daily Living in the Twelfth Century* (Madison, 1952), pp. 41, 270.
[2] Thorne's chronicle is most conveniently consulted in the annotated translation by A. H. Davis (Oxford, 1934).

the antiquity of a Christian foundation we should not now consider it necessary to go back to the Creation, but it was the scholastic way to begin at the beginning and go on to the end, and the general public in the fourteenth century would not have taken seriously any chronicle which deviated from the *Brut* tradition.

John of Canterbury can hardly be said to have a style. He writes a difficult prose, with awkward syntax and strained word-order. When translating from Latin he made no attempt to give any elegance or even clarity to his French.

GESTE DE BURCH

Besides the *Polistorie*, then, there are other monastic chronicles written for purely propaganda purposes. The earliest of these is the *Geste de Burch*,[1] an abridged translation of the *Peterborough Chronicle* by Hugh Candidus. This may have been made at the end of the twelfth century. A possible occasion for its composition, the editor points out, is the visit of Edward, Prince of Wales, and Piers Gaveston to Peterborough in 1302. On linguistic grounds it is impossible to date, as the Cotton manuscript in which it was contained was amongst those which perished in the fire, and the text survives only in a transcript by Sparke which was made in 1723, most fortunately, though naturally it is not always reliable. Mr. Bell's edition might well be taken as a model by the editor of the *Petit Bruit*.

The poem is in *laisses* of alexandrines. It is charitable to assume that the versification has suffered in transmission. A prologue of eleven lines points out the merits and wisdom of studying 'aunciene geste'. It is addressed to the laity— 'A seinur e a dame'. The poem is a *chanson de geste*, with an abbey as hero:

> De une aboie ert la geste: Burch est anumé.   (12)

(This tale of deeds will be about an abbey; it is named [Peter]-borough.)

What is left is only a fragment; evidently the manuscript was

---

[1] A. T. Bell in *The Peterborough Chronicle of Hugh Candidus*, ed. W. T. Mellows (Oxford, 1949).

defective. The foundation of the abbey is described, and the history of the Saxon kings, the Danish invasions, and the reign of William the Conqueror are briefly told. Those who were brought up on Kingsley will meet old friends in Abbot Turold and Hereward the Wake. The poem breaks off just after an exciting account of an invasion of the woods between Peterborough and Stamford one Lent by enormous apparitions, quite black, like huntsmen with black hounds, with horns and with big eyes. They went in bands of twenty, thirty, ten, or eight—

<blockquote>E en grant anguisse furent les moines de Burch.   (612)</blockquote>

(And the monks of Peterborough were sore oppressed by it.)

HISTORY OF WIGMORE ABBEY

The *History of the Foundation of Wigmore Abbey* is a straightforward prose work which purports to give an account, derived from tradition, of the foundation of the monastery in the twelfth century, and this is followed by an involved story of the relations between the abbey and the House of Mortimer, including the mysterious circumstances surrounding the gift of a croft called Mortimer's Treasure. The exact purpose of all this is not clear, but it has the appearance of a pamphlet composed to remind the Mortimers of their connexion with and obligations to the abbey. The last event mentioned is a donation made by Roger de Mortimer, who died in 1214. His wife, who died before 1252, is mentioned in the past tense. The extant copy is early fourteenth-century, and is to be found in a handsome manuscript made at Wigmore. Other items to do with the Mortimers were added to it. These are a Latin *Brut*, genealogies of the Royal House and the House of Mortimer, and a few other things. These were designed to show that Roger Mortimer, Earl of March, who was killed in Ireland in 1398, was heir to Richard II. The *Brut* is found in association with similar genealogies, such as the great roll in Corpus Christi, Cambridge, MS. 98, where the *Brut* is in French, and is wrongly identified by Vising with the *Livere de Reis de Brittanie*. It was regarded as a political document.

The Wigmore manuscript (Univ. of Chicago 224) as a

whole is therefore illuminating on the subject of the relationship between a religious house and its patrons.[1]

The Roll type of Chronicle, of which an example has just been mentioned, was a French summary of history and genealogy—Latin and ultimately English were later used—apparently kept in noble houses from the mid-thirteenth century onwards.[2] There is one curious example of a roll of arms combined with prayers (Fitzwilliam 7. 1953).

THE *DELAPRÉ CHRONICLE*

Somewhat similar, but much clearer in its import, is the *Delapré Chronicle*,[3] written early in the thirteenth century but known only in a transcript (Bodleian Dugdale 18). Delapré was a house of Cluniac nuns whose patrons were the Earls of Huntingdon. In 1237 John le Scot, who had succeeded his father Earl David, to whom William the Lion had given Huntingdon, died without heir of his body, and the question arose whether the King of Scots or the King of England was the superior. Matters were complicated by the fact that for ten years, 1174–84, the earldom had been forfeited and given by the King of England to Simon de Senlis, who was descended, like the Kings of Scots, from Waltheof, Earl of Northumberland. The nuns were anxious to show that the earldom was held of the King of Scots, and their chronicle was written to prove it. It is not necessary to assume that one of them actually composed it; they may have asked their chaplain or some other man to do it for them. It is in French, not for their own benefit but for the benefit of a lay public. Some of the early part of the chronicle, dealing with Siward and his son Waltheof, is very similar to the Latin account in a Croyland chronicle, but it is interesting to note that a reference to a Life of Siward 'en les lyveres as Engleys, que est en Notynghamsyre, que Richard le Chanteur de Notyngham

---

[1] Text in Dugdale, vi. 344–8, Thomas Wright, *History of Ludlow* (Ludlow, 1852), pp. 102–32; description of manuscript, cf. M. E. Giffin, 'A Wigmore MS. at Chicago', *National Library of Wales Journal*, vii (1952), pp. 316–25, and *Studies in Chaucer and his Audience* (Quebec, 1956), pp. 93–96 and plates vi, vii; B. Smalley, 'Andrew of St. Victor', *Recherches de théologie ancienne et médiévale*, x (1938), pp. 364–7.

[2] Thomas Wright, *Feudal Manuals of English History* (London, *passim*).

[3] N. Denholm-Young, *Bodleian Quarterly Record*, vi (1931), pp. 225–30.

eut' ('in the book of the English, which is in Nottingham-
shire, which belonged to Richard the Cantor of Nottingham')
is not in the Croyland material. Croyland comes into this
story because Waltheof had been a benefactor, and his tomb,
regarded as that of a martyr, was in the abbey.

Various details are given about the holdings of Delapré,
how 'les dames' were disseised of this and that, and how it was
afterwards restored to them, and how Henry II was wroth
with them when they refused to pay the Scutage of Toulouse,
which was levied for the expedition of 1159: 'et les dames
furent poverez, et rien ne vouloient doner; et le roy de ceo
se corrousa.' The unfortunate ladies suffered losses through
the frequent changes of ownership, but they had no doubt
that the claims of the King of Scots were justified, and these
are reiterated like a refrain at the end of each section of the
narrative. It ends triumphantly with the words:

Et pour veir le sachez, que pour ce que le conte Simon le darrayn
morust sans heire de sei, reverti la terre al roy William d'Escoce, fitz le
conte Henry, frere Simon le Malvein et uncle Simon le darrayne, unke
fu fait homage au roy d'Engleterre par ceus d'Escoce deske Simon[1] le
avantdit conte fu mort sanz heir de sey.

(And know for very truth, that because Earl Simon the Last died
without heir of his body, the land reverted to King William of
Scotland, son of Earl Henry the brother [i.e. half-brother] of Simon le
Malvein and uncle of Simon the Last. Never was homage done to the
King of England by the Earls from Scotland down to the time when
John the aforesaid Earl died without heir of his body.)

It is possible that the chronicle was submitted as evidence
to Henry III's council, when it was considering the claims
of Alexander II on the death of his cousin Earl John. While
these were rejected, Alexander was allowed the earldom with
the exception of four manors—a typically English way out
of the tangle. Besides the general interest of this little pamphlet, it gives details of local history which would otherwise be
unknown, and gives a precious insight into the feelings of the
members of a religious house, whose fortunes were tossed
about like a ball when kings went to war and nobles got into
the hands of usurers, and whose stability ultimately depended
on such apparently remote affairs as the eternal question of

[1] Error for John.

the kind of homage paid by Kings of Scots to Kings of England.

TOPICAL PIECES

The reign of Edward I, when literacy had become common and people of every class understood French, whatever they talked in the kitchen and the nursery, saw an increase in a kind of journalistic chronicle. The earliest of this class, dealing with contemporary events, and with a flavour of propaganda, is Jordan Fantosme's *Chronicle of the War with Scotland*, written in the late twelfth century in the style of a *chanson de geste*.[1] A century later publicity was attained in a different way. The *Itinerary of Edward I in Scotland* in 1296 reads like an official diary, but it exists in two different Anglo-Norman manuscripts[2] and was also translated into English. It may have been copied and distributed for better conservation. For the topography of Scotland at the date it is invaluable, but it is merely a catalogue of place-names and dates.

It is perhaps not surprising that there should be an account of the *Entrevue d'Ardres* in 1396,[3] when the marriage between Richard II and Isabelle of France was arranged.

The famous and glittering *Roll of Arms of Caerlaverock* is accompanied by descriptive verses in octosyllabic couplets, which also give a few details, not altogether reliable, about the great siege of the castle in 1300. The writer was probably a herald in Edward I's train, and it has been suggested that he was a Frenchman. The arms include some French ones.[4]

Mention has already been made of the satirical songs preserved in Langtoft's Chronicle. These are not the only ones which survive, and there are both political poems and lyrics.[5] Langtoft, or a contemporary, put into alexandrine rhyming couplets the replies of Edward I and the magnates to the Pope on the subject of the relationship between the

[1] Cf. above, pp. 75–81.

[2] Edited in two Bannatyne Club volumes—*Bannatyne Miscellany I* (1827) and *Instrumenta publica super Scotorum factis* (1834).

[3] Ed. P. Meyer, *Annuaire Bulletin de la Société de l'Histoire de France*, xviii (1881), pp. 209–24.

[4] Ed. Thomas Wright (London, 1864). Cf. A. R. Wagner, *A Catalogue of English Mediaeval Rolls of Arms* (London, 1950), pp. 29–34.

[5] Cf. below, pp. 351–7.

kingdoms of England and Scotland.[1] Everything, down to the
sealing clauses, is included, and the result inevitably strikes
a comic note:

> En testmoigne a ceste lettre penduz sunt nos seals,
> Pur nous avantnomez e pur touz iceaus
> Qe sunt de la tere dount nous sumes neez.
> Doné a Nichole devant noz parentez,
> En meis de Februare, le jour pur veir duzisme,
> En l'an le fiz Marie mil e trescentisme.

(In witness hereof we have appended our seals, for us aforenamed and
for all those who belong to the land where we were born. Given at
Lincoln, before our kindred, in the month of February, on the very
twelfth day, in the one thousand and three hundredth year of Mary's
son.)

In considering such things, it is as well to remember that
there existed in England a public for the *fabliaux*. There are
not only copies or versions of continental specimens, but a few
written in the country. They demonstrate, if they do nothing else, a very great familiarity with French on the part of
all classes of society, since many of them depend for their
enjoyment on *double entendres*.[2] It was no waste of time
writing political satire for a public capable of appreciating
these niceties.

NICHOLAS TREVET

A Dominican friar and the son of a Chief Justice, Nicholas
Trevet, was responsible for a new departure in vernacular
chronicles. His voluminous writings include, besides many
on religious subjects, commentaries on Seneca's tragedies
and the *Consolatio* of Boethius, and three historical works,
which alone concern us here.[3] These are the *Annales Sex
Regum Angliae*, a *Historia ab orbe condito ad Christi Nativi-
tatem*, and a *Chronicle* in Anglo-Norman. Only the first is in
print.[4] It is a remarkably accurate and judicious compilation
of extracts relating to English history from French and

[1] Printed in Appendix I to Wright's edition of Langtoft.
[2] See the bibliography in Vising's *Manual*, nos. 216–24, 266–82. It is amusing
to note that St. Augustine's, Canterbury, owned *Le chevalier, sa dame et un clerc*!
[3] A list is given in E. Brock, *Originals and Analogues* (Chaucer Society, 2nd
Series, VII), pp. i–v.
[4] Ed. Thomas Hog (E.H.S., 1845).

Norman chronicles he found in Paris during a period of study there, combined with others from English sources. The six kings are the Angevins, but the Annals begin with the year 1136, when Stephen was on the throne. The later part was used by subsequent historians, including Thomas of Walsingham. The other two have often been confused; yet, as Edmund Brock had pointed out, they are distinct works, and one is not a translation of the other. The Latin work is dedicated to Hugh of Angoulême, Archdeacon of Canterbury and Papal Nuncio. It must therefore have been completed between 1327 and 1329. Again, it is a compilation from various sources. The period covered is the First Five Ages into which St. Augustine had divided the pre-Christian era. Trevet's immediate inspiration came from the *Speculum Historiale* of his fellow Dominican Vincent of Beauvais. It is interesting to note that the one undoubted Dominican writer in Anglo-Norman is in a category by himself, solely on account of his training and environment. Towards the end of the *Historia* are a few items of British history, such as an account of Julius Caesar's invasion, from Bede, and of Cymbeline's reign, from Geoffrey of Monmouth.

The *Chronicle* was in all probability his last work. It awaits a publisher.[1] It is a popularization made for Mary, daughter of Edward I, a nun at Amesbury. She entered that convent in 1285, before she was seven years of age, in order to be a companion to her grandmother, Queen Eleanor of Provence, who retired there in her last illness. She had no vocation, and though she was generous to objects of charity, she was also, thanks to her father and later to her brother, Edward II, able to indulge her extravagant taste in plate and furniture and for gambling. Trevet's *Chronicle* is not a child's guide to history, as might have been expected in the circumstances, and the reason why the work was undertaken is not apparent. The dedication was not an afterthought, and it is clear that the person for whom it was intended was a member

[1] Miss R. J. Dean has long had an edition in contemplation, and I have to thank her for permission to consult her thesis (unpublished), *The Life and Works of Nicholas Trevet* (Oxford, 1938). Professor R. C. Johnston hopes to publish the text in her stead. I have perused the unpublished thesis of A. Rutherford, *The Anglo-Norman Chronicle of Nicholas Trivet* (London, 1932). The quotations which follow are from MS. B.N. fr. 9687.

of the royal family and a close connexion of Edward I. Mary died on 29 May 1332,[1] and as Trevet refers to the year 1334 he must have completed his book after her death. It was well worth his while to do so, for it became widely known and quoted.

The *Chronicle* has something in common with both the Latin histories. It was, like them, a compilation. The first part covers the same ground as the *Historia*, and the later some of that covered by the *Annales*. In character, the *Chronicle* has more in common with the *Historia*; that is to say, it is a universal history with items of interest to English readers dovetailed into it. In the *Chronicle*, however, the aim is to please rather than to instruct. Place is given to picturesque details and anecdotes (though here Trevet's training as a preacher in the use of *exempla* may count for something), and the reign of Edward I receives fuller treatment than any other.

Trevet explains his purpose in a short prologue, which begins:

Ci comencent les cronicles qe frere Nichol Trivet escrit a ma dame Marie la Fille moun seignour le Roy d'Engleterre Edward le filz Henri. Pur ce que nos sumes avisez de ceux que sont pereceous en estudie q'il sont enoiez de la prolixité d'estories et que plusurs en ount defaute des livres, il nous plust requiller brevement la conte des lynes que descenderent del primer piere Adam.

(Here begin the chronicles which Friar Nicholas Trevet wrote for my lady Mary the daughter of my lord the King of England Edward FitzHenry. Because we are aware of those who are backward in study, that they are vexed by the prolixity of the histories, and that many lack books of these, it has pleased us to gather together in brief the tale of the lines which descended from the first father, Adam.)

Then follows a history from the creation of the world until the death of Christ, then the 'gestes des apostles, emperours et rois' down to contemporary times. There is a description of Mary's entry into the convent in 1285, and a table of genealogy tracing Edward I's descent from Adam.

A short chapter from this part, about the Church in Wales

---

[1] *Calendar of Close Rolls 1330-3*, p. 511. Cf. M. A. E. Green, *Lives of the Princesses of England*, ii (London, 1849), pp. 404-42.

in the time of Augustine, and just after his death, with a Latin translation, was printed by Spelman in his *Concilia*.[1]

Of the anecdotes which have had some influence on writers in Middle English, the most important is the Tale of Constance, which is the source for Chaucer's *Man of Law's Tale* and, with more modification, for a section of Gower's *Confessio Amantis*.[2] Trevet's text, with an English translation, is printed by Brock.[3]

The *Chronicle* was evidently popular in the fourteenth century, for besides the testimony of the English borrowings there is the fact that the text survives in at least six complete manuscripts and in extracts in two more. Unfortunately, no complete list has been published. Most are known to Vising, with the exception of the Paris manuscript used in this chapter, which was pointed out to the writer by Miss Dean. In the fifteenth century the chronicle was translated into English, and the Constance episode from this translation was published by Edmund Brock.[3]

As an historical source this particular work of Trevet's is valueless. Its importance lies in his treatment of the subject-matter and in his use of anecdote. His style is clear and direct, and his vocabulary wide. In the absence of an autograph manuscript it is impossible to tell how Anglo-Norman his language was. His sojourn in Paris may have made him more fluent, though there he would have chiefly made use of Latin. Occasionally he quotes something in English for the sake of effect, adding a French translation, as in his account of Hengist's treacherous act near Amesbury: 'Draweth youre sexes, que fust a dire, treietz voz cotels.'

The treatment of history from a universal viewpoint was something new in Anglo-Norman, and is the direct result of Trevet's Dominican training. It had long been the custom to begin *Brut* chronicles with the creation, but such works

---

[1] Vol. i (London, 1639), pp. 111–12.

[2] Cf. A. B. Gough, 'The Constance Saga', *Palaestra*, xxiii (Berlin, 1902); M. Schlauch, *Chaucer's Constance and Accused Queens* (New York, 1927), pp. 132–4; L. H. Hornstein, 'Trevet's Constance and the *King of Tars*', *Modern Language Notes*, lv (1940), pp. 354–7.

[3] In the Chaucer Society volume cited on p. 298; see also volume xv, pp. 223–50. and the *Report of the Royal Historical Manuscripts Commission*, vi (1877), pt. 1, pp. 344–5.

end as accounts of the history of one particular country or province. This is true even of the *Scalacronica*. Though towards the end the affairs of England loom large, Trevet's remains a world history. The emphasis on rulers, partly brought about by patronage, paves the way for the interest in the Fall of Princes.

FRENCH CHRONICLE OF LONDON

French, the non-clerical professional, legal, and business language, was used not only in Parliament, but in municipal councils, particularly at ports.[1] It is therefore not surprising to come across annals of London kept in French.[2] They cover the period 44 Henry III to 17 Edward III, 1259–1342, and were written about the middle of the fourteenth century, probably by some official, as a record of events. Each year is headed by the names of the mayor and the two sheriffs. As in the monastic chronicles, national and local events are mingled, but the fact that the capital was naturally the scene of so many happenings of more than local interest means that often no distinction can be drawn between national and domestic events. Items that have nothing to do with London include a fantastically horrible and patently untrue account of the death devised by Eleanor for Fair Rosamond (already La Bele Rosamonde), battles in Scotland, the execution of Harcla at Carlisle, and expeditions across the Channel. Details of minor importance are the records of the tower of St. Bartholomew's being struck by lightning, and of the conduit at Cheap running red and white wine all day on the occasion of Edward I's coronation. The real value of this chronicle lies in what it has to tell of local events of national importance—such as the lengthy and dramatic account of Edward III's surprise return to London in 1340. Who would have thought that 'Out of town' goes back to that date? Certainly, no reader of the *O.E.D.* Yet, when Edward stormed into the Tower, and found the Constable not at his

[1] Cf. P. Studer, *The Oak Book of Southampton* (Southampton Record Society, 1910, 1911); K. M. E. Murray, *Register of Daniel Rough, Common Clerk of Romney 1353–80* (Kent Records, XVI, 1945).
[2] *French Chronicle of London*, ed. G. J. Aungier (Camden Society, 1844).

post, these were the words which sprang to the lips of the Under-Constable. 'Monsieur,' he said, falling on his knees, 'il est hors de vile.' A soft answer which did not turn away wrath.

THE *SONG OF DERMOT AND THE EARL*

The Anglo-Norman colony in Ireland produced two works on the recent history of the island, both in verse. The more important is known as the *Song of Dermot and the Earl*.[1] It has been called a *chanson de geste*, but it is in the romantic form of the octosyllabic couplet. There survive 3,459 lines, but unluckily it is extant in only one manuscript (Lambeth, Carew 596), from which the beginning and end are missing. Probably not very much is lacking, but the prologue as it stands is impossible to interpret, and there is a chance that some mention of the occasion for which it was composed was made at the end. The action commences with the elopement of Devorguilla in 1152, and breaks off in the middle of the siege of Limerick in 1175, though the destruction of Slane Castle, which did not occur until 1176, had already been mentioned. The poem may have covered the death of Strongbow in that year. There are reasons for thinking that it was not written until after 1230, but how much later cannot be guessed. There is no evidence that it was based on other than written sources frequently mentioned. That the chief source was a Latin chronicle based on information supplied by Maurice Regan, secretary to King Dermot, may be suspected but not determined. The editor had, very naturally, an exaggerated idea of its historical value, and probably its information must be regarded with caution when not corroborated by other accounts. The introduction and notes to the edition are admirable, but the text could be more intelligibly printed, and the notes on the language are sketchy.

The poem is a stirring affair, consisting chiefly of descriptions of the battles and sieges which took place during the invasion of Strongbow and of Henry II in person, but makes mention of current affairs in Europe when they are relevant. The title was invented by Orpen, and it is misleading, for

[1] Ed. G. H. Orpen (Oxford, 1892). Cf. criticism and a rejoinder in *Irish Historical Studies*, i (1938), by J. F. O'Doherty and M. J. de C. Dodd, pp. 4–20, 294–6.

the poem has no hero. It is simply the story of a campaign. Paul Meyer suggested in his review[1] that it was written for Dermot's granddaughter and Strongbow's daughter, who married the great William Marshall and died in 1220. But it was almost certainly written by and for the Anglo-Norman community in Ireland, quite likely at Waterford, since in later times the manuscript is known to have been there, together with another containing an English translation of the French *Secretum Secretorum* made by Jofroi de Waterford, a Dominican. Not far away was Ross, where Adam de Ros, possibly a Cistercian of Dunbrody, who wrote one of the versions of the *Vision of St. Paul*, may have been born.[2]

Ross itself is the subject of a less interesting poem *On the Erection of the Walls of New Ross* in 1265.[3] The language is not markedly Anglo-Norman and the author may have been a French monk or friar in Ireland.

The government in Ireland, like the government at home, was carried on in Latin and French. Anglo-Norman documents relating to William of Windsor's lieutenancy (1369–76) have been published.[4]

One is on safe ground in saying that the Anglo-Norman colony in Ireland was just that, and reproduced on a small scale all the characteristics of life at home, including literature. It is perhaps not surprising that that great compendium, a private library in itself, Cambridge University Library Gg. I. 1, which includes twenty-five items in Anglo-Norman, may have been copied in Ireland.

BIOGRAPHIES

An offshoot of the chronicle is the historical biography, of which the Anglo-Norman society was particularly fond, though, curiously enough, the best works in this class may be by continental Frenchmen. Certain saints' Lives have some claim to be considered here. The *Life of St. Edmund,*

---

[1] *Romania*, xxi (1892), p. 448.

[2] Cf. *Anglo-Norman in the Cloisters*, pp. 78–80, 53. I am grateful to M. Jacques Monfrin for letting me read his unpublished edition of Jofroi de Waterford.

[3] Cf. A. G. Little, *Franciscan Studies*, ix (1927), p. 121, and St. John D. Seymour, *Anglo-Irish Literature* (Cambridge, 1929), pp. 22–29.

[4] M. V. Clarke, 'William of Windsor in Ireland', *Fourteenth-Century Studies* (Oxford, 1937), pp. 146–241.

king and martyr, is largely mythical, but the *Lives* of Edward the Confessor, of Becket, of Edmund Rich, and Richard of Chichester are all factual. Of these, however, only the *Life of St. Thomas* by the Frenchman Guernes de Pont-Sainte-Maxence has any independent value. The rest contain nothing of historical importance which was not already in their sources.[1]

The Crusade and Death of Richard I[2] is an interesting prose chronicle. The sources are chiefly Howden, Wendover, and Paris, and possibly Trevet. If the author made use of this last, he cannot have been working before about 1320. If, however, he made use of some common source, he may have been writing as early as 1240. The two manuscripts (Bodleian Fairfax 10 and Cambridge, Trinity O. 4. 32) are both fourteenth-century. Historically speaking, the chronicle is of little value; the interest lies in the method of adaptation. As is the case with other popular versions of chronicles, the writer omitted details which he considered uninteresting, and copies of official documents. He also often suppressed proper and place names. To make up for this he added picturesque incidents and personal details from some unknown source, perhaps, as the editor thinks, from a lost Anglo-Norman chronicle in prose—possible evidence for the early use of prose in Anglo-Norman. The style of these passages is more vivid and romantic than in the parts translated from the Latin. The liveliness may be illustrated by the description of Richard's theft of a hawk.

D'illoeqes passa le Roi ove un soul chivaler par une petite villette, si oist un espervier crier en une meson, dont il estoi molt confortez, et commencea penser des envoisures et deduitz de son paiis, et molt lui poisa q'il n'eust l'esperver, si se ferist ignelment dedeinz la dite meson et prist l'esperver et le mist courtoisement au poigne, dont molt feust lez (p. 14).

(Thence the King passed with a single knight through a little townlet, and heard a sparrowhawk calling in a house, which encouraged him much, and he began to think about the pleasures and sports of his own country, and it grieved him greatly not to possess the

[1] Cf. above, pp. 185–7, 244–52, 268–71.
[2] Ed. R. C. Johnston (A.N.T.S., xvii, 1961); cf. his article in *Studies . . . Presented to A. Ewert* (Oxford, 1961), pp. 259–78.

sparrowhawk, so he dashed quickly into the said house and took the sparrowhawk and put it in courtly fashion on his wrist, which made him very joyful.)

The king was set upon by the inhabitants, but he beat them off with the flat of his sword, for he was too courtly to slay villeins, just as, according to Béroul, Tristan was too courtly to slay the lepers.

The object of the author all through is not to write history but to give the picture of a hero in action.

WILLIAM MARSHALL

The great glory of Anglo-Norman biography is the survival of two poems which are primary sources for the history of the times.

The earlier of these is the *Histoire de Guillaume le Maréchal*.[1] William Marshall died in 1219, and his eldest son commissioned this biography very soon afterwards. Obviously he hired the best writer he could for the purpose, and the man he secured came from the Cotentin. Most of the information was supplied by the marshal's squire, John of Early, who was an eyewitness of the later events and had heard about the rest from the marshal's own lips. He seems, fortunately, to have been given to reminiscence, and Early had been in close contact with him for many years. The poem was probably begun in 1225 and finished in 1226. It consists of 19,254 lines, in octosyllabic couplets.

This poem is now extremely well known. It has been pillaged for information about the characters not only of the marshal, but of the Young King and Richard I, for the events of the Regency and the invasion by the Dauphin Louis, and for details about tournaments. Through it all the strength of character of the marshal, whom one is tempted to think of as the only honest man of his times, shines like a beacon. The author knew his trade, and the form is conventional enough, but he has been carried away by his subject. There is a short prologue of the usual pedantic type, and the action is occasionally held up by further pedantic reflections on Fortune and such favourite subjects. Action begins with the 'enfances'

---

[1] Ed. P. Meyer (Paris, 1891–1901).

of the hero, goes on to describe his life as a landless knight, a 'chevalier qui vit de proie', or ineligible bachelor forced to make a living out of pot-hunting at tournaments. War and his attachment to the Young King gave him his chance, and the poem goes on to describe his rise to fame, his *mariage de convenance* which turned out to be a love-match, as occasionally may happen, and his ultimate acknowledgement as the first subject in the kingdom. It ends with his edifying death, with his family round him, and shows him firm and unselfish to the last. There can have been few 'self-made' men in history who were so little self-seeking as William Marshall.

A perhaps surprising feature of the work is the great interest shown in children. The stories of the innocent little William, when he was hostage for his father at the court of Stephen, though carefully arranged, are not artificial in themselves. Mistaking a catapult for a swing, making Stephen play 'knights'—we call it 'soldiers' today—with plantain-stalks: such little incidents are told with charm and freshness. Henry III's knighting and coronation give a further opportunity for tenderness—he made a sweet little knight. As for good stories, they are legion. William's absent-mindedness, when he was so engaged in chatting with the Young King that he failed to notice that the captured knight, whose horse he was leading, had caught hold of an overhanging gutter and swung himself out of the saddle, and the mischievous behaviour of the Young King on that occasion, is perhaps the best of them.

The superb quality of this work must not blind one to the fact that in its own day it may not have been widely known. In fact, its public may have been restricted to the family and their friends. One family copy is known to have found its way to St. Augustine's, Canterbury.[1] The only extant manuscript (now in the Pierpont Morgan library) is an attempt to reproduce exactly what was in front of the scribe, down to the number of lines in the column. From his misreadings it is evident that he was copying a hand almost indistinguishable from his own, which is, to say the least of it, ambiguous. It

---

[1] G. L. Hamilton, 'Un Ms. perdu de l'*Histoire de Guillaume le Maréchal*', *Romania*, xli (1912), pp. 601–5.

has been gone over very carefully by a corrector, but has still many blemishes.

The metre employed is the standard one for romances, the octosyllabic rhyming couplet, which is here often broken.

From every point of view this is one of the outstanding productions in Old French. It is well known to historians, less well known to students of literature, and this is a pity.

THE BLACK PRINCE

Some sixty years later, in 1385 or thereabouts, a similar biography was written of the Black Prince.[1] The author was the herald of the great Chandos, writing after the latter's death, which is referred to in the poem. He was not an eye-witness of all that he relates, but does not appear to have made use of written sources. He seems to have gathered his material in conversations, which he would be well placed to do. This is almost certainly a commissioned work, but no mention is made of who paid for it. From the historical point of view the value of the poem is unequal, depending on the reliability of the information. The sections dealing with Poitiers and the Spanish campaign are important, and Froissart probably used them as a source for the period 1366–7.

The poem is in the same form and style as the *Histoire de Guillaume le Maréchal*, but it is not so fine. The latter was more likely to have been the work of a professional poet, while the herald, trained to keep records, like the supposed author of the *Siege of Caerlaverock*, would never have written a romance in his life. *Guillaume le Maréchal* has all the qualities, good and bad, of the turn of the century. With the *Black Prince* these qualities are in a state of decadence. When the former was written the continuators of Crestien's *Perceval* were still at work. The latter is contemporary with Froissart's wretched *Méliador*. Part of the blame must be laid on the tastes of the age. It must be confessed, too, that the Black Prince is a less attractive hero than the marshal, and a kind of invisible barrier shuts off a royal

[1] Ed. M. K. Pope and E. C. Lodge (Oxford, 1910). Another manuscript has been described by E. J. Arnould, 'Un manuscrit méconnu de la Vie du Prince Noir', *Études dédiées à Mario Roques*, ii (Paris, 1953), pp. 3–14.

personage, and the poem is a record of events, not a portrait study.

Both the surviving manuscripts (at Worcester College and in the possession of H.R.H. the Duke of Windsor) are Anglo-Norman, but the origin of the herald is a matter for speculation. Miss Pope made out a case for his having been a Hainaulter, therefore a compatriot of Froissart. There is nothing unlikely about this, since the Black Prince's mother was Philippa of Hainault, and England was full of Hainaulters in Edward III's reign.[1] Froissart mentions Chandos Herald several times, but gives no clue to his identity. As Professor Arnould points out, there is a mysterious payment of 20 crowns (55s. 10d.) by the Black Prince in July 1355, to 'Haneray, herald-of-arms, who came from beyond the seas in the company of Sir John Chaundos, on the information of Sir John de Wengefeld'.[2] But even if this entry does supply the possible name of the herald, it does not give much help in establishing his identity. The matter may rest there for ever, unless some new reference turns up.

In view of the discovery of a fresh and better manuscript, and the fact that Miss Pope's edition was made long years before Bédier enunciated his famous principles, a new edition of the text would not be superfluous.

DOCUMENTS

This historical literature must be viewed against a background of a widespread use of French. There is a vast amount of documentary material, in the shape of enrolments and missives of all kinds, official and private letters, and wills. French was used in Parliament, except on rare occasions, down to the time of Henry IV. The rough rule was Latin for letters under the Great Seal and French for those under the lesser. Diplomatic correspondence with French-speaking courts was usually carried on in French, and such peace as there was on the Scottish Border was maintained in that language.

[1] Cf., for the relations between English and Hainaulters, J. M. Manly, *Some New Light on Chaucer* (New York, 1926), pp. 200 ff., and Froissart, I. xxxi and xxxii.
[2] *Register of the Black Prince*, iv (P.R.O., 1933), p. 167.

YEAR-BOOKS

For the sheer joy of reading conversational exchanges in Old French there is nothing, on either side of the Channel, to beat the year-books. These were reports of the pleadings in the Court of Common Pleas, and sometimes of the Eyres, and were sold by the stationers for the use of the Apprentices at Law. They exist in almost unbroken series from the reign of Edward I to that of Henry VIII. Demand for them was created by the foundation of the Inns of Court, and they continued to be reproduced until their replacement by Reports and Quaeres compiled by the Judges. In the early period Judge and Counsel were on quite informal terms, and would prove their points with the aid of proverbs and even stories which the modern editors sometimes leave untranslated. The reporters were careful to add a note when irony was used. In this way, the tone in which a remark was made, and the facial expression which accompanied it, can almost be recaptured.

While none of this can be classed as literature in the shape of *belles lettres*, it cannot be passed over in complete silence.[1]

[1] Cf. F. J. Tanquerey, *Recueil de lettres anglo-françaises* (Paris, 1916); M. D. Legge, 'Anglo-Norman and the Historian', *History*, xxvi (1941), 'The French Language and the English Cloister', *Studies Presented to Rose Graham* (Oxford, 1950), 'Ouster-le-mer', *Studies Presented to John Orr* (Manchester, 1953), 'In fere of Werre', *Scottish Historical Review*, xxxv (1956); year-books in black-letter editions and in editions for the Rolls Series, the Selden Society, and the Ames Foundation.

XII

THE ANGLO-NORMAN DRAMA

At the beginning of this century it would have been considered an act of madness to attempt to write a chapter under this heading. It has, however, gradually become plain that during the Middle Ages plays in French were written and performed in England, though so far only the fragments of four plays have been recovered; all are of clerkly origin. There is no trace of comic drama.

The earliest record of the performance of a play in England after the Conquest is the result of an accident which occurred before 1119. A native of Maine, Geoffrey of Gorham, was invited to St. Albans to take charge of a school. Delayed by a storm, he found the post filled and opened a school at Dunstable while awaiting the next vacancy. He borrowed some copes from the sacrist of St. Albans as costumes for 'quemdam ludum de Sancta Katerina quem "Miracula" vulgariter appellamus', which was performed under his direction. This would not be known if his house had not caught fire in the night, causing the loss of all his books and the borrowed copes. Geoffrey was so upset by this that he entered the abbey as a monk. He ultimately rose to be abbot, and it is interesting to note that the material prosperity of the abbey increased greatly during his reign, which lasted from 1119 to 1146, and the copy of *St. Alexis* may belong to this time.[1] As this was a school performance, the play may have been in Latin, but if the pupils were little boys, it may possibly have been in French. The choice of St. Catherine for schoolboys was not inappropriate. The name-part would have been given to a boy with an unbroken voice, and the martyr's arguments with the pagan doctors are merely scholastic disputations which would be excellent training to get by heart. The play may have been part narrative, and the

[1] Thomas of Walsingham, *Gesta Abbatum Monasterii Sancti Albani*, ed. H. T. Riley (Rolls Series), i. 73 ff.; cf. above, pp. 243–4.

Life discovered by E. C. Fawtier-Jones could be the text of something which was both narrated and acted.[1] Even if the play was in Latin, there may have been snatches of French incorporated in it. The use of the word 'Miracula' as the ordinary, or vernacular, word for play is noteworthy.

'About 1130' is the date assigned to the first known use of French passages in a Latin play. These occur in the Lazarus and St. Nicholas plays of Hilarius, a pupil of Abaelard who is believed to have been an Englishman. At about the same time the *Sponsus* mixed drama was copied at Limoges. What is apparently the oldest surviving play with the dialogue entirely in French is almost certainly due to an Anglo-Norman writer.

THE *ADAM* PLAY

The *Mystère d'Adam*[2] is generally supposed to have been written in England about 1140, and copied there more than once. Thence it seems to have made its way to the south of France. A text by a Provençal scribe was then copied in Anjou. These comings and goings could be explained by the nature of the Angevin Empire. The survival of even part of this remarkable text is a miracle. The only extant manuscript (Tours 927) is thirteenth-century, on soft cotton paper waxed to take ink, an extremely fragile substance, with the disadvantage that if the waxed surface flakes off, the ink goes with it, and ultra-violet rays are useless to recover the text. The scribe made use of some blank space near the beginning of the manuscript for his copy. It breaks off before the end, and he may have had before him a manuscript which was already defective. The next item is a copy of the well-known poem on the *Quinze signes du jugement*, which appears, as it often does, as a separate piece, but since it is related to the Sibyl's prophecy in the Pseudo-Augustinian Sermon to the Jews, its presence here is not inappropriate.[3] The beginning part of the *Adam* is written as prose. Anglo-Norman scribes of the twelfth and early thirteenth centuries often wrote verse as prose, with the ends of the lines marked by a full

---

[1] Published in *Romania*, lvi (1930), pp. 80 ff.

[2] Ed. P. Studer (Manchester, 1918, reprinted); P. Aebischer (Geneva and Paris, 1963).   [3] But see W. W. Hirst, *The Fifteen Signs before Doomsday* (Michigan, 1952).

stop. This remained the custom in Provence. The Angevin scribe may have followed his Provençal model in its layout, and later changed to the normal northern French way of writing verse. This method takes up more room, and may possibly account for the loss of the end of the play.

Although the history of the text makes localization and dating extremely difficult and hazardous, the patient work of successive editors has made the above reconstruction plausible. Yet it is based upon conjecture, and it is perhaps salutary to recall the words of no less a person than Joseph Bédier, who once dismissed the whole question of dating, localization, and literary merit in one contemptuous sentence: 'Je ne vois pas de raison positive pour attribuer à l'Angleterre ce petit mystère qui ne me paraît pas antérieur au commencement du xiiie siècle.'[1] Much about the same time Sir Edmund Chambers made a statement which is unacceptable today: 'But even if the writer was an Anglo-Norman clerk, the play must have been written for performance in France. I doubt if it was ever actually performed or finished.' It is difficult to see why, even at the time when he was writing, he could not realize the possibility of plays being performed in French in England, since he refers later to the Anglo-Norman Resurrection play, without suggesting that it was written for performance in France.[2] Just as people who knew no Latin and little French were required to sit through sermons in these languages, so they were expected to enjoy plays performed in them. This would be easier, since the acting would help and most people would understand French even if they did not speak it. The rhyme *criator* : *dur* (lines 231, 232) seems to be decisive on the point of Anglo-Norman authorship, since the rhyming of u:ù is difficult to attribute to a Frenchman. A telling point in favour of the Anglo-Norman origin of the play is the part allotted to Satan, here probably confused with Lucifer, who appears as well as the serpent. This looks like a legacy from Anglo-Saxon tradition.[3] The date and literary merits of the play will be discussed later in this chapter.

---

[1] *Romania*, xxxii (1903), p. 637.
[2] E. K. Chambers, *The Mediaeval Stage* (Oxford, 1903), ii. 71, 85.
[3] O. Pächt in *The St. Albans Psalter* (London, 1960), p. 57.

The play is of the type known as semi-liturgical.[1] It consists of a series of scenes illustrating some of the lessons and responses for Septuagesima Sunday and the week following, rearranged to form a narrative of the Fall and the murder of Abel. Though they are not in what is now their proper order, it must be pointed out that there were formerly local variations in the reading of these lessons, and there may have been less editing than appears. Each scene is introduced by the lesson and chanted response in Latin. Then follows a dialogue in French. The question arises whether these scenes were not once independent and played within the church, and later arranged to form a connected narrative in chronological order played outside it. The extant text is divided into three parts of unequal length. The first covers the Charge, Temptation, Fall, and Expulsion from Paradise; the second, the Sacrifice of Cain and Abel, the murder of the latter, and the Curse of Cain; the third is based not on the liturgy of the present day but upon the Pseudo-Augustinian Sermon which was used in England as a lesson on the Fourth Sunday in Advent. The first two parts consist of ordinary theatrical scenes; in the last, each prophet appears in turn after the reading of his prophecy in Latin, and pronounces a paraphrase of it in French verse. Isaiah is interrupted by a Jew who provokes a short argument. Otherwise, the Procession gives rise to a series of monologues. Shakespeare in *Macbeth* uses much the same technique for the Apparitions and Show in the Witches' cave. The Procession of Prophets breaks off in the middle of Nebuchadnezzar's speech. Then follows the *Quinze Signes*, whose appearance here may be no more than a coincidence, though it is just possible that the scribe was copying from a tattered manuscript with gaps towards the end, and that the poem had been interpolated into the play. It is usually thought to have been written at the end of the twelfth century, and may be later than the play. How this ended is a matter for debate. It may have been either a Passion or a Christmas play. In view of the interpolation of references to the redemption of Adam into several of the prophecies, it is tempting to see in it an Easter

---

[1] For the fullest and most recent description of it, with an up-to-date bibliography, cf. G. Frank, *The Medieval French Drama* (Oxford, 1954), pp. 74–84.

play, going down at least as far as the Harrowing of Hell.
The modern title of *Le Mystère d'Adam* has been criticized
as inadequate, but the heading in the manuscript is *Ordo
Representacionis Ade*. The emphasis all through is on the fate
of Adam. It is perhaps unnecessary to postulate a complete
Passion play. It may have been a diptych, one wing being
the Old Adam, the other the New.[1]

Inevitably, the plan of this work recalls the great sculptured church façades and porches of the twelfth century.[2]
The particular glory of Poitou, they occur sporadically all
over France, but are extremely rare in England, and, where
they occur, seem to be due to influences from western
France. Most of them, apart from Malmesbury, seem to be
associated with Henry of Blois, Bishop of Winchester,
brother of King Stephen. This rarity is an argument for the
Anglo-Norman origin of the play, for, just as the hangings
painted on the wooden lining of the rooms characteristic
of sixteenth-century Scotland prove that panelling was an
alternative to tapestry, so the frozen drama of the sculptured
façades would make the performance of plays unnecessary.
In the case of the *Adam*, the separate scenes are represented
in sculpture by the little reliefs in linked medallions which
so often decorate the surroundings of the doorways, while
the Procession of Prophets finds its counterpart in the rows
of statues placed above them. Possibly the rows of apostles
sometimes found were also inspired by their appearance in
drama, and, as our play may have been an illustration of the
theme of the Old Adam and the New, the apostles may have
been introduced in the part which has been lost, to correspond with the prophets of the Mosaic dispensation.

That the play belongs to an early date is suggested by the
elaborate stage-directions at the beginning. It seems to be
implicit that neither stage-director, actors, nor audience were
familiar with the technique of performing a play. The stage
was formed by the porch and landing outside a church-door,
either at the west end or at the north side. The church itself
served as the retiring-room, and it is likely that the choir

---

[1] Cf. for a discussion on these points, G. Frank, op. cit., pp. 80–82.
[2] Cf. especially E. Mâle, *L'Art religieux du xiie siècle en France* (Paris, 1928),
ch. iv, *et passim*.

stood and chanted just outside. Presumably the reader of the
lessons was outside in order to be heard. On the other hand,
as the placing of neither the choir nor the reader is mentioned, they may both have had lecterns just inside. Paradise
was on the right, that is to say, to the spectators' left. It was
elevated and enclosed by curtains, so that only the head and
shoulders of the actors inside were visible. Opposite and at
a lower level, perhaps on the ground, was Hell, from which
smoke could rise, and where the demons could make a noise
by beating on pots and kettles, but whether it was made to
look like a fortress or whether it already took the form of a
dragon's mouth is not stated. At the foot of the steps was
a clear space where Adam and Eve could pretend to till the
ground and where the scene between Cain and Abel took
place. The demons were to cause a diversion by running
about this place and amongst the audience. It does not sound
as though the spectators were thought of as being very
numerous.[1] Later in the play, mention is made of a door
representing the synagogue. There was a little scenery and
a few properties. The curtains enclosing Paradise were to be
made of silk, and within were branches and flowers and trees
bearing fruit, one being the Forbidden Tree, up which a
counterfeit serpent could be hauled. Adam and Eve were to
dig the ground with spade and mattock, and to sow seed.
The Devil was to plant thorns and thistles when they had
done. Cain and Abel were each to be provided with a stone
to serve as an altar of sacrifice. Abel was to have a lamb to
sacrifice, and he was also to conceal a pot in his clothes,
which Cain was to smash when he struck him. Whether this
pot was to contain blood which would be spilt, or merely to
make a crunch as if bones were being broken, is not stated.

Many of the costumes are prescribed, and the church vest-
ments, as in the case of the St. Catherine play at Dunstable,
were laid under contribution. Thus, the Figura representing
the Saviour, as Jehovah is called, wore a dalmatic, a vestment
worn by deacons and prelates, and when about to pronounce
the doom he added a stole. In the fabliau *Estula*, it will be
remembered, the exorcizing priest has no time to pull on his

---

[1] For the latest discussion on these points, see R. Southern, *The Medieval Theatre
in the Round* (London, 1957), pp. 227–35.

boots, but throws on his stole. It seems plain that this part was assigned to a member of the clergy. Adam wore a tunic of red, an expensive colour worn by the nobility and symbolical of the Passion, whereas Eve, who was played by a youth, was dressed like a woman in white, the colour of innocence and virginity, and her veil or wimple was of white silk, a costly and noble material. After the Fall they crouched down behind the curtains and put off this festal garb, to reappear in poor clothes sewn with fig-leaves. Not merely was the wearing of clothes as well as fig-leaves a concession to decency, but the change from noble to poor garments was symbolical of their changed estate.[1] The Angel wore an alb, a vestment. Cain, like Adam, was in red, here the colour of wrath, but Abel, like Eve, was in white. The contrast here was evidently between the worldly and the unworldly man, the guilty and the innocent. Nothing is said about the appearance of the devils, of whom there were three or four besides Satan, but they carried chains and shackles. Whether at this date they already wore skins and had horns and a tail it is impossible to say, but it seems unlikely that in the Temptation Scene Satan could have been repulsively ugly. Any reader of the *Adam* who goes to Strasbourg feels a shock of recognition when confronted with the Tempter and the Foolish Virgin of the cathedral façade, though these statues are dated 1280. The instructions for the clothes and symbols of the Prophets resemble those for the Rouen Procession, but are more detailed.[2] Abraham was an old man, with a long beard and wearing wide garments; Moses carried a rod in his right hand and the Tables of the Law in his left; Aaron, dressed like a bishop, had a rod with flowers and fruit in his hand; David and Solomon bore royal insignia and wore crowns; Balaam, an old man, was dressed in wide garments and was riding on his ass; Daniel was a young man dressed like an old one; Habakkuk was another old man; Jeremiah carried a scroll in his hand; Isaiah had a book, and wore a large cloak; the Jew's clothes are not described; Nebuchadnezzar was adorned like a king.

[1] Cf. G. F. Jones, 'Sartorial Symbols in Mediaeval Literature', *Medium Ævum*, xxv (1956), pp. 63–70.
[2] Cf. M. Sepet, *Les Prophètes du Christ* (Paris, 1878), pp. 43, 44.

Almost every gesture was prescribed. Adam was to stand
near the Figura, with a composed countenance, and Eve a
little farther off, looking subdued. Anyone who mentioned
Paradise was to turn towards it and point it out with his
hand. This mention of pointing demonstrates, as so often,
the influence of staging upon medieval art; in miniatures
people are often represented as pointing. Pointing at people
is an indication that a conversation is taking place; in the
drawings accompanying the Matthew Paris *Life of Thomas
Becket*[1] this is particularly striking, and in the representation
of the quarrel between King Henry and Thomas, the courtiers and the archbishop are all pointing and speaking at
once, while the king is ticking off the arguments on his
fingers. In the play, the devils, who except for Satan are not
given speaking parts, were to indulge in dumb show, which
is meticulously described. Eve was to incline an ear to the
artificial serpent, to give the illusion that it was speaking.
Satan was to smile ingratiatingly at Eve, Cain to show a
threatening countenance to Abel when he attacked him, and
so on. Little is left to discretion or to chance, and this makes
the few omissions the more remarkable. The Prophets, except
for Balaam, mounted on his ass, and Habakkuk, who was
so old and frail that he appeared somehow already seated,
advanced one by one and sat down on a stool before speaking.
As they announced their prophecies first in Latin and then
in French, they must have been clerks. The Figura was probably played by a priest, the Angel perhaps by a deacon,
Adam, Satan, Cain, and Abel also by deacons or clerks in
minor orders, Eve and the devils by choir-boys.

Neither actors nor audience seem to have been expected to
have any previous knowledge of the manner of performance
of a play. Some of the most striking directions concern the
speaking of parts:

Let Adam be well taught when he should answer, lest he should
answer too soon or too late. Not only he, but all the actors are to be so
taught that they may speak composedly and make gestures appropriate
to the matter being mentioned; and, in reciting the verses, they should
not add or omit any syllable, but pronounce them all distinctly, and say
what is to be said in the right order.

[1] Ed. P. Meyer (S.A.T.F., 1885).

This last remark has been interpreted to mean that the poet
was proud of his skill as a versifier, and that Anglo-Norman
actors might be expected to mangle syllabic versification.
But taken in its context the passage must mean something
much more elementary. Perhaps there was a stage in the
history of the drama where, after the reciting of a Latin lesson
or even dialogue, the action was mimed and the performers
'gagged' in the vernacular. Hilarius, the author of the
Sponsus,[1] and the writer of the *Adam* were perhaps pioneers
in providing written parts in French, just as Shakespeare was
a pioneer in providing written parts for his clowns. Moreover, it is clear that the man who took the part of Adam,
singled out as the actor who was first to talk with the Figura
(who alone seems to have been expected to know better), and
by inference all the subsequent speakers, were in the state
of Flute, and, if they had not been instructed to the contrary,
would have spoken all their parts at once, cues and all. In
fact, the best commentary on the opening directions of the
Adam is provided by the rehearsal and performance scenes
in *A Midsummer-Night's Dream*.

If, however, the author of the *Adam* took pride in his skill
as a poet, he did right. So much has already been written
(since 1903) about the literary merits of this play that it
is unnecessary to add much here. The writer had every
possible qualification for his task. His dialogue is lively
or solemn as the occasion requires. The lines, as in so
many romances, are often divided between speakers, making for quick exchanges. This obvious device is surprisingly
rare in medieval plays. For dialogue and narrative speeches,
the octosyllabic rhyming couplet is employed, while for
reflective speeches and lamentations, quatrains of decasyllables are used. The character-drawing is excellent. Abel
is a pious, mild young man, completely at the mercy of
his cynical, jealous, and cunning elder brother. Today,
Abel seems like a prig and Cain is the more sympathetic
character, but this was not the author's intention and
the contemporary spectators would share his view of the
two brothers. The temptation scenes are the triumph of the
play. Satan first approaches Adam, and tries to rouse his

[1] Ed. L. P. Thomas (Paris, 1951).

curiosity. When Adam finally responds to his advances he is
in no hurry to tell him what is incomplete in the life in
Paradise. Then he urges Adam to taste the fruit of the
Forbidden Tree, which Adam refuses to do, so Satan leaves
him alone again, hoping that he will reflect on what he has
been told, and yield. When Satan returns to the charge he
is met by an even fiercer refusal. With a look of discourage-
ment he goes off to find Eve. He flatters her by telling her
how much cleverer she is than her husband, but goes too far,
and Eve suddenly rallies to the defence of Adam. Quickly
realizing his mistake, he abandons his first manner of approach and tries the effect of a reference to her physical
charms. Not without the churchman's disapproval of courtly
love does the poet put into Satan's mouth lines which might
come from any troubadour song:

> Tu es fieblette e tendre chose,
> E es plus fresche que n'est rose;
> Tu es plus blanche que cristal,
> Que neif que chiet sor glace enval.   (227–30)

(What a delicate and dainty creature you are, fresher than any rose;
whiter than crystal, than the snow which falls on the ice below.)[1]

Only the idea of the woman's weakness is foreign to the love-
song, but this insinuation that the wife is tied to a husband
of coarser fibre, who does not appreciate her at her true
worth, has been made by seducers since the beginning of
time, and its antiquity does not make it less effective at whatever date it is employed. Eve, conforming to the medieval
idea fostered by the fathers that the woman is more sensual
than the man, is now being approached on the right level.
When Satan goes on to describe the powers that eating the
fruit will confer upon Eve, who will be given the position in
life which she merits, she brushes his arguments aside with
the interruption 'Quel savor a?' ('What does it taste like?').
And he replies 'Celestial', and, again realizing his mistake,
goes on to say that such an adventure will suit her appearance, for by that she is well fitted to rule the world. As he
had formerly done with Adam, he allows time for his lure

---

[1] Cf. *Horn* 4428, Peil blanc cumme neif sur gravier; *Aliscans* 2853, Ele est plus
blanche ke n'est noif sur gelee; *Sir Launfal* 241, Whyt as snowe on downe.

to work, but Adam appears, alarmed at the interview, and all might have been lost. His attempts to give Eve good advice, however, merely decide her to trust the devil. She takes the apple, and when Adam is still distrustful, tells him to leave it alone. Instantly he desires it, and she finally persuades him to eat by insisting on tasting it first. But the whole scene must be read again and again to appreciate its finer points. If the actors were amateurs, the writer most certainly was not.

Except for the Procession of Prophets, based on the Pseudo-Augustinian Sermon to the Jews, the only source for the play is the Bible. In this it resembles the early parts of the Norman sermon *Grant mal fist Adam*.[1] All that the author does is to trope the lessons and responses in French verse. A similar technique is employed for stories from the Bible told in the B.B.C. Friday morning religious programme for schools. But the anonymous writer of the *Adam* play was a genius, and the result is one of the finest works in the whole history of Old French literature. No general history can afford to ignore it, and it finds a place here also because it was almost certainly written in England, and was undoubtedly copied and presumably played there.

THE RESURRECTION PLAY

Some time early in the thirteenth century the history of the drama in England was marked by another accident. At Beverley Minster, the performance of a Resurrection play was in progress in the churchyard on the north side. A door into the church had been left open, and some boys took advantage of this to climb the tower in order to get a better view. The sacristans caught sight of them. The windows were glazed, and glass was precious; the boys might break it. Accordingly, the sacristans gave chase, caught, and beat them. One, trying to escape, went up higher, put his foot upon a rocking stone and crashed down on to the pavement of the church, where he lay as one dead. While his parents were weeping over his apparently lifeless body, he recovered his senses, so that those who had been prevented by the size

---

[1] Cf. above, pp. 180–1.

of the crowd from being present at a performance of the Resurrection outside the church, saw a more miraculous symbol of resurrection within it.[1]

In the account of this accident nothing is said about the language of the play, but this may perhaps have been French. There is evidence that the play known as the *Seinte Resureccion*[2] was popular for a long time in England, and played in more than one locality, so that it may have been a performance of this very play that the boys were anxious to see. The date when it was originally written is unknown. Some authorities place it earlier than the *Adam*, but, as will be seen, it appears to belong to a more elaborate tradition of staging and to have a longer history of performance of a similar kind behind it. Some put it as late as the thirteenth century. If the *Adam* is really mid-twelfth century, it would seem likely that the *Resurrection* is late twelfth, but of this there can be no certainty. Again, there is nothing comparable in continental French literature, and again, there is evidence for the manner of staging which is invaluable for the history of the European stage in general.

This play has been known for some time through a mid-thirteenth-century copy in a Paris manuscript (B.N. fr. 902) containing a considerable number of Anglo-Norman and other texts, mainly Norman in origin. The play is incomplete, and seems, curiously enough, to be the transcript of a manuscript of which the end was already missing, and the last sheet of which must have been loose, so that a whole column has been misplaced and copied in the wrong order. Now there is available a later, longer, but still incomplete version in a magnificent and earlier copy made at Canterbury (B.M. Add. 45103). This version contains an addition, an allusion to St. Bartholomew, which can hardly be explained except as an adaptation made for a performance at Canterbury itself, thus proving beyond all manner of doubt that French plays were not out of place in England. The history of this version is complicated. It has gone through two stages of development since the Paris version, which itself has been

---

[1] 'Miracles of St. John of Beverley', *Acta Sanctorum*, May, ii. 187–8.
[2] Ed. T. A. Jenkins, J. M. Manly, M. K. Pope, J. G. Wright (A.N.T.S., iv, 1943), exhaustive from every point of view.

modified from the original. The Canterbury version, where it is most closely connected with the Paris one, has been modernized, but it has also passed through the hands of a more drastic *remanieur*. The editors of the Anglo-Norman Text Society's publication have wisely printed both versions, one above the other, on the same page, and the differences, linguistic and other, have been analysed.

From the aesthetic point of view the *Resurrection* is not the equal of the *Adam*, but it has merits of its own. The whole, including prologue and stage-directions, is in octosyllabic rhyming couplets, with a few minor exceptions. The prologue describes the setting. This is more elaborate than that of the *Adam*, and requires more room. Like the *Adam* and the *Resurrection* performed at Beverley, whatever that was, it was probably intended to be played outside a church porch. Behind was a row of mansions and posts—these two expressions 'mansions' and 'lius' are not meant to be alternatives: the 'lius' seem to have been raised. In front of these, in the 'place', the open level space, were others. There has been argument whether this prologue and the stage-directions were recited to the audience by the stage-manager, who in medieval plays was present in view of the audience, with a white wand in one hand and a prompt-copy of the play in the other, for all the world like a conductor with his baton and score. There can really be little doubt that the author intended this to be the case. It has been objected that most of the stage-directions are in the past tense. But the action did take place in the past. It is not a play about contemporary life, but an enacting of the Bible story, and there can be no incongruity in the action being first described in the past and then performed in the present. It looks as though this is a development from the old system of miming the lessons in dumb-show. The prologue of the Paris version opens as though the audience was being addressed, though towards the end it has apparently been altered to suit later conditions. The Canterbury prologue has been rewritten from the start. Thus the Paris prologue begins with the lines:

> En ceste manere recitom
> La seinte resureccion. . . .

(In this fashion we recite the holy resurrection. . . .)

By the time the play was performed in Canterbury this had
been altered to

> Si vus avez devociun
> De la seinte resurrectiun
> En l'onur Deu representer
> E devant le puple reciter . . . .

(If you have the devout intention of representing the holy resurrection in God's honour and of reciting it before the people . . . .)

By that time, evidently, everybody was expected to be more
familiar with the performance of plays than in the days when
the *Adam* and the *Resurrection* were first written. Yet to the
end of the history of medieval plays some help was given to
the audience, who, after all, had no printed programmes. In
its most exaggerated form the prologue was parodied in *A
Midsummer-Night's Dream*, but the old technique could be
adroitly used, as it was by Sir David Lindsay of the Mount
in the *Satire of the Thrie Estaits*, where the prologue and the
characters in order of appearance contrive to embrace the
other players and the audience in their address. It is so
naturally done that the artifice is hardly apparent. It seems
strange that there is still difference of opinion about the
function of the prologue and the stage-directions in the
Resurrection play. Miss Pope thought the directions were
read during the performance, Mrs. Frank disagrees.[1] It
seems that Miss Pope has more likelihood of being right.
Just as the scenes in the *Adam* illustrated the preceding
lesson and response, here the scenes illustrated the lines
telling people what to expect. That this spoils the dramatic
effect according to present-day ideas has nothing to do with
the case. In the same way the writers of epic and romance
were obliged by the fact that their works were heard, not
read, to anticipate events and do without the element of
surprise. So in the Balain episode in the *Huth Merlin*, the
auditor is told Balain is about to engage in mortal combat
with his own brother, whereas a modern author would be
able to let the reader's recognition keep pace with Balain's
own. No risks of misunderstanding could be taken. It is an

[1] Edition, p. cxxiv; G. Frank, op. cit., p. 89. For a third view, cf. W. Noomen,
'Passages narratifs dans les drames médiévaux français', *Revue belge de Philologie
et d'Histoire*, xxxvi (1958), pp. 761–85.

application to literature of the golden rule for preaching and lecturing: 'Tell them what you're going to say, say it, and then tell them what you've said.'

The description of the staging in the prologue is the earliest full description of the simultaneous setting which survived in France into the seventeenth century. The germ of it was already in the *Adam*, but the *Resurrection* shows it fully developed. Though they were fewer in number, the mansions were arranged, stretching from Heaven on the dexter side to Hell on the sinister, with very little use of depth, just as they do in the famous miniature, the sixteenth-century Passion of Valenciennes, in which they number twenty-two. Owing to the slight changes made in the Canterbury version the number and arrangement of the mansions differ in the two versions of the *Resurrection*. These are conveniently illustrated by plans in the Anglo-Norman Text Society edition.

The versification is archaic. The line most used is the octosyllable, with a caesura after the fourth syllable. About as many feminine couplets are of the lyric type (with only seven syllables according to modern reckoning) as are of the ordinary narrative kind. A further group of feminine couplets can be scanned either way. It is evident that the poet considered himself free to employ either type as he pleased. Some of the 'stage-directions' are in couplets of decasyllables, but all the dialogue is in octosyllabic rhyming couplets. The same rhyme can be used twice, or even as many as six times, running. This common feature of Norman and Anglo-Norman verse is here used for dramatic effect. Sometimes a link between speeches is obtained by using the same sequence of rhymes in both. The lines are never broken up between the speakers (except in interpolations or added passages in the later version), and the couplet is only occasionally divided. The result is stiffer and more formal, but a certain amount of variety and characterization is achieved by differences in the language. In the opening scene Joseph of Arimathea and Pilate greet one another in the third person. This formal salutation over, they are able to converse in the second person. Here the Paris version sheds some light on the history of the polite use of the plural form. The author

began by using 'tu', as in Latin, but after a few lines was
unable to keep it up, and unconsciously slid into what was
evidently already more natural to him, and substituted 'vous'.
This is not just the usual confusion between the forms, a hap-
hazard mixture such as one so often finds. In the Canterbury version 'vous' is used straight away, and the order of
the words and the rhymes have had to be changed in consequence. But in both versions 'tu' makes spasmodic reappear-
ances in the first scene. The soldiers use 'tu' to Longinus and
address him as 'frere', for they regard him as their social equal
or inferior. Even when they are taking him off to prison, there
is a kind of jovial familiarity in their treatment of him:

> Ça, frere, ça, en chartre irras;
> Malvais hostel huimes avras. (159–60)

(There, brother, there, you're going to prison; from now on you'll
have an uncomfortable lodging.)

Pilate speaks roughly to the soldiers:

> Taisé'us, bricons, ne ditez plus. (130)
> (Be quiet, fools, say no more.)

> Diva, vaissal, trai tai en sa. (141)
> (Get on, fellow, come over here.)

When the watch is set four soldiers boast in turn about what
they will do to any robber who ventures near. Longinus is
a dignified figure, and his prayer of thanksgiving when he
receives his sight is almost eloquent. The soldier who describes the miracle rises to the occasion:

> Longins li ciu, quant out nafré
> Cel pendu de lance el costé,
> Prist del sanc, a sez oils le mist:
> A bon hure a son os le fist,
> Car ainz fut cius e ore veit.
> N'est pas merveille c'il en lui creit. (145–50)

(Longinus the blind, when he had struck the hanged man in the
side with a lance, took some of the blood and put it on his eyes; it was
a happy and profitable thing he did for himself, for once he was blind
and now he sees. It is no wonder if he believes in him.)

There are a few anachronisms, and naïve touches. Joseph
of Arimathea calls on the God of the Old Testament, Pilate

replies by invoking Hercules, also a miracle-worker.[1] Jesus is referred to as 'le fiz Marie'. Pilate orders Longinus to be taken to prison as a dangerous agitator:

> Alez tost, metez le en prison,
> Que ne voist prechant tel sermon. (155–6)

(Go quickly and put him in prison, lest he should go on preaching this sermon.)

When the watch is set Caiaphas calls for the Roll of the Law, and makes the soldiers 'take their Bible oath' on it. 'Dan', it is interesting to note, is used as a title of respect. In south-western dialects this did not take on a pejorative sense, but 'sire'—our 'sirrah'—did.[2] In the *Resurrection* 'sire' is possibly higher in the social scale than 'dan', but the choice seems to be decided by metrical considerations. In Deposition scenes on the stage and in art Joseph of Arimathea's traditional place is at the head, that of Nicodemus at the feet. In this play Nicodemus explains why this should be so:

> Sire Joseph, vus estes einz nez:
> Alez al chef, jo vois as piez. (269–70)

(Master Joseph, you are the senior. Go to the head, I am going to the feet.)

This Resurrection play is the simplest of those which survive on the subject. Owing to the sketch of the action in the prologue, it is known that it included the scene at Emmaus but nothing later, and the play's title is no misnomer. Like the *Adam* it is an expansion of the Biblical text, and there is nothing which is not a legitimate addition, save for the legend of Longinus, here represented as a blind beggar who will do anything for a dozen pence. The author fails to explain why the soldiers press him to perform an act which seems peculiarly appropriate to their own calling. The introduction of the legend here is interesting from the point of view of date. It occurs in a simple form, and there is no hint of the lengths to which it would go when it became combined with the Grail story. The other interpolated scenes are

---

[1] Cf. the tradition exploited, unpleasantly by modern ideas, by Ronsard in his hymn 'Hercule chrestien'.

[2] M. K. Pope, 'Titles of Respect in the Romance of *Horn*', *Studies Presented to John Orr* (Manchester, 1953), pp. 226–32.

admirably contrived. The passer-by who questions the soldiers hurrying to take up their watch, a scene which is omitted from the later version, is beautifully natural. Here, even more than in the *Adam* with its demons who may have caused amusement as well as fear, is the germ of the comic interludes which took on the proportions of the farce in later plays.

Were it not that the *Adam* sets a standard of comparison which it is impossible to attain, the *Resurrection* would be hailed as a minor masterpiece. Its existence in two forms, one fairly close to the original and the other considerably revised, adds to its interest. It seems clear that an early play, written for some particular occasion at some particular place, became more widely known and was borrowed and adapted to suit local conditions elsewhere. There is no evidence that this play was known, as the *Adam* was, on the Continent.

TWO BILINGUAL FRAGMENTS

Before 1921 these two plays were the only specimens known of Anglo-Norman drama. In fact, the history of early plays in general is sketchy where England is concerned. This is so puzzling that Mr. R. M. Wilson has devoted several pages to it in his *Lost Literature of Medieval England*.[1] He has gathered there an anthology of stray allusions to the performance of plays. Most of the extant plays in English date from the fifteenth century, and it is impossible to tell whether any of these are late versions of plays of the same title mentioned in the earlier documents. Mr. Wilson thinks that the choice of language for the plays lay between Latin and English, but there is another alternative; some of the lost early plays referred to may have been, like the two extant plays which are so much earlier than anything in English, in Anglo-Norman. After all, as late as the fourteenth century friars preached in French. It would not be surprising if the clergy did also produce plays in that language. In 1921 the gap between Anglo-Norman and English was narrowed: fragments of two bilingual plays have been recovered.

[1] (London, 1952), especially pp. 215–20.

The earlier is late thirteenth-century, and is therefore the earliest direct evidence for performance in English.[1] It consists of twenty-two lines of Anglo-Norman, followed by the same number in English. The English is a paraphrase, not a translation, of the French. The fragment is the prologue of a play. The harbingers of a pagan Emperor call for silence in the customary fashion and demand a clear space for the performance. Evidently the audience crowded the 'place' until they were ordered to the edge or to their 'boxes'. The Anglo-Norman begins:

> Oez, seygnur, oez, oez,
> Escoutez tant cum wus poez. . . .
> Fetes place e tene'us coy.

(Oyez, oyez, oyez! Listen, lords, as well as you can. . . . Make room! Silence please!)

The other fragment, recovered earlier, belongs to the next century.[2] It is written on the back of a manorial roll from Ricklinghall, Suffolk, and seems to have been a piece of scrap parchment used for the accounts at the manor. This fragment, like the other, is the beginning of a play. The prologue is in stanza form. There are two stanzas in Anglo-Norman, rhyming aab, ccb, followed by nine lines of paraphrase in English, rhyming aab, ccd, eed. Then follows a stage-direction in Latin, and the beginning of the first speech in Anglo-Norman only. The prologue is spoken by a king, probably Octavian. He calls for silence, ostensibly from his court, but indirectly from the audience:

> Ore escutez, seignurs cheris,
> Cuntis e barouns e chivaleris,
> E tus qui sunt en cour.

(Now listen, dear my lords, earls, barons, knights, and all who are present in court.)

After this appeal, the king calls his messenger:

> Tunc dicet Nuncio: Venet sa, moun messager,
> Vous dirray, pur turney
> I vous covent tout aler.

---

[1] R. H. Robbins, 'An English Mystery Play Fragment', *Modern Language Notes*, lxv (1950), pp. 30–55.

[2] J. P. Gilson, *Times Literary Supplement*, 26 May 1921, p. 340.

(Then shall he say to the Messenger: Come here, my messenger. I tell you, you must go at once on an errand.)

There is no clue to the place of origin of the earlier fragment, which has been used as a fly-leaf, but as the later one comes from Suffolk it has been suggested that it belonged to Bury, an abbey where there had been great interest in the teaching of French in the schools under its jurisdiction.[1] Perhaps the play was a scholastic one.

It will have been noticed that in both cases the French and English speeches alternate. The whole play is not first copied in one language and repeated in the other. It is difficult to understand the point of this, but it is probably a method of copying. The same thing happened in the case of bilingual lyrics.[2] The most likely explanation is that the plays were first written in French, and that an English version, not a literal translation, was made later. Both versions were then copied in this peculiar fashion, and the plays performed in whichever language was most convenient. It is possible that only the stage-manager had a written text, and that he taught the parts to the actors. In this case, the dovetailing of the French and English versions might not have been as inconvenient as appears.

The chance preservation of these two tiny scraps shows the fate which must have befallen all the plays, whether in Latin, French, or English, which we know (from the allusions referred to above) were performed in England before the fifteenth century. As soon as the drama left the direct control of the church, and became the peculiar property of towns and their guilds, English probably began to prevail, except in towns like London and other big ports, where French was kept up for convenience in trade and international relations.[3] It is unlikely that there was any French drama of a purely secular nature written in England. It was probably all either religious or scholastic, though, as has appeared above, a comic element in the serious plays may not have been lacking.

[1] Cf. a copy of the *Manière de langage*, made there in 1386, ed. J. Gessler (Brussels, Paris, Louvain, 1934), p. 88.

[2] Cf. below, p. 354.

[3] Cf. above, p. 302.

The fragmentary character of these remnants of the Anglo-Norman drama must not be allowed to disguise the fact that the two early plays, the *Adam* and the *Resurrection*, are works of considerable literary merit, besides being of capital importance for the history of the Western stage.

XIII

THE LYRIC AND ITS BACKGROUND

OF all the classes into which literature may be divided the lyric has been most neglected where Anglo-Norman is concerned.[1] Undoubtedly, this is partly due to the fixed belief that Anglo-Norman literature was largely the work of clerks. This, however, is true of all medieval literature, and clerks, like other men, fell in love and frequented taverns. Since, at the same time, it is contended that Anglo-Norman literature was directed at the upper classes only, it seems strange that the existence of a kind of poetry which was so frequently of a courtly type should not have been the subject of an inquiry. There was, as will appear in the course of this chapter, an Anglo-Norman lyric, but no collection of it was ever made at the time, and in consequence its remains are both scanty and scattered. The surviving specimens, however, give some indication of what the desire for it was; and how that was fulfilled. In view of the fact that Northern French courtly lyric poetry has its beginnings in the second half of the twelfth century, it is hardly to be expected that any would be written in England before the time of Henry II.

Henry II's train always included women singers,[2] but what their nationality was and what they sang is left to the imagination. They were evidently thought not to be respectable. Thomas Becket's footmen on his famous progress through northern France in 1157 sang in their own tongue according to their countries.[3] Henry's sons were well known amongst the troubadours, and Richard I is supposed to have written songs himself in French and Provençal. The Blondel legend has a kind of verisimilitude about it. It is possible

[1] This was something which the late Professor Pope always hoped to see remedied.
[2] Peter of Blois, 1177, Migne, *Pat. Lat.*, vol. ccvii, cols. 42–51.
[3] William Fitzstephen in *Materials for the History of Thomas Becket*, ed. J. C. Robertson (R.S.), iii. 31.

that some of the lyric poetry of various categories which would obviously be fashionable in the noble courts as well as the king's was written by Anglo-Norman writers. Most of it, however, was probably imported from the Continent by travelling minstrels. Some of the nobility may have imitated those of the Continent and tried their hands at poetry, but the only certain example of this kind of indoor amusement is a tençon (*Scottice* 'flyting') of 1270. Whether it is permissible to deduce from its existence that it was representative of a widespread custom is a matter for debate. Most of the poems which survive were preserved by clerks, and some of them are students' songs, but in the absence of any *chansonniers* such as were compiled in France in the late thirteenth and early fourteenth centuries for wealthy patrons, it would be unwise to attribute too much importance to the role of clerks in the history of the Anglo-Norman lyric. The safest generalization is to say that some lyric poetry was written and sung in circles which were accustomed to use French in daily life; these would include both courts and communities of clerks, and, by the accident of committal to writing, a high proportion of what survives is clerkly. The very great variation in the text of such lyrics as have survived in more than one manuscript is evidence of the fact that lyric poetry, even at a late date, was more likely to be preserved by oral transmission than any other kind.

The background to the courtly lyric can be abundantly illustrated from Anglo-Norman literature. There has been a tendency to exaggerate the difference in attitude between the continental and Anglo-Norman writers of romances,[1] for which, as has been shown above, there was some political foundation. Romance, however, is not the most convenient means of expressing courtly ideas, and for the illustration of these one must look elsewhere. There are, in Anglo-Norman, a few doctrinal works.

DEBATES

The *Donnei des Amants* has already been discussed.[2] Whether or not ironical in intention, it was written for an

---

[1] Cf. C. B. West, *Courtoisie in Anglo-Norman Literature* (Oxford, 1938), *passim*, and above, pp. 139–41.   [2] Above, pp. 128–32.

audience well broken in to the pastime of discussing love. Debates on that favourite theme, first treated in Latin poems, of whether a knight or a clerk is the better lover, terminating by convention in a combat between bird champions of the antagonists, are represented in Anglo-Norman by *La Geste de Blancheflour e de Florence* and *Melior e Ydoine*.[1] These belong to the thirteenth century.

Melior e Ydoine follows the usual pattern, and may owe something to the continental *Hueline e Aiglantine*, of which only a fragment survives. In the Anglo-Norman poem the names are symbolical, and the second, it will be remembered, had already been used for the heroine of the romance *Amadas e Ydoine*, whose real name is never revealed. The form used is, as in the continental debates, the octosyllabic rhyming couplet. This gives it lightness and a swift pace and underlines the resemblance to the pastoral poem and the *fabliau*. The scene is laid at Lincoln, and the poet, like the clerk of the *Donnei des Amants* and the author of *Florance et Blancheflor*, pretends to have been an eyewitness of the dispute. The conclusion is the expected one:

> Mieuz est li clers a amer
> Qe li orgoillouse chivaler.

(The clerk is better to love than the arrogant knight.)

Debates of this kind did not, in the minds of their authors redound to the credit of clerks, as is sometimes implied.

Blancheflour et Florence is quite different. It is probably a rehandling of the continental *Florance et Blancheflor*, though the poet claims to be translating from English:

> Banastre en englois le fist,
> E Brykhulle cest escrit
> En franceois translata.
> A verrois amaunz soit honour,
> Beautee, bountee e valour,
> E joye eit qe mieuz amera! Amen.

(Banastre made it in English, and Brykhulle translated this writing into French. Honour, beauty, goodness, and worth to true lovers, and joy to him who loves the best! Amen.)

No trace of a poet named Banastre has been discovered, or

[1] Both edited by C. Oulmont (Paris, 1911).

of an English poem of this nature at this early date.[1] Moreover, the lines will bear another interpretation, that both the
English and Anglo-Norman writers were making use of the
same source, possibly in Latin. The meaning of this final
stanza is obscure and it cannot be used, for the present at
any rate, to prove anything. Mr. Russell has suggested that
the Anglo-Norman poet may be identified with a certain
Elias of Brichulle, canon of Hereford.[2] This identification is
less unlikely than appears at first sight. In the French poem
the clerk's champion wins the battle, the usual outcome in
these cases. In the Anglo-Norman poem the reverse is the case,
for to indulge in the love of a clerk is 'vivre en hountage',
'to live in shame', and it is the knight's champion who wins,
causing Blancheflour to die of shock. The change of metre
from the swift-flowing octosyllabic couplet to the tail-rhyme
stanza, giving more scope for development and reflexion,
is a move away from the characteristics of the *fabliau*, for a
fabliau in stanza-form is rare.[3] Finally—and this suggests
that, whatever Brykhulle was doing, he was not making a
literal translation of an English poem—this version is an
exercise in vocabulary. Many of the stanzas are hardly more
than lists of names of musical instruments, precious stones,
fruits, trees, and birds, and so apparently the didactic intention was twofold: to teach French and morality at one and the
same time by means of a sugared pill. The violent language
used by both parties to the debate is, like the language of
flytings, not to be taken seriously. It is the conclusion which
matters, and the only difficulty is to decide whether it is
ironical or not.

In both the Anglo-Norman debates a more serious turn
is given to the question under discussion by the use of the
term 'clerk' in a narrower sense than in the older works of
this nature: to mean someone who has actually taken the
vow of chastity. The late Edmond Faral dismissed them

[1] Mr. J. C. Russell, *Dictionary of Writers of Thirteenth Century England* (London,
1936), pp. 183–5, has confused the supposed debate with the later English romance
with the same title in the Vernon MS., for which see J. E. Wells, *Manual of the
Writings in Middle English* (Yale and Oxford University Presses, 1916), pp. 139–41.

[2] Op. cit., pp. 24–25, cf. *Modern Philology*, xxviii (1931), p. 259.

[3] Professor T. B. W. Reid goes so far as to exclude *Richeut* from the genre: *Twelve
Fabliaux* (Manchester, 1958), p. x.

somewhat contemptuously as presenting 'sous une forme dégénérée le débat primitif'.[1] 'Degenerate' is perhaps too strong a word to use of a legitimate development of the original idea.

There exists a third debate, in lyric stanzas, between a girl and her mother this time, on another perennial theme.[2]

> Bele mere, ke frai?
> De deus amanz su mis en plai:
> Li uns est beaus cum flur de may,
> Li autre est riche, ben le sai.

(Fair mother, what shall I do? My mind is divided between two lovers: one is as beautiful as the mayflower, the other is rich, as I know well.)

The conclusion is moral:

> Aver est en aventure:
> Mut est fous ke trop l'aseure.
> Mes honur e bunté dure
> Coment ke del aver alt:
> Ke seit entendre mesure,
> Cil est riche ke mout valt.

(Possessions are subject to chance, he is a great fool who trusts in them too much. But honour and goodness are lasting, whatever becomes of possessions. Because he understands moderation, he is rich for it is worth much.)

THE NIGHTINGALE ALLEGORY

Le Russinol voleit amer[3] is an allegorical poem which owes an obvious debt to Guillaume de Lorris. The nightingale stands for the lover, but the bird is soon forgotten and the lover's heart is shut up in a tower—the lady—which has twelve guardians, Nobility, Purity, Beauty, and so on. There is nothing remarkable about it, but its existence is significant. Except for the first ten lines, which are in octosyllabic couplets, it consists of tercets of seven-syllable lines.

---

[1] *Recherches sur les sources latines des contes et romans courtois* (Paris, 1913), p. 239.
[2] Ed. P. Meyer, *Romania*, xiii (1884), pp. 512–13.
[3] Ed. P. Meyer, *Romania*, xv (1886), p. 242.

THE ORCHARD WALK

Much more graceful is a charming poem[1] (Cotton Caligula A. xviii) which begins:

> En un verger m'en entrai qe mult fu replenye
> De flurs e de oysels que fesoient melodie;
> E joe mournes alay pensant de ma amye,
> Si luy ateindroie a nul jour de ma vie.

(I entered an orchard which was full of flowers and of birds making
melody and I was thinking sorrowfully about my love, wondering
whether I should attain to her any day of my life.)

A little bird brings comfort, and the poet catches sight of

> Lestres bien escrites sur une foille . . .
> Disant: 'Li Deu de amur a bele seignurie
> Kant tous finz amanz ad en sa baillie,
> E les fauz amans si des liens lie
> Qe a sei les tire de bien amer en partie.
>
> Amur se joint a dreite naturesse;
> Kar leauté norist e donne pruesse,
> Curtoisie voet, chasteté e largesse,
> Et a ses sogés tout udiveté e peresse.'

(Letters well written on a leaf... saying: 'The God of Love has a fair
lordship, since he has in his sway all true lovers, and he binds the false
lovers so fast that he draws them to himself so that they may love well.
Love is joined to kindly nature, for it nourishes loyalty and confers
prowess. It desires courtesy, chastity, and generosity, and takes from its
subjects idleness and laziness.')

THE DREAM OF THE CASTLE OF LOVE

To the fourteenth century belongs an allegory inspired
by Guillaume de Lorris which is longer and more elaborate
than *Le Russinol*. It consists of 1,333 octosyllables,[2] in
couplets. The writer is unknown, but it has mistakenly been
attributed to Walter of Henley, because it occurs in the
same manuscript as his *Husbandry*—a manuscript which is
not easily accessible since it belongs to the College of Arms
(Arundel XIV). The author visits the Castle of Love in a
dream and receives instruction from the God of Love. The

---

[1] Ed. Francisque Michel, *Rapports au ministre* (1839), p. 134.
[2] Ed. O. Södergård, 'Un Art d'Aimer Anglo-normand', *Romania*, lxxvii (1956),
pp. 289–330. Cf. C. B. West, *Courtoisie in Anglo-Norman Literature*, pp. 144–50.

symbolism is complicated and the prominence given to bright colours, to gold and jewels, is a sign of a decadent tradition. As so often happens, the imitator lacks the invention of his model and tries to compensate for this by the multiplicity of his images. He shows no great originality in the choice of these, but a long development of the theme of the 'magic mirror'[1] is handled with skill. By means of this device Jealousy is able to spy upon the castle of the God of Love. Roger Bacon's invention of the telescope caused him to be credited with the possession of such another mirror, and it is possible that the author, like Bacon, was a Franciscan. While the love he describes appears to be courtly, it has to be blessed by the Church. What begins as an art of love ends as an exhortation to married couples to serve God and so 'a la joye saunz fine venir'.

DEFINITIONS OF LOVE

Before an art of anything can be composed its subject must be defined. Definitions as well as arts of love therefore exist. They are, however, a later manifestation when they occur separately. Arts of love originally opened with a definition. Chapter i of Andreas Capellanus's treatise bears the title 'Quid sit Amor'. It was the increasing influence of scholasticism, coupled with the spread of courtly ideas, that caused the separation between the mere definition and the treatise on love which supposes that a person desirous of knowing how to conduct a love-affair was already acquainted with the nature of his malady. John of Garland (*fl.* 1230) composed four lines in Latin defining love, which exist in both a French and an English translation.[2] The play upon words in the Latin can be reproduced in French, but is lacking from the English translation. Unfortunately, the last line is missing from the French translation in the only manuscript in which it survives:

> Amur est une pensee enragiee
> Ke le udif homme meyne par veie deveye,

---

[1] For the fullest bibliography of this subject, cf. W. A. Clouston, 'On the Magical Elements in Chaucer's Squire's Tale', Chaucer Society, Series II, xxvi (1889), pp. 299–333.

[2] Edited by P. Meyer, *Romania*, iv (1875), pp. 382–3.

Ke a seyf de delices ne beyt ke tristesce
[Crebris doloribus commiscens gaudia.]

(Love is a mood of madness, which leads the idle man out of his way, who when athirst for delights drinks only sorrow, and with abundance of griefs dilutes his joy.)

Another, much longer, definition is in prose and has affinities with continental treatises. Their relationship and history are obscure. The Anglo-Norman treatise is prefaced by a few remarks on the nature of courtly love which deserve to be better known.[1] This type of definition belongs to the tradition of Andreas Capellanus, but is heavily marked by a scholastic tradition which had barely touched the earlier work. Andreas twice enumerates regulations for loving. There are thirteen precepts and thirty-one rules, and these figures relate to the subject-matter and have no significance in themselves. The numbers in the Anglo-Norman *Definition* are three, thirteen, nine, six, four, and twelve, and it is impossible not to be struck by the resemblance between the method used and that employed in the religious treatises of the thirteenth and fourteenth centuries.

The treatise begins with the definition proper, and lists thirteen properties of courtly love, with the blazon of its arms added for full measure. Love is, amongst other things, like the lynx which can see through nine walls. It has six servants, who have English names all ending in *-ing*, linked in pairs by alliteration. This does not mean that the treatise has an English source, any more than the fact that Bozon gives English names to some of the eight Hounds of the Devil means that he was translating from English, but it does suggest that the Anglo-Norman author was not slavishly dependent on a continental work. A short middle section is devoted to the four qualities by which a loyal friend may be assayed. The last section lists the twelve points of love which distinguish a true lover.

Professor Studer observed that the middle section resembles the end of a later continental treatise, *La Puissance d'Amour*, but he was unaware that this was itself merely a re-working of an earlier continental work, *L'Amistiés de*

---

[1] Edited by P. Studer, 'Une Définition d'amour en prose anglo-normand', *Mélanges Antoine Thomas* (Paris, 1927), pp. 433–6.

Vraie Amour,[1] which begins with the list of twelve points. The editor is uncertain whether the Anglo-Norman writer is to be accused of plagiarism or whether there were once a number of little independent works of the same kind, proceeding from the same source. The *Amistiés* is thirteenth-century. Paul Studer thought that the *Definition* belonged to the beginning of the fourteenth century or perhaps the end of the thirteenth, but we now know that it is earlier, probably mid-thirteenth-century, since a fragment of it—the middle section and part of the last—occurs in the Bodleian MS. Digby 86, which was begun in 1272 and finished in 1283. It seems idle to talk about priority, and there may have been some lost Latin source of all these French treatises.

The inspiration for them comes ultimately from Cicero's *De Amicitia*, which was given a Christian transformation by Ailred of Rievaulx. The immediate source of the French treatises, especially the list of twelve points contained in them, is the *De Amicitia Christiana* by Petrus Blesensis, which is an expanded modernization of Ailred. When it is remembered that Peter was Archdeacon of Bath and frequented Henry II's court in England—it was he who said that there was no more peace in that court than there is in hell—it is apparent that it was equally open to French and Anglo-Norman writers to be the first to exploit one of his works. The substitution of 'fins amors' for Christian charity and friendship is an obvious step to take, but whether that step was taken in French or in Latin, in France or in England, is a point which cannot be decided on the evidence.

In view of the date of the treatise, and its derivation from a religious work, it is not surprising that although it professes to treat of courtly love—destructive, ruthless, consuming—self-centred, and irresistible, but yet a 'pleisante maladie', the 'points' and the qualities are based upon a strict morality. The seventh point—that lovers must be 'per a per, tut soit l'un de greindre estat que l'autre' ('they must be the equals of one another, even if one be of higher rank than the other')—has a matrimonial air. Professor Studer ascribed this attitude to Anglo-Norman decadence, and said

---

[1] Edited by J. Thomas, *Revue Belge de Philologie et d'Histoire*, xxxvi (1958), pp. 786–811, see especially 787–93.

that the author 'fait appel au bon sens plutôt qu'à l'autorité des anciens, et ses conseils s'adaptent à la moralité bourgeoise plutôt qu'à l'idéalisme chevaleresque'. This attitude, it is now plain, was neither decadent nor Anglo-Norman, and the morality is rather clerical than middle-class.

The style of the *Definition* is epigrammatical and not without charm. Much of it is an anthology of pithy sayings:

Amur est un doutz disir et une dolerouse pensé. . . . Amur est lunge esperance, curte joye.

(Love is a sweet desire and a grievous idea. . . . Love is long hope, short joy.)

The conclusion has a Biblical ring:

Celi que tint ses pointz, ou cele, il est verroie amaunt.

(He who keeps these points—or she—is the true lover.)

A LESSON FOR LOVERS

There is a song of about 1300 on much the same subject.[1] It consists of thirteen stanzas of eight octosyllables rhyming abababab, the first line being masculine and the next feminine. The feminine lines have only seven syllables by modern reckoning, a characteristically lyric feature. In the first stanza the poet states that he is going to write a song in Romance:

> La lessoun a leals amantz
> Vus y comencez a lyre.

(In it you are about to read the lesson for loyal lovers.)

The seventh begins:

> Entre amis seit owelté,
> Senz e curteysie.

(Between lovers let there be equality, wisdom, and courtliness.)

The poem ends:

> Ore pri a touz lais e clers,
> Si ne me chaut qe l'oye,
> Qe nul ne prenge le travers
> De fyn amour verroie;

---

[1] Edited by Th. Wright, *Specimens of Lyric Poetry* (Percy Society, **xix**, 1842), pp. 18–22, and, from another manuscript, by E. Stengel, *Zeitschrift für französische Sprache und Literatur*, xiv (1892), pp. 158–9.

Car leal cuer n'est pas divers,
Eynz ayme droite voie;
Ly *tu autem* est en ce vers,
Ly respounz soit de joye. Amen.

(Now I pray all laymen and clerks, I don't care who hears it, not to take the wrong turning in true love, for the loyal heart is single in purpose, and only loves the straight way; this versicle is the *Tu autem* of the lesson, let your response be of joy. Amen.)

HOW TO CHOOSE A LOVER

A letter addressed to the 'Tresnoble Dame Desyree' on how to choose a lover[1] can fortunately be dated, 23 June 1299. It is more cynical in tone and lacks the charm of the *Definition*. The lady is given a list of the six qualities to look for in a lover, and taught how they may be tested. If the lover conforms to the right type a probationary period of seven years is prescribed. Before the final acceptance by the lady a pact must be made before a witness. What the lady in this case requires is not so much devotion as material rewards. The lover must pledge his body, chattels, and everything that he possesses before winning the favours of a tyrannical dame who has already imposed such tests as a journey to Rome at his own expense merely to gratify her whim. The mock letter ends with a sealing-clause:

Doné dens les quatre mers de Engletere, en vyle de la Seint Johan le Baptist, le aan du regne le roy Edward fiz le roy Henry vint e seitime.

(Given within the four seas of England on the Eve of St. John the Baptist in the twenty-seventh year of the reign of King Edward the son of King Henry.)

LOVE-SONGS

So much for the background to courtliness in Anglo-Norman. Of the works mentioned, only the *Donnei des Amants* belongs to the period when the most spontaneous expression in lyric form is to be expected. The number of love-songs surviving is not great, and none of them can be claimed as being of outstanding merit. A few, however, are pleasant enough. Five stanzas, with music,[2] have an agreeable

---

[1] Ed. J. Koch, 'Anglonormannische Texte im MS. Arundel 220 des Britischen Museums', *Zeitschrift für romanische Philologie*, liv (1934), pp. 47–56.

[2] Text and music in J. Stainer, *Early Bodleian Music* (London, 1901).

refrain of two lines beginning with the words 'Trop s'esluine' ('She—or it—goes too far off'). There is no depth of feeling, but the song can be described as pretty (MS. Ashmole 1285).

A gayer song, a ballete of five stanzas, has perhaps been falsely claimed for Anglo-Norman. This has the refrain:

> E! dame jolyve,
> Mun q[u]er sauns faucer
> Met en vostre balaye,
> Qe ne say vos per.

(Ah! lady gay, my heart without deceiving puts itself in your power, for I know not your equal.)

Paul Meyer first published this song[1] from a copy written in a fourteenth-century English hand on a flyleaf of an Italian manuscript of the Code of Justinian, now Gonville and Caius College MS. 11. The first four stanzas have since been discovered in the Lorraine Chansonnier in the Bodleian (MS. Douce 308), and the melody has been recovered from the tenor part of a motet in Montpellier (Bibliothèque de l'École de Médecine MS. 196). Thus the song was evidently very well known on both sides of the Channel, and probably circulated amongst students. The refrain is quoted in *Renart le Nouvel*, in one manuscript with the same tune as the Montpellier tenor, in another with a different one. It is also parodied in the 'correspondance amoureuse' of a clerk published, by a coincidence, at the same time as the song itself by Paul Meyer. A love-letter in verse ends with the lines:

> Ey, Mergrete jolie,
> Mon quer sans fauser, etc.

This correspondence is Anglo-Norman. Professor Gennrich, who published the Lorraine version and the music with commentary,[2] states categorically: 'die ürspringliche Heimat des Liedes ist natürlich Frankreich, nicht England.' This simply cannot be proved. It has already been mentioned that the Lorraine copy lacks the final stanza, and there are other

---

[1] In *Romania*, xxxviii (1909), pp. 438–41.
[2] *Rondeaux, Virelais und Balladen* (Gesellschaft für Romanische Literatur, Dresden), i (1921), ii (1927), no. 178.

minor variants of interest. In particular, in one couplet the rhymes differ, according to the dialect. The Anglo-Norman has

> Dame a gent cors avenaunt
> Pur Deu, ne creez pas taunt.

In the Lorraine text the same couplet reads:

> Tres douce dame a cors gent,
> Por Dieu, nes croiez pas tant.

Anglo-Norman was one of the dialects in which -en and -an remained undifferentiated in pronunciation. It seems unlikely that an Anglo-Norman writer would be at pains to correct a continental rhyme, whereas a continental writer might change these rhymes to get what he considered a better line. Some songs from England did find their way to the Continent, those with English words being sometimes given a rough French translation,[1] so the possibility of this ballete having an Anglo-Norman origin cannot be ruled out.

Other songs of fixed form include a Rondeau from the flyleaf of B.N. fr. 19525, 'Margot, Margot', published with some of its music by F. Gennrich,[2] and a Rotrouenge 'Quant primes me quintey de amors' ('When first I knew love well'), published from a flyleaf of B.M. Add. 16559 by Paul Meyer.[3] The southern form 'goie' is to be noted in the refrain of another song published, with a facsimile of the music, by A. T. Baker[4] from a blank leaf in a copy of Juvenal and Persius in Cambridge, Pembroke College MS. 13.

In a copy of Peraldus which once belonged to Bury, now Cambridge, St. John's College MS. 138, is bound a leaf from a thirteenth-century song-book on which are the French and Latin versions of two songs. The Latin songs are religious, the French are love-songs. The versions are written in alternate lines for convenience in singing the music.[5] Elsewhere, lyrics and plays are found written in alternate stanzas

---

[1] Cf. M. F. Bukofzer in the *New Oxford History of Music*, iii (1960), pp. 130–3; F. H. Harrison, *Music in Medieval Britain* (London, 1958), pp. 133, 134 (for the Montpellier MS.); P. Meyer, *Bulletin de la Société des Anciens Textes*, x (1885), pp. 65 ff. (for a Provençal copy).   [2] Loc. cit., no. 24.

[3] In *Romania*, xix (1890), pp. 102–5.

[4] In *Revue des Langues Modernes*, li (1908), pp. 39–43.

[5] Cf. M. R. James, *Catalogue of MSS.* (Cambridge, 1913).

of French and English. A similar leaf in Cambridge, Corpus Christi College MS. 8, contains songs in Latin and English, and a French love-song.[1] The 'Bury Manuscript', now Bodleian MS. e Mus. 7, has two motets with one part having French words, in one case the tenor, 'Doucement mi reconforte', and in the other the duplum, 'Parfundement plure Absolon'. While the music was almost certainly composed at Bury, the origin of the French words is unknown.[2] French was much used at Bury; saints' Lives were written there and one of the *Manières de langage* comes from there. A song with the refrain:

> A li dunt ai peine e delit
> Cri merci qu'ele ne m'ublit.

(To her, from whom I have pain and delight, I cry mercy that she forget me not.)

has four stanzas with alternating masculine and feminine lines rhyming in -*u*. It ends with a couplet rhyming with the refrain:

> Brief est a metre en escrit
> La joie dunt mis queors vit.

(Short it is to put in writing, the joy by which my heart lives.)

An incomplete song of the thirteenth century with the refrain:

> Jeo sui li plus traiz del munt
> Ki maignent de tuz cels ki sunt.

(I am, of all the people in existence, the man in the world the worst betrayed.)

in Bodleian MS. Rawlinson G. 22 is probably Anglo-Norman. The rhymes are all feminine except in the refrain. Some fifteenth-century songs in Bodleian MS. Douce 381, 'Les euz overt, la bouche close' and 'Mon cuer n'averoye', are more likely continental, though the spelling is Anglo-Norman.

French songs also circulated in Ireland. Amongst the profane songs to which Richard Lederede, the Franciscan

---

[1] Cf. M. R. James, *Catalogue of MSS.*, i (Cambridge, 1912).
[2] See especially F. Ll. Harrison, *New Oxford History of Music*, iii. 94–95. Text and music of this and the next five songs are in J. Stainer, *Early Bodleian Music* (London, 1901).

Bishop of Ossory from 1317–60, composed Latin words more appropriate for singing by the cathedral clergy, two were French. As in the case of the English songs, only the refrains of the originals are given for the purpose of identification, and unfortunately no musical notation is provided. The inference is that the tunes were too well known for this to be necessary. The French refrains are

> Harrow, jeo su trahy
> Par fol amor de mal amy.

   (Harrow! I am betrayed by the foolish love of an evil lover.)

and

> Heu, alas, pur amour
> Qy moy myst en taunt dolour.

   (Alack, alas, for Love which has put me in such grief.)[1]

The songs without refrains are duller. Some are in lines of equal length, of ten or eight syllables, with very little variety in the rhyme pattern. The subjects are either the poet's address to his sovereign lady, who alone has the power to solace and cure him, or a complaint describing his situation and perhaps the charms of the lady. They are purely conventional, and are rarely distinguished in any way. One, which may possibly be continental, though it does not survive in a French manuscript, contains a stanza comparing the poet and his lady to the unicorn captured by the maiden. This comparison, derived from a favourite theme in the *Bestiaires*, also occurs in a poem by no less a writer than Thibaut de Champagne.[2] Another, whose Anglo-Norman origin is betrayed by its metre, in spite of Paul Meyer's doubts, is perhaps the unique example of a reverdie or spring song. It begins with a description of the spring, with the woods turning green and the birds singing to their mates. The lady's complexion is compared to hawthorn blossom, to roses, to a swan. It is well done, but it is scarcely more than an exercise in rhetoric. The last stanza contains the traditional play on the words 'mordre' and 'mourir', 'cœur' and

---

[1] *The Red Book of Ossory, Historical MSS. Commission Report*, x, appendix, part v (1885), pp. 244, 248.

[2] P. Meyer, *Romania*, xv (1886), p. 248; cf. *Les Chansons de Thibaut de Navarre*, ed. A. Wallensköld (S.A.T.F.), pp. 112–16.

'corps', and finishes with a parody of testamentary phraseo-
logy. The poem is a remote and light-hearted ancestor of
Villon's *Testament*.

> Jo sui si mortelement mors
> Ke le quer m'estuit tut fendre,
> Puisk'ele ne voet pité prendre,
> Ben crei ke men seit le tort.
> Valer ne me poet nul jur
> Puis ke mort me voet esteyndre,
> Mes a Deu voil l'alme rendre
> E a ma dame mun cors.

(I am so mortally stung that my heart will cleave in two. Since she
will not take pity on me, I believe that the fault is mine. I can never
be hale, since death wishes to destroy me, but I will yield my soul to
God, and my body to my lady.)

RHETORICAL SONGS

This last example shows that Anglo-Norman writers knew
not only the right things to say but how to say them in the
right way. There are other and even more elaborate rhetorical fireworks. Five stanzas built round three rhyme schemes
form a song of antitheses, of the kind made celebrated by
one of the contests at Blois in which Villon took part, and
were later used in sonnet-form by Renaissance writers, particularly by Du Bellay. The Anglo-Norman poem begins:

> Malade sui, de joie espris,
> Tant suspire que ne repos[e].

(I am sick, afire with joy, I sigh so much I cannot rest.)

Another song of five stanzas and an envoy is proudly
entitled 'Ryme Bon'. The rhymes are nearly all of the 'grammatical' type. These are described in the *Leys d'Amors* and
are used in lyrics by the Countess of Die and Bernart de
Ventadorn. In narrative verse they occasionally occur as
ornaments.[1] The Anglo-Norman writer has succeeded in
using rhymes of this kind for both masculine and feminine
endings, except in the first stanza, where only the masculine
lines have them. The same rhyme is used, in the masculine

[1] G. Lote, *Histoire du vers français*, II. ii (Paris, 1951), pp. 87, 148–50;
J. Anglade, *Las Leys d'Amors* (Toulouse, 1919), ii. 112–17; G. Kussler-Ratyé, 'Les
Chansons de la Comtesse Béatrix de Dia', *Archivum Romanicum*, i (1917), p. 176.

and the feminine, twelve lines running, in the last stanza and
the envoy. This last may serve as an example of the whole:

> Ma chaunson et ma repris[e]
> Envoy a ceux enpris,
> E si je ai rien mespris
> Bien voil[e] q'el[e] soit mesprise.

(My song and my refrain I send to those in love. And if I have done
anything wrong I hope that it will be overlooked.)

Les Dytees Moun Syre Gautier de Bybeswurthe, by the author
of the treatise on French and of a debate with Earl Henry
de Lacy, is an exercise in 'grammatical' rhymes addressed,
possibly, to the same lady as the treatise. It is headed:
'Regardez, Lyssez, Apernez' ('Look, read, learn') and ends
as follows:

> Gabriel, bone ryme as
> E ta chaunçon ben rymé as,
> Qar qy la rymera
> En paradis rymera
> Ou nous trestouz rymerons
> Par *Ave* qe nous cryerons.
> Ore vous ay, Dame, rymee,
> Veyez si jeo ay bein rymee.

The pun here on *rymer* 'to rhyme' and 'to set a course' was
probably overworked. It was a godsend to medieval versifiers.[1]

The *Débat* refers to the Crusade of 1270. Henry de Lacy,
Earl of Lincoln, the patron of Ralph de Bohun, had taken
the Cross, but held back—on account of his love for a lady,
according to the poem. Bibbesworth took part in the expedition.[2] One stanza is a kind of 'anti-Chevrefoil' in which the
author of the treatise displays, as might be expected, a more
accurate knowledge of natural history than Marie de France:

> Beau sire quens, jeo truis en un foil,
> Qe amur ressemble au chevrefoil
> Qe en destreignaunt fait setchir
> Le plus bel arbre de un haut broil,

---

[1] Cf. J. Orr, *Le Lai de l'Ombre* (Edinburgh, 1948), p. 31.

[2] *Reliquiae Antiquae*, i. 134–6. Cf. *C.P.R. Henry III*, p. 480; A. C. Baugh, 'The
Date of Walter of Bibbesworth's *Traité*', *Festschrift für Walther Fischer* (Heidelberg, 1959), pp. 25–26.

Et pus ausi cum en somoil
Sanz porter fruit le fait murrir.
Mais qi voudra l'arbre garir,
Et faire le ben revenir,
Les cordes coupe pres du soil.
Lors purront les braunches flurir,
Et li fust a grant ben venir;
Ensi le ferez, a mon voil.

(Fair sir Earl, I find on a leaf in a book that love is like the honey-suckle, which by strangling withers up the fairest tree of a tall coppice, and then afterwards as if in sleep it makes it die without bearing fruit. But he who would cure the tree, and make it recover, cuts the bonds close to the ground. Then the branches will blossom and the wood come to a healthy state. Thus will you do, if you take my advice.)

Vising condemned this effort as 'somewhat ludicrous'.[1] So it is, but it was never meant to be very much else. (Vising treated everything on the same level always, and was incapable of seeing the difference between serious poetry and 'two gentlemen daffing over their wine'.)

MACARONIC VERSE

With three languages in one country to play with it is not surprising that the rhetorically inclined took to macaronic verse. Pastorals are rare in Anglo-Norman, so it is curious to find a specimen in Anglo-Norman and Latin:

En may quant dait e foil e fruit Parens natura parere.

Each of the seven stanzas of this poem ends with a line from a hymn—'Jam lucis orto sidere', and so on. This is obviously a student's effort. Two famous love-letters in three languages are well known through their appearance in *Early English Lyrics* and *The Oxford Book of English Verse*.[2] The last stanzas of the *De Amico ad Amicam* and of her *Responsio* are as follows:

Jeo vous pry par charité,
The wordes that here wreten be
Tenete;

---

[1] *Anglo-Norman*, p. 38.
[2] E. K. Chambers and F. Sidgwick, *Early English Lyrics* (London, 1907), nos. viii, ix; *Oxford Book* (ed. 1929), nos. 2, 3.

> And turne thy herte me toward
> O a Dieu que vous gard!
> Valete!
>
> Vous estes ma morte et ma vye,
> I preye you for your curteisie
> Amate,
> Cestes maundes jeo vous pry
> In youre herte stedefastly
> Notate.

The lady, it will be observed, knew her *Tristan*, and an even closer reminiscence of Thomas's couplet occurs in a *Littera amorose composita* included in a formulary with the usual students' begging letters in prose:[1]

> Vous estez ma mort, vous estez ma vie,
> En vous est toute ma druerye.

(You are my death, you are my life, in you is all my love.)

DRINKING-SONGS

A few more love-songs are preserved in the *Manière de langage*[2] together with some drinking-songs celebrating 'la bone vinee' or 'la cerveyse', wine or ale.

RELIGIOUS LYRICS

Religious poems followed the same patterns as the secular. There are several translations of proses, and some original hymns. The translations usually occur along with both the Latin text and the music, and it is not at all clear whether they were actually meant to be sung, as *St. Eulalia* was, or whether they were just 'cribs', used perhaps in the song-schools.[3] The song beginning 'Quant le russinol se cesse',[4] and ending with a prayer to God and the Virgin, of which the music is preserved, is undoubtedly a parody of a love-song on the lines of our *Gude and Godly Ballats* and the Ossory Latin songs. Another parody begins like a woman's

---

[1] E. Stengel, 'Die ältesten Anleitungsschriften', *Zeitschrift für neufranzösische Sprache und Literatur*, i (1879), p. 10.

[2] Last ed. J. Gessler (Brussels, Paris, Louvain, 1934).

[3] P. Meyer, *Romania*, iv (1875), pp. 370–4; E. V. Mead, 'Two Anglo-Norman Devotional Poems', *Medium Ævum*, xxviii (1959), pp. 87–90.

[4] Edited by H. Petersen, *Neuphilologische Mitteilungen*, xiii (1911).

love-song, and it is quite a shock to find as it goes on that it is addressed to God. Presumably it was intended for nuns.[1] It begins:

> En une matine me levoye l'autre er,
> Pensif de amorettes ke fet a preiser.

(The other day I rose up in the morning, meditating on love-affairs which are to be prized.)

The second stanza opens:

> Mei ke sui ameruse, ne suy a blamer;
> Kar je ay tel amy ke n'ad poynt de per.

(I who am in love, am not to be blamed, for I have a lover who has no equal.)

The last two stanzas are addressed to 'mun tresduz amy', and Amen is written at the close. The poem consists of four quatrains of decasyllables. The date suggested for it is early thirteenth century, but this seems too soon, and it may be mid thirteenth century, like Thomas of Hales's *Luve Ron*. Indeed, the poet, like Thomas, may have been a Franciscan.

The Christmas carol is represented by a wassail-song which can hardly rank as religious, though it is connected with a church festival. In wording it is very close to one which has remained popular to the present day, 'Here we come a-wassailing', though it is no longer used for its original purpose. The Anglo-Norman song[2] begins:

> Seignors, ore entendez a nus;
> De loins sumes venuz a vous
>   Pur quere Noël.

It concludes with the couplet:

> Si jo vus di trestoz: Wesseyl!
> Dehaiz eit qui ne dira: Drincheyl!

(And so I say to you all: Wassail! A curse on him who will not say: Drinkhail!)

POLITICAL SATIRES

Of no great literary merit, but of great historical interest, are a considerable number of political satires and songs. The

---

[1] *Reliquiae Antiquae*, i (London, 1841), p. 104.
[2] Ed. P. Meyer, *Recueil d'anciens textes* (Paris, 1877), p. 382.

'male chanson' was a form of medieval lampoon which drove men to fury. The late Monsieur Faral's attempt to prove that it was a mere figure of speech takes no account of the historical evidence.[1] Verbal insults were often dearly paid for. When the garrison of Alençon thrust raw hides over the walls with cries of 'Hides for the tanner!', William the Bastard retorted by flinging the hands and feet of his prisoners into the town. Henry I drove a man to suicide who had written scurrilous songs about him.[2] After the Battle of Bannockburn, Scottish maidens danced a mock sea-shanty in commemoration of Edward II's low taste in sport and his escape to Dunbar in a fishing-boat.[3]

The evil song might be in Latin, French, or English. Langtoft has happily preserved many from both sides in the wars of Edward I against the Scots. When Edward took Berwick in 1302:

> Le fet environer de fosse large e lee,
> En reprovaunt le Escot, ke ad de ly chaunté
> E par mokerye en Englays rymeye:
> Pykit him
> An diket hym
> On scoren sayd he.
> He dikes, he pikes
> On lenche als hym likes. . . .[4]

(He causes it to be surrounded with a wide and broad foss, in reproval of the Scots, who had sung of him, and in mockery made verses in English:

> 'Let him pick
> And let him dike'
> In scorn said they.
> He dikes and he picks
> As long as he likes. . . .)

---

[1] 'Sur trois vers de la *Chanson de Roland*', *Modern Philology*, xxviii (1941), pp. 235–42. Cf. T. A. Jenkins, *La Chanson de Roland* (Boston, New York, Chicago, and London, 1924), p. 83; R. M. Wilson, *The Lost Literature of Medieval England* (London, 1952), pp. 192–214.

[2] William of Jumièges, Migne, *Pat. Lat.* cxlix. 858; Wace, *Roman de Rou*, ed. H. Andresen (Heilbronn, 1879), ii. 4336 ff.; Ordericus Vitalis, ed. A. Le Prevost, iv. 460 ff.

[3] F. W. D. Brie, *The Brut* (E.E.T.S., o.s., 131, 136), p. 208. Cf. H. Johnstone, *Letters of Edward Prince of Wales* (Roxburghe Club, cxciv, 1931), p. xxxviii, and *Edward of Carnarvon* (Manchester, 1946), pp. 130, 131.

[4] Ed. Th. Wright (R.S.), ii. 235–6.

The original Scots song ran thus:

> Kyng Edward, wanne þu havest Berwic,
> > pike þe,
> Wanne þu havest geten,
> > dike þe.[1]

King Edward is said to have speeded the digging operation by wheeling barrows of earth about with his own hands.

Langtoft's songs are all in the same sort of tail-rhyme and short metre, and could all be sung to the same tune. They were probably well known through oral transmission, for there is much variation both in wording and in length in the different manuscripts and in the translation by Robert of Brunne and the prose *Bruts*. In Langtoft most begin with a French version, with a last stanza in English. One is entirely in French, and a French snatch about John Balliol seems to be a composition of Langtoft's own in the same style:

> . . . tel est la bounté
> Dount li rays Eduuard
> Du ray Jon musard
> > Est rewerdoné.
> De Escoce sait cum pot;
> Parfurnyr nus estot
> > La geste avaunt parlé. . . .[2]

(Such is the goodness by which King Edward is by King John the Fool rewarded. Let it be as it can about Scotland; we must complete the story begun before. . . .)

Most of these songs are said to have originated with the armies, but a nasty gloating celebration of the execution of Sir William Wallace may belong to London.

It has sometimes been assumed that the songs were all in English and that Langtoft translated them, and that he got tired before the end and left part untranslated. This cannot be concluded with certainty. There exists so much macaronic verse, and so much bilingual too, that it is possible that two versions existed. It would be strange if Langtoft's patience regularly gave out just before the last verse of a song.

---

[1] W. Rishanger, *Annales Angliae et Scotiae*, in *Chronica Monasterii S. Albani*, ed. H. T. Riley (R.S.), ii. 373.   [2] Ed. ii. 222.

Mention has already been made of two curious examples of what appear to be alternative versions of plays and hymns,[1] and amongst the group of songs next to be described the same phenomenon is to be observed.

Sixteen political songs and satires, known through editions by Thomas Wright, have now been magnificently republished by the late Miss I. S. T. Aspin.[2] They are very varied. Some are in octosyllabic couplets and some in stanzas. An *Elegy on the Death of Edward I* occurs in both English and French, and the probabilities are that the English is a contemporary translation of the French. *Against the King's Taxes* (?1337–40) is, from the versification point of view, a *tour de force*. It is in five-line stanzas. The first four lines of each are grouped as a quatrain, with the first hemistich in French and the second in accented Latin, with internal rhyme. The final line is a Latin hexameter or pentameter. This is in imitation of the goliardic stanza 'with authority', the first part being accentual and the final line quantitative. This song, therefore, smells of the lamp and is in no wise a popular one. *Vulneratur Karitas*, late thirteenth century, like the religious poems already mentioned, is in alternate stanzas in Latin and French, the one being translated from the other. The arrangement stanza by stanza is the same as that for the bilingual prologues to plays in French and English. *On the Times*, fourteenth century, is a collection of proverbs in Latin, French, and English all mixed up and probably intended to scan as English, but scansion is comparatively unimportant in such a case, where the tune would override any differences. All the songs are anonymous except the poem ascribed to Edward II just before his murder,[3] which took place in 1327. The mysterious reference to 'la Bise du par Kenire' may be best interpreted as an allusion to a mistress and is one of the arguments in favour of the attribution to the king. The heading in the manuscript may have been inserted by a partisan for propaganda purposes—'De le roi Edward le fiz roi Edward, le chanson qe il fist mesmes'—

[1] Cf. above, p. 330.

[2] A.N.T.S., xi (1953).

[3] The authenticity or otherwise of this ascription has been hotly disputed, but the balance is in favour of it. To the bibliography given by Miss Aspin add H. Johnstone, *Edward of Carnarvon*, p. 20.

but as it was probably written before 1340 this seems unlikely. This song is one of the few with any claims to be
judged as poetry, and opens conventionally:

> En tenps de iver me survynt damage,
> Fortune trop m'ad traversé,
> Eure m'est faili tut mon age.

(In winter-time harm overtook me. Fortune has much thwarted
me. Good luck has failed me all my life.)

Only one is a true song, which cries out for a tune and to be
sung, and that is *Trailbaston* (1305–7), of which these are
the fifth and twenty-fifth—and last—stanzas:

> Pur ce me tendroi antre bois, suz le jolyf umbray;
> La n'y a fauceté ne nulle male lay,
> En le bois de Belregard, ou vole le jay
> E chaunte russinole touz jours santz delay. . . .

> Cest rym fust fet al bois, desouz un lorer,
> La chaunte merle, russinole e eyre l'esperver;
> Escrit estoit en perchemyn pur mout remenbrer
> E gitté en haut chemyn qe um le dust trover.

(Therefore I will keep within the shaws, under the merry shade;
there is no falseness there, nor any evil law, in the forest of Belregard,
where the jay flies and the nightingale sings without stint every day. . . .
This rhyme was made in the greenwood, beneath a laurel tree. There
sing blackbird and nightingale and hovers the sparrowhawk. It was
written on parchment so that it should be well minded, and flung on
the high road for all to find.)

The other subjects are: laments for the dead—Simon de
Montfort and Edward I; topical events—*The Song of the
Barons* against Montfort's enemies, the execution of the
traitor Thomas of Turberville, the breach of Magna Carta;
satire on abuses, some on the Church and of course on the
religious orders—*L'Ordre de Bel Ayse*; others on the state
of society—the Three Estates and the ingratitude of the
great.

A song which unfortunately escaped the notice of Wright
and of Miss Aspin contains one of the few English allusions
to the legend of Scota and the Stone of Destiny.[1] Written

---

[1] M. D. Legge, 'La Piere d'Escoce', *Scottish Historical Review*, xxxviii (1959),
pp. 109–13.

soon after the death of Edward I, it tells the history of the
Stone, its rape by Edward I, and his presentation of it to
St. Edward. Presumably designed to put the case of Westminster Abbey as owners of the Stone, it may have been
useful when the king proposed to return it to Scotland in
1328. The song consists of six quatrains of monorhymed
alexandrines.

Nearly everything mentioned so far is either thirteenth
or fourteenth century. In other words, the best period of the
Old French lyric is not represented at all. Yet it must not be
deduced that no earlier lyric was written—apart from the
efforts of the sons of Henry II, which rank as continental.
The only copy of the earliest crusading song, 'Chevalier,
mult estes guariz', a French recruiting song written for
the crusade of Louis VII in 1147, happens to be Anglo-
Norman.[1] This cannot have been the only song circulating in
England, and some may have been composed there. More
than anything else, songs must have been transmitted orally,
and there is no Anglo-Norman *chansonnier* to correspond
with the great collections made for the French nobility in
the fourteenth century. Nearly everything mentioned here
has been preserved by accident, either by being used as part
of a motet or by incorporation into a *Manière de langage*
or written on a blank page in a manuscript, even in a Latin
theological work. This is evidence that songs ran in people's
heads. It must have been some idle law-student who wrote
in a copy of the Code of Justinian imported from Italy that
charming song 'E! Dame jolyve'. For one song which
survives, hundreds must have been lost. There is one
miraculously preserved example of the written form these
songs originally took, the tiny pocket roll, only two and a
half inches wide and five and a half long (B.M. Add. 23986).
It looks for all the world like a computus roll, and may owe
its escape to being mistaken for one. How many of these
little scraps may not have rolled off the table and been swept
up with the rushes or been put to the innumerable uses for
which a small piece of parchment was suitable in times past!

---

[1] Text and music, J. Bédier and P. Aubry, *Les Chansons de Croisade* (Paris,
1909), pp. 3–16; F. Gennrich, *Altfranzösische Lieder*, i (Halle/Saale, 1953),
pp. 1–4.

Perhaps the writer of *Trailbaston* was thinking of a roll like this.[1]

THE *BALADES* OF JOHN GOWER

Though, therefore, the Anglo-Norman lyric begins in obscurity and the earliest survivals are not of the highest order, its end is magnificent, and the last writer surpasses his French contemporaries by a long way. John Gower[2] shows what French poetry in England might have become if Chaucer had not flung his cap over the windmill and plunged into the English language. Gower (*c.* 1330–1408) is usually refused a place as an Anglo-Norman writer on two grounds—that he wrote good French and that he struck out a fresh line. Neither of these reasons will stand scrutiny. Gower wrote an Anglo-Norman dialect, influenced, as had been the case from 1066 onwards, by continental French, and as he was an educated and intelligent man of some wealth, he obviously had opportunities of reading widely and of mixing with people, even if he never travelled. The *Mirour de l'Omme*, his French prose work, as has been pointed out, follows the tradition of Anglo-Norman religious literature. All that is new and might be considered un-Anglo-Norman is his use of the balade. But this is ridiculous. The balade was not adopted in northern France until the time of Gower himself, and its best exponents, Charles of Orleans and Villon, wrote after his death. It is with Deschamps and Machault alone that he can be compared as a lyric poet, and he is their superior. It is a curious fact that the balade does not well survive its transference into English—even Chaucer's experiments with it are not very successful, and his use of the form is another reason, besides his use of the French language, why Gower would have been ranged with the 'attardés et égarés', supposing Lanson had ever written a history of literature in England.

Gower's output is not very great. He used the balade in sequences, the *Cinkante Balades* (fifty is a round number; there are fifty-one besides two dedicatory ones and a

---

[1] Cf. K. Sisam, *Fourteenth Century Prose and Verse* (Oxford, 1955), pp. xxxiv–xxxviii.

[2] *French Works*, ed. G. C. Macaulay (Oxford, 1899), i; cf. above, pp. 220–2.

concluding one), and the *Traitie*, a series of eighteen, making a grand total of seventy-two. This is not very much to set against the three hundred of Christine de Pisan, or the eleven hundred odd of Eustache Deschamps, but it is quality, not quantity, that counts. Charles of Orleans wrote only a hundred and twenty-two, and Villon thirty, if one excepts the ones in jargon.

The *Traitie selonc les auctours pour essampler les amantz marietz* forms a kind of sequel in French to the English *Confessio Amantis*, written just before his marriage at the beginning of 1398. Many of the *exempla* had already appeared in the earlier poem. In this collection it is 'moral Gower' speaking, and the poems are less attractive than those in the longer sequence. Most of the personages mentioned come from the Bible or from classical writers, but the fifteenth balade draws upon the 'well-known chronicle and story of Lancelot and Tristram'. It is here that there occurs the description of the Fair of Love, where Cupid has hearts to sell or give away. None of these balades has an envoy except the last:

> Al Université de tout le monde
> Johan Gower ceste Balade envoie:
> E si jeo n'ai de François la faconde,
> Pardonetz moi qe jeo de ceo forsvoie:
> Jeo sui Englois, si quier par tiele voie
> Estre excusé; mais quoique nulls en die,
> L'amour parfit en Dieu se justifie.

(To the community of the whole world John Gower addresses this balade; and if I have not fluency in French, forgive me if I go astray; I am English, and seek in this way to be excused; but whatever anyone says of it, perfect love is justified in God.)

This envoy is followed by two poems in Latin.

The *Cinkante Balades* are more difficult to date. They were first noticed by Thomas Warton, who thought they were a youthful work of about 1350, apparently believing that only the young are likely to write about love. The dedication and conclusion are both addressed, however, to Henry IV. True, they might have been later additions, but it seems unnecessary to assume this, and Gower was not writing because he himself was in love. As he had become blind and had ceased to write by 1401, it seems probable that the collection was made soon after Henry's accession in 1399.

These poems are not personal. They were written, like so much of Marot's poetry, for the court. The surprising thing is that in spite of this they are so fine. Gower divides them into two classes, those written for persons about to be married, and those of universal application. Five poems are put into the mouths of ladies. Though this series contains the most poetical of Gower's works, they bear the unmistakable stamp of his personality. Number xliii, addressed by a lady to her lover, begins:

> Plus tricherous qe Jason a Medee,

and is a catalogue of faithless lovers, Æneas, Theseus, Lancelot, Tristram, and many more. The bestiary is drawn upon for comparisons with the falcon, 'caladrius', sparrowhawk, chameleon, phoenix, blackbird, and popinjay. The months and seasons are mentioned again and again. Discreet use is made of rhetorical devices. The refrain of iv* is

> Sanz departir tu es ma joie maire.
>
> (Without question thou art my greatest joy.)

and the first, third, and fifth lines of each stanza begin with the words 'Sanz departir'. Number v contains lines in the old courtly tradition:

> Elle est ma vie, elle est tout mon avoir,
> Elle est m'amie, elle est toute ma joie,
> Elle est tout mon confort matin et soir.

(She is my life, she is all my wealth; she is my love, she is all my joy; she is all my strength morning and evening.)

Gower speaks of 'fin amour' and 'joie' like any troubadour, and the lover is the lady's knight. It is really astonishing how much new wine Gower is able to pour into old bottles without bursting them.[1]

It is quite impossible to quote sufficient to give any idea of the philosophy of these poems—a philosophy of love—but here is the envoy of the last balade but one: 'De vrai

---

[1] Cf. J. Audiau, *Les Troubadours et l'Angleterre* (Paris, 1927), pp. 103 ff., and G. Kar, *Thoughts on the Mediaeval Lyric* (Oxford, 1933), pp. 55–63.

honour est amour tout le chief', and the last stanza of the concluding address to the Virgin:

> N'est qui d'amour poet dire le final;
> Mais endroit moi c'est la conclusioun,
> Qui voet d'onour sercher l'original,
> Amour s'acorde a nature et reson.

(There is no one who can say the last word on Love, but according to me this is the conclusion: if anyone would seek the original of honour, let Love agree with Nature and with Reason.)

> De tout mon coer jeo l'aime et serve et prise,
> Et amerai sanz nulle departie;
> Par quoi j'espoir d'avoir ma rewardise,
> Pour quelle jeo ma dame ades supplie:
> C'est, quant mon corps lerra la compaignie
> De m'alme, lors lui deigne en remembrance
> D'amour doner a moi le pourpartie,
> Dont puiss avoir le ciel en heritance.

(With my whole heart I love and serve and prize her, and always will without ceasing; by which I hope to have my reward, for which I continually beseech my lady; it is, that when my body leaves the company of my soul, she will deign to give the share of love by which I may obtain the inheritance of Heaven.)

Gower's versification is peculiar to himself. Unlike his immediate predecessors in Anglo-Norman, he wrote syllabic verse, but on a system of his own. Apart from the fact that he was freer than continental writers in making grammar give way before the requirement of metre and rhyme, he has more feeling for rhythm and a tendency to write in iambics. The editor refers to his 'attempt to combine the English accentual with the French syllabic measure', but it is more likely that he was influenced by Latin verse. His English verse is also syllabic, and differs from Chaucer's in several respects. A comparative study of the versification used by Gower in his three languages would prove of interest.

The deliberate use of different languages for different purposes was nothing new. Thomas of Hales had done exactly the same thing in the thirteenth century, and there were doubtless many more whose names are unknown. It so happens that Gower's is the last name on the roll of Anglo-Norman writers. Chaucer's could have stood beside it, but it was he who sounded the death-knell of Anglo-Norman literature, and cast off the tradition which Gower was content to foster. Latin, of course, remained as an alternative to a vernacular for a long time to come. Writers like Milton and Herbert changed from English to Latin at will; what is more relevant here is the fact that Charles of Orleans used Latin for his serious poetry, and it was in Latin that Du Bellay expressed his most intimate feelings. Language, like style, could be varied to suit the occasion and the mood of the moment. From this point of view the present-day concentration on the mother-tongue results in loss.

XIV

CONCLUSION

ANGLO-NORMAN literature has now been treated from the beginning of the twelfth century to the end of the fourteenth, from the reign of Henry I to that of Henry IV, and the time has come to assess the importance of these three centuries of activity.

On its first appearance Anglo-Norman literature was in the van of progress, and part of the movement towards courtliness just beginning in the north of France. Many will remember the late Professor Pope's paper, 'The Precocity of Anglo-Norman Literature'.[1] She confined her attention to three subjects, Historical Literature, Prose, and the Drama. In the case of history, she pointed out that Gaimar is the earliest writer in French, only possibly preceded in the field by David, who also wrote in England, and that Fantosme is the earliest writer of a different kind of history, describing events in which the writer has participated (perhaps one should rather say, in which his informants had taken part). Gaimar was at least fifteen years ahead of Wace, a Norman, and Fantosme about twenty years earlier than Ambroise, another Norman. It is a case of England first, Normandy second, and the rest nowhere. Interest in the biography of the recently deceased is shown by the *Histoire de Guillaume le Maréchal* written for an English family by a Norman writer. For prose, Miss Pope cited the example of the *IV Livre des Reis*, in which prose, which had begun 'in rather stammering fashion' with interlinear glosses to the Psalter, really came into its own. The continental prose translation nearest to it in date is the *Dialogues of Gregory the Great*, apparently from Liège, which is too literal to count as a specimen of real French prose. For the drama, there are only two examples she could use, the *Adam* and the *Resurrection*, but both are invaluable for the history of the growth

---

[1] This paper was unfortunately never printed. Miss Pope handed the script of it to the writer for use in this book.

of vernacular drama in general. Miss Pope suggested four reasons for this precocity: the prestige of the Conqueror's language; the influence of the courts of Henry I and Henry II and of the Norman barons, 'active-minded, intelligent, greedy for knowledge'; the activity of a Church which was animated by a missionary spirit; English influence. Against the first argument, that French was in a privileged position, must be opposed the plain fact that Latin, not French, supplanted English as a written language.[1] The second argument carries more weight. The family of the Conqueror, the knights and barons who accompanied him, and later on the Angevins, were all ruthless but enterprising and inquiring people, else they would never have come, would never have settled down, but would have plundered the country and gone home like the Viking grandfathers of so many of them. Some did, but their younger brothers remained to make a career for themselves in a land they soon regarded as their own. Miss Pope's statement that historiography was chiefly inspired by the need for propaganda requires a little modification. It has been pointed out above that equally important was the urge of the immigrants to feel that they had roots in the country. The Church was undoubtedly energetic, and prelates were shocked by what they considered to be laxity on the part of the clergy they found installed, but some of the churchmen of all ranks were just as much adventurers as the laity. At the beginning clerks may have outnumbered jongleurs as vernacular writers, but it will have become evident from what has been said above that the impression people sometimes have that all Anglo-Norman literature is dreary religious and didactic stuff ground out by a few monks cut off from the world is quite erroneous. There was in England and Normandy in the twelfth century a great outpouring of saints' Lives and sermons in verse, and in England the tradition of these persisted in the thirteenth century and was given fresh impulse by the Fourth Lateran Council, but there were also plenty of other things: chronicles, romances, and lyrics. It is perhaps possible, as Miss Pope says, that the drama developed early in

---

[1] Cf. R. R. Darlington, *Anglo-Norman Historians* (Birkbeck College, 1947), pp. 5–7.

England because in the case of English-speaking audiences it was found useful to reinforce sermons by an appeal to the eye. But some preaching was always done in English, and rustic congregations accustomed to services in an incomprehensible Latin would probably welcome French as an alternative, since an understanding of that language spread rapidly after the Conquest. As for English influence, it is quite true that Gaimar made use of English sources, especially the Anglo-Saxon Chronicle, of which he saw two copies, one of them being at Winchester. The chronicle, however, was not made for the benefit of lay patrons, as Gaimar's own work was. It is a curious coincidence that Fantosme lived in the Winchester diocese.

It is, therefore, difficult to account for the precocity of Anglo-Norman literature, though that precocity is undoubted. It is possible that the invasion and subsequent colonizing of the country had a stimulating effect. The most striking point which emerges from the consideration of the problem is the importance of patronage. What counted for more than the quality or nationality of the writer was the taste, the power, and the riches of the patron. This had bad results as well as good, and the preference shown by Henry II for Benoit over Wace can only be deplored by posterity. It was very often the queens who created the demand for vernacular literature, and when Miss Pope talks of the courts of Henry I and Henry II it must be remembered that an important part in the creation of a literature was played by the Queens, Maud and Adeliza, and the three Eleanors. The kings held the purse-strings, and therefore exerted some control and won the gratitude of the writers. In speaking of the court of Henry II especially it is impossible to distinguish between what was written in England and what was written in the continental provinces which made up the Angevin Empire.[1] Continental writers were patronized to such an extent that some, like Marie de France and Guillaume le Clerc, seem to have written exclusively to please English taste. Marie may have followed the court in its peregrinations, but Guillaume seems to have made his home in England.

[1] Cf. W. F. Schirmer and U. Broich, *Studien zum literarischen Patronat im England des 12. Jahrhunderts* (Cologne and Opladen, 1962).

Due recognition is not always given to the precocity of Anglo-Norman literature. It is shocking to find Professor Angelo Monteverdi saying that Wace's *Brut* 'est peut-être le plus ancien récit profane ainsi versifié (i.e. en vers de huit syllabes à rime plate) que l'histoire de la poésie française nous présente'.[1] For Wace did but follow in the steps of Gaimar, who had preceded him by fifteen years or more. And it would be no use to argue that Gaimar cannot count as belonging to the history of French poetry, because it may well be that Wace was imitating him, and there is some suggestion that his lost *Estorie des Bretuns* was known in France. The later developments in Anglo-Norman versification must not be allowed to obscure the fact that in the twelfth century Anglo-Norman writers were experimenting with various kinds of short lines, which were all ultimately abandoned in favour of the octosyllabic rhyming couplet, which they did much to popularize. Because of their precocity in the adopting of new kinds of literature they were obliged to find the most suitable form in which to express them.

The Anglo-Norman patrons had at their disposal not only works especially written but others imported from abroad and recopied in England. The *Roland*, the *Gormont*, the *Willame*, the *Pelerinage de Charlemagne*, and *St. Alexis* are well-known examples. Sometimes, as in the case of the *Roland* and the *Roman de Thebes*, the scribes worked on early continental prototypes, sometimes, as in the notorious case of the *Willame*, on a late 'remaniement'. It may have come as a surprise to some people to read in the foregoing pages how often an Anglo-Norman work crossed the Channel and circulated in France. Early examples of this traffic may have been due to the association of England with the north-east through the wool-trade, since more texts seem to have found their way there than to central France. Later texts written when Anglo-Norman had reached a barbarous stage may have been valued for their illustrations, since the tradition of the well-written and superbly decorated manuscript survived the Conquest and later on the East Anglian school was a pioneer in a new sort of decoration.[2] Through the marriages

---

[1] 'La laisse épique', *La Technique littéraire des chansons de geste* (Liège, 1959), p. 139.   [2] J. Baltrušaitis, *Le Moyen Âge fantastique* (Paris, 1955), p. 18 *et passim*.

of Henry II's daughters and Henry III's alliance with Haakon IV of Norway Old French literature, especially as represented by Anglo-Norman, became known in the courts of Germany, Spain, Sicily, and Norway.

It may seem curious that it now appears, contrary to former belief, that the works of Crestien de Troyes were unknown in England for some time after they were written, and had little influence on Anglo-Norman writers. The explanation is probably, as Madame Rita Lejeune says, that the court of Marie de Champagne rose to pre-eminence as a literary centre only after her mother's disgrace,[1] and until after her stepfather's death there would be little interchange between his court and her own. If Hue de Roteland, for instance, had any knowledge of Crestien, it was used only to turn to ridicule courtly ideas.

This interchange of texts has led to two misconceptions. M. Maurice Delbouille would have it that the Anglo-Norman reader was old-fashioned in his tastes, and M. Pierre Le Gentil finds evidence that the continental Frenchman early thought the Anglo-Norman writers were old-fashioned and provincial.[2] As we have seen, Anglo-Norman taste in the twelfth century was actually in advance of continental French, but quite naturally texts took time to migrate. Geoffrey of Monmouth's *Historia* indeed seems to have reached Normandy in a sort of advance copy, but as a rule a text did not become known for several years outside the small circle for which it was composed. Sometimes it was copied just as it was, sometimes it was brought up to date. It is doubtful whether Anglo-Norman was regarded as on a different footing from other French dialects much before the end of the twelfth century. The earliest acknowledgement that it was a dialect at all is the Nun of Barking's statement which cannot be earlier than 1163 and may be 1169 that she knew a false French of England; some would make it

---

[1] 'Rôle littéraire de la famille d'Aliénor d'Aquitaine', *Cahiers de Civilisation Médiévale*, i (Poitiers, 1958), pp. 324–8.

[2] M. Delbouille, 'Sur la genèse de la *Chanson de Roland*' (Brussels, 1954), p. 31, 'Les chansons de geste et le livre', *La Technique littéraire des chansons de geste* (Liège, 1959), pp. 325–6; cf. M. D. Legge, 'Archaism and the Conquest', *Modern Language Review*, li (1956), pp. 227–30; P. Le Gentil, 'A propos d'*Amadas et Ydoine*', *Romania*, lxxi (1950), pp. 359–73.

later. It was about this time that Marie de France and Guernes de Pont-Sainte-Maxence were calling attention to their French origin. The French of Guernes did not stand up against the insular influences to which he was exposed during his stay in England. About 1180 the famous incident occurred at the French court when they made fun of Conon de Bethune's use of dialect. This applies to language, not to substance, and the French were ready enough to borrow the Nun's *Life* of Edward the Confessor. Anglo-Norman scribes modernized the work of their own countrymen. The Picard scribe was not the only one to add a syllable to the short feminine lines in Benedeit's *St. Brendan*. Change in domestic arrangements caused someone to make alterations to the text of *Horn*. In line 2470 'les tables funt oster' is substituted for 'la nape fu cuillie', and in the next line 'chevalier' has been changed to 'chevalerie' to get a correct rhyme.

The question of scribal responsibility for indifferent versification and incorrect grammar is constantly raised where Anglo-Norman is concerned. Some Anglo-Norman scribes, especially at the end of the twelfth century and the beginning of the thirteenth—ordinary scribes, that is to say, not calligraphers engaged upon *de luxe* copies, who are in a class apart—are as good as any anywhere. Some, especially at a later period, seem to be infuriatingly inefficient. Mr. F. B. Agard's study[1] of the manuscript tradition of the *Roman de Toute Chevalerie* is illuminating on this point, provided that his remarks are taken as referring to the scribes and not, as he intends, to the poets. They should be read in conjunction with Dr. H. J. Chaytor's chapter[2] on reading and writing. The best scribes, as he points out, did not think, but memorized their model word by word and many imposed their own orthography, for they memorized by ear and not by eye. Some Anglo-Norman scribes seem to have been educated above their station, and to have memorized not word by word, but sentence by sentence. As a safeguard against omissions the initial letter of each line of a verse text was usually written first in a separate column. The height of

---

[1] *Romanic Review*, xxxiii (1942), pp. 216–35.
[2] *From Script to Print* (Cambridge, 1945), pp. 5–21.

perfection is reached when the same procedure is adopted for the last letter of each line, as is the case for part of one of the manuscripts of *Horn*. This makes the text awkward to read, since the lines are of varying length and the last letter is sometimes a considerable distance from the rest of the word, which is perhaps why this system is rarely seen. The scribe of *Guillaume le Maréchal*—an Anglo-Norman—worked from a copy which he tried to reproduce exactly, column by column. If he omitted a line this was at once apparent, and in most cases the omitted line or lines have been added later, by himself or his reviser. But if a column is complete and a line is missing it must already have been lacking in his model. Some scribes were mechanical to a fault. The copyist of Béroul—not an Anglo-Norman—imposed his own spelling on the text, but copied both his model's mistakes and the reviser's version one after the other, without noticing that they were alternatives, and that the first version had probably been expunged. The case of the *Willame* scribe is one of the most interesting. It is known from his other work that he gave a more or less accurate reproduction of what was in front of him. The chaotic state of the *Willame* text is none of his making. Some time previously the poem seems to have passed through the hands of someone who memorized sentence by sentence, and this explains why the word in assonance has often been removed from the syntactically unnatural position which the poet gave it and has been put back in its normal place in the sentence. It may seem odd that this copyist did not memorize the rhythm as well as the words, but medieval readers proceeded more slowly than we do, and he may have had in front of him a text written as prose. When continental scribes came later on to copy the prose romances, they worked in the same way, and variants are far more numerous, but often of less importance, than in the case of texts in verse. This kind of variant is of use in the study of the changes in vocabulary. Slowness in reading partly accounts for the use of the octosyllabic couplet for texts meant to be read aloud by amateurs. They are easier to read in this form. Whether the jongleurs who chanted the *chansons de geste* read from books is doubtful, though they may have carried copies about with them to refresh their

memory. Romances written in similar form were read and
not chanted, and Thomas in *Horn* suggests this when he says
of the lost *Aaluf*:

> Seignurs, oi avez le[s] vers del parchemin,
> Cum li bers Aaluf est venuz a sa fin.   (1–2)

One of the reasons why early copies, like the Oxford *Roland*,
are so rare is that oral transmission leaves no trace. The
Roland, as Mr. Richard Hunt of the Bodleian (whom I
quote by permission) pointed out to me, had the good
fortune to find a place on the shelves of the medieval equivalent of a public library (Oseney Abbey), and so escaped
destruction.

Another minor point which must be made before leaving
the question of the relationship between Anglo-Norman
literature in particular and Old French literature in general
is that there were acknowledged women writers, Marie de
France, Clemence of Barking, and the Nun of Barking, if
she is not to be identified with Clemence, and Marie of
Chatteris(?). The Nun speaks as though women writers
were exceptional:

> Si requiert a toz les oianz,
> Ki mais orrunt cest soen rumanz,
> Qu'il ne seit pur ço avilé,
> Se femme l'ad si translaté.
> Pur ço nel deit hoem pas despire
> Ne le bien qu'il i ad desdire.   (5312–17)

(So all those hearers who will ever hear this romance of hers must
not hold it base if a woman has thus translated it. For this reason it
should not be despised, or the good in it disdained.)

It is, however, uncertain whether she really means to insist
on the fact of her sex or on her humility as a nun. In any
case, she was much given to false modesty; it is she who
speaks of her 'false French' and parades the concealment of
her name. There is no similar case of a nun known to have
been writing on the Continent; the first woman writer to
make a name in northern France was Christine de Pisan—
and she was an Italian!

To turn now to English literature. Anglo-Norman fills
a gap which all too often occurs in general histories of it. It

is useless to lament the change in taste and manner brought
about by the Norman Conquest, a hard fact which cannot be
ignored. But for the Conquest there would not have been
a Chaucer—a writer with whom France can show no one to
compare. Within a generation Normans and Saxons were
hopelessly mingled and most were bilingual up to a point.
Anglo-Norman literature was not the prerogative of a few.
It is significant that romance in English did not begin to
proliferate until the ruling classes were feeling the strain of
keeping up their French. A glance at the parallel chronological tables printed by Schofield,[1] out of date though they
may be, is instructive. From 1100 to 1250 the same kind of
religious and didactic works were being produced in both
English and Anglo-Norman, but there is not a work in
English written purely for entertainment before 1250, the
date ascribed to *King Horn*. From the end of the century
translations and adaptations of French and Anglo-Norman
works abound and the gap in time between the composition
of a work and its appearance in English shrinks and shrinks
until it practically disappears. There are, naturally, other
factors to be taken into account. If *The Owl and the Nightingale* was written for the Young King, this means that courtly
literature of an astonishingly accomplished and original
nature was being written in English in the twelfth century,[2]
and makes the existence of Banastre, author of the pretended source of *Blancheflour e Florence*, less incredible than
would appear. Then there is the question of the lost literature of medieval England. Oral transmission may have preserved many romances which have completely disappeared
since. But this is known to have been true also of French and
Anglo-Norman, so that the picture given by the tables is not
far out if it is taken as a rough guide to the situation. *Sir Orfeo*
and *Sir Gawain and the Green Knight* amongst other works
have been supposed to be based upon lost Anglo-Norman
works. A study of the differences between the French or
Anglo-Norman source and the Middle English adaptation

---

[1] W. H. Schofield, *English Literature from the Norman Conquest to Chaucer*
(London, 1906), pp. 458–65.
[2] S. d'Ardenne, 'That Underyat the King Henri', *Moyen Âge*, liv (1948),
pp. 249–56.

of it would be both useful and interesting, for the adaptation was never slavish. This has been done for individual works, but no comprehensive study has yet been made.

Moreover, a distinction needs to be made between the adaptation of Anglo-Norman and of French works. At the time, it seems clear, neither the French nor the English were conscious of any difference. Both Anglo-Norman and continental French works were French to them. Yet the Normans and the English had tastes in common before the Conquest, and this accounts not only for the emergence of an Anglo-Norman literature, but for the adaptation of Anglo-Norman works by English writers. History, romance, and devotional writing were the main interests shared by the English and the Normans, and the Anglo-Norman influence in Middle English may be traced in all these directions. In the case of saints' Lives, the influence was chiefly in the substitution of verse for prose. Through Anglo-Norman English seems to have come into contact with the French traditions in lyric and drama. Direct influence is most clearly seen in the case of history and romance, where there are many translations, sometimes very close. It is no accident that the earliest major adaptation into Middle English is Laȝamon's but *Brut*. Wace, it is true, was not an Anglo-Norman writer, he wrote to please the English court, and may be imitating the example of the Anglo-Norman Gaimar. When there is an Anglo-Norman version of a romance independent of the French one, as in the case of *Amis e Amilun*, the English adapter will probably choose it, though both may be used, as for the *Alexander* romances. *Beves of Hampton* follows the Anglo-Norman very closely; the author of *Amis and Amiloun* may have known an earlier version than the one which is preserved. The Middle English versions are more vigorous and sometimes coarser than their models, and this is sometimes ascribed to the fact that they were addressing a public of lower social order than the French and Anglo-Norman writers. It may, however, be simply due to the demands of a wider public. There is a similar development to be observed in France.

It will be seen that there are many questions which cannot be satisfactorily answered within the scope of this book.

A further subject which would repay study is the contrast between Gower, the last of the Anglo-Normans, and Chaucer, the first of the modern English.

What is new in this book may prove to be matter of contention, but this will not be considered a drawback by scholars. It has suffered from two major handicaps. The first is that there is no general history of Old French literature which is as detailed, so that comparative study has been a matter of bits and pieces. The present work, like its predecessor *Anglo-Norman in the Cloisters*, has only been possible because Anglo-Norman is by definition merely a part of a very big whole. For that very reason, however, it may act as a pilot to a larger work, if someone ever had the courage and patience to undertake it. The second handicap is, that the chronology of the Old French romances has suddenly been flung into the melting-pot. A quarter of a century ago everything looked nice and tidy. The romances of antiquity, of which *Thebes* was obviously the oldest, preceded the courtly romances, of which Crestien de Troyes was the pioneer and principal exponent. Now it is not at all clear what priority, if any, should be given to the romances of antiquity, and *Thebes* may very well turn out to be the latest of them and to follow Crestien. Crestien himself may have been far less well known among his contemporaries than has been thought, and his romances may all have been compressed into a decade or so, which makes much better sense of his career than the older view. Every month brings forth fresh surmises based on evidence which had been overlooked, and where it will all end no one can foresee. It is therefore no longer possible to date Anglo-Norman works by the simple expedient of declaring them to show traces of borrowing from this or that continental work, and there may have been more independent development than was formerly thought. Occasionally there are clues which provide a date, or a writer may even give the date himself. Thus the chronology of Gaimar and Wace is firm and settled. But such good fortune is rare.

It is claimed in this survey that the study of both Old French and Middle English literature must gain from the separate consideration of Anglo-Norman. This literature was a far more living thing than the purely derivative and imitative Franco-Italian literature with which it is sometimes compared. Anglo-Norman writers were creative from first to last, and often pioneers where Old French is concerned. The influence of their patrons sometimes caused them to diverge from the lines followed on the Continent, but it is a superficial judgement to dismiss them as 'provincial' on that account. Writers in English, French, German, Italian, Spanish, and Norse did not disdain to borrow from them. The legacy of Anglo-Norman is of European significance, and it is only fitting that its literature should receive some honour in the land which gave it birth.

INDEX

Names of characters in works under discussion do not necessarily
appear in the Index. Manuscripts are not listed.

PRINTED IN GREAT BRITAIN
AT THE UNIVERSITY PRESS, OXFORD
BY VIVIAN RIDLER
PRINTER TO THE UNIVERSITY